THE NORTH SEA:
PERSPECTIVES ON REGIONAL ENVIRONMENTAL CO-OPERATION

SPECIAL ISSUE
OF THE INTERNATIONAL JOURNAL OF
ESTUARINE AND COASTAL LAW

Edited by

David Freestone
Senior Lecturer in Law, University of Hull, UK;
formerly Adviser, Government of Antigua and Barbuda

Ton IJlstra
Netherlands Institute for the Law of the Sea (NILOS),
University of Utrecht, Netherlands

Graham & Trotman / Martinus Nijhoff
Members of the Kluwer Academic Publishers Group
LONDON/DORDRECHT/BOSTON

First published in 1990 by
Graham & Trotman Limited
Sterling House
66 Wilton Road
London SW1V 1DE
UK

Graham & Trotman
Kluwer Academic Publishers Group
101 Philip Drive
Assinippi Park
Norwell, MA 02061
USA

British Library Cataloguing in Publication Data
The North Sea : perspectives on regional environmental co-operation : special issue of the International journal of estuarine and coastal law.
1. North Sea. Environment. Conservation
I. Freestone, David II. IJlstra, Ton III. International journal of estuarine and coastal law.
333.9164170916336

ISBN 1–85333–413–8

Library of Congress Cataloging-in-Publication Data
The North Sea : perspectives on regional environmental co-operation/ edited by David Freestone and Ton Ijlstra.
p. cm.
"Special issue of the International journal of estuarine and coastal law."
Includes bibliographical references.
ISBN 1–85333–413–8
1. Environmental protection—North Sea—International cooperation.
2. Marine pollution—North Sea. 3. Marine pollution—Law and legislation—North Sea. I. Freestone, David. II. Ijlstra, Ton.
TD171.5.N775N67 1990
363.73'9456'0916336—dc20

89–77578
CIP

Typeset in Times by Promenade Graphics Ltd, Cheltenham
Printed and bound in Great Britain by
Bell and Bain Ltd, Glasgow

Contents

Foreword

The lack of romanticism in the Dutch attitude to the North Sea can come as a surprise to other seafaring peoples. True, we boast of salt water in our veins. True, the sea has always been a source of our prosperity and the backdrop for historical heroics. But healthy respect rather than sentiment has always coloured our relationship to the often far-from-still waters. And never has our respect for the North Sea stopped at lip service; it has always been matched by commitment and investment. In medieval times, maintaining the dikes was the duty of all but the least able-bodied. Those who shirked their contribution to the survival of the population faced swingeing penalties and ostracism. The Storm Surge Barrier, inaugurated by Her Majesty the Queen in 1987, was a tangible sign that the commitment across our community continues.

Now, the scene has shifted. The sea itself is the victim, and the effects are starting to rebound on the culprits—the users. We have polluted an essential natural resource through a combination of short-sightedness, neglect and greed. Cold realization of the implications for posterity grows with every new glimpse we get of the damage caused, with every additional—often enigmatic—clue.

Swift, decisive action is required nationally, internationally and at the individual level. Precisely what this entails became clear during the political consultations at the first two North Sea Conferences. 1984 and 1987 also exposed differing priorities and capabilities. All agree on the need to halt and repair damage to the eco-system, but national interests prevent a consensus and differing national infrastructures limit practical scope and achievement.

Compounding the lack of a concerted programme is basic ignorance. We are only just starting to comprehend the complexity of the system which is the North Sea.

The need for a joint approach was established in Bremen and the policy objectives were elaborated in London two years ago. It is now essential that all governments involved in the 1990 North Sea Conference in The Hague demonstrate that fine intentions can be matched by concerted endeavour. This is the message I intend to emphasize from the chair; and as the Netherlands Minister of Transport and Public Works I shall do my utmost to prove the willingness and the determination of my fellow countrymen.

This book covers past North Sea conferences. It is up to all of us to ensure that 1990 provides adequate material for a positive and forward-looking sequel.

Hanja Maij-Weggen
Minister for Transport and Public Works,
The Netherlands

Acknowledgements

The editors would like to acknowledge the assistance of a number of individuals in the preparation of this volume: particularly Paul Ymkers but also Gerard Peet, NILOS, David Shaw and Dr. Uwe Jenisch for their contributions to the bibliography.

The opinions expressed in this volume are the opinions of the authors alone and should not be taken to represent the opinions of the organizations or institutions for which they work, or with which they are associated.

List of Contributors

The Editors

David Freestone is a senior lecturer in law at the University of Hull. He has established research interests in the law of the sea, European Community law, coastal and environmental law. From 1987 to 1989 he was Adviser to the Ministry of Foreign Affairs, Antigua and Barbuda. He is Managing Editor of the *International Journal of Estuarine and Coastal Law*. In addition to this Volume, he is also editing with Ton IJlstra a complementary book of documents entitled *The North Sea: Basic Legal Documents on Regional Environmental Co-operation*, to be published in 1990 by Graham & Trotman/Martinus Nijhoff.
Ton IJlstra graduated from the Erasmus University, Rotterdam in public and administrative law, and pursued postgraduate studies in international law at the University of Paris (II). Since then he has worked for the Netherlands Institute for the Law of the Sea (NILOS) as assistant researcher and subsequently as Research Associate. He has published in the field of protection and preservation of the marine environment of the North Sea, navigation, maritime safety, offshore and user conflicts. In addition to his present post, he is a member of the Dutch North Sea Commission (an advisory body to the Dutch minister) and legal adviser to the Dutch Environmental Impact Assessment Commission.

The Contributors

Steinar Andresen, programme director at the Fridtjof Nansen Institute, is a political scientist from the University of Oslo. He has worked with various aspects of ocean management, law of the sea and international resource management. Among his publications is *Power and Law of the Oceans*, Norwegian UP, Oslo, 1987 (in Norwegian). He has been affiliated to the Fridtjof Nansen Institute since 1979, since 1987 as senior research fellow. In 1987/88 he was visiting research scholar at the Institute for Marine Studies, University of Washington.
Professor Patricia Birnie has, since October 1989, been Director of the IMO International Institute of Maritime Law in Malta. She was previously lecturer in public international law at the University of Edinburgh (1973–83) and then senior lecturer in law at the London School of Economics. Her extensive publications on the law of the sea, the North Sea and international environmental law include: with R. Barston (eds), *The Maritime Dimension* (1980); *International Regulation of Whaling* (2 vols, 1985).
Dr. Sonja Boehmer-Christiansen was educated in both Germanies, and has degrees from the Universities of Adelaide, Australia (Geography), and Sussex (International relations). She has lectured in Australia and the UK, from 1981–1983 undertook research in Munich. Since 1984 she has worked at the Science Policy Research Unit, University of Sussex, where her current research is on comparative environmental politics (UK/FRG) primarily in relation to air pollution.
Dr. Robin Churchill is a senior lecturer in law at the Cardiff Law School University of Wales, where he has worked since 1977. He is author of *EEC Fisheries Law* (1987), and (with AV Lowe) of *The Law of the Sea* (2nd edition, 1988) as well as a number of articles on marine law matters.
Scott Davidson recently took up an appointment as a senior lecturer in law at the University

of Canterbury, New Zealand. Prior to that he worked, from 1979, at the Law School of the University of Hull. He has published widely in the field of EC law and public international law, and was until 1989 Deputy Managing Editor of the *International Journal of Estuarine and Coastal Law*.

Aline de Bievre is currently Deputy Editor of the *Hazardous Cargo Bulletin*. Previously she was a core research member of a UK Department of Transport sponsored project on the human element in shipping casualties. She contributed an independent study report to COST 301 on the legal aspects of Vessel Traffic Services operations and the question of liability. From 1980–85 she advised the European Environmental Bureau on ship safety and pollution matters, and since 1983 she has been a regular adviser to the Friends of the Earth International (FOEI) delegation at IMO.

Folkert de Jong has an MSc in biology. From 1985 to 1989 he was managing co-ordinator of the North Sea Working Group Foundation (an environmental protection association). He is now Managing Director of the Seas at Risk Federation, and is also Editor of the *North Sea Monitor*.

Professor Dr. Peter Ehlers joined the Maritime Shipping Administration of the Federal Republic of Germany in 1970. He was Under-Secretary in the Maritime Transport Department of the Federal Ministry of Transport before being appointed, in March 1989, President and Professor of the German Hydrographic Institute (a Central Maritime and Marine Federal Authority). As part of his marine environmental protection responsibilities, he was Chairman of the Helsinki Commission and was Head of Delegation to the IMO Marine Environmental Protection Committee and the Oslo Commission. He attended both North Sea International Conferences, and chaired several preparatory expert groups. He has published widely on marine and marine environmental problems.

Dr. Erik Franckx holds the Licentiaat and Doctorate degrees from the Free University of Brussels and has an MA in Eastern European Studies, as well as an LLM (Athens, Georgia). He has published widely on the law of the sea, mainly relating to USSR state practice and legislation. He is presently involved in a comparative ocean boundary delimitation project organised by the American Society of International Law.

John Gibson has been a lecturer in law at the Cardiff Law School since 1978, where he specialises in research, teaching and consultancy in UK coastal law. He is the author of many publications on that subject.

Dr. Susan Gubbay is a marine biologist, with a PhD in marine ecology from the University of York. She is Conservation Officer for the UK based Marine Conservation Society and is actively involved in promoting the establishment of voluntary marine conservation areas around the UK coast. She compiled the first *Directory of Sites of Marine Conservation Interest*, and in 1989 published a *Review of Techniques for Coastal and Sea Use Management*.

Dr. Lothar Gündling is a Senior Research Fellow at the Max-Planck-Institute for Comparative Public Law and International Law, and a Lecturer at the Universities of Heidelberg, Mannheim and Frankfurt 'Main. His major areas of work are in law of the sea, international environmental law, European environmental policy and comparative environmental law. His publications include *Tendenzen des Umweltrechts im internationalen Vergleich*, 1978 (2nd ed forthcoming); *die 200 Seemeilen Wirtschaftszone*, 1983; *Forest Resource Management*, 1984; *Dicke Luft in Europa, Aufgaben und Probleme der europaischen Umweltpolitik* (with Beate Weber), 1988.

Peter Hayward joined the staff of the Oslo and Paris Commissions in 1977, and was their Secretary from 1980–1989. He was previously an administrator in the British civil service, having studied geography and town planning at London University. He now runs an environmental consultancy partnership.

Dr. Uwe Jenisch is based in Kiel, West Germany. He is a legal counsellor, and advisor to the Law of the Sea Delegation of the Federal Republic of Germany. He is a member of the Law of the Sea Institute, the American Society of International Law, the Deutscher Seerechtsverein Hamburg and the Council on Ocean Law. He has published extensively on law of the sea and North Sea issues.

Dr. Neville Jones is Director of the Institute of Estuarine and Coastal Studies, and senior lecturer in applied biology, University of Hull. From 1959–62 he worked with the British Antarctic Survey as meteorologist/biologist, and subsequently worked at the University College of North Wales at Bangor before moving to Hull. He is Honorary Secretary of the Estuarine and Coastal Sciences Association and a member of the Humber Estuary Technical Management Committee. He has written widely on Antarctic birds, freshwater and estuarine ecology and pollution.

Dr. George Kasoulides has a first class honours degree in Political science from Pantios, Athens, Greece, and LLM and PhD degrees from London University. He has worked as an independent consultant in collaboration with the Sea Foundation Ltd and as a part-time Research Assistant at the London School of Economics (LSE). Since March 1989 he has been an LSE Research Officer on a project developing databases of national legal material for comparative research on state practice in the law of the sea.

Professor John Kemp is currently Editor of the *Journal of Navigation* (the Journal of the Royal Institute of Navigation, UK). Prior to this he was Dean of the Faculty of Transport at the City of London Polytechnic. He contributed extensively to the research work of the European COST 301 project on Shore-based Maritime Navigation Aid Systems and was leader of the Risk Analysis Task Force. He acts as occasional consultant to the Friends of the Earth delegation at IMO.

André Nollkaemper studied Political Science and Law at the Erasmus University of Rotterdam. Subsequently he was research assistant at the Netherlands Institute for the Law of the Sea (NILOS) University of Utrecht. He is currently preparing a thesis on international instruments for the control of transboundary water pollution at the University of Utrecht. He has published on topics concerned with international environmental co-operation and law.

Dr. Philip Reid is the North Sea Scientific Co-ordinator at the Department of the Environment, London, and heads the UK delegation to the North Sea Task Force. Initially trained as a geologist, he lectured in geology at Fourah Bay College, Sierra Leone before moving to Edinburgh to work with the Continuous Plankton Recorder project—monitoring plankton in the North Atlantic and North Sea. He then worked at the Plymouth Marine Laboratory on a number of other North Sea projects before taking up his present post.

Gerard Peet is Director of the S.E.A. Foundation (Rotterdam, Netherlands) and is also a Research Associate at the Netherlands Institute for the Law of the Sea (NILOS). He is an adviser to Friends of the Earth International and in that capacity attends meetings of the IMO and other organisations at which FOEI has observer status. He has written widely in the field of protection of the environment, sea use management and planning.

Jean-Luc Prat works in the Centre de Droit et d'Economie de la Mer, University of West Brittany, and is a lecturer at the Institut Universitaire de Technologie, Brest. He is currently preparing a doctoral dissertation on state competence in the field of protection of the marine environment and has published on a number of other law of the sea issues.

Dr. Victor Sebek is the Executive Secretary of the London-based Advisory Committee on Pollution of the Sea (ACOPS), and has represented ACOPS at IMO and UNEP diplomatic conferences. He is the author of *East European States and the Law of the Sea* (Oceana, 2 vols) and of numerous articles on the law of the sea and environmental law. He is a member of the Editorial Board of *Marine Policy*.

Dr. Hance Smith is a senior lecturer in the Department of Maritime Studies, University of Wales College of Cardiff. He has teaching and research interests in maritime geography, development of maritime communities and integrated sea use management. He is a member of the RICS Marine Resource Management Committee, Secretary of the International Geographical Union Commission on Marine Geography, and a member of the Planning, Development and Management Group of the Irish Sea Study Group established by the Royal Society of Arts.

Professor Eddy Somers is professor of Public International Law and Law of the Sea at the State Universities of Ghent and Antwerp. He is Head of the Study and Documentation

Centre for Port and Maritime Science (RUG), and Director of the Research and Training Project on the Law of the Sea, Ocean Management and Marine Policy at the University of Nairobi, Kenya. He is a member of the Juridical Committee of the Belgian Red Cross, and the Belgian Society for International Law, and has published widely on public international law, law of the sea and environmental law.

David Symes, an Oxford graduate, is currently senior lecturer in Geography and Assistant Director of the Institute of Estuarine and Coastal Studies, University of Hull. His research interests include the economic, social and political aspects of North Atlantic fisheries, as well as the impact of agricultural modernisation in Europe. He has worked on fisheries-related problems in the UK, Norway, Iceland, the Faroes and Newfoundland.

Professor Yves van der Mensbrugghe is Professor Extraordinary at the Katholieke Universiteit, Leuven. He is a specialist in international law (especially law of the sea) and in European law (external relations and environmental law) on which he has written widely. He is also a consultant.

Mrs. Mr. Ir. J. Vennekens-Capkova was born in Czechoslovakia. She received her Masters degree in chemical technology at the Technical University of Eindhoven in 1971, and from then until 1980 worked for Cindhu Chemie BV (Uithoorn). She then entered the Ministry of Housing, Physical Planning and Environment at Leidschehndam, and since 1985 has worked for the EEC Commission in the Directorate-General for Environment, Nuclear Safety and Civil Protection.

Jorgen Wettestad, research fellow at the Fridtjof Nansen Institute, is a political scientist from the University of Oslo. He has been associated with the Fridtjof Nansen Institute since he graduated. He has worked with various aspects of environmental politics both at the national and international level, with special emphasis on organizational aspects. Among his publications is *Multilateral Aid Agencies and the Environment: Principles, Implementation and Possible Nordic Policy Options* 1987, Fridtjof Nansen Institute (in Norwegian).

John Woodliffe is a senior lecturer in law at the University of Leicester. He has written widely on the law of the sea; on national, international and EC aspects of energy and natural resources law; and on the civil and military aspects of nuclear power.

Karel van der Zwiep has been, since 1976, legal adviser to the Dutch Wadden Sea Society, and since 1978 its foreign secretary.

Table of Cases

Decisions of International Courts and Tribunals

Table of Statutes

Table of Secondary Legislation

Statutory Instruments

Denmark

UK

EEC Directives, Decisions and Regulations

Table of Agreements, Conventions and Treaties

Introduction

Legal measures for the protection and the preservation of the marine environment have advanced considerably in the last two decades. Global and regional treaties have been introduced for marine-based sources of pollution such as vessel-source pollution (MARPOL 73/78) and dumping at sea (London Dumping Convention). However, experience seems to suggest that the other, possibly more significant, sources of marine pollution, such as land-based, river and atmospheric pollution, are likely to be better regulated at a regional level. With the establishment of the Oslo Commission on dumping and the Paris Commission on land-based pollution, the littoral states of the North-East Atlantic have taken the lead in the development of a regional policy, which has been followed by other regions (e.g. the Mediterranean). In the North-East Atlantic this regulatory response has been paralleled by the emergence of extensive formal and informal consultative forums. So extensive has this regional system become that even the emergence of the 1982 Law of the Sea Convention (although it contains some new elements likely to be of interest to the North Sea littoral states) did not substantially affect the regional framework for the protection and preservation of the marine environment of the North Sea.

Thus the institutional apparatus of the North Sea regional system seems impressive—but is it as effective as it could be? Notwithstanding the fact that there has been a reported steady decrease in the quantity of polluting materials, it is apparent that the marine environment of the North Sea is still degrading. This process is evidenced by a number of phenomena, including an increase in fish diseases, viral infections among marine mammals, as well as reproduction problems (due to the presence of PCBs in coastal waters), overfishing, discharges of oil and chemicals from offshore installations polluting surrounding sediments, and significant inputs of nutrients leading to eutrophication and oxygen depletion. All these issues raise significant questions about the role and powers of existing environmental regulatory systems.

In 1984 North Sea Ministers met at Bremen and agreed what has become known as the Bremen Declaration. They did the same in London in 1987, adopting what many felt to be a rather limited declaration. They intend to meet next on 7 and March 1990 in The Netherlands, and a further meeting has been scheduled for 1995 at which a revised Quality Status Report on the North Sea will be available. These International North Sea Conferences (INSCs) are still essentially *ad hoc*—in the sense that they are not the result of an institutional obligation to meet, but rather of a high level of political concern about the state of the North Sea. The fact that these Ministerial meetings now seem to be assuming a regular pattern prompts a number of questions about the emergence of a new North Sea forum. It suggests that the participants at least feel that the existing systems are no longer adequate and it also suggests that it may be opportune to subject these meetings to more critical scrutiny. However, it is surprising to note that there has been only limited interest in these developments among the legal community, and indeed in non-scientific circles generally. The reasons for this may well be the difficulties inherent in any form of exercise which involves an appreciation of developments in other disciplines, be they those of the scientist in the strict sense, the political scientist, or even contemporary techniques of exploration and exploitation.

Another relatively recent phenomenon of interest is the appearance of new actors on this stage. What will be the future role of the European Community (EC), which as an international (or some say supranational) institution not only has a legal status different from individual states, but is also developing increased competence in the field of the environment—most recently through the Single European Act? In addition we seem to be witnessing the emergence of an increased role for Non-Governmental Organizations (NGOs)—which have played an important part in raising public awareness of environmental threats. Their influence is already known, but their status in the new decision-making processes is still unclear.

The INSC Declarations themselves also prompt questions about the nature of environmental regulatory instruments. In the past the traditional international convention has been seen to be the proper legal form for such instruments. But in the environmental field, as well as in other fields of international relations, new forms of "agreement" are developing. Not only do the INSCs not fit into any pre-existing institutional framework, but their "Declarations" do not fit into conventional classifications of international agreements. Debate continues as to the extent of the legal obligations they impose on signatories. Another example is the Memorandum of Understanding on Port State Control—which is also an instrument which does not fit into a traditional framework. It too, however, is concerned with the protection of the marine environment

Despite all these new inputs to the system, we are still facing increasing environmental problems in the North Sea, and the regulatory responses in very important areas still do not seem to be adequate. It is clear that new perspectives are badly needed. These new perspectives can relate as much to the goals of marine pollution control as to their means—although in this volume we are particularly concerned with means—the means which contribute to the better functioning of the whole regional system for the protection and preservation of the marine environment.

In putting this volume together the editors made a survey of previous publications with similar aims. It was noticeable that interest in North Sea affairs reached a high point in the mid-1970s—spurred by the "boom" of the offshore oil and gas industry and the resulting literature. Wider concerns were raised by the publication of Young's pamphlet on sea-use planning in the North Sea (1975), and by the David Davies Institute study (ed. M. Sibthorp) *The North Sea: Challenge and Opportunity* (1974). This "boom" in North Sea literature seemed to fade at the beginning of the 1980s, despite the publication of important volumes edited by

D. C. Watt (*The North Sea: A New International Regime* (1980)) and C. Mason (*The Effective Management of Resources* (1979)). Renewed academic interest—primarily environmental in nature—was spurred by the first INSC in Bremen in 1984, but the resulting literature has been primarily at a scientific rather than a legal and policy level. We trust that this volume will demonstrate that we have again reached a point at which policy-orientated authors may have a useful contribution to make.

David Freestone and Ton IJlstra

Part I
The International North Sea Conferences in Perspective

Chapter 1

The History of the International North Sea Conferences

Professor Peter Ehlers

Introduction

When dealing with the history of the International North Sea Conferences, it is helpful to start with the Baltic Sea, however paradoxical that may appear. In 1974, with the Convention on the Protection of the Marine Environment of the Baltic Sea (Helsinki Convention), for the first time comprehensive measures for a sea area were laid down in order to combat all relevant pollution sources.[1] At the same time, the Convention—with the setting-up of the Helsinki Commission—created an organizational framework establishing close co-operation between the bordering coastal states for the protection of the Baltic Sea.[2]

Development in the North Sea region has proceeded differently. Here there also exist Conventions which serve the protection of the marine environment, although, in most cases, they are not limited to the North Sea but are applicable to larger sea regions. Moreover, these Conventions deal with individual sources of pollution, so that there is no comprehensive overall system.[3]

Chronologically the first international instrument was the Agreement for Co-operation in Dealing with Pollution of the North Sea by Oil of 9 June 1969 (Bonn Agreement). A new agreement in 1983, superseding the 1969 agreement, which extends co-operation to other harmful substances, entered into force in 1989. Whereas this Agreement is limited to the North Sea, two further Conventions go

[1] For details see H. Rotkirch, "Ten Years of Environmental Co- operation in the Baltic Sea", *Aqua Fennica* 14; P. Ehlers, "Zehn Jahre Helsinki-Uebereinkommen—ein Bericht", (1984) *Natur & Recht* 138.

[2] In this connection see the yearly reports about the activities of the Commission, published in the Baltic Sea Environment Proceedings by the Helsinki Commission.

[3] If J. Side, "The North Sea Conference, Bremen 1984—London 1987", (1986) *Marine Pollution Bulletin* 394, calls the Conference on the Protection of the North Sea a "unique regional initiative", he fails to notice the development in the Baltic Sea area as outlined.

far beyond it and cover the entire North-East Atlantic region: the Convention for the Prevention of Marine Pollution by Dumping from Ships and Aircraft (Oslo Convention) of 15 February 1972,[4] as well as the Convention for the Prevention of Marine Pollution from Land-Based Sources (Paris Convention of 4 July 1974).[5]

The International Convention for the Prevention of Pollution from Ships 1973 as modified by the protocol of 1978 relating thereto (MARPOL 73/78) contains world-wide applicable regulations for the limitation of the discharge of oil, noxious liquid substances, packaged goods, ships' sewage and garbage.[6] Unlike the Baltic Sea, the Convention does not declare the North Sea a Special Area.

In the field of marine mining exploration and exploitation, there is to date no comprehensive compulsory regulatory system in the North Sea region.[7]

However, a certain organizational unification of different international endeavours for the protection of the North Sea and the North-East Atlantic has been attained in that the Commissions established by the Oslo and Paris Conventions maintain a joint Secretariat that simultaneously undertakes the Secretariat functions for the Bonn Agreement. Of course, this has led to administrative improvement but hardly to the degree of international co-operation which takes account of the special concerns of the North Sea.[8]

The First International Conference on the Protection of the North Sea

Background

By the beginning of the eighties—at the latest—there were growing indications that the North Sea, at least in problem regions, was becoming severely polluted by harmful substances.[9] Particularly affected were coastal regions such as the Wadden Sea off the Netherlands, and the German and Danish coasts. On the basis of the hydrographic conditions in the North Sea, it was obvious that national measures taken by the coastal state concerned would not be sufficient by themselves. Also,

[4] In this connection see Ehlers and P. Kunig, *Abfallbeseitigung auf Hoher See* (Hamburg, 1978).

[5] With regard to Paris Convention, see e.g. P. Ehlers, Internationale Regelungen zum Schutz von Nord- und Ostsee vor radioaktiven Einträgen, in N. Pelzer, Friedliche Kernenergienutzung und Staatsgrenzen in Mitteleuropa, 1986, p. 206.

[6] With regard to the MARPOL Convention cf. e.g. Ehlers, "MARPOL", (1985) *Gefährliche Ladung* 363, 393.

[7] Some very special items are dealt with in Annex I of MARPOL 73/78; the Paris Commission also deals with several items, without covering the total area.

[8] As regards the activities, for details see the Annual Reports issued by the Oslo and Paris Commissions.

[9] Cf. e.g. *Umweltprobleme der Nordsee: Sondergutachten June 1980; Der Rat von Sachverständigen für Umweltfragen*. This is a comprehensive expert report about the quality status of the North Sea, compiled by a group of experts on environmental questions—appointed by the Deutsche Bundestag (Parliament of the Federal Republic of Germany). Compared with this, the environmental protection, for example, at the 5th Annual Conference of the Greenwich Forum, 1979, has had—at best—only marginal importance. See *Greenwich Forum V: The North Sea. A New International Regime* (1980).

the continuing work of the Oslo and Paris Commissions did not suggest that, without additional political impetus, immediate radical measures could be initiated to stop a further burdening of the North Sea and to reduce the pollution which had already occurred.

That is why in 1983 the Government of the Federal Republic of Germany took the initiative of inviting the North Sea coastal states to an International Conference on the Protection of the North Sea (INSC) at ministerial level. They were of the opinion that it was essential that the loads hitherto ascertained in individual regions should be prevented from having negative repercussions upon the entire ecological system of the North Sea. One should not wait until large-scale harmful effects had been proved. On the contrary, with the application of the precautionary principle, all measures should be taken as early as possible within the framework of the co-operation of all the neighbouring states in order to avoid irreversible damage. It would not be the aim of the Conference to create a new set of international agreements. On the contrary, it would provide political impetus for the intensification of the work of the competent international commissions and bodies, and for the more efficient implementation, in all the neighbouring states, of the existing international rules.[10]

Preparation

At a preparatory meeting of all the North Sea coastal states in December 1983 in Bonn, an important agreement was reached that the Conference should not restrict itself to general principles but should examine all pollution sources and adopt definite decisions.

In preparation, international Groups of Experts compiled resolution proposals on the range of subjects of the Conference up to the summer of 1984. Subsequently, a hearing took place in August 1984, at which international associations could present their suggestions. In September 1984 the preparatory work was concluded in Wilhelmshaven at a meeting of the permanent Secretaries of State responsible.

Progress of the First International Conference on the Protection of the North Sea

The First International Conference on the Protection of the North Sea took place in Bremen from 31 October to 1 November 1984. All the Ministers of the North Sea Coastal States[11] responsible for the protection of the North Sea participated as well as the Commission of the European Communities. Several international organizations attended as observers as well as representatives of the rest of the contracting

[10] On the preparation of the First Conference see also G. Peet, "The 1984 North Sea Conference, A Preview" (1984) 8 *Marine Policy* 259–270.

[11] These are Belgium, Denmark, the Federal Republic of Germany, France, the Netherlands, Norway, Sweden, and the United Kingdom.

parties of the Oslo and Paris Conventions and of the EC Member States.[12] Under the chairmanship of the Minister for the Interior of the Federal Republic of Germany, at that time responsible for environmental protection, several public plenary sessions took place to discuss basic positions. At the Heads of Delegation level, even more controversial individual questions were clarified in tough debates which extended far beyond the temporal framework originally intended. The Conference closed with the adoption of a comprehensive declaration concerning the protection of the North Sea.[13]

Results of the First International Conference on the Protection of the North Sea

The Declaration is subdivided into a programmatic introductory part which gives a general summary of the Conference results, as well as the actual operative part which consists of a multitude of detailed declarations.[14]

In Section A, the operative part deals with the problems in the form of considerations. Then follow decisions of a basic type (Section B), which are supplemented by individual measures in Sections C to J. In a comprehensive Annex, a part of the measures are concretized further. The following findings and results should be given prominence.

Status of the North Sea

The North Sea and in particular its natural resources constitute an important, irreplaceable environment. A Quality Status Report, worked out by experts from all the North Sea Coastal States,[15] came to the conclusion that the central and the northern part of the North Sea on the whole did not seem to be considerably affected, but that pollution has been identified particularly in the estuaries and coastal regions. The inputs of pollutant loads mainly come from land-based sources via rivers, coastal waters, and the atmosphere; moreover, pollutant inputs via direct discharges, dumping and the operation of ships may cause serious local damage to the North Sea.

Basic principles

The Conference emphasized that the coastal states and the EC bear joint responsibility—for present and future generations—for the conservation of the important marine ecosystem of the North Sea region, including the Wadden Sea and other

[12] Observers were present from Finland, Greece, Ireland, Italy and Portugal as well as from the International Maritime Organization, the United Nations Environment Programme, the Secretariat of the Bonn Agreement, the Helsinki Commission, the International Council for the Exploration of the Sea, the Oslo Commission, the Paris Commission, and the Secretariat of the Memorandum of Understanding on Port State Control.

[13] *Declaration of the International Conference on the Protection of the North Sea*, published by Bundesminister des Innern of the Federal Republic of Germany, 1985.

[14] See in this connection the summary by Side, "The North Sea Conference". For details see Ehlers, "Die 1. Internationale Nordseeschutz-Konferenz" (1985) *Natur & Recht* 102.

[15] *Quality Status of the North Sea. A Report compiled from Contributions by Experts of the Governments of the North Sea Coastal States and the Commission of the European Communities prepared for the Conference on the Protection of the North Sea*, Supplement No. 16 to *Deutsche Hydrographische Zeitschrift*.

highly sensitive coastal areas. The environment is best protected against pollution by timely preventive measures. As damage to the marine environment can be irreversible, or remediable only at considerable expense and over long periods, it is not prudent to await proof of harmful effects before taking action. The precautionary principle is thereby acknowledged by the First International Conference on the Protection of the North Sea.

The existing international agreements for preventing marine pollution should be implemented without delay, and appropriate initiatives in international bodies should be taken with regard to the prevention and further marked reduction of marine pollution. With regard to its legal character, the Declaration makes it clear that it contains no legally binding international agreements but that the results of the Conference should be considered as the basis of further environmental political action for the North Sea and that the Ministers accept the conclusions of the Conference for concerted action in the competent international bodies.

Pollution via rivers and from coastal waters

Recognizing that pollution via rivers and coastal waters needs to be prevented or markedly reduced, mandatory regulations for the control of substances contained in "black" and "grey" lists, particularly organohalogen compounds and heavy metals, should be adopted within the framework of the EC, the Paris Commission, and the River Commissions concerned, if possible as early as 1985. In these regulations, methods for the prevention of pollution of sediments should be included. With regard to additional regulations, potentially hazardous substances, particularly new synthetic organic compounds, are to be continuously examined as to their potential deleterious effects. Activities aiming at the phasing out of the use and discharge of PCBs should be intensified without delay. Normally, emissions should be limited at source; emission standards should take into account the best technical means available and quality objectives should be based upon the latest scientific data. The different approaches of uniform emission standards and the environmental quality objectives, based either upon the principle of immission or emission, should be reviewed periodically, to bring them closer together.

In order to reduce radioactive discharges into the marine environment from all nuclear industries, the North Sea coastal states declared their firm intention to respect the recommendations of the competent international organizations applicable and to take account of the best available technology.

Pollution via the atmosphere

A joint initiative, in the Paris Commission, should be taken to adopt in 1985 an additional protocol to the Paris Convention relating to the prevention, reduction or elimination of marine pollution via the atmosphere. This initiative should also cover the adoption of corresponding joint programmes and measures.

Waste disposal at sea

Wastes, including sewage sludge, containing amounts of substances which are or could be harmful to the marine environment, should not be dumped into the North Sea.

Pollution from ships

To prevent marine pollution from operational discharges, the system of reception facilities should be established and comprehensive and practicable procedures for their use be introduced. The North Sea States agreed to do their utmost within IMO so that appropriate international regulations for harmful substances in packaged form and for garbage from ships (Annexes III and V of MARPOL 73/78) will enter into force as soon as possible. The detection, prosecution and punishment of violations against anti-pollution regulations should be intensified.[16] In the light of the "Mont Louis" accident, IMO should be requested to consider additional measures for ships which, due to the nature of their cargo, pose a potentially grave and imminent threat of marine pollution, including ships carrying radioactive substances. No agreement could be reached about an initiative to declare the North Sea a MARPOL Special Area.[17]

Airborne surveillance

National and international efforts to introduce airborne surveillance systems, independent of visibility, in the North Sea area should be intensified. The desirable objective should be to develop or improve airborne surveillance systems which can function even at night and in bad weather when visibility is poor.

Oil pollution from platforms

Any technical equipment for exploration and exploitation should be constructed and operated in conformity with the best technology available. The improvement on existing platforms, in principle, should be completed within a period of 3 years. Marine pollution by drilling mud and drill cuttings should be avoided or prevented to the greatest extent possible. For the prevention of oily waste waters, the best available technology should be applied. Precautionary measures should be taken for emergencies and accidents.

Environmentally sound technologies and products

The exchange of information and experience on low-waste and non-waste technologies, on waste management, and on substitutes, as well as the technical co-operation with regard to recycling, reprocessing and waste disposal on land should be intensified. Regulations should be agreed which aim at the development and introduction of environmentally sound technologies, products, and substitutes.

Monitoring programmes

The Conference underlined the urgency to make more coherent and to develop intensively the Joint Monitoring Programme of the Oslo and Paris Commissions to provide the basis for a better knowledge of the state of the North Sea's marine environment.

[16] The intensive co-operation is to take place especially within the framework of the Bonn Agreement and the Memorandum of Understanding on Port State Control.

[17] MARPOL 73/78 provides for more stringent discharge prohibitions and restrictions for special areas in Annexes I, II, and V.

Assessment

Reaction to the results of the First Conference by the North Sea coastal states was varied. In the Federal Republic of Germany especially, where even before the Conference the public discussion was marked by an extraordinarily high degree of expectation, negative comments predominated. The main criticism was that the decisions were not formulated sufficiently precisely, and that for the most part they contained only declarations of intention for future international activities and therefore would hardly provide the motivation for concrete measures.

Nevertheless, when one takes a more realistic approach, the Conference can be regarded as being a success. For the first time all the coastal states' ministers responsible for the protection of the North Sea had assembled around one table and had committed themselves to taking joint measures. In consideration of the different ecological and economic prerequisites and individual interests, and—until that time—the very different evaluations of the situation in the North Sea, it can be viewed as a decisive breakthrough that all the participants affirmed the joint responsibility and the necessity of united action, that they reached agreement about first measures, and decided upon further concerted action.

In this connection, the agreement to hold a follow-up Conference was important. Thereby the coastal states placed themselves under an obligation to translate the resolutions into action as quickly as possible and to develop them further in the light of the latest knowledge.

The Second International Conference on the Protection of the North Sea

Preparation

The specialized preparation for the Second Conference began internationally in autumn 1985. From January 1986, a Scientific Technical Working Group worked on the compilation of an up-to-date Quality Status Report of the North Sea as a basis for the Conference.[18]

The report describes the physical oceanography of the North Sea, the major inputs of pollutants and contaminants and their theoretical dispersion pattern. The report identifies, as issues of concern, the large inputs from land-based sources, the inputs of nutrients, and oil pollution from illegal discharges or accidents. It reports that, in general, deleterious effects are only to be seen in certain regions, in the coastal margins, or near to identifiable pollution sources.

From January 1986, a Political Working Group compiled a survey concerning the implementation of the First Conference's resolutions and considered the themes to be discussed in detail at the Second Conference.

Despite different views at the beginning, it was agreed unanimously that the Second Conference should not limit itself to a few issues but should deal anew with the whole scope of problems and should take into account all the pollution sources.

[18] *Quality Status of the North Sea*, A Report by the Scientific and Technical Working Group (September 1987).

The international preparation was concluded at a meeting of the Permanent Secretaries of State in Edinburgh on 15 and 16 September 1987.

Progress of the Conference

The Second International Conference on the Protection of the North Sea took place in London on 24 and 25 November 1987, under the chairmanship of the British Minister of the Environment. The circle of those participating corresponded with that of the First Conference. After a highly esteemed opening address by the Prince of Wales, the individual Heads of Delegation delivered statements of principles. Subsequently, speakers from the environmental and industrial associations had the opportunity to state their opinions. Afterwards, a generally formulated report about the implementation of the resolutions of the First Conference was approved. The priority was the debate about further concrete measures for the protection of the North Sea. After intensive, and frequently extremely controversial discussions, a comprehensive Ministerial Declaration was ultimately adopted.[19]

Results[20]

The Declaration is divided into 16 sections. Sections I to XIV deal with the general grounds for consideration which serve as a basis for the Ministers' specific decisions. Here, the precautionary principle is once more expressly acknowledged. In section XV the reduction of pollution at source, i.e. the emission principle, is given priority. Section XVI—where the actual decisions are listed—contains (in 11 individual sections with a total of 56 paragraphs and 7 annexes) a comprehensive catalogue of specific decisions.

Land-based pollution

By the use of the best available technology and other appropriate measures, inputs of substances that are persistent, toxic, and liable to bioaccumulate should be reduced urgently and drastically, with the aim of achieving a substantial reduction of the order of 50 per cent between 1985 and 1995. With regard to other types of discharges which may pose environmental risks, the Paris Commission should evaluate the extent to which further action is required.

Inputs of nutrients

A substantial reduction of the order of 50 per cent in inputs of phosphorus and nitrogen into areas where these inputs are likely to cause pollution should be achieved between 1985 and 1995.

The best available technology should be used to reduce nutrients in discharges from waste water treatment plants; the use of phosphate in detergents should be regulated; the nutrient inputs from agriculture and industry should be reduced.

[19] *Second International Conference on the Protection of the North Sea, London, 24–25 November 1987, Ministerial Declaration, issued by the Department of the Environment of the United Kingdom, April 1988.*

[20] See in this connection E. C. Kasoulides, (1988) *Marine Pollution Bulletin* 97; Ehlers, "Wichtige Fortschritte beim Schutz der Nordsee—Bericht über die 2. Internationale Nordseeschutz-Konferenz" (1988) *Natur & Recht* 126.

Inputs of pollutants via the atmosphere
Additional measures on a national or international basis, in particular within the framework of the Paris Commission, should be envisaged as appropriate, in particular covering a long-term monitoring programme, the identification of priority sources by an emission inventory, the use of strict emission standards based upon the best available technology, and the phasing out of the use of petrol containing lead.

Dumping and incineration at sea
The Ministers agreed, as a matter of principle, to end the dumping of polluting materials in the North Sea at the earliest practicable date. The dumping of industrial wastes should be phased out by 31 December 1989, except for inert materials of natural origin or other materials which can be shown in the competent international organization to cause no harm to the marine environment. Governments should adhere strictly to Oslo Commission guidelines on dredged material in order to prevent dumping of contaminated dredged material. Those countries that dispose of sewage sludge in the North Sea should take urgent action to reduce the contamination of sludges and to ensure that the quantities of such contaminants do not increase above 1987 levels.

By 1 January 1991, incineration of wastes at sea should be reduced substantially by not less than 65 per cent, and incineration operations should be phased out totally by 31 December 1994.[21]

Pollution from ships
The Ministers agreed to initiate action, within the International Maritime Organization, for designating the North Sea a Special Area for the purpose of Annex V of MARPOL 73/78, with the consequence that the disposal of garbage into the North Sea would be prohibited.[22] The ready availability, capacity, and standards of service of reception facilities should be kept under permanent review. The use of shore reception facilities should be promoted by making such facilities available at reasonable cost or without charging special fees to the individual ship. Ships reported for an alleged pollution incident should be subject to stringent and wide-ranging inspection procedures in ports; the prosecution of violations should be facilitated.

The North Sea States should continue their efforts, within IMO, to bring into force Annexes III (packaged goods) and V (garbage) of MARPOL 73/78 at the earliest possible time;

Annex V should be implemented on a regional basis as from 31 December

[21] In the mean time, corresponding decisions were taken by the Oslo Commission during their 10th Annual Meeting in June 1988, regarding the termination of incineration at sea, and during their 11th Annual Meeting in June 1989, regarding the termination of the dumping of industrial wastes.

[22] In the mean time, the Marine Environment Protection Committee of the IMO during their 28th Session in October 1989 agreed to the proposal of the North Sea Coastal States to modify Annex V of MARPOL 73/78 correspondingly.

1988.[23] Within the International Maritime Organization and the International Standards Organization action should be initiated leading to improved quality standards of heavy fuel, aimed at reducing marine and atmospheric pollution.

Pollution from offshore installations
The Paris Commission is invited to tighten the criteria for the use of oil-based muds, to establish strict standards to reduce the oil content of discharged cuttings, to agree upon specific criteria to prohibit or strictly limit the discharge of chemicals, and to continue its work on the introduction of cleaner technologies.

Discharges and disposal of radioactive wastes
The North Sea states should apply the best available technology in order to minimize any pollution caused by radioactive discharges from nuclear industries. The design and construction of repositories for the disposal of radioactive wastes should aim to prevent pollution of the North Sea.

The Wadden Sea
The vulnerability of the Wadden Sea and its importance to the North Sea as a whole are expressly recognized. As its ecological value is threatened by a variety of factors, high priority should be given to the implementation of measures particularly significant for the protection of the Wadden Sea.

Airborne surveillance
Co-operation on airborne surveillance is an aid to enforcing anti-pollution regulations. The North Sea States should take appropriate action, with the aim of improving and extending bilateral and multilateral co-operation on airborne surveillance, in particular using the Bonn Agreement as the appropriate international forum. In addition, the Ministers for the Environment of Belgium, Denmark, the Federal Republic of Germany, and the Netherlands decided to improve further their co-operative work in airborne surveillance and to come to a separate agreement on this subject.

Scientific knowledge and understanding
The Conference endorsed the need for further development of harmonized methods for monitoring, modelling, and assessment of environmental conditions. They requested ICES[24] and the Oslo and Paris Commissions to consider together the optimal means to achieve these aims, including the possible benefits of a joint working group or task force[25] and to prepare and publish further reports on the quality of the North Sea at regular intervals, perhaps every five years—commencing in 1991.

[23] Annex V was ratified in the mean time by a sufficient quorum of states and came into force on 31 December 1988; additional regional measures are not required.
[24] International Council for the Exploration of the Sea.
[25] The Task Force started its work in 1988.

Assessment

At the Second Conference not all the demands made by the individual countries (notably those of the Federal Republic of Germany) were met. Nevertheless, as a whole, a political action programme with far-reaching measures for the protection of the North Sea was achieved. This constitutes a very considerable step forward. This is obvious from the decision to impose clear-cut targets for the reduction of all inputs from land and for the termination of the disposal of wastes at sea. The implementation of these measures in the North Sea coastal states necessitates the most supreme efforts and is linked up with colossal capital expenditure.[26] The fact, however, that sewage sludge can continue to be dumped in the North Sea is deplorable. The initiative to declare the North Sea a Special Area with regard to ships' garbage is a first step towards giving greater prominence for the special need for protection of this sea area in the field of shipping. Further steps must follow, so that in future the stringent Special Area Prohibitions will be in force for oil and chemicals also. With the Declaration it has become clear that the coastal states do take seriously their responsibility for the North Sea—which they had acknowledged during the First Conference—and are determined that this acknowledgement will be followed by action.

Preparation of the Third International Conference on the Protection of the North Sea

At the Second INSC, the Ministers, as a follow-up, decided to hold a Third Conference in the Netherlands in early 1990. The objectives of this Conference, in particular, should be to evaluate the measures agreed in the Declaration, especially the progress made in the implementation of the 50 per cent reduction plans, in the field of dumping and incineration at sea, and on measures taken to protect the Wadden Sea.

Since then, the date for the Third INSC has been fixed as 7–8 March 1990. The international preparations began with a high-level Government executives' meeting in October 1988 at the Hague. A Preparatory Working Group with several subgroups is carrying out the preparatory work for the Conference. Owing to the significance of the input via the rivers, participation of the German Democratic Republic, Switzerland, and the CSSR—if necessary, as observers—is being sought. NGOs should again have the opportunity of giving an oral statement at the beginning of the Conference.

Underlying the preparatory work are the reports of the individual governments and the competent international organizations about how the decisions of the Second INSC have already been implemented and what further steps are to be taken. Additional measures which are to be discussed[27] concern joint lists of

[26] In the Federal Republic of Germany, the most important measures for the implementation are embodied in a 10-item catalogue for the protection of the North Sea and the Baltic Sea in June 1988, issued by the Federal Minister for Environment, Nature Conservation and Nuclear Safety.

[27] As per 1 August 1989.

substances and minimum requirements for treatment plants in view of the 50 per cent reduction of nutrients and harmful substances, the accelerated application of Annex IV of MARPOL 73/78, the identification of the North Sea as a MARPOL Special Area for oil and chemicals, and intensive control measures with regard to tankers. Furthermore, additional measures for offshore platforms, the extension of territorial jurisdictions at sea, and the termination of dumping of sewage sludge belong thereto.

At the Third Conference, the future of the International Conferences on the Protection of the North Sea is also to be debated as a question of principle. In particular, the relationship of these Conferences to the Meetings of the Oslo and Paris Commissions is to be clarified, the more so as the Commissions' Meeting in 1992 will also be held at ministerial level.[28] Here, the substitution in the future of the Conferences on the Protection of the North Sea by joint Meetings of Ministers within the framework of the Oslo and Paris Commissions and the Bonn Agreement will come under consideration. Of course, that could lead to problems, because the member states of these Commissions are not identical with the North Sea coastal states and, in substance, the Commissions have a narrower competence. It is also conceivable that the Conferences on the Protection of the North Sea will continue—at intervals of several years—in addition to the Commissions' Meetings. These would then fix political action programmes at a high level, which would then be carried out in the Commissions. Of course, that could lead to the situation that the Commissions would become technical executive bodies of the Conferences on the Protection of the North Sea. In turn, that could encounter problems at least with those Commission members which do not border the North Sea.

Finally, it appears not to be out of the question that the measures and the framework of international co-operation for the protection of the North Sea will be legally consolidated by means of a North Sea Convention following the example of the Baltic Sea. In this case also, its relationship to the Bonn, Oslo and Paris Conventions will need to be clarified. Provided that the Conferences for the Protection of the North Sea continue to take place, there is much to be said for institutionalizing them more intensively than hitherto and for laying down rules of procedure.

There are good reasons for continuing the Conferences. They appear to be the best guarantee of further progress by additional political initiatives and for effective control of the timely implementation of existing decisions.

[28] During the 11th Joint Meeting of the Oslo and Paris Commissions in June 1989, France issued a formal invitation.

Chapter 2

Legal Status of International North Sea Conference Declarations

Professor Yves van der Mensbrugghe

Introduction

The legal status of declarations is a controversial issue. Such declarations belong to the wide world of international texts the legal status of which is questionable. That world is expanding: today, many ministerial meetings end with a declaration, a statement, a press release or whatsoever. It is also extremely heterogeneous: some of these declarations are purely informative in nature; some announce an agreed policy; others imply legal obligations. It often happens that the three aspects are involved in the same document and, generally, the precise extent of the commitments subscribed to, if any, is properly passed over in silence. Ambiguity is an often-used ingredient in international relations. One is then obliged to rely on the intention of the Parties, the circumstances, the wording of the document, etc. Sometimes the conclusion is obvious, sometimes doubts remain as to the degree of legal implications.

There is also a problem of semantics. A declaration may have a legal value because of the legal obligations it implies but it may also have one because, although not binding in strict legal terms, it has nevertheless a legal significance. Indeed, the way international norms are growing is not a matter of indifference to the internationalist, even if this happens outside the scope of international law. Looseness of terminology only adds to confusion.

International jurisprudence

This being said, international law is not that formal: states may choose the way they want to undertake commitments. They may have recourse to the traditional treaty form or engage themselves through unilateral declarations. And what they can do individually, they also can do collectively. This means that a concerted declaration may entail legal obligations. All depends on the intention of the Parties.

International jurisprudence gives some indications in that respect.

(a) The famous oral declaration, later set down in writing, made on 22 July 1919 by Mr. Ihlen, Norwegian Minister of Foreign Affairs, to his Danish colleague was considered to be binding upon Norway by the Permanent Court of International Justice in its judgment of 5 April 1933 concerning the *status of East Greenland.*[1]

(b) In its judgment of 20 December 1974 in the *nuclear tests case*, the International Court of Justice also considered that the declarations by which France renounced nuclear testing in the atmosphere was an obligatory unilateral act because that promise had been made publicly and with the intention to be binding.[2]

(c) In the *Aegean continental shelf case*, the Court's judgment of 19 December 1978 stated that no rule of international law prevented a joint communiqué constituting an international agreement even if, in casu, the joint communiqué made on 31 May 1975 by the Prime Ministers of Greece and Turkey did not amount to a commitment to submit the dispute to arbitration or rule of Court.[3]

Doctrine

On the doctrinal level, the matter has been examined very thoroughly and with great subtlety by the late Professor Virally in a report for the Institute of International Law entitled, "La distinction entre textes internationaux de portée juridique et textes internationaux dépourvus de portée juridique".[4] Several members of the commission made valuable contributions,[5] but the resolution of the Institute only took note of the conclusions of the rapporteur without endorsing them. Further study of the problem was postponed until better times, when practice and doctrine would allow it. This of course reveals hesitations and divergences in the approach to an indeed very complex question.

It is not suitable, in the framework of this paper, to present a résumé of Virally's views with all its intricacies and nuances. Suffice it to say, that, according to him, there are, roughly speaking, and apart from traditional treaties, two great categories of instruments: those which are to be situated in the realm of law although they are but weakly compulsory and largely discretionary (so-called soft law) and those which have a purely moral or rather political character and do not entail legal commitments even if they too have to be respected bona fide.

The difference between both categories lies certainly not in the higher degree of

[1] PCIJ Rep. Series A/B, no. 53 (1933).

[2] *Nuclear tests cases* (Interim Protection) (Australia, New Zealand v France) ICJ [1973] 99; see also B. Bollecker-Stern, "L'affaire des essais nucléaires français devant la CIJ", *Annuaire Français de Droit International*, 1974, pp. 299–333, esp. pp. 328–333.

[3] (Greece v Turkey) ICJ [1978] 3; see also M. Bettati, "L'Affaire du plateau continental de la mer Egée devant la CIJ", *Annuaire Français de Droit International*, 1978, pp. 303–320.

[4] Later, the title was changed to "La distinction entre textes internationaux ayant une portée juridique dans les relations mutuelles entre leurs auteurs et textes qui en sont dépourvus", *Annuaire de l'Institut de Droit International*, Vol. 60, I, Session de Cambridge, 1983; rapp. provisoire, pp. 166–257; rapp. définitif pp. 328–357.

[5] *Ibid.* 258–282, 358–374. See also W. Wengler, "Efectos de los acuerdos no juridicos entre Estados", *Anuario Derecho Internacional* (Navarre), 1985, pp. 17–37.

precision of the first one: political instruments also can be very precise in their wording.

It is rather the intentions of the Parties that count, although it may be very difficult to discern them, taking into account the fact that in the same instrument stipulations may occur which belong to both the above categories.

This does not make the task of analysis any easier and the battle is raging on. Some authors defend the view that there is no clear distinction between binding and non-binding norms and that the notion of a spectrum with intermediate categories would be preferable,[6] whilst others refuse a watering-down of international law and maintain the difference between what is not legal and what is legal, however feeble the constraints of the latter may be.[7]

Other authors contest the assimilation between "legal" and "obligatory". For them, non-conventional concerted acts[8] or concerted declarations[9] are non-binding ex natura: the non-compliance with their provisions cannot engage the international responsibility of their authors, and resort to the rule of Court is out of the question. Nevertheless, those acts are—albeit partly—submitted to international law: for instance, the principle of estoppel could be invoked and signatories cannot have recourse to the domestic jurisdiction exception concerning the matter that has been dealt with. The non-enforceability of such acts derives from the fact that states simply do not wish to bind themselves in too precise and constraining a manner because they think the object of the engagement requires a flexible legal approach. Is this running away from the rule of law? In a sense, certainly, but one has to admit that such instruments—which are often carried out scrupulously—are a handy tool in managing changing international relations.

The partial submission of the said acts to international law, however, is not generally accepted and Professor Virally in his final report made some reservations about it, although he recognizes, in case of purely political engagements, the possibility of estoppel and the non-application of the domestic jurisdiction exception.[10]

The legal status of the INSC declarations is thus not to be determined by their belonging to, let us say, the category of a declaration issued at the end of an international conference. They will have to be weighed on their own merits.

Recent state practice

Before examining these declarations, it may be interesting to look at some seemingly analogous texts in recent state practice.

(a) By the Bonn Declaration on Hijacking made on 17 July 1978[11] the Heads of State and Government of the seven major industrialized countries agreed on the

[6] See esp. R. R. Baxter, "International Law in her Infinite Variety", (1980) ICLQ 550.

[7] See esp. P. Weil, "Vers une normativité relative en droit international?" (1982) *Revue Générale de Droit International Public* 5; see also Weil's comments on Virally's report, *op. cit.*, 366–373.

[8] Quoc Dinh Nguyen, P. Daillier, and A. Pellet, *Droit international public* (Paris: LGDJ, 3rd ed., 1987), pp. 351–358.

[9] D. Carreau, *Droit international* (Paris: Pédone, 1986), pp. 183–194.

[10] *Op. cit.*, pp. 341–348.

[11] Followed by the Declaration of Montebello of 21 July 1981.

imposition of a boycott of the air traffic of countries offering sanctuary to aircraft hijackers. Despite the apparently quite radical character of that joint statement but taking into account the imprecision of its terms, most authors do not consider is as legally binding.[12]

(b) The Hague Declaration of 11 March 1989 on the protection of the atmosphere, signed by 24 states and several international organizations,[13] is to be seen as an appeal, a message calling for the establishment of a new world authority and indicating some principles the signatories intend to promote. It is not a legally binding instrument.

(c) The same may even be said of the conclusions of the so-called "Sommet de l'Arche", adopted in Paris on 16 July 1989 by the seven major industrialized countries. The section devoted to the environment was relatively substantial for that kind of document.[14]

(d) When the Commission of the European Communities signed the Basel Convention of 22 March 1989 on the control of transboundary movements of hazardous wastes and their disposal, it was duly mandated thereto by the Council. But, on the same occasion, the Commission also signed a declaration, initiated by the Dutch minister for the environment, which was intended to add some strength to the Convention. That declaration, being of a purely political nature and along the lines of the Commission's own policy, was signed by the Commission without any formal mandate by the Council.

(e) But, on the other hand, the joint statement made by France and Great Britain on transit passage in the Straits of Dover on 2 November 1988[15] is unmistakably an instrument that binds both states. More, it is a clear legal commitment *vis-à-vis* third states to observe the principles of the regime of international straits laid down in Part III of the Montego Bay Convention of 1982.

(f) There is also some analogy to be drawn between the North Sea declarations and the environmental programmes of the EC. Four of these have been adopted hitherto, in 1973[16], 1977[17], 1983[18] and 1987.[19]

Although the Commission duly pursued the execution of these programmes, it

[12] See J. Busitill, "The Bonn Declaration on International Terrorism: A Non-binding International Agreement on Aircraft Hijacking", (1982) ICLQ 474–487; K. Chamberlain, "Collective Suspension of Air Service with States which Harbour Hijackers:. (1983) ICLQ 616–632, esp. p. 627; J. L. Magdalenat, "Le Terrorisme international contre l'aviation civile et la valeur des déclarations de Bonn et Montebello en droit international public" (1982) *Revue français de droit aérien*, 448–466; W. Schwenk, "The Bonn Declaration on Hijacking", *Annals of Air Space Law*, 1979, pp. 307–322.

[13] NTIR 1989, pp. 69–72; (1989) *Revue Générale de Droit International Public* 538–539. Besides, the text specifies that the declaration is not eligible for registration under art. 102 of the Charter of the UN.

[14] *Le Monde*, 18 July 1989.

[15] (1988) *Revue Générale de Droit International Public* 1043–1044, repr. (1989) 4 IJECL 155–158.

[16] OJ, C 112, 20 December 1973. "Declaration of the Council and of the Representatives of Member States of 22 November 1973".

[17] OJ, C 139, 13 June 1977. Resolution of the same of 17 May 1977.

[18] OJ, C 46, 17 February 1983. Resolution of the same of 7 February 1983 taking note of the programme and approving its general orientations.

[19] OJ, C 238, 7 December 1987. Resolution of the Council of 18 March 1987.

does not seem that they entail any legal obligation. In reality they fix political orientations, which are not compulsory and are preparatory acts to later formal decisions.[20] However, the resolutions accompanying those programmes are not deprived of legal effect. By their mere adoption they engage the Community in a certain direction and authorize Member States and the Community's institutions as well to rely on that engagement and to draw all consequences as to future action.[21]

The Declarations of Bremen and London

Looking now at the declarations of Bremen and London themselves, some indications have to be underscored.

1. Both declarations are preceded by a statement of the ministers responsible for the protection of the North Sea wherein it is stated that they have reached agreement on (further) measures necessary for the protection of the North Sea and that they have agreed to take (further) timely preventive measures to maintain the quality of the North Sea. To this end they have adopted a comprehensive and detailed set of protective measures.

At first sight, one could get the impression that this terminology shows a firm determination which may involve a legal commitment.

2. That impression must be corrected when one looks at the terms of the declarations.[22]

First, nowhere is mention made of contracting parties. The expression used is: "the participants at the Conference", and just under the title of the Bremen declaration one finds the words: "Conclusions of the Conference". Now this does not preclude—*per se*—the existence of a binding commitment which may be concealed under the most various terms. Nevertheless, it hints at much looser engagements.

Further, the substance of these engagements is policy-oriented. In the Bremen declaration the ministers declare their firm determination "to make every effort" (B.1), "to implement existing international agreements" (B.3), "to set clear objectives" (B.4), "to lay down quality standards", (B.5), "to prevent waste from production and consumption as far as possible" (B.7), "to intensify research and development" (B.10), "to ensure . . . develop . . . analyze . . ." (B.11, 12, 13), "to take initiatives in international bodies" (B.15), "to use their best endeavours" (B.18).

They "consider it necessary to make the results of this Conference the basis of

[20] See E. Germain, "Les Instruments juridiques et financiers de l'action communautaire en faveur de l'environnement", in J. Charpentier, (ed.), *La Protection de l'environnement par le communautés européennes* (Paris: Pédone, 1988), esp. pp. 22–25; and H. J. Glaesner, "L'Environnement comme objet d'une politique communautaire", *ibid.* esp. pp. 5–6.

[21] P. Daillier, "Droit communautaire et protection de l'environnement marin", Annuaire de droit maritime et aérien, 1982, pp. 277–278.

[22] The Bremen statement is followed by the indication of the focal areas of joint action which is nothing else than a résumé of the declaration. The London statement limits itself to a mere enumeration of the fields of action.

their environmental political action" (B.19) and "resolve . . . to take the conclusions of this Conference as a basis for concerted action in the competent international bodies" (B.20).

There are proclaimed intentions to act—later on—in a certain way, at the national level, at EC level or, more especially, in the framework of international commissions like those of Oslo and Paris (e.g. C. 1–5).

The declaration then goes further with a set of "principles for the approaches: environmental quality objectives and uniform emission standards" (C. 6–11), before considering different kinds of pollution, practically always with due reference to international bodies or conventions (C. 12, D,E,F). The declaration also handles some other items like airborne surveillance (G), measures to prevent or reduce oil pollution from platforms (H), research and development (I) and monitoring (J).

In the Annex many aspects are detailed and specified, some of them in a very precise way but always in the framework of existing bodies, conventions and programmes.

The London Declaration follows the same pattern. The Ministers decide "to reaffirm", "to ensure", "to carry forward these conclusions by inviting" (XV). They agree to "accept the principle", "take or intensify measures", "establish appropriate procedures", "invite the appropriate international bodies" , etc.

It is true that, in the section devoted to dumping and incineration at sea, the ministers "accept as a matter of principle that . . . as from 1 January 1989, no material should be dumped in the North Sea unless there are no practical alternatives on land and it can be shown to the competent international organizations that the materials pose no risk to the marine environment" (XVI.21). True, also, that they agree "to take steps to minimize or substantially reduce, by not less than 65 per cent, the use of marine incineration by 1 January 1991" (XVI.24.b) and "to phase out such operations by 31 December 1994 and to seek agreement to such a date within the Oslo Convention by 1 January 1990" (XVI.24.c). But the wording makes it sufficiently clear that political decisions are involved which have still to be crystallized and implemented. The annexes A to G do not contradict this conclusion. In other words, the declaration indicates the objectives which have to be pursued, be it along the figures and dates mentioned.

Furthermore, the Ministers agreed to evaluate at the next Conference in the Netherlands, in 1990, "the measures agreed in this Declaration from a policy viewpoint" (XVI.55.a) and to "recognize that appropriate measures will need to be made available to the Oslo and Paris Commissions and ICES for the implementation of the measures agreed in this Declaration that fall to them" (XVI.56).

European Community practice

The EC's attitude towards the Declaration seems to confirm this analysis.

The Community, represented by the Commission, participated in the Bremen and London Conferences. Six Member States did not participate and, hence, the conclusions do not concern them directly. The Commission signed the Declarations because their general sense corresponded to the basic policy of the Commission.[23] A formal mandate by the Council was deemed superfluous owing to the political nature of the Conference and the absence of legally binding commitments in the conclusions.[24] This does not mean that the Community is not inspired by the Declarations of Bremen and Hamburg: many points of the fourth environment programme are a direct application of their principles. In the framework of international conventions to which the Community is a party or acts as observer, it has made endeavours to realize, whenever possible, the aims set forth in the declarations.[25] More specifically, a resolution of the Council of 28 June 1988 on the protection of the North Sea and of other waters in the Community invites the Commission to submit proposals on the reduction of nutrients and for the treatment of municipal sewage and as regards industrial waste waters. The resolution ends with a specific reference to the London conclusions.[26]

Conclusions

What, then, is the legal status of the Declarations? Clearly, they are not legally binding instruments: no international responsibility, no resort to the rule of court. However, they too have to be carried out in good faith, which is a notion not limited to the sphere of international law, although with other requirements. As such, they certainly have a legal significance in so far as they announce an action which will (it is hoped) be cast in legal terms, later and elsewhere, at the appropriate levels, international, European or national. Leaving aside the rather speculative question (raised above under the section on the doctrine), as to whether they are purely political texts or submitted in part to international law, it seems that, in any case, some legal consequences could be attached to them, namely, as it has been mentioned, estoppel and the domestic jurisdiction exception. Let us assume, for instance, that a participant Minister, invoking budgetary difficulties, persistently refuses to make appropriate resources available to the Oslo Commission, according to point XVI.56 of the London Declaration. Of course, his colleagues could not bring him before a court but they would be released from their obligation to do the same and, when urged by his colleagues to come forward with the finance, the reluctant Minister could not answer that the domestic jurisdiction of his country is at stake.

Undoubtedly, the proliferation of instruments of this kind creates a rather confused situation that impairs the normativity of rules. But, on the other hand, states are free to determine the extent to which they consent to engage themselves. Of

[23] Written Question 2852/87, Hughes, OJ, C 114, 8 May 1989.

[24] J. L. Prat, "La CEE et la protection de la mer du Nord", Coll. Cedece, *La Communauté européenne et la mer* (Brest, 1988).

[25] Prat, *op. cit.*

[26] OJ, C 209, 9 August 1988.

course, a clarification of their intention would be most welcome in order to know exactly who is obliged to do what.

In the present state of international relations, however, it is not evident that such a clarification would be generally accepted.

Chapter 3

The Status in International Law of the Principle of Precautionary Action

Dr. Lothar Gündling

The principle of precautionary action at the north sea conferences

The principle of precautionary action played a considerable role in the debate on the appropriate protection policy for the North Sea.[1] However, it has not always been clear whether the issue was the principle itself or, rather, a specific regulatory approach usually linked to the principle of precautionary action, namely that of control of emissions at source using the best available technology.

There are good reasons to believe that the heart of the controversy was the uniform emission standards approach as opposed to the environmental quality objectives approach.[2] But, while it is true that uniform emission standards have to be seen in connection with the principle of precautionary action which means that they constitute an appropriate regulatory approach to implement the principle, one should bear in mind that uniform emission standards are not identical with the principle of precautionary action.[3]

Recognition at the North Sea Conferences of the principle of precautionary action was a major negotiation goal of the Federal Republic of Germany. In the Federal Republic the principle of precautionary action ("Vorsorgeprinzip") is considered one of the most important principles of environmental policy,[4] some even consider it the primary one.[5] And there is no doubt that the principle of precaution-

[1] See P. Ehlers, "Die erste Internationale Nordseeschutz-Konferenz" (1985) *Natur & Recht* 102; *id.*, "Wichtige Fortschritte beim Schutz der Nordsee" (1988) *Natur & Recht* 126; G. Winter, "Der Schutz der Nordsee als Problem internationaler übereinkommen und EG-Richtlinien" (1988) *Natur & Recht* 265.

[2] See Boehmer-Christiansen, *below*.

[3] See section II, *below*.

[4] Umweltprogramm 1971, Bundestag-Drucksache VI/2710; Umweltbericht 1976, Bundestag-Drucksache 8/3713; Leitlinien Umweltvorsorge 1986.

[5] H. von Lersner, Vorsorgeprinzip, *Handwörterbuch des Umweltrechts*, Vol. 2, p. 1086.

ary action is also a principle of law although there is considerable disagreement as to the scope and the limits of the principle.[6]

In 1980, the German "Council of Experts on Environmental Matters", in its report on "Environmental Problems of the North Sea",[7] considered the principle of precautionary action a "requirement for a successful environmental policy for the North Sea ecosystem".[8] The Council even argued that the principle of precautionary action was "required in international, supranational and national law".[9] In 1987, giving a preparatory report on the forthcoming Second INSC,[10] the Federal Government announced that it would make every effort to ensure that all participating countries "pay more attention to the principle of precautionary action",[11] and that it would pursue the goal that emissions of hazardous substances are reduced at the source using the best available technology.[12]

Following each Conference it has been said that "the principle of precautionary action had been recognized".[13] A closer look at the Final Declarations[14] reveals that a judgment of this kind might be justified only with regard to the Second INSC.

The Final Declaration of the First Conference[15] deals only little with principles of protection policy. Concerning the principle of precautionary action one can only refer to one phrase in the preamble which reads:

> "They [the Ministers] agreed to the timely preventive measures to maintain the quality of the North Sea and to closely cooperate herein."

Interestingly, the notion of "precautionary action" is not used. The German text, however, speaks of "Vorsorgemass-nahmen". Since "preventive action" does not necessarily correspond to "Vorsorgemassnahmen",[16] one has to ask the question whether all participating states shared a common understanding, or whether the German translation was some concession to the German delegation and its negotiating goals. Except for this one phrase quoted above there is no reference to the

[6] See E. Rehbinder, Allgemeines Umweltrecht, in J. Salzwedel (ed.), *Grundzüge des Umweltrechts* (1982), p. 81; *id.*, "Das Vorsorgeprinzip im internationalen Vergleich" (unpub. manuscript, 1988 Umweltbundesamt, F. & E-Vorliaben No. 10106022); H. von Lersner, "Vorsorgeprinzip", in *Handwörterbuch des Umweltrechts*, Vol. 2 (1988), p. 1086; R. Breuer, "Umweltschutzrecht", in *Besonderes Verwaltungsrecht* (8th edn., 1988), p. 601; H.-W. Rengeling, *Die immissionsschutzrechtliche Vorsorge* (1982); H.-W. Rengeling, *Umweltvorsorge und ihre Grenzen im EWG-Recht* (1989); C. Schröder, *Vorsorge als Prinzip des Immissionsschutzes* (1987); H.-H. Trute, *Vorsorgestrukturen und Luftreinhalteplanung im Bundesimmissionsschutzgesetz* (1989); P. Marburger, *Atomrechtliche Schadensvorsorge* (1983).

[7] *Der Rat der Sachverständigen für Umweltfragen, Umweltprobleme der Nordsee* (1980).

[8] op. cit. p. 444.

[9] op. cit. p. 445.

[10] Bericht der Bundesregierung an den Deutschen Bundestag zur Vorbereitung der 2.Internationalen Nordseeschutz-Konferenz, Bundestag-Drucksache 11/878.

[11] op. cit. p. 24, D. I.

[12] *Ibid.* 24, D. II.

[13] Ehlers, *op. cit.*

[14] On the legal nature of the *Final Declaration* see van der Mensbrugghe, *above*.

[15] *International Conference on the Protection of the North Sea, London, 31 October and 1 November 1984, Ministerial Declaration, issued by the Department of the Environment of the United Kingdom.*

[16] "Preventive action" corresponds to "präventive Massnahme" rather than to "Vorsorgemassnahme".

principle of precautionary action. The Declaration does not mention emission control at the source or any other specific regulatory approach which might imply recognition of the principle of precautionary action.

The Final Declaration of the Second INSC[17] is much more detailed as to both principles and specific measures. The principle of precautionary action is mentioned several times. The first reference might even be considered a definition:

> "Accepting that, in order to protect the North Sea from possibly damaging effects of the most dangerous substances, a precautionary approach is necessary which may require action to control inputs of such substances even before a causal link has been established by absolutely clear scientific evidence."[18]

Then, the Declaration recognizes that this approach requires both reduction of pollution at source and establishment of environmental quality objectives.[19] This combination of emission control policy and environmental quality objectives is again stressed in another provision which reads:

> "[The participants] accept that by combining, simultaneously and complementary, approaches based on emission standards and environmental quality objectives, a more precautionary approach to dangerous substances will be established."[20]

Finally, the ministers agree, as far as pollution from rivers is concerned, on the application of emission standards "especially" where precautionary action is required:

> "[The ministers] accept the principle of safeguarding the marine ecosystem of the North Sea by reducing pollution emissions of substances that are persistent, toxic and liable to bioaccumulate at source by the use of the best available technology and other appropriate measures. This applies especially when there is reason to assume that certain damage or harmful effects on the living resources of the sea are likely to be caused by such substances, even where there is no scientific evidence to prove a causal link between emissions and effects ('the principle of precautionary action')."[21]

"Precautionary action": an elusive concept

The principle of precautionary action has a variety of aspects which makes it difficult to develop a common understanding. Things become even more complicated in an international context where problems of concept are increased by linguistic difficulties. There is controversy at least with regard to the following questions:

[17] *Second International Conference on the Protection of the North Sea, London, 24–25 November 1987, Ministerial Declaration, issued by the Department of the Environment of the United Kingdom, April 1988.*

[18] Item VII. The German text speaks of "vorbeugende Vorgehensweise", not of "Vorsorge".

[19] Item VIII.

[20] Item XV (ii); the German wording "ein vorbeugender Umgang", again, is not exactly what is meant by "precautionary approach".

[21] Item XVI (1); here, the German text speaks of "Vorsorgemassnahmen".

- What is the specific content of the principle of precautionary action?
- What are the functions of the principle of precautionary action?
- Does the principle of precautionary action require specific instruments or regulatory approaches, and, if yes, what are these?
- Where are the conceptional and other limitations of the principle of precautionary action?

Also in the Federal Republic where the principle of precautionary action plays an eminent role—at least in political rhetoric—the concept is far from being clarified. Government statements were hardly precise in the past,[22] and neither were the statutory provisions which referred to the principle.[23] As to the functicns it is often said that the principle of precautionary action serves several purposes: on the one hand, it allows—or even requires—governmental action even if there are scientific uncertainties with regard to hazards of specific activities or substances; on the other hand, it requires that governments do not exhaust the loading capacity of the environment in order to retain reserves for future uses including those by future generations.[24]

However, this view is not shared by all; some believe that the principle of precautionary action cannot have this kind of "planning aspect" which is implied by the last mentioned purpose.[25]

As to specific instruments, there is certainly no doubt that emission control at source using the best available technology may be an appropriate instrument. However, there is no consensus on whether there are other instruments or regulatory approaches which may also be considered appropriate to implement the principle of precautionary action.[26]

For the purpose of this study the following understanding of the principle of precautionary action is submitted: "Precautionary action" is a more stringent form of preventive environmental policy. It is more than repair of damage or prevention of risks. Precautionary action requires reduction and prevention of environmental impacts irrespective of the existence of risks. This, however, must not be understood in the sense that aspects of risks are not relevant; the crucial point is that environmental impacts are reduced or prevented even before the threshold of risks is reached. This means that precautionary action must be taken to ensure that the loading capacity of the environment is not exhausted, and it also requires action even if risks are not yet certain but only probable, or, even less, not excluded.

The emission control approach is an appropriate approach to implement the principle of precautionary action. However, there is no guarantee that it will always lead to a true preventive environmental policy; emission control will be ineffective—from an environmental point of view—if the "best available technology" is

[22] See n. 4, above.
[23] e.g. Para.1 Bundesimmissionsschutzgesetz.
[24] Von Lersner, *op. cit.*
[25] Breuer, *op. cit.*
[26] Rehbinder, "Vorsorgeprinzip", pp. 3 *et seq*.

not advanced, or if the positive effect of an advanced technology is compensated by an increase of sources. Furthermore, there are a number of other regulatory approaches to implement the principle of precautionary action, like, for example, stringent environmental quality objectives, the principle of non-degradation, strict prohibition with regard to hazardous substances, prohibition of shifting environmental impacts from one area to another or from one environmental medium to another, comprehensive and timely environmental impact assessments for all governmental and private activities with a potential impact on the environment, or integration of environmental policy into all other policies with a potential impact on the environment.[27]

Therefore, it is important not to identify the principle of precautionary action with a specific regulatory approach, for example, the control of emissions at source. A variety of other approaches—if not all—may also be used for a "precautionary policy", and, therefore, the secret of a successful environmental policy lies in the appropriate combination of the various regulatory options.

Precautionary action: required by international law?

Significance of the question; methodology

Although the principle of precautionary action has been recognized at least at the Second INSC the question remains whether the principle is also one of international law, given the fact that the "ministerial declaration" cannot be considered a legally binding instrument.[28] Is precautionary action required by international law as the German "Council of Experts on Environmental Matters" seemed to suggest in 1980?[29] Do treaties and/or norms of general international law applicable to the protection of the North Sea contain the principle of precautionary action? And if yes: what is the content of the principle?

An answer to these questions faces a number of methodological difficulties. It is very rare that treaties, declarations and resolutions of international organizations, or other elements of state practice which may be considered constitutive for the formation of general international law, expressly recognize the principle of precautionary action. This does not mean, however, that the principle does not exist in international law; it may be recognized as an "underlying" or "implied" principle. Therefore, one has to analyse the texts with regard to instruments or approaches which may be an indication of precautionary action. This, however, is not an easy undertaking. As has been said earlier, there are a variety of instruments or approaches to implement the principle of precautionary action, but they do not always serve this purpose. It depends on whether they are specifically designed to implement the principle of precautionary action—which is not always the case.

Therefore, it will be difficult to give any definitive answer to the question raised

[27] *Ibid.* 3; Winter, *op. cit.*
[28] Winter, *op. cit.*; van der Mensbrugghe, *above*.
[29] See n. 7, *above*.

above; there remains considerable uncertainty and, here too, a "precautionary approach" will be necessary in drawing conclusions.

Treaty law

Looking at the treaties applicable to the protection of the North Sea, we find no express reference to the principle of precautionary action. The 1974 Paris Convention on marine pollution from land-based sources requires reduction of marine pollution which, *inter alia*, endangers human health or damages the living resources or the marine environment (Article 1). This is not a reference to the principle of precautionary action but, rather, to the principle of prevention of risk. On the other hand, the Convention contains several provisions which may be related to precautionary action, like the obligation in Article 4 to eliminate pollution from certain substances (blacklist) and to strictly limit pollution from other substances (grey list),[30] or the obligation in Article 6 to reduce existing pollution and to avoid new pollution in order to conserve and improve the quality of the marine environment.

However, it is far from being certain that the reasoning behind these provisions was the precautionary approach; they may also reflect the conviction of the Contracting Parties that the quality of the marine environment had reached a critical stage, that it had to be improved, and that pollution from particularly dangerous substances had to be eliminated.

This uncertainty with regard to the precautionary approach as well as an "invitation" made by the Second INSC[31] form the background for two Recommendations of the Paris Commission of 22 June 1989 in which the Contracting Parties of the Paris Convention formally accept the principle of precautionary action[32] and formally agree on the use of the "best available technology".[33] The Resolution on the principle of precautionary action simply repeats the provision of the Final Declaration of the Second INSC on pollution from land-based sources which has been cited above. The second Resolution on the use of the "best available technology" clearly designs this approach as a precautionary one:

> "the application of the best available technology, should be applied in such a way as to prevent pollution in Convention waters, any increase in pollution in other sea areas or in other parts of the environment, or any increased risk to the health of industrial workers or the general public."

The provision of the Resolution on the definition of "best available technology" makes express reference to the "precautionary principle", and the final clause provides that application of the "best available technology" has to lead to an improvement of the environment: "If the reduction of emissions resulting from the use of best available technology does not lead to environmentally acceptable results, additional measures have to be applied."

[30] Rehbinder, "Vorsorgeprinzip", p. 266.
[31] *Ministerial Declaration*, at item XV (vi).
[32] PARCOM Recommendation 89/1 of 22 June 1989.
[33] PARCOM Recommendation 89/2 of 22 June 1989.

The 1972 Oslo Convention on dumping follows a similar regulatory structure as the Paris Convention, particularly it contains the same distinction between substances of a "blacklist" and those of a "grey list". Here, again, it must be said that this does not necessarily imply recognition of the principle of precautionary action.

The 1973/78 MARPOL Convention contains regulations which—at least at first glance—seem to reflect the principle of precautionary action, especially those regulations on the construction of ships or those on "special areas". However, one has to bear in mind that the purpose of the construction regulations is the protection of the marine environment against pollution from dangerous substances (oil, chemicals), and that the reasoning behind "special areas" is the protection of extremely loaded or extremely endangered areas. In both cases it is hard to discover any precautionary thinking.

General international law

With the exception of the most recent developments within the Paris Commission, treaty law is not very specific as to the principle of precautionary action. The question, therefore, arises whether general customary international law contains any norms which require application of the precautionary principle. Evidence of general international law may be found in the general treaty practice of States and in the various activities of international organizations dealing with environmental matters. Limited space does not allow for a comprehensive survey of State practice but only for a few general observations.[34]

Treaties dealing with international environmental problems, in particular transboundary pollution or protection of international commons, in general serve the purpose of preventing damage and coping with risk. It is certainly fair to state that in most cases the damages and risks are known, and that the agreements confine themselves to dealing with these known damages and risks. There is only one case which may be considered an application of the principle of precautionary action: the protection of the ozone layer by the 1985 Vienna Convention and the 1987 Montreal Protocol. These instruments were negotiated and adopted although there had been considerable scientific uncertainties as to the risks and possible damages resulting from destruction of the ozone layer. The basic reasoning is that the possible damage to man and the environment may be so serious that it has to be avoided at all costs, that it must not occur, and that it would have been an irresponsible policy to wait for complete clarification of all scientific uncertainties.

Resolutions, declarations and other instruments adopted at international conferences or within international organizations contain a number of references to the principle of precautionary action or at least to aspects of it. Only a few examples can be given. The Final Declaration of the 1972 Stockholm Conference[35] contains several Principles which may be considered an application of the precautionary approach: conservation of natural resources for present and future generations

[34] For more details, see Rehbinder, "Verursacherprinzip", pp. 259 *et seq*.
[35] The Results from Stockholm, Beiträge zur Umweltgestaltung A 10, (1973).

(Principle 2), maintenance of the capacity of the earth to produce vital renewable resources (Principle 3), non-exhaustion of non-renewable resources (Principle 5).The 1982 Nairobi Declaration adopted by the UNEP Governing Council[36] stressed the necessity of environmental management and assessment of environmental impacts (No. 3) as well as the necessity of "preventive action" which "should include proper planning of all activities" (No. 9). The "World Charter for Nature" adopted by the General Assembly of the UN in 1982[37] is certainly the most elaborate instrument with regard to the precautionary principle. The "Charter" expressly recognizes the principle and, in addition, contains various provisions in which the principle is further developed, like the provisions on the protection of unique areas, habitats and species, on sustainable use of natural resources, or on planning.

In addition to these instruments, one could refer to a number of Resolutions adopted within the OECD,[38] the Action Programmes of the EC,[39] or to the Amendment of the EC Treaties by the Single European Act[40] which all contain references to at least aspects of the principle of precautionary action. Nevertheless, the numerous and in some cases elaborate instruments do not justify the conclusion that there exists a norm of general international law requiring application of the principle of precautionary action. All instruments which have been mentioned are, as such, non-binding, and, consequently, cannot constitute the basis for a legal obligation. They may reflect the conviction of States that precautionary action is needed, but in order to have a binding rule additional law-creating acts are necessary.

Conclusion

Both the status and the content of the principle of precautionary action are still surrounded by uncertainties. Therefore, it is essential that the North Sea states reach agreement on this basic principle of environmental policy. It will not be sufficient, however, simply to recognize the necessity of precautionary action; it will also be necessary to agree on the specific contents, limitations and instruments of implementation. The Resolutions of the Paris Commission of 1989 are to be considered a first step. Further steps should follow.

[36] (1982) 9 *Environmental Policy and Law* No. 9, p. 45.
[37] The World Charter for Nature, Beiträge zur Umweltgestaltung A 90, (1983).
[38] See *OECD and the Environment (1986); Environment Policies for the 1980s* (1980).
[39] OJ C 112, 20 December 1973, p. 1; OJ C 139, 13 June 1977, p. 1; OJ C 46, 17 February 1983, p. 1; OJ C 328, 7 December 1987, p. 1.
[40] See Art. 130 r,s,t of the EEC Treaty.

Chapter 4

The Second International Conference on the Protection of the North Sea: National Implementation.

Folkert de Jong

Introduction

At the second Ministerial Conference on the Protection of the North Sea (London 1987) a number of specific decisions were taken:

- riverine inputs of dangerous substances to the North Sea will be reduced by the order of 50 per cent in the period 1985–1995;
- inputs of nutrients to vulnerable areas will be reduced by 50 per cent between 1985 and 1995;
- dumping of industrial wastes will be phased out;
- incineration at sea will be phased out by 1995;
- the North Sea will be declared a special area under MARPOL 73/78 Annex V.

As regards the amounts of pollutants the first two decisions are by far the most important. The dumping of industrial wastes accounts for only a small percentage of total dumping. Dumping of dredge spoils, the major source of contamination via direct inputs, continues. The decision to phase out the incineration of chemical wastes must be judged as a political decision rather than one that will have substantial beneficial effects on the North Sea ecosystem. The same can be said for the decision to declare the North Sea a MARPOL Annex V special area, at least as long as the availability of port reception facilities is as poor as at present.

In this contribution emphasis will therefore be laid on the first two decisions. It will also address the precautionary principle, since the decision to accept this principle as a starting-point can be regarded as an important international policy shift. An overview will be given of the implementation of the decisions on the reduction of inputs of nutrients and dangerous substances by the North Sea states and by the EC (which is a full party to the North Sea Conferences). The review of national actions will be preceded by overviews of the national administrative situation with regard to control of water pollution. The last is very important for the practice of implementation.

The information presented in this paper is based on the (limited) material that was published by the various governments and on the material collected by the national organizations participating in the Seas at Risk Federation. The material of the Preparatory Working Group (PWG)[1] is not publicly available. This seriously limits the opportunity to present a thorough evaluation of the implementation process. No information is available on the situation in France.

Belgium

Administration

Belgium is divided into three Regions: Flanders, Wallonië and Brussels. Each district has its own government which is to a large extent independent of the central government. The undertakings signed at the North Sea Conferences by the Belgian Minister Smet can therefore not be imposed on the regional governments.

The regional governments are in charge of issuing discharge consents. Discharge limits are fixed for various sectors of industry. They are based on uniform emission standards. Exceptions are made when no economically feasible technologies are available. The permits are often issued for a very long period (30 years), and their content is secret. The regional water purification boards are in charge of the control of discharges. The control is almost exclusively directed to emission standards and not to the quality of the receiving waters.

Recently a report on the efficacy of the Flemish purification board leaked out.[2] The survey was commissioned by the Flemish Minister of the Environment. The report concludes that the condition of the surface water in the Flemish region is very bad: 75 per cent can be considered to be biologically dead. Poor control on discharges is criticized: at the most plants are checked once a year. In 10 per cent of the checks violations of the permits are found but there are hardly any prosecutions. Only 54 per cent of sewage is treated and only 57 per cent of the population is connected to the sewer system. The situation in the Brussels and Wallonië regions is no better. The sewage of the Brussels region, for example (with over 1 million inhabitants), is discharged untreated.

Implementation

On 20 May 1989 an agreement for co-operation on the protection of the North Sea between the Belgian State and the Regions was signed by the Belgian Ministers of the Environment and Agriculture, and the regional Ministers responsible for the

[1] PWG officials from North Sea countries prepared the Third North Sea Conference.

[2] "Werking van de Vlaamse Maatschappij voor Waterzuivering (VMZ), May 1989": Consultatieopdracht van de Gemeenschapsminister van Leefmilieu. Eindrapport.

Environment.[3] In the agreement the Ministers decided to "strive for a substantial reduction of inputs to the North Sea via rivers and estuaries, of bio- accumulating, persistent and toxic substances". The same wording is used for the reduction of the inputs of nutrients. There is little further elaboration of these agreements in the document itself. No specific aims are given, nor is there any indication as to the substances for which discharges will be reduced.

Reduction of dangerous substances has to be effected by "starting treatment of waste streams where necessary", by "executing a strict control", and by a revision of the existing system of general and sectorial norms.[4]

Reduction of nutrient inputs will be realized by "a coherent and balanced reduction of various waste streams through the elaboration and application of appropriate measures".[5] *In agriculture* the use of manure and fertilizer will be attuned to the nutritive requirements of the crops, new techniques will be stimulated and over-concentration of farms will be avoided. *In the urban* sector plans will be developed for the realization of primary and secondary treatment of sewage by 1997; possibilities for tertiary treatment will be investigated; further limitations of phosphate contents of detergent will be enforced.

The acceptance of the Precautionary Principle is specifically mentioned in the document. The Precautionary Principle has been defined in precise accordance with the London Declaration.[6]

Denmark

Administration

The administrative system responsible for water protection in Denmark is rather decentralized. Depending on the size of the discharge, permits are issued by regional or local authorities. Only discharge permits for larger plants are issued by the National Agency for Environmental Protection (NAEP). The authority which issues the permit is also responsible for the control. Limits are set according to guidelines from the Environmental Protection Act (EPA). Regional or local authorities may impose tighter limits than indicated by the guidelines. This can be the case when the quality of the receiving water is deteriorating. In fact a combination of the uniform emission approach and the environmental quality approach is used. The decentralized system makes it hard to approach the protection of the water quality in a uniform way. It also hampers implementation. Since 1974 when the EPA became effective, a lot of illegal discharges occurred without action being taken by the responsible authorities. In 1987 the Danish Parliament decided that illegal discharges should be ended within 6 months.

[3] Plechtige verklaring inzake het ontwerp-regeringsakkoord tussen de staat en de gewesten met als doel een verhoogde bescherming van de Noordzee tegen verontreiniging (Ostend, 20 May 1989).

[4] *Ibid.* 4 n. 3.

[5] *Ibid.* 5 n. 3.

[6] See *Second International Conference on the Protection of the North Sea, London, 24–25 November 1987, Ministerial Declaration, issued by the Department of the Environment of the United Kingdom, April 1988*, xvi. 1.

Implementation

In May 1987 the Danish Parliament accepted an Action Plan for the Marine Environment. The major goal of the plan was to reduce inputs of *nitrogen* and *phosphorus* to Danish waters by 50 per cent in the period 1987–1990. In 1988 a new Danish Parliament decided on a relaxation of the Plan: Agriculture should meet the goals before 1993; Municipalities were offered two more years but refused, their planning makes it possible to meet the demands before 1993; Industry has until the end of 1994. The plan focuses mainly on agriculture and urban discharges, the major sources of nutrient pollution. In *agriculture* rules for spreading manure, use and application of fertilizer, and covering of fields in the winter period are imposed on farmers. Discharge limits for *municipal sewage treatment* plants have been tightened to 8 mg/l of nitrogen and 1.5 mg/l of phosphorus. *Industry* must use the best available technology to reduce nutrient discharges. Although the Action Plan is the most far-reaching nutrient reduction plan of the North Sea states, it is already generally recognized that the goals will not be reached. This is mainly due to insufficient reductions of agricultural inputs.

The Danish Government has laid most emphasis on the reduction of nutrient inputs. The required reduction of discharges of *dangerous substances* will be achieved by the already mentioned improvement of municipal sewage treatment: "Denmark has a fairly low level of industrial activity, but intensive agriculture; thus point source discharges of toxic or persistent, etc. substances are small, and most industrial plants discharge their waste water through the municipal treatment system.[7] Denmark has submitted a priority list of dangerous substances to the PWG. The provisional list contains 69 substances. On the basis of this list specific reduction programmes for individual substances will be drawn up.[8] Agricultural pesticides are subject to a reduction programme on a voluntary basis which aims at reducing the use of pesticides by 25 per cent in 1990 and 50 per cent in 1997.[9]

The NAEP has proposed a revision of the guidelines in the Danish national water protection policy, "to give greater prominence to the *Precautionary Principle* and to the use of best available technology".[10]

Federal Republic of Germany

Administration

The Federal Republic of Germany (FRG) comprises 11 Länder. For the pollution of the marine environment (North Sea, Baltic Sea), the Länder bordering these seas and those in the catchment areas of the rivers Rhine, Elbe, Weser and Oder

[7] National follow-up of the *Ministerial Declaration of the Second International Conference on the Protection of the North Sea*. National Agency of Environmental Protection, Denmark (29 September 1988).

[8] "Progress Report for Denmark on Inputs of Substances that are Persistent, Toxic and Liable to Bioaccumulate", National Agency of Environmental Protection, Denmark (24 April 1989).

[9] *Ibid*. n. 5.

[10] *Ibid*. n. 6.

are important. Discharges of substances to the German waters are covered by a framework law, the Wasserhaushaltsgesetz (WHG). The various Länder are responsible for the implementation of the WHG through regional Acts. According to the WHG all effluents must be treated with the Best Available Technology (BAT);[11] dangerous substances have to be treated with the Best Technical Means (BTM).[12] BATs and BTMs for different sectors[13] are drawn up by the central Government and have to be ratified by the individual Länder. The Governments of the Länder are responsible for the issuing of discharge permits and for the control of discharges.

The federal system under which the Länder have a great deal of administrative power makes the national implementation of international agreements an extremely slow process.

Implementation

In the summer of 1988 the German Minister of the Environment, Töpfer, announced a 10-point catalogue for strengthening the efforts to protect the North Sea and the Baltic Sea. The Minister was very specific on reductions of *nutrient* inputs from sewage treatment plants: as of 1 January 1989 discharge limits for phosphorus will be tightened to 1 mg/l for large installations (100,000 population equivalents and more) and 2 mg/l for smaller installations (20,000 equivalents and more); ammonium emissions may not exceed 10 mg/l and as of 1991 all sewage treatment plants of 5,000 equivalents and more must have denitrification facilities. As regards the reduction of *dangerous substances* the Minister announced a state-of-the-art limitation of hazardous substances in industrial waste. For at least 10 important industrial sectors new requirements are planned to be set by mid–1989.

On 17 January 1989 the German Government presented its intentions with regard to the implementation of the Second INSC to the German Parliament.[14] A variety of measures together with the necessary legal adaptations was announced. The above-mentioned new requirements for *sewage treatment plants* are confirmed. Financial support for the Länder to carry out the improvements was promised. It is estimated that the Länder will have to spend 3 billion DM extra in a 5-year period. The Central Government, however, cannot force the Länder to use the money in the way it wants. By the end of 1988 80 per cent of the detergent market is phosphate free. Requirements for nutrient reduction in the *industrial* sector will be comparable to those for the urban sector. A study group has been established to investigate the introduction of BAT for the reduction of nutrient discharges.

[11] Allgemein anerkannten Regeln der Techniek (aaRdT).
[12] Stand der Techniek (SdT)
[13] Abwasserverwaltungsvorschrift (AbwVwV)
[14] Bericht der Bundesregierung über den Stand der Arbeiten zur Umsetzung der Beschlüsse der 2. Internationalen Nordseeschutz- Konferenz (2.INK) vom 24. bis 25. November 1987 in London. Deutscher Bundestag. 11. Wahlperiode. Drucksache 11/3847. 17 January 1989.

A catalogue with measures for the reduction of nutrient inputs by *agriculture* is presented. It includes rules for spreading of manure the application of fertilizer according to "good practice", the creation of stripes of land along waters where no manure may be applied, and "extensivation".[15] Research into alternative agriculture will also be set up. The effect of all these measures cannot be estimated.

Reduction of discharges of *dangerous substances* has to be achieved by tightening the WHG by enacting new implementing orders for the various sectors. Thirty study groups have been established to elaborate the orders. As to the reduction of *diffuse inputs* of dangerous substances the German Government intends to investigate the possibilities prohibiting the production, use and distribution of certain dangerous substances. It is noted that problems may be expected within the EC context. As of 27 July 1988 a regulation is operative prescribing a standstill of new active ingredients for pesticides and limiting the use of existing active ingredients.

The German Government gives a clear definition of the *Precautionary Principle*: inputs of accumulating, persistent and toxic substances must be reduced at source by using BTM. The already-mentioned ban on the production, use and distribution of certain dangerous substances is also part of the German view on the implementation of the Precautionary Principle.

Netherlands

Administration

Directorates of the Ministry of Transport and Public Works are responsible for issuing permits for discharges to State Waters; these are the major rivers, estuaries and lakes. The Provinces are responsible for discharges to other waters. The authorities have to make a public announcement before issuing a permit and to consult interest groups. There is institutionalized co-ordination between central and regional authorities. The Dutch water quality policy is based on a combination of an emission approach and a water quality approach: discharges of blacklist substances must be eliminated using BTM; for a number of blacklist substances discharge limits have been set in accordance with EC Directives. Effluents containing other substances must be treated with BAT. Here the standstill principle applies: the quality of the receiving waters must not deteriorate.

Enforcement is the responsibility of the authority which issues the permits. Despite a relatively centralized administrative system and fairly good communication between the various responsible departments, the implementation and enforcement of Dutch water quality policy must be regarded as insufficient. This was the conclusion of a survey by the Dutch Auditors Office.[16] The recently pub-

[15] "Extensivation" means here making less intensive use of natural resources, i.e. by increasing the area of fallow land or reducing animal density.

[16] Milieubeleid Oppervlaktewateren. Algemene Rekenkamer. Tweede Kamer der Staten-Generaal. TK 1986–1987, 20 020, nos. 1–2.

lished Third Memorandum on Water Management,[17] covering the period 1990–1994, concluded that, despite an improvement in the situation with regard to discharges of blacklist substances, water quality must be regarded as poor. Nutrients, pesticides and organic micropollutants like PAHs cause particular problems.

Implementation

In January 1989 the Dutch Minister of Transport and Public Works published the proceedings of the Rhine Action Programme (RAP) and the North Sea Action Programme (NAP)—the Dutch implementation of the Eighth Ministerial Rhine Conference and the Second INSC. There is a clear interrelationship between the two plans, even more so since the Dutch Government has decided to apply the agreements of the Rhine Conference to all other Dutch waters.

In accordance with the agreements of the Ninth Rhine Conference (Bonn, 11 October 1988) new requirements for *municipal sewage treatment plants* were fixed: the limit value for *phosphorus* will be 1 mg/l for large plants (100,000 p.e. and more) and 2 mg/l for plants of 20,000 equivalents or more. This must result in a 75 per cent reduction of inputs of phosphorus from urban sources in the period 1985–1995. Two Dutch phosphate fertilizer industries have agreed to reduce phosphate inputs by 50 per cent by 1995. Effluents of municipal sewage treatment plants of 5,000 p.e. and more may contain at most 10 mg/l of *ammonium*. This is also in accordance with the Ninth Rhine Conference. No specific measures were announced to reduce inputs of *nitrogen*. Agriculture is the major source of nitrogen pollution. With the present legal instruments (i.e. for handling of manure) a maximum reduction of 25 per cent by 1995 is expected.

The Dutch Government has published a priority list containing *40 dangerous substances*. For the Rhine catchment area input data for the reference year 1985 have been fixed. 1985 data for discharges to other Dutch rivers are expected by the end of 1989. In the already mentioned Memorandum on Water Management the future goal for reduction of *heavy metals* has been set at 50 to 90 per cent; in 1995 the intermediate goal of a 50 per cent reduction (compared with the situation in 1985) must be reached. The final reduction goal for *organic micropollutants* has been set at 90 per cent with an intermediate 50 per cent (and for some substances 90 per cent) reduction by 1995. These reductions must be reached through strict emission reduction whereby prevention has priority. Policies for the reduction of inputs of *pesticides* are being developed; the policy goal for the year 2000 is a reduction of the use of at least 50 per cent.

The Dutch Government has not indicated how it will elaborate the *Precautionary Principle*. In the implementation of the RAP and the NAP the importance of the acceptance of the Precautionary Principle by all North Sea states is stressed.

[17] Water voor nu en later. Derde Nota Waterhuishouding. Tweede Kamer der Staten-Generaal, TK 1988–1989, 21 250, nos.1–2.

Norway

Administration

Norway is divided into 19 Regions and about 450 Municipalities which all have their own authorities and some degree of self-government. Discharge permits for all private and state owned factories are issued by the State Pollution Inspectorate (SFT),[18] which operates under the responsibility of the State Environmental Department (MD).[19] Regional and local authorities as well as special interest organizations are consulted before permits are granted. Regional authorities are responsible for discharge control of agriculture, aquaculture and sewage treatment plants. Municipalities are responsible for sewage and refuse treatment. Until recently municipalities had no specific body concerned with environmental protection. To date in 80 municipalities pollution divisions operate on an experimental level. The body that issues the discharge permit is also responsible for the control.

The Norwegian water quality policy is based neither on the emission approach nor the water quality approach. There are quality standards for drinking-water and bathing-water and there are discharge limits for a few substances. In general an environmental capacity approach is followed meaning that action is taken once pollution is clearly obvious. The last becomes clear from the results of a survey into the quality of Norwegian waters.[20] It concluded that over 1,000 square kilometres of Norwegian fiords are seriously polluted.

Implementation

In October 1988 the Norwegian Government published a preliminary working programme to follow-up the Second INSC.[21] In the programme plans are announced for the construction of sewage treatment plants in the area between the Swedish border and Stavanger, with a total capacity of 1.1 million p.e.s. The result of this, together with the modernization of existing plants, means that a 60 to 70 per cent reduction of *phosphate* inputs between 1985 and 1995 is expected. A 20 per cent reduction of nutrient inputs from *agriculture* is expected to result from planned use of fertilizers, more effective control of point emissions and improvement of ground levelling practices. The *artificial fertilizer industry* is a major source of nitrogen inputs into Norwegian waters. The Hydro Porsgrunn plant must reduce nitrogen inputs by 50 per cent by the end of 1990 and must investigate further reductions at a later stage.

As for the inputs of *dangerous substances*, the Norwegian Government announced a systematic review of industrial permits in the course of 1988/1989 with

[18] Statens Forurensingstilsyn.

[19] Miljöverndepartementet.

[20] This is concluded in the report of a survey by the SFT into the pollution situation of Norwegian waters. The survey was carried out in 1987.

[21] "Preliminary Working Programme for Norwegian Follow-up of the International Conference on Protection of the North Sea, London 24–25 November 1987". Ministry of Environment, Norway (October 1988).

the aim of improving the water quality of the most exposed fiords. It is estimated that this will result in a more than 50 per cent reduction in the period 1985–1995. Based on the results of the above-mentioned survey by the SFT, 13 priority substances have been selected for which the reduction measures must be carried out.

No reference is made to the *Precautionary Principle*; however, a special paragraph in the Working Programme deals with product control. In the period to 1995 measures will be introduced for the reduction of the use of products containing mercury, cadmium, PCBs and organic tin compounds. Also a national system for the collection of used batteries is announced.

United Kingdom

Administration

In England and Wales discharges of effluent to rivers, estuaries and coastal waters require consent from one of the ten water authorities. The Ministry of Agriculture, Fisheries and Food (MAFF) advises water authorities on the limits for discharges to estuaries and coastal waters. The discharge of effluent from a sewage works also requires a consent by Her Majesty's Inspectorate of Pollution (HMIP) on behalf of the Secretary of State for the Environment. The Water Act 1989 transfers the water pollution control functions of the present Water Authorities to the new National Rivers Authority (NRA).[22] Similar provisions apply in Scotland where seven river purification authorities control the system, and in Northern Ireland, where responsibility rests with the DOE for Northern Ireland.

In England and Wales control of discharges to rivers and through coastal outfalls is exercised by the 10 water authorities under the responsibility of DOE. The Scottish Development Department (SDD), Department of Agriculture and Fisheries for Scotland (DAFS) and the DOE for Northern Ireland have similar responsibilities in their territorial areas.

The general principle governing the control of discharges has been a system of Environmental Quality Standards (EQS), defined in terms of use, for different stretches of water. EQSs are fixed in such a way that "unacceptable damage" is prevented "wherever practical".[23]

The UK Government considers that "the environmental quality approach . . . has served us well." "The 1985 River Quality Survey showed that 90 per cent of the rivers in England and Wales were of 'good' or 'fair' quality and only 2 per cent remained of poor quality. A similar picture applies to estuaries."[24] A recently pub-

[22] "Inputs of Dangerous Substances to Water: Proposals for a Unified System of Control": the Government's consultative proposals for tighter controls over the most dangerous substances entering the aquatic environment ("The Red List"). Department of the Environment, July 1988. See also generally, Chapter 6.

[23] "Controlling Pollution: Principles and Prospects", Department of the Environment, 1984, p. 2.

[24] *Ibid*. 2 n. 20 (para. 5).

lished Greenpeace survey reveals that the quality of UK rivers has rapidly declined: between 1985 and 1989 there was a net deterioration of 895 kilometres of rivers.[25]

Implementation

In February 1988, the UK Department of the Environment published its "Guidance Note on the Ministerial Declaration"[26] in which the ideas of the British Government as to the implementation of the London Declaration are presented.

With regard to inputs of *nutrients* it is noted that the Wadden Sea and the Skagerrak are the areas most affected by nutrient pollution. The UK will review nutrient concentrations in its coastal and estuarine waters before considering reduction measures. By now the results of the survey are known; it is concluded that British waters in general are hardly affected by nutrients.[27] The UK Government will "prepare the plan required by the Declaration to combat any problems identified."[28] The plan will cover the source emissions of NOx from vehicles, emissions from large combustion plants, nitrates in drinking-water and phosphates in fresh water.

In the Guidance Note reference is made to a "Red List" of *dangerous substances* to be reduced by 50 per cent between 1985 and 1995. The list is contained in the Government's proposal for a unified system of control.[29] It includes 26 dangerous substances. According to the Guidance Note the proposal for a unified system of control is consistent with the complementary use of EQSs and UESs, as adopted at the 1987 INSC. In advance of new legislation, action must be taken by water authorities and industries to reduce discharges of dangerous substances. Water authorities must draw up action plans according to Guidelines issued by the Government. The plans must contain proposals for achieving the 50 per cent reduction, the 1985 baseline values, a timetable for the implementation of existing legislation and information on diffuse sources. At the national level, quality objectives for rivers and estuaries for the Red List substances must be set and diffuse sources identified.

According to the Guidance Note, the *Precautionary Principle* involves both the use of BAT for point sources as well as controls on the manufacture, marketing, use and disposal of products containing such substances for diffuse sources. The definition of BAT is specified by the addition that economic availability is taken into account.[30]

[25] T. Birch, *Poison in the System. Water Pollution: A Critical View on the Role of Industry, Water Authorities, the Public and the Control of Pollution Act* (London: Greenpeace UK, 1989).

[26] *Second International Conference on the Protection of the North Sea, London, 24–25 November 1987, Ministerial Declaration, issued by the Department of the Environment of the United Kingdom, April 1988.*

[27] *North Sea Monitor*, 89–3.

[28] *Ibid.* n. 26 (para. 14).

[29] *Ibid.* n. 22.

[30] *Ibid.* n. 26 (para. 7).

Sweden

Administration

For large-scale activities consent from the Franchise Board, an environmental court, is necessary. County administrations issue permits for activities on a smaller scale. The Environmental Protection Board is responsible for monitoring seas and rivers. County administrations control discharges to local sea areas and rivers in their Counties. In Sweden the Uniform Emission approach is the basis of the water quality policy. According to the Swedish Environmental Protection Act disturbances of the environment shall be prevented as far as is practically feasible; unnecessary disturbances should not be tolerated under any circumstances.

In August 1986 the Swedish Government appointed a Task Force on marine pollution. The Task Force commissioned the National Environmental Protection Board to produce an action plan. The plan was submitted to the Government in May 1987.[31] According to the Action Plan the marine areas surrounding Sweden are seriously threatened. Discharges originating in Sweden affect primarily the Swedish coastal waters and contribute relatively little to the overall pollution load in the open sea, with the exception of chlorinated organic substances originating from the pulp and paper industry, certain metals and nutrients (to the Kattegatt). The plan gives therefore highest priority to the limitation of discharges of stable organic substances and nutrients.

Implementation

The conclusions of the Action Plan are reflected in the Swedish contribution to the preparatory work of the Third INSC. In the Statement, presented at the Preparatory Meeting of Senior Officials (The Hague, 19–20 October 1988), Sweden announced a 50 per cent reduction of *nutrient* inputs to particularly sensitive areas before the end of the century. For discharges from *municipal sewage treatment plants* to coastal areas that are particularly affected a 50 per cent reduction in *nitrogen* discharges should be effected before the end of 1992. Discharges to other coastal areas should be halved before 1995. Reduction of nutrient leakage from *agriculture* is covered by a separate agricultural Bill aiming at a 50 per cent reduction of nutrient discharges by the end of the century. The Bill gives regulations for the keeping of animals, fertilizer use and crop cultivation. The use of fertilizers is to be reduced by 20 per cent by the end of the century. The Government proposes that the environmental levy on fertilizers and pesticides should be doubled.

With regard to *dangerous substances* the following plans are revealed in the Statement. In the long term, discharges of stable organic chlorine compounds from pulp and paper mills are to cease entirely. In the initial phase discharges are to be cut by 60 to 70 per cent. Licences of existing plants will be reviewed before the end

[31] "Action Plan for Marine Pollution", National Swedish Environmental Protection Board, Solna (May 1987).

of 1990. Discharges of mercury and cadmium must be reduced by 50 per cent by 1995. Discharges of copper, lead and arsenic are to be considerable reduced.

Sweden has screened the various priority lists that have been proposed by the North Sea states.[32] It has used a selection procedure in which persistence is the most important discriminating factor.

> "[F]or compounds, which are persistent and bioaccumulating, restrictions should be applied even if we have not found any effects of them. We cannot afford building up increasing concentrations of substances which may have effects we are not aware of yet."[33]

By this Sweden has given a practical elaboration of the *Precautionary Principle* with regard to dangerous substances.

European Community

Administration

The role of the EC with regard to water quality management is primarily expressed through a number of Directives on the quality of water used for specific purposes and on discharges of dangerous substances into water. There are now Directives giving quality standards for drinking-water, fishing waters, shellfish water and bathing-water. Discharges of dangerous substances to the waters of the Community are covered by the 76/464 framework Directive. The Directive aims at the elimination of discharges of blacklist substances by fixing uniform emission standards and water quality objectives.

The implementation of the EC Directives cannot be regarded as very successful. Since the ratification of the framework Directive 76/464 only six daughter Directives covering twelve substances have come into force. The implementation at the national level is an even slower process.[34] The enforcement of the EC Directives is very problematic. A recent example is the non-compliance of the UK with the Directive on drinking-water quality. After 10 years of violation of the Directive the EC decided in September 1989 to begin a case against the UK before the European Court.

Implementation

The role of the EC as a party to the North Sea Ministerial Conferences is a rather peculiar one. The EC is the only supra-national body which is a full party to the Conference. The EC is also party to the Paris Convention and the Rhine Convention. The position of the EC in these forums is important for the bringing about and

[32] "Report on the Meeting of the Informal Working Group on Guidelines for the Reporting on the Implementation of the HELCOM Declaration. Baltic Marine Environment Commission—Helsinki Commission. 27–28 February 1989". See also F. de Jong, "Policies for Effluent Waters. Proceedings of the Third North Sea Seminar", in C. T. H. Ten Hallers (ed), *Werkgroep Noordzee* (Amsterdam. 1989).

[33] *Ibid.* 2 n. 32.

[34] *Ibid.* 2 n. 33.

implementation of international agreements, but this is beyond the scope of this contribution.

In June 1988 a Ministerial Seminar on the future Community water policy announced that actions will be prepared in the *industrial and municipal* sector with regard to the treatment of *waste water*. A commission of the EC DG XI department is presently working on the elaboration of emission standards and quality objectives for *18 priority substances*, compiled from the original list of 129 potential blacklist substances, annexed to the 76/464 Directive. At the end of 1988 the Commission published a proposal for a Directive on *diffuse nitrate* pollution.[35] The Directive gives rules for application of manure, capacity of manure storage and maximum application rates for fertilizer. The total nitrogen content of effluents from municipal sewage treatment plants of 5,000 p.e. and more may not exceed 10 mg/l. This only applies to vulnerable zones, which should be designated by the Member States within a 2-year period following the notification of the Directive. The criteria for vulnerable areas are rather weak.

Discussion and Conclusions

Introduction

It is at this stage hard to present a thorough evaluation of the implementation of the Second INSC. It is even harder to evaluate the practical results. There are several reasons for this. The time-lag between the Second and the Third Conferences is too short: the results of the Conference must be transferred and delegated to many different levels of the administrative system; this part of the implementation process can be frustrated by resistance from regional and local authorities, administrations and politicians. In many cases new legislation must be developed and enforced; this is a time-consuming process; resistance may be expected from industries, farmers, local and regional authorities. In most cases only plans have been produced by Governments, often based on rough estimates. It is therefore hard to judge these plans although it is fair to assume that they will in general present a too optimistic view as to the expected results.

Still, it is possible to describe some general lines in the material that has been presented. The following three issues will be addressed: "dangerous substances and nutrients", "*The Precautionary Principle*", and "effects on existing policies".

Dangerous Substances and Nutrients

The decision taken at the Second INSC to reduce inputs of nutrients and dangerous substances by 50 per cent is a new concept because it is about the reduction of *loads* instead of concentrations. A major problem is the fixing of the baseline input data of the reference year 1985. Half a year before the Third Conference only the Netherlands had produced 1985 data. Most states do not make a clear distinction

[35] "Commission of the European Communities. Proposal for a Council Directive Concerning the Protection of Fresh, Coastal and Marine Waters against Pollution Caused by Nitrates from Diffuse Sources", Brussels (22 December 1988).

between the "nutrient" and the "dangerous substances" decision. Both are part of the priority list. A notable exception is the UK which concludes that there are no eutrophication problems in its coastal waters.

In general it can be concluded that the follow-up plans are most specific about new conditions for sewage treatment plants, especially with regard to phosphates. This seems logical since in most cases central Governments can have direct influence on the implementation of those plans, unlike the industrial and agricultural sectors. The UK is a clear exception: in the Guidance Note most emphasis has been laid on the reduction of dangerous substances. Nutrients are not considered a serious problem, at least not as to salt water. In the plans of the FRG, The Netherlands and Belgium (further) reduction of phosphate-containing detergents is a policy goal. It should, however, be kept in mind that present reductions have primarily been the result of market developments. Hardly any specific plans for the reduction of nitrate inputs have been announced. This is especially the case for nitrate inputs from agriculture, the major source. Sweden and Denmark are here the positive exceptions. With regard to nutrient reductions it can be concluded that there is a fair chance that most states will fulfil the 50 per cent reduction goal for phosphorus, but that a 50 per cent nitrate reduction will not be achieved in any country. Sweden might be the exception here.

The proposed EC Directive on nutrients will hardly have a noticeable effect: in the first place because the proposed measures in agriculture are far from sufficient; this is even more disappointing since the EC is the appropriate body to tackle problems of agriculture. Secondly, national implementation will certainly not be effective before 1995.

The implementation of the "dangerous substances" decision depends to a great deal on the ability of the administrative system to tighten discharge licences of industries. In many cases this will be hard in the short term, at least on a legal basis: they can probably not base themselves on the London decisions since these are probably not legally binding (see Chapter 2). Governments will therefore have to negotiate with industries to achieve the necessary reduction figures. The long-term result of these negotiations is uncertain since the agreements are generally not legally binding.

The Precautionary Principle

The *Precautionary Principle* as defined in the Final Declaration of the Second INSC[36] is more a reduction principle than a precaution principle. Even worse, the reduction goal in the *Principle* is weakened by the caveat that "throughout this Declaration, the term 'Best Available Technology' is understood to take into account economic availability".[37] It seems necessary to come to clear internationally agreed definitions of BAT, BTM and BPM (Best Practical Means). BAT now

[36] *Second International Conference on the Protection of the North Sea, London, 24–25 November 1987, Ministerial Declaration, issued by the Department of the Environment of the United Kingdom, April 1988*. xvi. 1.

[37] *Ibid*. 7 n. 26.

seems to have become downgraded to BPM. This development was confirmed by the Paris Commission in its meeting of June 1988. The Commission recommended that BAT should be understood to take into account economic availability. The FRG made a reservation because "this recommendation does not reflect the principle of precautionary action contained in paragraph xvi. 1 of the London Conference Declaration".[38]

Some states (FRG, UK) specifically indicate that product control is part of the Precautionary Principle; the FRG mentions a *ban* on production, use and control of certain dangerous substances whereas the UK uses the word "control". Norway also includes product control in its working programme. In Sweden, Denmark and The Netherlands some form of production control is already operative. The Netherlands have, for example, forbidden the production and use of certain PCB-substitutes;[39] in Sweden a law is operative which forbids the use of substances for which less dangerous alternatives exist.

Most states have announced that they will reduce the use of pesticides. Sweden and Denmark are again the leading states: Sweden already imposes levies on pesticides and has announced its intention to double those levies; in Denmark a voluntary reduction programme is operative.

Various developments in agriculture must also be regarded as "precautionary actions". The reduction of the use of pesticides has just been mentioned. Extensivation, "alternative" agricultural practices, and reduction of fertilizer use are other examples.

Effects on existing policies

Existing policies for the protection of the quality of fresh and salt waters so far have been completely insufficient: in most countries surface water, ground water and marine waters are polluted with nutrients and a variety of heavy metals and organic micropollutants; moreover, sediments have accumulated large amounts of toxic substances which will leak into the water in the next decades.[40] The INSCs, and particularly the Second Conference, have certainly set things in motion in most North Sea states. Still, public opinion, especially after the 1988 algal blooms and seal epidemic, have had far more impact on Governments. Exceptions here are Belgium and the UK. It is therefore not surprising that these countries have produced the weakest sanitation programmes. An evaluation of national implementation also reveals the differences between the present sanitation situation in the North Sea states. Belgium and the UK lag far behind the other countries. Enormous investments will be necessary to make up for this. But the most striking is the fact that, despite a certain speeding up of implementation and a possible improvement of enforcement, resulting from the gatherings of the North Sea Ministers, the actual reduction of the pollution of fresh and salt water systems will be totally

[38] Paris Commission. 1989. Tenth Annual Report, Annex 1: Parcom Recommendation 88/3 of 17 June 1988: "As a First Approach on the Use of Best Available Technology".

[39] *Ibid*. n. 33.

[40] *Ibid*.

insufficient. A 50 per cent reduction of inputs of a limited number of dangerous substances may be reached, but inputs of thousands of other toxic and persistent chemicals will continue; the gap between the substances for which legislation has and has not been achieved is increasing every day.

It is already obvious that the 50 per cent reduction of nutrient inputs will not be reached. Recent studies indicate that even if a 50 per cent reduction was to be reached, the eutrophication situation would still get worse; reductions of some 90 per cent for both nitrates and phosphates are necessary to improve the marine ecosystem.[41]

The Second INSC has produced a very limited and completely insufficient answer to the present problems of polluted fresh and saltwater ecosystems. The *Precautionary Principle*, potentially the most important instrument for the effective protection of the water quality, has been defined in a very poor way. From this it must be concluded that the North Sea Conferences have not really altered the existing policies.

The Third North Sea Conference should therefore not simply confine itself to the evaluation of the implementation of the London Final Declaration. It should set the basis for a fundamental policy change by clearly defining and elaborating the Precautionary Principle. Some North Sea states have already started this process by proposing and implementing more fundamental solutions like preventing production and use of potentially dangerous substances, the reduction of the use of fertilizers and pesticides by agriculture, the introduction of environmentally sound agricultural practices and an extensivation of common agriculture.

[41] B. J. E. Ten Brink, "Amoeba-approach: A Method for Description and Assessment of Ecosystems" (Poster presented at Third North Sea Seminar, Rotterdam 1989).

Chapter 5

Problems of Implementation of the North Sea Declarations: A Case Study of the United Kingdom*

J. Gibson and Dr. R. R. Churchill

Introduction

In considering the impact of the Bremen and London Declarations, an important question is obviously the extent to which the North Sea states have implemented the various undertakings given in these Declarations. The aim of this chapter is to look at this question of implementation, focusing in particular on the United Kingdom. Of the North Sea states, the UK is particularly appropriate as the choice of such an implementation study, both because it is one of the major polluters of the North Sea and because it is commonly regarded as being the North Sea state least keen on stricter controls on pollution of the marine environment.

To study the degree to which the UK (or any other North Sea state) has complied with or implemented the various undertakings in the Bremen and London Declarations is not, however, a straightforward matter. First of all, it is not always easy to determine exactly what obligations the Declarations contain. A number of the provisions of the Declarations (particularly of the Bremen Declaration) are vague and imprecise. Nor, as will be seen below, are the provisions of a Declaration on a particular topic always internally consistent. A second problem is the difficulty in some cases of making a judgement as to whether a particular obligation of the Declarations has been complied with: for example, whether as required by paragraph XVI. 39 of the London Declaration, "best available technology" is being applied to "minimize" any pollution caused by radioactive discharges from nuclear industries; or, in the case of dumping of waste at sea, whether there are "practical

* This chapter is based on a report on implementation of the INSC Declarations by the UK which the authors are preparing for Greenpeace International as part of an independent international assessment on implementation of the Declarations, to be presented to the Third INSC Conference. Funding from Greenpeace towards preparation of the report is gratefully acknowledged.

alternatives" on land which would therefore mean that no dumping should take place. A final difficulty in making an implementation study is that in assessing whether there has been compliance or implementation, it is usually not enough simply to look at the relevant legislation of the state concerned. In most cases it is essential, and often more important, to look as well at administrative policy and practice: however, information on these matters (at least in the UK) is not always easy to obtain.

Although the British Government has not, as far as the authors are aware, made any public statement about the legal status of the INSC Declarations,[1] it is likely that it does not regard the Declarations as being legally binding. Nevertheless the Government has said that it "attaches considerable importance to implementing" the Declarations.[2]

Much of this implementation is being done through the existing legislative and administrative framework, although major new legislation is planned in order to regulate inputs to rivers and estuaries of substances that are persistent, toxic and liable to bioaccumulate. It is also noteworthy that in February 1988 the Department of the Environment published a "Guidance Note" on the London Declaration,[3] the purpose of which was to set out the Government's thinking about the implications of each section of the Declaration, and to indicate what action was expected to follow as a result.

For reasons of space this chapter cannot look at all the matters dealt with by the Bremen and London Declarations and see how far the UK has complied with or implemented them. Instead it concentrates on looking at compliance and implementation in two areas—inputs of dangerous substances into rivers and estuaries and dumping. These two areas have been selected for study because, first, they illustrate rather well some of the problems involved in doing an implementation study which were referred to above, and second, these two areas are ones with which it might be expected beforehand that the UK would have difficulty, or show some reluctance, in complying. By looking at these areas, therefore, some idea of the impact of the Declarations can be gained.

Inputs via Rivers and Estuaries of Substances that are Persistent, Toxic and Liable to Bioaccumulate

The provisions of the Bremen Declaration[4] on the reduction of pollution from land-based sources were primarily directed towards the EC and the Paris Commission. It

[1] Though the then UK Secretary of State for the Environment, Mr. Ridley, has been reported as saying that the London Declaration was not legally binding but a common declaration of political will. See (1988) 19 *Marine Pollution Bulletin* 3.

[2] Government Observations on the Third Report of the Environment Committee, House of Commons Paper (hereafter HC) (1987–1988), 543, p. xiii.

[3] *Guidance Note on the Ministerial Declaration, Second International Conference on the Protection of the North Sea, London, Department of the Environment, 1988.*

[4] Part C.

was left until the London Conference to deal more specifically with proposals for national action.

Paragraphs 1–9 of point XVI of the London Declaration concern inputs via rivers and estuaries of substances that are persistent, toxic and liable to bioaccumulate. In paragraph XVI. 2, the Ministers agree to:

> "take measures to reduce urgently and drastically the total quantity of such substances reaching the aquatic environment of the North Sea, with the aim of achieving a substantial reduction (of the order of 50 per cent) in total inputs from these sources between 1985 and 1995."

It is characteristic of the somewhat equivocal wording of the Declaration that it does not simply refer to a "50 per cent reduction", but instead uses the adjective "substantial", which it then defines parenthetically as signifying something "in the order of 50 per cent". The target is accordingly not identified with absolute precision, but would seem to allow for some flexibility of interpretation. Nor is it explicit whether the figure should be calculated as an overall average whereby successes might offset failures, or, at the other extreme, as applying to every individual discharge. In practice, the UK has adopted a middle course, aiming for a 50 per cent reduction in the aggregate input of each substance.

The actions envisaged in order to reach this objective are described in paragraph XVI. 3. First, it is agreed to "intensify, to this end, measures in hand to reduce inputs of the substances listed in Annex A, which are already the subject of specific action". These are substances for which directives, decisions or recommendations currently exist in the European Community or the Paris Commission, and are identified as mercury, cadmium, PCBs/PCTs,[5] CTC,[6] organotin compounds, biocides,[7] wastes from the titanium dioxide industry, and oil from refineries and reception facilities. The second commitment is to "take positive action by setting concrete targets to reduce inputs of other potentially significant pollutants of the North Sea, including those from the sectors exemplified in Annex B". The examples of potentially significant pollutants listed in Annex B are: (a) persistent halogen compounds from the organic chemical industry, the pulp industry, pesticides manufacture and use, and the paper-making industry; (b) the use of chemical products (including PACs)[8] (c) dioxins; and (d) Grey List metals.[9]

An essential difference between the two Annexes is that Annex A prescribes a fixed list of identified substances, whereas Annex B illustrates an open-ended category whose components remain to be determined. Nevertheless, it might be

[5] Polychlorinated biphenyls/polychlorinated triphenyls.

[6] Carbon tetrachloride.

[7] HCH (hexachlorocyclohexane, e.g. lindane), DDT (an organochlorine insecticide), PCP (pentachloro phenol), PCC (polychlorinated camphenes), drins (a group of organochlorine insecticides).

[8] Polychlorinated aliphatic hydrocarbons.

[9] i.e. metals identified in Annex, List II, to the Council Directive 76/464/EEC of 4 May 1976 on pollution caused by dangerous substances discharged into the aquatic environment of the Community, OJ, L 129, 18 May 1976, p. 23, and Annex A, Part II, to the Convention of 4 June 1974 for the Prevention of Marine Pollution from Land-Based Sources (Paris Convention), Treaty Series No. 64 (1978), Cmnd. 7251.

supposed that the examples contained in Annex B should represent the minimum content of any such list, since paragraph XVI. 3 applies the word "including" to them. In practice, however, the UK regards Annex B as exemplificatory only, and considers itself free to select the particular pollutants appropriate for national action.

The "Red List"

In July 1988, the Department of the Environment and the Welsh Office published a joint consultation paper,[10] which proposed a screening system intended to identify a "Red List" of the most dangerous substances entering the aquatic environment;[11] a similar document relating to Scotland was issued by the Scottish Development Department in December 1988.[12] The selection procedure was initially applied to the 129 candidate substances for inclusion in List I of the EC Dangerous Substances Directive.[13] The properties and inputs of each substance are classified as either high, medium or low on scales that measure persistence, acute and chronic aquatic toxicity, toxicity to higher organisms, bioaccumulation, production, source, solubility and volatility. These classifications are then incorporated in three decision trees representing short-term, long-term, and food-chain scenarios in order to determine priority substances (see Figure 1). The exercise originally resulted in a provisional "Red List" of 26 such substances, with an additional 23 proposed as first priority candidates. Following consultation, however, the "Red List" has itself been reduced to 23 by the deletion of five substances[14] and the inclusion of another two.[15] In particular, although it was initially intended for administrative convenience to include all 12 substances[16] that possess full List I status under the EC Dangerous Substances Directive irrespective of the outcome of the screening process, chloroform and carbon tetrachloride have now been omitted because they failed to demonstrate priority need. The amended version of the "Red List", which was announced in Parliament on 10 April 1989,[17] is set out in Table 1.

In order to show compliance with the agreed 50 per cent reduction between 1985

[10] "Inputs of Dangerous Substances to Water: Proposals for a Unified System of Control", Department of the Environment/Welsh Office, July 1988.

[11] For an appraisal of the proposals, see "Control of Inputs of Dangerous Substances to Waters in the UK: A Response by the Marine Conservation Society", *North Sea Monitor*, January 1989, pp. 2–7.

[12] "Inputs of Dangerous Substances to Water: Proposals for a Unified System of Control", Scottish Development Department, December 1988.

[13] See *above*, n. 9. The substances are listed in the Communication from the Commission to the Council on dangerous substances which might be included in List I of Council Directive 76/464/EEC, OJ, C 176, 14 July 1982, p. 3.

[14] Chloroprene, 3-chlorotoluene, triorganotin compounds, chloroform, carbon tetrachloride.

[15] Tributyltin compounds, triphenyltin compounds.

[16] Mercury, cadmium, gamma-HCH (lindane), DDT, pentachlorophenol (PCP), carbon tetrachloride, hexachlorobenzine (HCB), hexachlorobutadiene (HCBD), aldrin, dieldrin, endrin, chloroform.

[17] HC, Vol. 150, Cols. 405–406 (WA), 10 April 1989; HL, Vol. 506, Cols. 121–123, 10 April 1989. See also HC, Vol. 157, Cols. 894–896 (WA), 27 July 1989, for the similar result of the Scottish consultation exercise.

Short Term Scenario

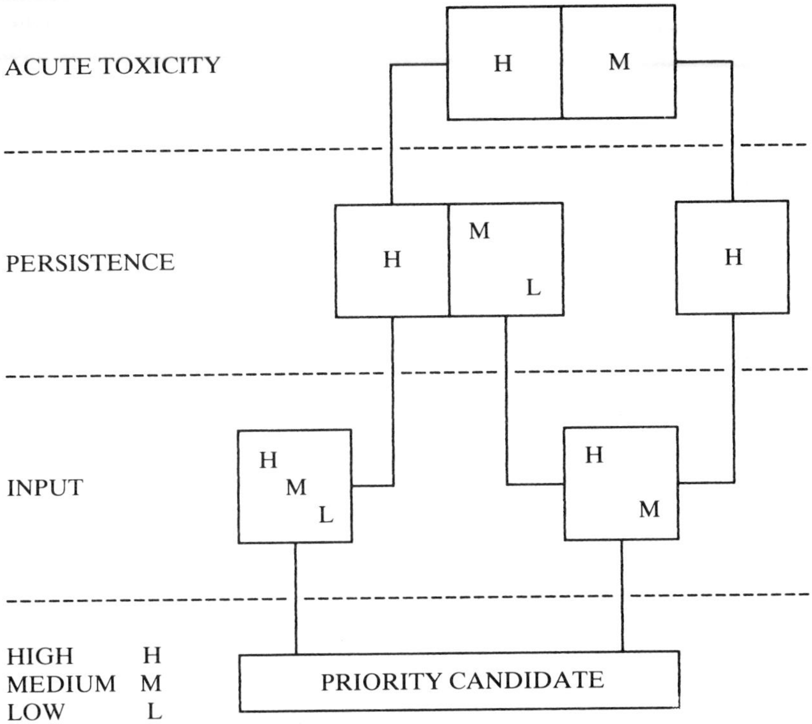

Figure 1 Selection of "Red List" Substances

TABLE 1 The "Red List"

Mercury and its compounds
Cadmium and its compounds
gamma-Hexachlorocyclohexane (Lindane)
DDT
Pentachlorophenol (PCP)
Hexachlorobenzene (HCB)
Hexachlorobutadiene (HCBD)
Aldrin
Dieldrin
Endrin
Polychlorinated Biphenyls (PCB)
Dichlorvos
1,2-Dichloroethane
Trichlorobenzene
Altrazine
Simazine
Tributyltin compounds
Triphenyltin compounds
Trifluralin
Fenitrothion
Azinphos-methyl
Malathion
Endosulfan

and 1995 in total inputs of substances that are persistent, toxic and liable to bioaccumulate, it will of course be necessary to compare data for the relevant years. There is an obvious difficulty in that the London Declaration adopts as its baseline a date two years before the agreement itself was signed. Moreover, it is unrealistic to expect all the necessary statistical information to be recorded until after each state has selected the substances for national action. In May 1988, the Scottish Development Department wrote to river purification authorities and regional councils in Scotland,[18] asking them to conduct surveys and prepare action plans for their areas. Likewise, in January 1989, the Department of the Environment issued detailed guidelines to water authorities in England and Wales.[19] The resultant surveys of "Red List" substances were expected to be complete by the end of 1989, and the information obtained provides the basis for drafting a national action plan for the UK.[20] Inevitably, however, data for earlier years is mainly confined to cases where monitoring has previously been required by the EC Dangerous Substances Directive.[21] Thus, in many instances, the reference year will necessarily be 1989, and the comparison will accordingly be too recent to prove conclusively whether the terms of the Declaration have been fulfilled.

Environmental Quality Objectives

Point XV of the London Declaration reaffirms the principles previously established in the Bremen Declaration[22] for the use of environmental quality objectives (EQO) and uniform emission standards (UES), and accepts that a simultaneous and complementary combination of both methods will establish a more precautionary approach to dangerous substances. The UK, unlike other European states, has traditionally favoured the application of environmental quality objectives to its rivers and estuaries, in order to obtain maximum economic advantage from the capacity of fast-flowing waters to assimilate pollutants. Thus, in the implementation of the EC Dangerous Substances Directive, Community EQOs are adopted for List I substances, specifying the concentration that must not be exceeded in receiving waters, having regard to the intended use of the area. For List II substances, water quality objectives are being set on a national basis by the Department of the Environment,

[18] River purification boards and islands councils are responsible for the control of water pollution in Scotland, whereas sewerage is undertaken by regional and islands councils. The Scottish water industry has not been privatized.

[19] Until 1 September 1989, water authorities were responsible for both sewerage and the control of water pollution in England and Wales. After privatization, their regulatory functions were transferred to the National Rivers Authority, which therefore took over the preparation of regional action plans. Continuity has been preserved, however, since the former staff of the water authorities are now employees of the NRA.

[20] Although Northern Ireland is outside the limits of the North Sea, action is also being taken there in order to comply with the requirement in point X of the London Declaration that there shall be no resultant increase in pollution elsewhere.

[21] In particular, mercury and cadmium.

[22] Paras. C6-C11.

and 17 have so far been established.[23] New guidance on the impact of the Directive was issued to authorities in England and Wales in March 1989.[24]

Under paragraph XVI. 3(c) of the London Declaration, it will be necessary to define strict environmental quality standards for all "Red List" substances where they do not already exist. Although Community EQOs are, of course, legally binding, the national water quality objectives have as yet no intrinsic legal status. However, the Water Act 1989[25] creates a new power for the Secretary of State for the Environment to establish statutory water quality objectives, and will place him and the National Rivers Authority under a duty to achieve and maintain them so far as practicable. In Scotland, the Control of Pollution Act 1974[26] has been amended to provide equivalent functions for the Secretary of State for Scotland and the river purification authorities. It was the Government's originally expressed intention that the statutory objectives should come into force for rivers and estuaries immediately upon enactment of the legislation privatizing the water industry in England and Wales.[27] Nevertheless, it has subsequently been decided that they will not now be introduced until Autumn 1992,[28] and their contribution towards the implementation of the London Declaration will to that extent be delayed.

Under British law, it is prima facie a criminal offence to discharge any trade or sewage effluent into "controlled waters", which include both inland and coastal waters up to three miles from the baseline of the territorial sea.[29] This strict legal formulation is, however, rather deceptive inasmuch as no offence is committed if a consent for the discharge has been obtained from the National Rivers Authority in England and Wales,[30] or from the appropriate river purification authority in Scotland.[31] Accordingly, the policy of the regulatory bodies in issuing consents is a more important factor in the control of pollution than the mere existence of legislation, and the function of water quality objectives is to guide them in the performance of that role.

In this context, the implementation of the INSC Declarations has been complicated by the competing demands of domestic political considerations. In 1987, the House of Commons Environment Committee revealed that 22 per cent of the sewage treatment works run by the English and Welsh water authorities were in breach

[23] Lead, chromium, zinc, copper, nickel, arsenic, boron, iron, pH, vanadium, tributyltin, triphenyltin, PCSDs, cyfluthrin, sulcofuron, flucofuron, permethrin.

[24] "Water and the Environment: The Implementation of European Community Directives on Pollution Caused by Certain Dangerous Substances Discharged into the Aquatic Environment", Department of the Environment Circular 7/89 (Welsh Office 16/89), 30 March 1989.

[25] ss. 105–106.

[26] ss. 30C-D, inserted by the Water Act 1989, Sch. 23.

[27] "The National Rivers Authority: The Government's Proposals for a Public Regulatory Body in a Privatised Water Industry", Department of the Environment/Ministry of Agriculture, Fisheries and Food/Welsh Office, July 1987, para. 4.6.

[28] HC, Vol. 143, Col. 401, 7 December 1988; Vol. 156, Col. 193, 4 July 1989. See also a letter from Andrew Lees, *The Times*, 7 June 1989, p. 15.

[29] Water Act 1989, ss. 103, 107 in England and Wales. The equivalent provisions in Scotland are Control of Pollution Act 1974, ss. 30A, 32, inserted by Water Act 1989, Sch. 23.

[30] Water Act 1989, s. 108.

[31] Control of Pollution Act 1974, s. 34, inserted by Water Act 1989, Sch. 23.

of their consents during 95 per cent of 1986 due to the inadequacy of past investment.[32] The ensuing privatization of those bodies would have been jeopardized if they had been offered for sale at a time when they were committing criminal offences. Accordingly, in November 1988, the Department of the Environment invited them to apply for a relaxation of the terms of their consents in order that they could claim to be complying with the law.[33] At the same time, an accelerated investment programme costing between £900 million and £1,000 million was announced with the aim of bringing almost all sewage works up to standard by March 1992.[34] In the mean time, the transition between public and private ownership has produced a temporary lacuna in the process of enforcement, since the successor companies are statutorily exempted from any criminal liabilities incurred in their previous capacity as water authorities,[35] and their obligation to comply with conditions in existing consents begins afresh from 1 September 1989.[36] Although prosecutions for past breaches may still be brought against the name of former water authorities, it is a fruitless exercise because they no longer have any assets from which to pay fines.[37] Moreover, compliance by the new companies is determined by the established "look-up table" procedure, which involves monitoring discharges over a period of one year to see whether they fulfil their consents for 95 per cent of the time.

This effectively means that they cannot now be prosecuted until 12 months after the transfer date. On the other hand, new regulations[38] do at least require them to refer to the Secretary of State for the Environment any applications that they themselves receive for permission to discharge trade effluents containing more than background concentrations of "Red List" substances into public sewers; and this also applies if they propose to vary existing consents so as to permit such discharges.

Uniform Emission Standards

In paragraph XVI. 3(a) of the London Declaration, the Ministers agree to "identify the best available technology for particular processes giving rise to point source discharges" of substances that are persistent, toxic and liable to bioaccumulate. The UK intends to implement this through the introduction of integrated pollution control proposed in the new Environmental Protection Bill. Under this system, certain industrial processes that discharge significant quantities of harmful wastes to air, land or water will be "scheduled" by the Secretary of State for the Environment,

[32] Third Report from the House of Commons Environment Committee, "Pollution of Rivers and Estuaries", HC (1986–1987), 183-I, p. xvi.

[33] See HC, Vol. 149, Col. 1018, 21 March 1989. Over 1,000 applications were received: *The Times*, 16 May 1989, p. 5.

[34] HC, Vol. 143, Cols. 199–200 (WA), 7 December 1988.

[35] Water Act 1989, Sch. 26, para. 58.

[36] *Ibid*. Sch. 26, para. 25(7).

[37] See a report of the conviction of the Severn Trent Water Authority in *The Times*, 14 September 1989, p. 5. The Government has now agreed to pay such fines itself: HC, Vol. 159, col. 800 (WA), 10 November 1989.

[38] Trade Effluents (Prescribed Substances and Processes) Regulations 1989, S.I. 1989 No. 1156.

and their operation will require the prior approval of Her Majesty's Inspectorate of Pollution (HMIP), who will impose technology-based emission standards.[39] The system will include processes discharging "Red List" substances to water, and in such cases, the consent of the National Rivers Authority must be obtained by HMIP before authorization can be granted, in order to ensure that water quality objectives are met. Related reforms are also being introduced in Scotland.[40]

A footnote to the London Declaration explains that the term "best available technology" is understood to take into account economic availability. This cautious qualification reflects an interpretation that has already become accepted in environmental usage,[41] although there remains uncertainty about the scope and significance of economic factors. However, in the context of integrated pollution control, the UK intends to apply instead the standard of "best available technology not entailing excessive cost" (BATNEEC). This formula is derived from the European Community framework directive on industrial air pollution.[42] One can, of course, argue that BATNEEC and "best available technology" are interchangeable, and that, since integrated pollution control extends beyond the ambit of the INSC Declarations, it is reasonable to adopt a single form of words for all media. However, once BATNEEC is given legislative force, it will become open to statutory interpretation. There may be a significant difference of emphasis between a definition that treats economic availability as one of the matters to be examined in identifying the appropriate technology, and a phrase that elevates it to the status of an overriding consideration.

It is also noteworthy that, for administrative and commercial reasons, a major new system of pollution control cannot be instantly applied to existing industrial operations. Initially, action will be directed towards new or refurbished plant, and interim consents reflecting the best available performance from installed equipment will be given to those that are already permitted to discharge "Red List" substances to water.[43] Moreover, on supposedly practical grounds, sewage works treating industrial effluent will not be regarded as scheduled processes, and so the sewerage undertakers need not conform to technology-based emission standards. Those standards will instead be imposed on the industries that discharge effluent into the

[39] See "Integrated Pollution Control: A Consultation Paper", Department of the Environment/Welsh Office, July 1988.

[40] See "Pollution Control in Scotland: Proposals for Changes", Scottish Development Department, July 1989. Processes would be prescribed by the Secretary of State for Scotland, and the enforcing authority for discharges to water would be the river purification board or islands council.

[41] For example, in 1985, the Paris Commission confirmed that the terms "best technical means available", "best available technology" and "best practicable means" should all be understood in that forum to take into account the economic availability of those means. See the Seventh Annual Report on the Activities of the Paris Commission, p. 19.

[42] Council Directive 84/360/EEC of 28 June 1984 on the combating of air pollution from industrial plants, OJ, L 188, 16 July 1984, p. 20.

[43] The existing consent system has already been amended so that it is possible to impose conditions on applicants not merely regulating discharges, but also dictating treatment and processes: Water Act 1989, Sch. 12, para. 2(3)(c). This power could be used as a transitional measure before the introduction of integrated pollution control. The equivalent provision in Scotland is Control of Pollution Act 1974, s. 34(4)(g), inserted by Water Act 1989, Sch. 23.

sewers, and the costs of BATNEEC will not be a burden to the privatized water companies. Only when the concentrations of "Red List" substances from scheduled processes are reduced will it be possible to tighten the discharge conditions for sewage works. Consequently, the benefits of integration are likely to be progressive rather than dramatic, and their contribution to the reduction of North Sea pollution will be gradual.

Diffuse Sources

One of the most difficult targets set by the London Declaration is the need to deal with pollutants that reach the aquatic environment by indirect pathways, in addition to those that are discharged straight into water from point sources. These include persistent, toxic and bioaccumulable substances in agricultural, industrial and household products, which pollute water courses through the sewerage system, by run-off from farm land or by leaching from waste disposal sites. Point VIII of the London Declaration recognizes that "simultaneous and complementary action is called for to reduce pollution at source . . . by restrictions on the manufacture, marketing and use of such substances and products containing" them. Furthermore, in paragraph XVI. 3(b), the Ministers agree to take positive steps by identifying the principal diffuse sources of those materials entering the North Sea via rivers and estuaries.

Implementation strategy in the UK has again focused on the "Red List", and the Government believes that existing legislation is largely sufficient to provide the necessary powers. Thus, the Control of Pollution Act 1974[44] enables regulations to be made prohibiting or restricting the import and supply of injurious substances, or their use in connection with a trade, business or manufacturing process. It is recognized, however, that this provision may be too narrow to cover storage or more general use, and amendments are proposed in the Environmental Protection Bill to bring existing chemicals within its scope. Likewise, the disposal of waste on land, which is currently governed by the Control of Pollution Act 1974,[45] is to be revised under the Bill. The Water Act 1989[46] already enables the Secretary of State for the Environment to regulate the storage of pollutants, and a statutory instrument is being made to deal with pesticides and oils. The same statute[47] also permits the designation of water protection zones, in which potentially polluting activities could be controlled, although similar powers in earlier legislation were never used.[48] In addition, pesticides are subject to approval under the Food and Environment Protection Act 1985,[49] and three "Red List" chemicals—chlordane, dieldrin, and

[44] s. 100.
[45] Part I.
[46] s. 110. The equivalent provision in Scotland is Control of Pollution Act 1974, s. 31A, inserted by Water Act 1989, Sch. 23.
[47] s. 111. The equivalent provision in Scotland is Control of Pollution Act 1974, s. 31(4)-(5), inserted by Water Act 1989, Sch. 23.
[48] Control of Pollution Act 1974, s. 31(5) (repealed).
[49] Part III.

aldrin—have recently been banned.[50] Further controls over the use, packaging and labelling of hazardous materials are provided by the Health and Safety at Work etc Act 1974,[51] and regulations oblige manufacturers and importers to report the marketing of new substances.[52]

Despite this abundance of legislation, the utility of the measures adopted by the UK to deal with inputs of pollutants to rivers and estuaries, whether from diffuse or point sources, must ultimately depend on the adequacy of the "Red List". The paucity of information on the impact of many chemicals might be thought to justify the inclusion of a wider range of chemicals, in order to comply with the precautionary approach adopted in the London Declaration. Paragraph XVI. 1 accepts that the principle of safeguarding the marine environment applies

> "especially when there is reason to assume that certain damage or harmful effects on the living resources of the sea are likely to be caused by such substances, even when there is no scientific evidence to prove a causal link between emissions and effects".

A difficulty with this statement is that a failure of information can too easily be represented as the absence of "reason to assume" that a problem may exist; and although the word "especially" does not preclude action in less definite circumstances, it may equally be used to explain inactivity. The Government argues, however, that by initially concentrating all its efforts on a limited target it is more likely to produce results, and that the "Red List" is in any case capable of revision in the future.

The INSC Declarations are inevitably compromise documents, and that quality is continued in the implementation policy of the UK. The Government's strategy suggests an uneasy desire to placate all who will be affected thereby, and, while emphasizing the environmental significance of its proposals, it simultaneously seeks to minimize their financial consequences for the economy. The provisions of the London Declaration on rivers and estuaries are sufficiently imprecise to accommodate significant differences of construction, and the UK may plausibly contend that its version lies somewhere inside those limits. There is less certainty that it has also chosen the best interpretation.

Dumping

In recent years the UK has been responsible for roughly half of all industrial wastes and about a quarter of all dredged spoils dumped in the North Sea beyond internal waters, and has been the only state to dump sewage sludge in the North Sea. Not

[50] The phased withdrawal of these pesticides was announced on 1 August 1988: MAFF News Release 312/88. Approval of chlordane products ceased after 1988, except for use on fine sports turf, which will remain until the end of 1992. Dieldrin was withdrawn from 30 March 1989. The three remaining uses of aldrin were originally to continue until 1992, but were subsequently banned on 18 May 1989: MAFF News Release 204/89. In contrast, however, a licence for the pesticide Nuvan (now called Aquagard), which contains the "Red List" substance dichlorvos, and is used by salmon farmers to kill sea lice, has been extended until June 1990 under the Medicines Act 1968, Pt. II: (1989) 20 *Marine Pollution Bulletin* 102, 422.

[51] s. 15, Sch. 3.

[52] Notification of New Substances Regulations 1982, S.I. 1982 No. 1496.

TABLE 2
Quantities of Waste Dumped by the United Kingdom in the North Sea 1979–87

	Liquid industrial waste	*Solid industrial waste*[1]	*Dredged spoils*[2]	*Sewage sludge*
		000 tonnes		
1979	455.8	5,515.0		5,793.1
1980	453.3	5,623.1		5,770.4
1981	380.9	5,488.5		5,795.7
1982	222.2	5,351.5		5,435.8
1983	218.3	6,003.7		5,070.2
1984	228.9	942.1		5,181.4
1985	262.9	3,865.5	22,747	5,218.8
1986	230.6	4,130.2	17,783	5,493.8
1987	223.4	3,974.4	17,864	4,734.3

[1] Colliery waste, flyash, etc.
[2] Figures for dredged spoils before 1985 are not available

Source: HC, Vol. 144, Cols. 527–528 (WA), 10 January 1989.

surprisingly, therefore, its dumping practices, particularly in relation to sewage sludge, have come in for considerable criticism from the other North Sea states.[53]

The Bremen Declaration includes a general exhortation to reduce dumping. Thus paragraph F1 states that "wastes including sewage sludges, containing such amounts of substances which are or could be harmful to the marine environment will not be dumped into the North Sea". Paragraphs 1 and A26 are in similar vein. This statement appears to be too woolly and imprecise to represent any kind of real undertaking with which states might be expected to comply; and this is borne out by the figures in Table 2, which show that except in relation to dredged spoils, there is no real trend to a reduction in the amounts of waste dumped by the UK since the Bremen Declaration was adopted in 1984. The same is true of those other states which dump waste in the North Sea.

At first sight the London Declaration contains much more precise and clear-cut obligations. In point XVI of the Declaration the Ministers

> " agree to . . .
> 21. accept as a matter of principle that:
> (a) it is important to end the dumping of polluting materials in the North Sea at the earliest practical date;
> (b) as from 1 January 1989, no material should be dumped in the North Sea unless there are no practical alternatives on land and it can be shown to the competent international organizations that the materials pose no risk to the marine environment;

[53] See the Dutch Government's criticisms in evidence to the House of Commons Select Committee on the Environment, HC (1986–1987) 183, p. xxiv; and more generally *The Guardian*, 19 November 1987 and *New Scientist*, 19 November 1987, p. 57.

22. take the following interim steps to this end:
(a) phase out the dumping in the North Sea of industrial wastes by 31 December 1989, except for inert materials of natural origin or other materials which can be shown in the competent international organizations to cause no harm in the marine environment;
(b) carry forward action to improve the quality of dredged materials disposed of in the North Sea, for example by reducing the inputs of toxic, persistent or bioaccumulable materials to rivers and estuaries, and ensure that, with immediate effect, Governments strictly adhere to the Oslo Commission Guidelines on Dredged Materials which have been agreed in order to prevent dumping of contaminated dredged material;
(c) take urgent action, in the case of those countries that dispose of sewage sludge in the North Sea, to reduce the contamination of such sludge by persistent, toxic or bioaccumulable materials, so that they pose no hazard to the marine environment, and to ensure that the quantities of such contaminants disposed to sea by this pathway in the immediate future do not increase above 1987 levels . . ."

These two paragraphs raise a number of difficulties when one considers their possible implementation. First, it is not clear what obligations (if any) are contained in paragraph 21. Second, there appear to be inconsistencies between the two paragraphs. Sub-paragraph (a) of paragraph 21 contains no very precise obligation. There is obviously room for considerable argument over what constitute "polluting materials" and what could be regarded as "the earliest practical date" for ending dumping. As a general exhortation and long-term aspiration, paragraph 21(a) should presumably be read subject to the more precise provisions in paragraphs 21(b) and 22. These two paragraphs are, however, to some extent inconsistent. In paragraph 22(a) the date is different from that in paragraph 21(b). Furthermore, paragraph 22(a) appears to permit the dumping of inert materials of natural origin without it being necessary to satisfy the two conditions set out in paragraph 21(b) and to permit the dumping of other industrial waste without it being necessary to satisfy the first condition of paragraph 21(b) (the absence of a practical alternative on land). However, subsequent to the London Declaration, in June 1989, the Oslo Dumping Commission (of which all North Sea states are members) adopted a decision "under which the dumping of industrial waste in the North Sea shall cease by 31 December 1989 . . . except for inert materials of natural origin, and except for those industrial wastes for which it can be shown to the Commission through the Prior Justification Procedure (PJP) both that *there are no practical alternatives on land* and that *the materials cause no harm in the marine environment*" (emphasis in the original).[54] In the light of this decision (although it is a moot point whether it is

[54] Oscom Decision 89/1 of 14 June 1989 on the Reduction and Cessation of Dumping Industrial Wastes at Sea, para.1.

legally binding),[55] it will be assumed for the purposes of this chapter that while the dumping of inert materials of natural origin is permitted under the London Declaration, the dumping of other forms of industrial waste is permissible after the end of 1989 only if both the conditions of paragraph 21(b) have been complied with.

A further difficulty arises in respect of sub-paragraphs (b) and (c) of paragraph 22. These paragraphs envisage the continued dumping of dredged materials and sewage sludge, at least for an unspecified interim period. Are they subject to the conditions of paragraph 21(b)? Unlike paragraph 22(a), paragraphs 22(b) and (c) contain no echo of paragraph 21(b) in their wording. It could be argued that, applying the *lex specialis* rule of interpretation, paragraphs 22(b) and (c) are not subject to the conditions of paragraph 21(b) (and such a view receives some support from the fact that the Oslo Commission was unable to agree to apply the decision referred to in the previous paragraph to dredged materials and sewage sludge). It is also significant that paragraph 21(b) uses the conditional tense ("no material *should* be dumped"), which is qualified by the phrase "accept as a matter of principle", whereas paragraphs 22(b) and (c) use the more obligatory present tense ("carry forward", "take urgent action"). Nevertheless, the matter is certainly not free from doubt.

It can be seen, therefore, that there is some difficulty in knowing precisely what obligations concerning dumping North Sea states should implement. The reason for the lack of clarity in the London Declaration's paragraphs on dumping is largely explained by the fact that these paragraphs are a compromise between those states that wanted an end to dumping (notably the Scandinavian states) and the UK, which wanted to be able to continue to dump sewage sludge.[56]

Having established, if only rather approximately, the obligations relating to dumping contained in the London Declaration, we must now turn to see what legislative and/or administrative action the UK has taken to implement these obligations. At the time of the adoption of the London Declaration the legislation regulating dumping was Part II of the Food and Environment Protection Act 1985. In essence, this prohibits the dumping of waste at sea unless a licence has been obtained from the Ministry of Agriculture, Fisheries and Food (MAFF) (or in Scotland from the Department of Agriculture and Fisheries for Scotland (DAFS)). Thus, to implement the London Declaration no legislative changes are necessary. All that is required are possible modifications in the policies followed by MAFF and DAFS in issuing licenses for dumping.

The Government has explained its general licensing policy in the following terms:

> "Sea disposal licences are not issued unless careful scientific examination shows the operation in question to be acceptable in terms of its impact on the

[55] For reasons of space this question cannot be discussed here. Suffice it to say that the Oslo Dumping Convention does not explicitly give the Commission the power to take decisions of the kind at issue here which are binding on its members.

[56] See T. IJlstra and F. de Jong, "The 1987 International North Sea Conference" (1988) 3 IJECL 249.

marine environment, the living resources it supports, and human health, and unless it conforms to the relevant international conventions. The practical availability of alternative methods of dealing with the wastes is also taken into account."[57]

Light is also shed on the Government's policy by its reply to a Parliamentary question as to why it had not supported a Nordic proposal made at the 1987 meeting of the Oslo Commission to end dumping of industrial waste and sewage sludge by the end of 1991. The Government said that it did not support the proposal because it was not satisfied that the proposal took

> "adequate account of the available scientific evidence which shows that the sea dumping of sewage sludge and certain industrial wastes causes no environmental harm and can be preferable to other disposal methods."[58]

Neither of these statements seems in accordance with the spirit of paragraph 21(a) of the London Declaration, and some would no doubt question the accuracy of the second statement. The first statement of policy is along the same sort of lines as paragraph 21(b), but there are differences in phrasing between the two which may be significant. Does an "acceptable . . . impact on the marine environment" amount to the same thing as paragraph 21(b)'s "no risk to the marine environment", or is it a less strict standard? Is taking into account "the practical availability of alternative methods of dealing with the waste" the same as establishing that "there are no practical alternatives on land", or, again, is it less strict?

Turning from general dumping policy, where there may be room for legitimate differences of opinion as to whether the UK complies with the spirit and wording of the London Declaration, we will now consider in turn each of the specific forms of dumping with which the London Declaration deals—industrial waste, dredged material and sewage sludge—and see what action the UK has taken or is taking in respect of each.

Industrial Waste

It will be recalled from the discussion above that paragraph 22(a) of the London Declaration permits the continued dumping of industrial waste which falls into the category of "inert material of natural origin". Such material includes colliery spoil (provided, as required by the Oslo Commission's decision referred to earlier, it has not been "contaminated by anthropogenic processes"), of which the UK dumps a considerable quantity each year. Although the London Declaration does not require any action to be taken in respect of this waste, the British Government has said that efforts will be made to find environmentally acceptable alternatives to dumping colliery spoil, provided such alternatives do not jeopardize the economic future of the pits from which the spoil is taken.[59] As part of these efforts, British

[57] HC, Vol. 121, Cols. 724–725 (WA), 4 November 1987; Vol. 129, Col. 524 (WA), 15 March 1988.
[58] HC, Vol. 123, Col. 412 (WA), 30 November 1987.
[59] "Guidance Note", *above*, n. 3, para. 21.

Coal has been required, as a condition of the licence it has been granted to dump colliery spoil, to produce a detailed analysis of the costs and benefits of practicable land-based alternatives. The results of this analysis are currently being studied by the Government and will be taken into account in any decision to renew British Coal's dumping licence.[60]

In relation to other kinds of industrial waste, paragraphs 21(b) and 22(a) require dumping of such waste to be phased out by the end of 1989 except for waste for which there is no practical alternative disposal on land and which poses no risk to the marine environment. Of these other kinds of waste, the UK dumps two types—fly ash from power stations and liquid industrial waste. The Government has said that no licences to dump such wastes after 1989 will be granted unless the conditions of paragraphs 21(b) and 22(a) are complied with.[61] Since this chapter was written in September 1989, it is obviously not possible to say whether this commitment has been honoured. In the mean time the electricity industry has been studying alternative disposal methods for fly ash and investigations have been carried out to find alternative treatment or land-based disposal methods for liquid industrial wastes.[62]

Dredged Materials

Paragraph 22(b), which was quoted earlier, calls on North Sea states to improve the quality of dredged materials which are dumped, for example by reducing the inputs of toxic, persistent and bioaccumulable materials to rivers and estuaries, and to ensure that the Oslo Commission's Guidelines on Dredged Materials are strictly adhered to. The question of reducing inputs of toxic, persistent and bioaccumulable materials to rivers and estuaries has already been dealt with in the previous section. Since paragraph 22(b) refers to such reduction only as one example of improving the quality of dredged spoils, and since no specific quantitative or qualitative reduction is prescribed, it would seem that the UK has done sufficient to comply with this aspect of paragraph 22(b). In relation to the other aspect, adherence to the Oslo Commission's Guidelines, the Government has said that "the licensing authorities [namely, MAFF and DAFS] will ensure that this is done through the licensing procedures".[63]

Sewage Sludge

Paragraph 22(c), quoted earlier, requires North Sea states to reduce the contamination of sewage sludge by persistent, toxic or bioaccumulable materials so that it poses no hazard to the marine environment, and to ensure that the quantities of such contaminants dumped at sea in sewage sludge do not increase above 1987 levels. It should be noted at the outset that there is some internal inconsistency in

[60] The Government's Reply to the Second Report of the Environment Committee: Toxic Waste, Cm. 679 (April 1989), p. 20.

[61] "Guidance Note", *above*, n. 3, paras. 22 and 23.

[62] *Ibid*.

[63] *Ibid*. para. 24.

this paragraph. On the one hand, it requires the contamination of sewage sludge by certain materials to be reduced: on the other, it says that the quantities of such contaminants dumped at sea should not increase.

As to how such a reduction (or non increase) is to be achieved, the Government envisages this being attained primarily through the action plans of water authorities for reducing inputs of dangerous substances[64] to rivers and estuaries (discussed in the previous section). In addition, the licensing authorities, in dealing with future applications for licences to dump sewage sludge in the North Sea, will have to take into account "the total load of dangerous contaminants carried by all licensed North Sea sludge dumping sites before granting individual licences".[65]

As no figures for 1988 (let alone 1989) have yet been published, it is impossible to say yet whether there has in fact been a reduction (or at least no increase) in the quantities of dangerous contaminants dumped in sewage sludge in the North Sea. A further complicating factor is that for some of these contaminants figures for the amounts dumped prior to 1988 do not apparently exist.

The Government has also said that it is investigating other methods of disposing of sewage sludge, and that water authorities applying for licences to dump sewage sludge must show that they have thoroughly examined alternative disposal options: licences will be refused in cases where satisfactory alternatives are available. Nevertheless in some circumstances, taking account of environmental and social factors as well as economic ones, the Government is of the view that dumping is often the best practicable environmental option. The Government has also asked HMIP to study sewage disposal operations and to publish guidance for assessing the best practicable environmental option in particular situations. This study would also look at opportunities for modifying trade waste treatment processes so as to reduce discharges to sewers of toxic substances from trade premises which in some places contaminate sewage sludge.[66]

It is interesting to note that in May 1986 MAFF told a House of Lords committee that

> "the key factor in choosing between sea and land disposal is the practical availability of suitable agricultural land within economic transport distance of the sewage treatment works concerned . . . Were it not for this constraint, virtually all of the sludge which the UK disposes of at sea at present could be safely spread on agricultural land."[67]

In the case of large conurbations, which tend to generate the most sewage sludge, a

[64] As to exactly what substances are covered by paragraph 22(c), the Government has said that it will draw up a list in consultation with the water industry, based on the substances in Annex I of the Oslo Convention and some of those in Annex II, and the "Red List" (referred to *above*). See "Guidance Note", *above*, n. 3, para. 26.

[65] *Ibid*. paras. 27 and 28.

[66] Government Observations on the Third Report of the Environment Committee, HC (1987–1988), 543, pp. xviii-xix.

[67] House of Lords Select Committee on the European Communities, "Dumping of Waste at Sea", HL (1985–1986) 219, p. 197.

further constraining factor is that transport of sewage sludge would generate extra heavy traffic and unpleasant smells.[68] It is an interesting point as to whether economic considerations of the kind referred to (the cost of transport) mean that there really is "no practical alternative on land" for disposing of such sludge, as would be required by paragraph 21(b) of the London Declaration, were it to apply to sewage sludge dumping (which, as was suggested above, is possibly not the case).

What conclusions can be reached regarding the UK's compliance with the London Declaration's provisions on dumping? The British Government has said that it will implement the various interim steps set out in paragraph 22 of the Declaration. In most cases it is too soon to say definitely whether this commitment has been honoured. The Government's general licensing policy is not fully in accord with the spirit and wording of paragraph 21, but as pointed out earlier, it may be that this paragraph has to be read subject to the more specific provisions of paragraph 22. For all these reasons, therefore, it is not yet possible to arrive at any final judgement as to how far the UK has complied with the London Declaration's provisions on dumping.

Conclusion

It is clear from the examples studied in this chapter that the implementation of the INSC Declarations presents problems that are both practical and semantic. To some extent, this is an inevitable consequence of undertakings that seek to reconcile the differing aspirations of the signatory states. Thus, generalizations and ambiguous commitments that are perceived as defects by an observer may represent diplomatic success to a negotiator, and are a price that probably has to be paid for the achievement of political unity. Provisions that contain apparently specific targets are found on closer inspection to be qualified in ways that give considerable scope for national discretion. In some cases, the data necessary to formulate more precise strategies were unavailable when the Declarations were signed; sometimes differences between the environmental circumstances in individual states may be thought to justify a flexible approach. There is less excuse, however, for the internal inconsistencies and contradictions within the texts, which make it difficult to understand particular obligations.

As a participant in the Bremen and London Conferences, the UK must share responsibility for the deficiencies of the Declarations. Where the provisions are obscure, however, the Government has not been reluctant to rely on its own powers of interpretation, and has rarely favoured the strictest possible construction. Many of the measures through which the UK is seeking to implement the Declarations have not been specifically designed for the North Sea, and some of these developments would probably have occurred without international agreement. It is true, however, that certain reforms have been accelerated in response to the timetable imposed by the London Declaration. That timetable does, of course, render it

[68] *Ibid.* 198.

premature to pass conclusive judgement on a particular state at a preparatory stage in its programme of compliance. The UK proclaims support for the North Sea initiative, and insists that it is discharging its undertakings. Whether those assertions will prove to be justified remains to be seen.

Chapter 6

The North Sea Environment: Features and Problems

Dr. N. V. Jones

The present North Sea has been formed by geological and glaciological events over the last 20,000 years. In common with other natural environments it involves the interactions between the physical, chemical and biological features of the area and the system as a whole can be seen as an integration of these aspects. An understanding of the functioning of such systems is necessary if we are to appreciate the effect man is having on them and to create a logical and sustainable management plan. A further complication in this case is the international nature of the North Sea.

This contribution aims to provide a general picture of the North Sea as an environment and to identify the problems involved in its study and management.

The North Sea

The southern part of the North Sea is shallow, being mostly less than 50 metres deep, whereas the central and northern parts become progressively deeper in a northerly direction (Figure 1).The clear waters of the northern basin become stratified in summer which gives rise to a productive and stable ecosystem. The waters of the southern basin are stirred by strong tidal currents which makes them turbid resulting in a less-productive, unpredictable and less-stable ecosystem. The main centres of human population are sited around this southern basin and it is into this area that most urban and industrial discharges take place which exacerbates the natural instability.

Physical features

In essence the North Sea is a semi-enclosed part of the Atlantic with the main entrance being to the north-west with a smaller opening in the English Channel. The tidal currents are due to water entering from the north-west as well as through the Channel and leaving along the Norwegian coast. These, along with the prevailing winds produce a general pattern of counterclockwise circulation of water within the North Sea (Figure 1); although local variations do occur. These currents are obviously of great importance in determining the nature of the water in various parts of the sea as well as in distributing sediments. They also influence the distribution of animals in a direct way as they are used to facilitate migrations as well as distributing developmental stages.

Surface currents may be moving in one direction while bottom waters are moving in the opposite direction. This phenomenon is shown where low salinity surface water near the coasts moves offshore and is replaced by deeper, denser water moving inshore along the bottom. Such salinity differences are created by the inflow of water from rivers, most of which enter in the southern basin of the North Sea. These currents move sediments of different sizes depending on current velocity. These physical features produce a mosaic of sediments on the bottom of the North Sea. They are mostly sand with patches of gravel and mud-filled holes. The latter were gouged by glaciers or are the submerged channels of rivers which existed before the sea-level rose to its present position. The deep trench along the Norwegian coast receives the fine material transported by the currents indicated in Figure 2.

These features of the sea floor reflect the history of the area and the more transient (in geological terms) and superficial effects of tides, currents and surface waves. These factors also shape the margins of the sea, creating the coastline of cliff, sandy beaches or estuaries. The whole system is dynamic with sediments being deposited, eroded, suspended and transported on the small or large scale in both time and space. These sediments transport chemicals such as metals attached to their surfaces and when deposited act as sinks which may accumulate natural contaminants as well as those from anthropogenic sources. They also constitute the environment in which many animals live and which in turn affect the sediments by their activities (bioturbation).

Chemical features

The salinity, or the total amount of dissolved salts, in Atlantic water is of the order of 35 grams per kilogram (or parts per thousand).The water entering the North Sea from rivers has a much lower salinity as a consequence of the dilution that has taken place in the estuaries. The salinity of water affects its density which in turn affects its capacity to hold particles in suspension and, therefore, has an effect on the physical features described above. Salinity also affects living organisms as it determines their osmotic or water balance. The pattern and changes in salinity of the North Sea are, therefore, important chemical features of the sea. In general, the northern section has Atlantic water and a salinity of over 35 parts per thousand all year round whereas the coastal areas, particularly the south eastern coast, have a salinity of about 29–30 parts per thousand. A tongue of high salinity water enters from the north and its extension depends on the relative strengths of the tides and freshwater flow. Salinity can be used as an indicator of the origin and nature of water masses and, along with temperature, may show quite sharp boundaries or fronts between different water masses.

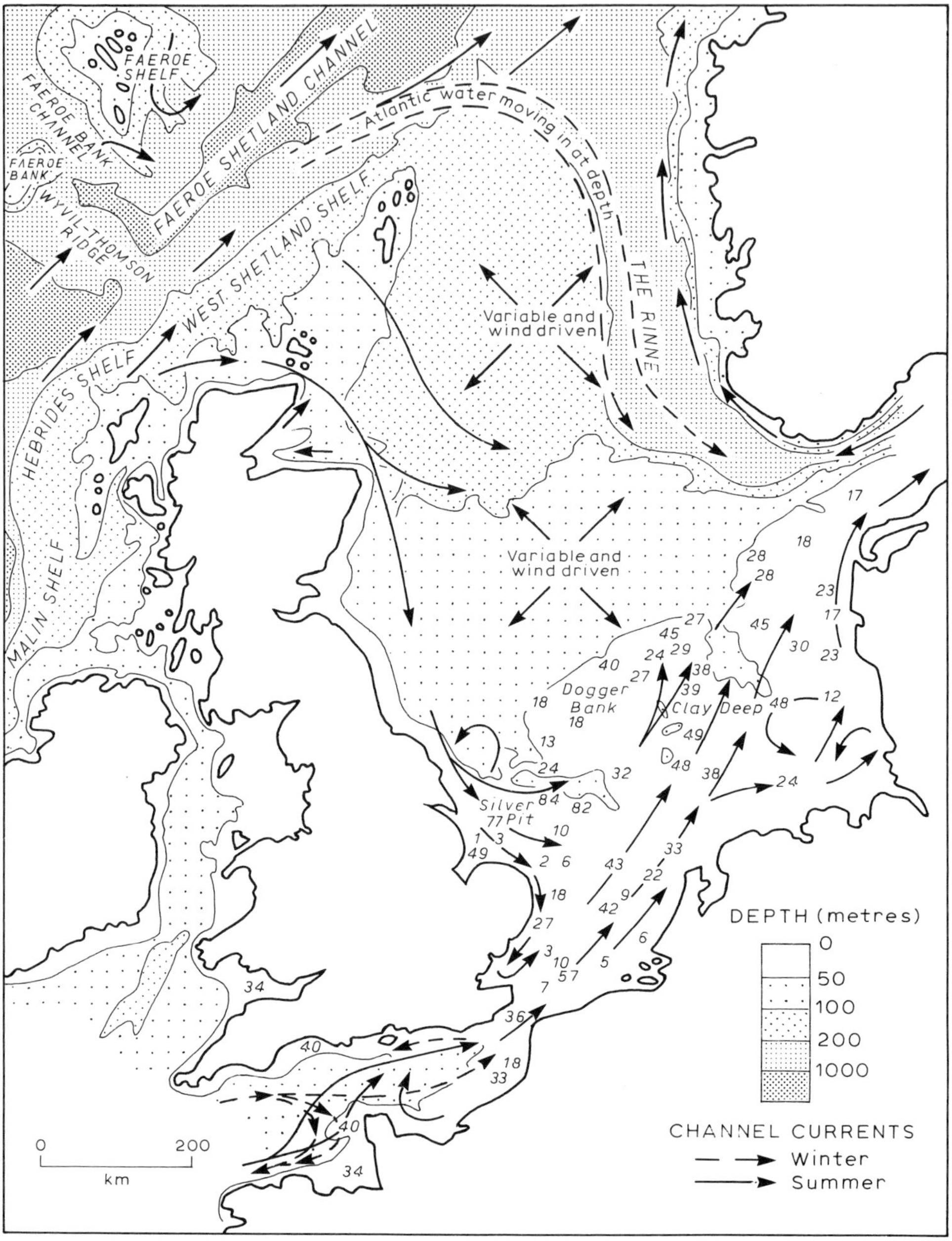

Figure 1 Bathsymmetry and currents of the North Sea
Source: based on Lee and Ramster, 1981

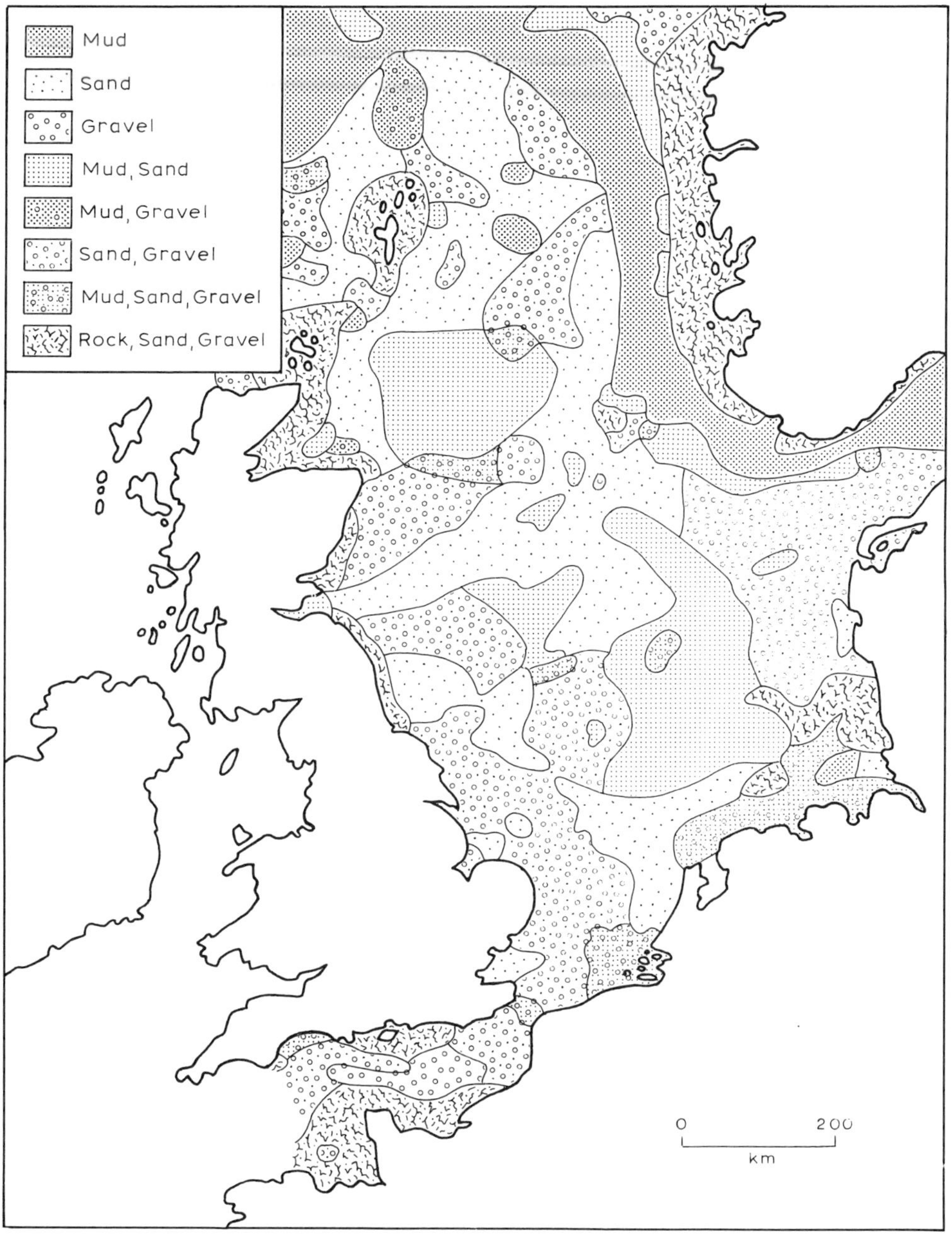

Figure 2 Sediment of the North Sea
Source: based on Lee and Ramster, 1981

These water masses also contain many dissolved substances required for life by plants and animals such as nitrates, phosphates and silicates as well as heavy metals, including some essential ones, such as zinc and copper. Most of these nutrients vary in their quantities during the year as they are used up by the photosynthetic activities of plants. This activity is affected by the availability of light and is, therefore, dependent on the clarity of the water which is in turn dependent on the currents. Levels of nutrients as well as other chemicals are affected by anthropogenic inputs from rivers and from the atmosphere. Table 1 gives an indication of the present estimates of the relative importance of the various sources.

The North Sea is clearly a complex system of physical and chemical characteristics which is affected by natural variations on both short and long time-scales. Added to this are the changes in chemistry and possibly in sediment dynamics which are caused by man and which are having their effect on the living part of the system.

Biological features

The living communities of the sea are based on the plants that create organic material by the process of photosynthesis. This requires chemical nutrients in available form and a suitable quantity and quality of light. The physical and chemical features already described restrict plant growth to the surface layers of the North Sea where light is available and to the shallow coastal fringe where plants can anchor to the bottom and still receive light. The plants are restricted to stable sites and are mainly the seaweed covered rocky shores and kelp beds which are features of the northern coasts of the North Sea. The sandy shores of most of the southern part are not suitable for the growth of these algae. These plant communities produce good quantities of material in a year but because they are restricted in area they are not as important as the algae that inhabit the surface layers of the whole sea. These small floating plants constitute the phytoplankton and the composition of the community will vary according to the nature of the water. The Atlantic water of the northern area will have a community which differs from that of the southern basin where the influences of freshwater and different physical conditions will have their effect. In between there will be a transition zone where the community will be characteristic of coastal shelf areas in such a temperate zone. The boundaries between these communities may be distinct but they are not always static as they will be affected by the changes in hydrography.

These plants are the basis of the trophic relationships (food chains) which have evolved in these environments. The first animals are the grazers that feed directly on the living plants. On the shore these are animals such as limpets and winkles whereas in the open sea they are swimming or floating animals that feed on the phytoplankton. These in turn are fed on by carnivorous animals leading up to the fish, birds and mammals at the end of the chain. Animals and plants that die together with faeces are processed by another group of organisms, the decomposers. These are mainly bacteria and protozoa helped by larger animals that shred the material and they operate largely on the bottom of the sea. They release the nutrients that

TABLE 1
Summary of Contaminant Inputs to the North Sea
(tonnes per annum)

	Nitrogen		*Phosphorus*		*Cd*		*Hg*	
Source	*Max*	*Min*	*Max*	*Min*	*Max*	*Min*	*Max*	*Min*
River Inputs	1,000,000	—	76,000	—	52	46	21	20
Direct Discharges	95,000	—	25,000	—	20	20	5	5
Atmospheric	400,000[2]	—	N/A	—	240	45	30	10
Dumpings								
Dredgings	N/A	—	N/A	—	20	—	17	—
Sewage Sludge	11,700	10,000	2,800	2,200	3	—	0.6	—
Industrial Waste[5]	N/A	—	N/A	—	0.3	—	0.2	—
Incineration at Sea[4]	N/A	—	N/A	—	0.1	—	Tr[6]	—
Total (Rounded)	1,500,000	—	100,000	—	335	135	75	50

	Cu		*Pb*		*Zn*		*Cr*		*Ni*	
Source	*Max*	*Min*	*Max*	*Min*	*Max*	*Min*	*Max*	*Min*	*Max*	*Min*
River Inputs	1,330	1,290	980	920	7,370	7,360	630	590	270	240
Direct Discharges	315	—	170	—	1,170	—	490	—	115	—
Atmospheric	1,600	400	7,400	2,600	11,000	4,900	900	300	950	300
Dumpings										
Dredgings	1,000	—	2,000	—	8,000	—	2,500	—	700	—
Sewage Sludge	100	—	100	—	220	—	40	—	15	—
Industrial Waste	160	—	200	—	450	—	350	—	70	—
Incineration at Sea	3	—	2	—	12	—	1.7	—	3	—
Total (Rounded)	4,500	3,000	11,000	6,000	28,000	22,000	5,000	4,200	2,100	1,450

	As		*HCH*		*Drins*		*DDT*		*PCB*	
Source	*Max*	*Min*	*Max*	*Min*	*Max*	*Min*	*Max*	*Min*	*Max*	*Min*
River Inputs	360	320	3	3	0.1	—	0.1	—	3	3
Direct Discharges	220	—	0	—	N/A	—	0	—	0	—
Atmospheric	120	40	N/A	—	N/A	—	N/A	—	N/A	—
Dumpings										
Dredgings	200	—	N/A	—	N/A	—	N/A	—	N/A	—
Sewage Sludge	Tr	—	N/A	—	N/A	—	N/A	—	N/A	—
Industrial Waste	40	—	N/A	—	N/A	—	N/A	—	N/A	—
Incineration at Sea	0.1	—	N/A	—	N/A	—	N/A	—	N/A	—
Total (Rounded)	950	820	3	3	0.1	—	0.1	—	3	3

Where the estimate of a contaminant load has been supplied as a range, this has been expressed in the table as a MAX (maximum) and a MIN (minimum) value. If only one value has been supplied as an estimate of the load, this has been assigned to the MAX value and a dash (—) has been assigned to the MIN value. Where no values have been supplied, an N/A has been assigned to the MAX value and a dash (—) to the MIN value. The MAX total is the sum of the values in the MAX column. The MIN total is the sum of the values in the MIN column with MAX values being incorporated in the totals where MIN values have not been supplied. It should be noted that all figures for inputs, with the possible exception of dumping, are subject to considerable uncertainty, the extent of which is variable and difficult to quantify.

1. The figures used in this table are the "rounded" totals taken from Tables 2B, 2D and 2E.
2. These totals do not include amounts entering the North Sea from the North Atlantic, the English Channel and the Baltic Sea.
3. Estimates as reported by the Fourth Meeting of the Paris Commission Working Group on Atmospheric Inputs.
4. Refers to material burnt and assumed to be discharged from the stack: this therefore represents the maximum amount which would enter the sea.
5. Includes liquid and solid.
6. Tr—trace.
7. Data is taken from different years, but is mainly 1983–1986.

Source: *Quality Status of the North Sea.* A Report by the Scientific and Technical Working Group (Second International Conference on the Protection of the North Sea, London, 24–25 November 1987).

ENVIRONMENT / COMMUNITY INTERACTIONS

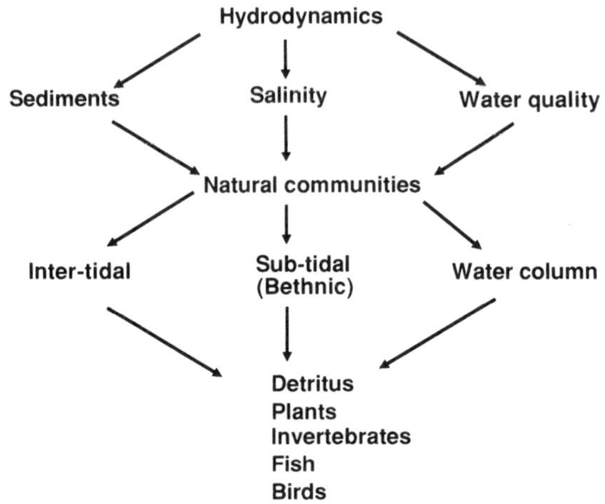

Figure 3

were locked up in the bodies of the dead organisms and thus make them available for further incorporation into plants. Their availability will depend on the physical conditions bringing them to the surface. The bottom-dwelling animals or benthos include many that filter fine particles from suspension or that feed on the detritus that has been deposited on the bottom.

The interrelationships that exist between the physical, chemical and biological aspects of the North Sea can be represented as shown in Figure 3 and their spatial links are diagrammatically shown in Figure 4. Figure 5 shows an example of the integration of various factors leading to the seasonal variations shown by phytoplankton.

The North Sea can be seen as a whole system, the functioning of which depends on the natural interactions outlined above. Parts of the system are usually regarded by man as being more important than others as they are of commercial value. These are mainly mineral and hydrocarbon energy resources which are finite and biological resources which can be renewable. The former are aggregates, oil and gas which have been deposited in certain areas by prehistoric events. The latter are mainly fish which have traditionally been taken by people living all around the North Sea. Fish of commercial importance are part of the pelagic (planktonic) system for at least some time in their life history. Plaice spawn in the southern, shallow part of the sea although the fishing area for adults is more extensive as the species is migratory. Sole are coastal spawners but the fishing areas extend out into most of the

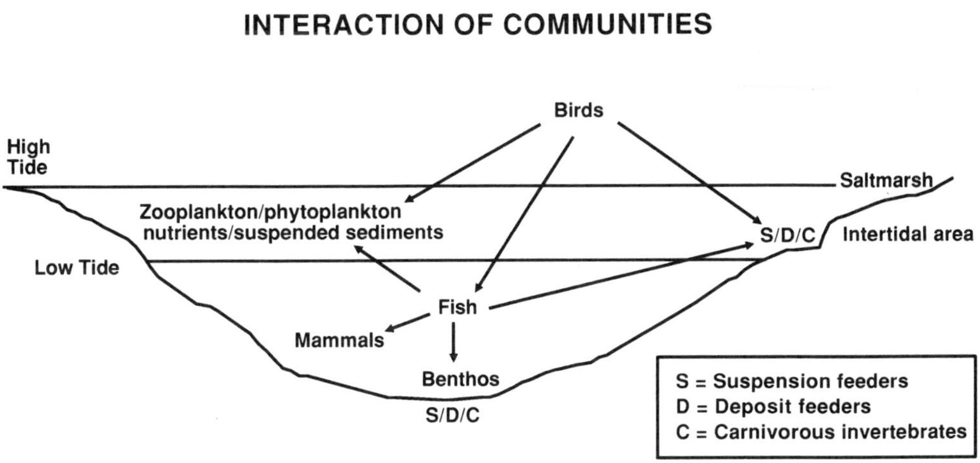

Figure 4

southern basin. Haddock, on the other hand, spawn in the area between Shetland and Norway but move south into the North Sea where they are fished in most of the deeper areas. Cod spawn in discontinuous areas mostly in the southern part of the North Sea and, after a period in the plankton, the fish settle to life on the bottom. They are fished over the whole area. This may serve to indicate the complex way that fish utilize the resources available to them added to which must be the time factor. All the species do not spawn at the same time although the important commercial ones do so during the period January to June (cod February-April, haddock March-May, sole April-June, plaice January-April). The fact that the larval stages have a different life style to the adults is important as different factors may operate on the species at different times.

Birds use the North Sea for breeding sites as well as for feeding in the winter. Sea birds of about 25 species with total numbers of over 4 million breed mainly on the rocky coasts. Waders and wildfowl which breed in the Arctic feed during the winter and while on migration on the sedimentary inter-tidal areas found mainly in the southern sector and in the estuaries. The North Sea is, thus, part of a much larger biological system which includes the Atlantic and Arctic areas of the Western Hemisphere.

Seals and other mammals also exploit the biological production of the North Sea. The Common and Grey Seals are mostly fish feeders and their distribution will be dependent on that of their prey. They need to come ashore to give birth in the same way as sea birds need land-based nesting sites. Dolphins and other small whales were much more common than at present and are, of course, a very mobile group which may use the North Sea on a seasonal basis.

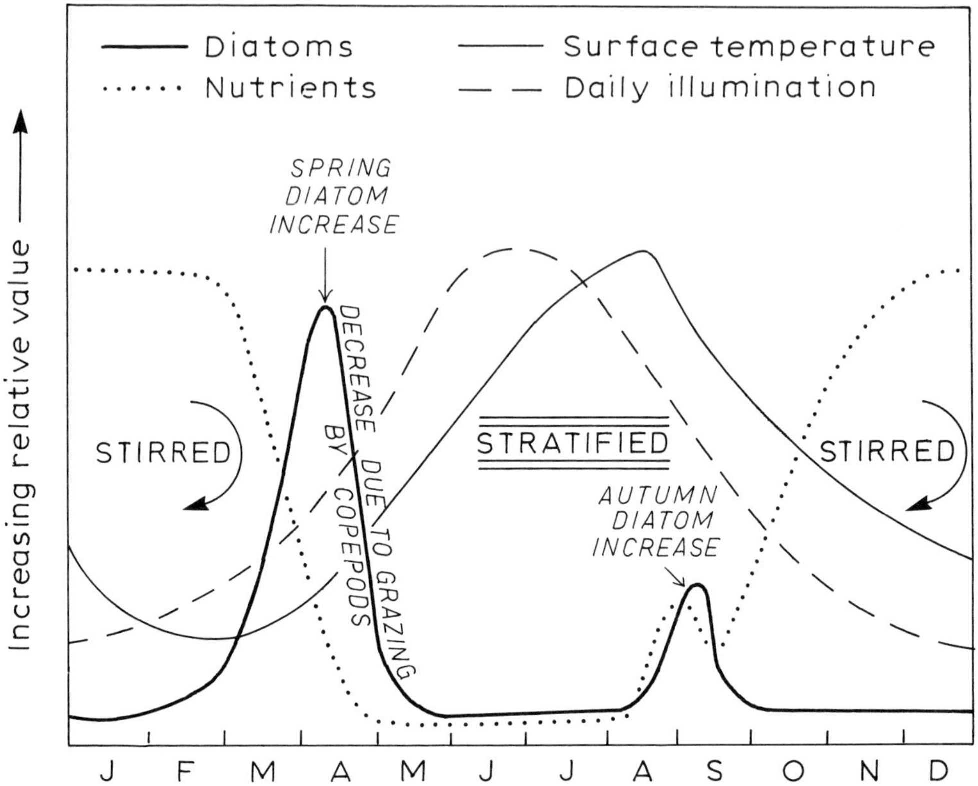

Figure 5 Seasonal variations in phytoplankton growth and nutrient concentration in the northern North Sea
Source: from Peet and Hey, 1986

Problems

The perception of the North Sea as presenting problems is, of course, a human phenomenon and the identification of such problems will be restricted to those of human origin.

Man has not been involved in large-scale interference with the physical features of the sea but he has had considerable influence in local areas, primarily on the sedimentary and low-lying coasts. These have been constrained by flood protection schemes notably in the Netherlands and along the southern shores of the North Sea. Such schemes may well have given rise to changes in the normal sediment dynamics of the adjacent areas and may be far reaching. Infilling or land-reclamation projects have also changed the shape of the coasts, particularly within estuaries, and have permanently removed some inter-tidal environments from the marine ecosystem. The dumping of dredged material and disposal of cuttings from drilling

TABLE 2
Typical Dissolved Concentrations (μg per litre) of Trace Metals in North Sea Areas with Average River and Ocean Data for Comparison

	Inshore Areas of the North Sea					
Element	*Netherlands Coast*	*German Bight*	*United Kingdom Coast*	*Central North Sea (Offshore)*	*Average Ocean*	*Average River*
Cadmium	0.10	0.05	0.03	0.02	0.01	0.02
Copper	0.60	0.60	0.30	0.20	0.10	1.5
Lead	0.05	0.05	0.05	0.03	0.003	0.1
Zinc	5.0	2.0	4.0	0.6	0.1	30
Nickel	1.0	0.8	0.7	0.3	0.2	0.5
Mercury	0.01	0.01	0.01	0.001	0.001	0.03

Source: Quality Status of the North Sea, 1987.

platforms may also produce sedimentary changes in localized areas but continued expansion of such activities may result in the area affected becoming significant within certain sectors.

Chemical changes due to human activity are, however, apparent over a larger scale because of the dispersal mechanisms involved. Effluent from urban and industrial areas are discharged either directly into the sea by pipeline or indirectly through estuaries, dumping from vessels or from atmospheric fall-out. Table 2 shows that the river and atmospheric inputs are the most significant for most chemicals although important contributions of metals come from the dumping of dredged material. This material originates from docks and estuaries which are, presumably, heavily contaminated. Atmospheric fall-out occurs over the whole area and the currents disperse the dissolved chemicals, as well as those attached to fine particles, along the paths outlined above.

River inputs represent less than 1 per cent of the volume of the North Sea but their effect on the levels of metals in the whole area is apparent from Table 2 which shows raised levels in coastal areas. A similar effect is shown in Figure 6 where the distribution of nitrite is shown. The distribution of radioactive material attributed to industrial discharges in France and England is also measurable in the North Sea.

Direct changes in the biology of the North Sea are mainly due to man hunting the predators. Removal of large numbers over a period of time causes a change in the food web and may result in the development of a different balance of species. This is the kind of problem caused by overfishing and is an example of an effect on a single species being followed by consequent effects on others. Man competes with birds and mammals for the fish resources and so overfishing results in reductions in the numbers of these other predators as well. If predation pressure is reduced then it may be possible for the prey to recover but this very much depends on the level reached by the population, the reproductive cycle of the species and the changes that may have been caused to its food supply.

These anthropogenic changes may be seen as causing problems at different levels

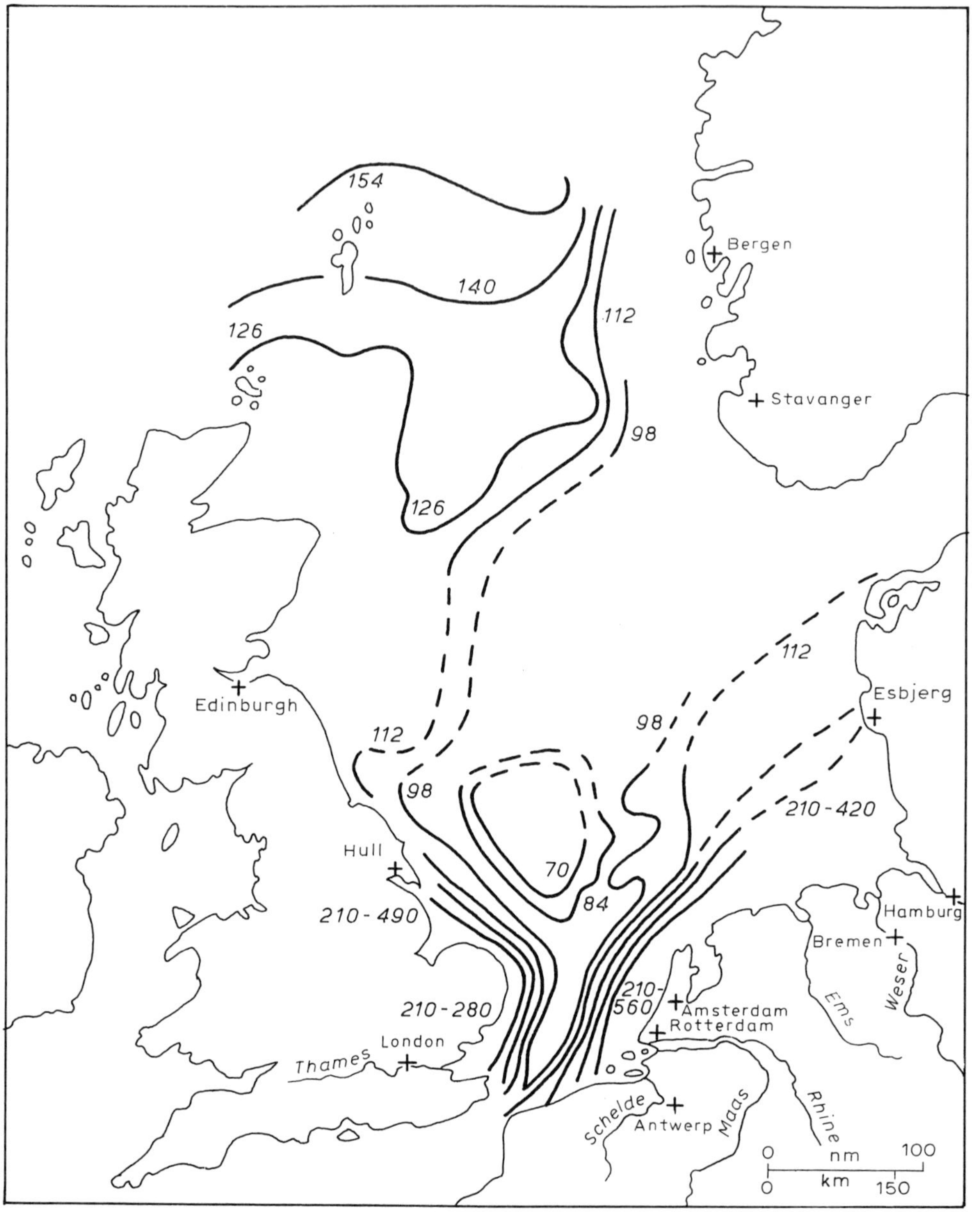

Figure 6 Distribution of NO_3N(A) and PO_4P(B) (both in mg/l) in the North Sea surface water in winter

Source: Peet and Hey, 1986

in the North Sea which can be summarized as follows. (i) Ecosystem changes: large-scale changes in the physical and/or chemical character of the area resulting in large-scale biological changes. (ii) Community changes: changes to more localized areas or type of environment resulting in changes in the living community of the site. (iii) Population changes: an effect seen on certain populations. Attention is usually drawn because of economic importance, aesthetic value, toxic nature or nuisance value. These issues will now be examined in a little detail to attempt to identify the main problems as they affect the North sea.

Ecosystem changes

The main large-scale changes to the physical features of the North Sea are likely to be a rise in sea-level due to global warming. Such changes could cause severe flooding problems around the North Sea as many large urban and industrial areas have been sited at or near to the present sea-level. There could also be secondary effects such as increased erosion. Such changes would have little effect on the main body of the North Sea but they would be very significant in redefining the coastline. Engineering works also have an effect on small stretches of coastline but their ramifications may extend further through their changes to sediment movement and their effects on animal life-cycles and interference with migratory patterns.

Large-scale chemical changes may be caused as outlined above due to the dispersion by currents of substances discharged either directly or indirectly into the sea. In general, the water of the North Sea is estimated to be renewed every 1–2 years, although the water in the Wadden Sea, in the south-eastern corner may be around for three years whereas that off the Norwegian coast will leave the area within a few months. The main problems caused by such discharges are due to increases in nutrients which encourage algal growth and which, thereby, increase the productivity of the area by the process of eutrophication. Toxic levels of chemicals, on the other hand, depress productivity and reduce the diversity of species. These changes lead to the next category.

Community Changes

The main changes of this kind that have been recognized are in the plankton which is expected as this part of the system is likely to be the first affected by the increase in dissolved chemicals, whether they are nutrients or toxins. The main changes have been described for phytoplankton in the southern North Sea but it is difficult to separate natural variations from those produced by man. An increase in flagellates (Protozoa) has been recorded concurrently with a decrease in diatoms. This has been ascribed to a decrease in silica which is required by diatoms and an increase in nitrates and phosphates during the last few decades. Such changes in the composition of a community may result in domination by a few species which upsets the normal trophic relations and produces an unstable system.

Blooms of algae cause problems when they die as their decomposition results in the depletion of dissolved oxygen which in turn may cause the death of other organisms. This has been recorded as the cause of death of fish on the Swedish and Norwegian coasts. Some flagellates exude toxins and mussels, which feed on these organisms, may become poisonous by accumulation of the chemicals.

Population Changes

The changes outlined above obviously include changes in populations but attention was being focused on their effects on the community as a whole. Other changes to populations attract attention because the animals concerned have become less available as in the case of fish or because their dead bodies become obvious as was the case with seals. The mortality of seals was variously ascribed to pollution either directly or indirectly through its effects on the resistance of the animals. This indicates the possible interactions that take place in these natural communities and our lack of information on them. The problem seems to have been due to a virus but it is still not clear whether or not this was entirely natural or contributed to by human activities. Fish have also attracted attention because of the development of disease and obvious external lesions. Some scientists have attributed these problems to pollution but others contend that they are naturally occurring phenomena. The matter, clearly, requires further study.

Bird populations have also suffered declines but some species are showing increases in the North Sea. One of the main problems is determining whether changes are occurring to long-lived animals as we rarely have long-term studies of their populations. One such study of the oceanic gull, the kittiwake, showed a considerable growth in population on the North-east coast of England until about 1965 when a decline set in which was attributed to a concurrent decline in the herring population.[1] The decrease in herring, which is a predator of the sand eel, resulted in an increase in the population of this species followed by an increase in the puffin population in Shetland. Since the late 1960s there has been a shift in fishing effort from demersal and pelagic fish to industrial fishing based mainly on the sand eel. This may have contributed to the decline in breeding performance of puffins in recent years. Such interactions are poorly understood but it has been suggested that fisheries have had greater impact on the North Sea ecosystem than the total flow of effluents.[2]

General Discussion

It is clear that the North Sea is a complicated system of interacting processes which is being affected by man at both the local and large- scale levels. Our understanding

[1] J Coulson and C. S. Thomas, "Changes in the Biology of the kittiwake *Rissa tidactyla*: A thirty-one-year study of breeding ecology", *Journal of Animal Ecology*, 54 (1985), pp. 9–26.

[2] C. ten Hallers, "Distress Signals: Signals from the Environment", in *Policy and Decision-Making: Basis Papers* (Werkgroep Noordzee, Amsterdam, 1989); G. Peet and E. Hey (eds.), *The Status of the North Sea Environment: Reasons for Concern*, Vol. i (Amsterdam, Stichting Werkgroep Noordzee, 1987); A. J. Lee and J. W. Ramster (eds.), *Atlas of the Seas around the British Isles*, Ministry of Agriculture, Fisheries and Food.

of the system as a whole is poor and a large-scale, multi-disciplinary and international effort is required to improve the situation.

Scientists in various countries have their own programmes and priorities but the interacting, integrating and international nature of the North Sea requires that scientific and managerial effort should show the same character. The present UK programme by the Natural Environment Research Council is a contribution of this kind. It is based on a multi-disciplinary approach to producing a transport model, a study of non-conservative processes and a definition of seasonal cycles within the system.

The system has a natural capacity to withstand changes which are a part of the natural environment but it is becoming increasingly clear that the system is showing signs of stress. The Third North Sea Seminar took as its theme a scientific understanding of signals from the environment as a basis for decision-making for the North Sea. Recognizing signs of stress, assessing their significance, attributing their causes and deciding on action requires complicated interaction between scientists, politicians and managers. The scientists, however, who have described changes in physics, chemistry, plankton, benthos, fish, birds and mammals do not always agree on the causes or significance of these changes. The formation of the North Sea Task Force following the Second INSC should facilitate co-ordination and exchange of information and views between scientists.[3]

There remains the problem of communication between scientists and policy makers which was highlighted during the Third North Sea Seminar. Such problems need to be addressed if we are to protect the North Sea environment which is being affected by our activities. The structure and function of the ecosystem should be the model for our activities and attempts at management of the sea that separates our countries but which unites the people.

[3] Ministerial Declaration, 2nd International Conference on the Protection of the North Sea, London 1987.

Chapter 7

The Work of the North Sea Task Force

Philip C. Reid

Introduction

An assessment of the "state of health" of the North Sea was produced as a "Quality Status Report" (QSR)[1] for the Second International Conference on the Protection of the North Sea held in London in November 1987. North Sea Ministers meeting at the Conference prepared a Declaration.[2] The United Kingdom published its response on the implications of the Declaration soon afterwards.[3] It was clear from the QSR and the parallel report on Oceanography[4] that the knowledge available at that time formed an inadequate basis properly to evaluate the North Sea. The report was compiled from piecemeal contributions by individual nations, of varying content and detail which often used different methodologies; areas of ignorance were particularly evident in some of the Tables in the report. A need to rectify this situation was recognized and Ministers therefore recommended in their Declaration[5] that a scientific "Task Force" be set up under the auspices of the International Council for the Exploration of the Sea (ICES) and the Oslo and Paris Commissions (OSPARCOM) to organize a co-ordinated programme of research and monitoring on the North Sea. A remit for the Task Force was set out as Annex G of the Declaration and includes the following objective: "To carry out work leading in a reasonable time-scale, to a dependable and comprehensive statement of circulation patterns, inputs and dispersion of contaminants, ecological conditions and effects of human activities in the North Sea".

The North Sea Task Force (NSTF) is comprised of delegates (scientists and senior administrators) from the eight coastal states of the North Sea (The United Kingdom,

[1] *Quality Status of the North Sea. A Report by the Scientific and Technical Working Group*. Second International North Sea Conference, London, September 1987.
[2] *Second International Conference on the Protection of the North Sea, London, 24–25 November 1987, Ministerial Declaration, issued by the Department of the Environment of the United Kingdom, April 1988.*
[3] *Guidance Note on the Ministerial Declaration*. Department of the Environment, London, February 1988.
[4] *Report of the Oceanography Subgroup*, Second INSC, September 1987.
[5] *Second International Conference on the Protection of the North Sea, London, 24–25 November 1987, Ministerial Declaration*, Annex G.

France, Belgium, The Netherlands, the Federal Republic of Germany, Denmark, Sweden, Norway), the Commission of the European Community (CEC), ICES and OSPARCOM. Observer status is granted to international organizations such as the Helsinki Commission and the Wadden Sea Secretariat and to OSPARCOM countries which do not border the North Sea. While primarily a scientific organization, NSTF is perhaps unique in providing a forum for interaction between policy-makers and scientists in furthering understanding of the North Sea.

After a preliminary meeting in London the NSTF was established at the first formal meeting in the Hague in December 1988 (hosted by The Netherlands) and has since held two further meetings, in Plymouth (United Kingdom) and Copenhagen (ICES). This new long-term organization has been given as its primary task the preparation of the next QSR for 1993 consideration of which may be timed to coincide with the Fourth Ministerial Conference in 1995 and, in the interim, reports to the Third Ministerial Conference in March 1990 (The Hague) on topics where significant scientific progress has been made since the London Conference.

This chapter summarizes progress made by the Task Force in defining objectives and research needs and putting into action a five-year plan to co-ordinate research, monitoring and modelling and other special projects leading up to the next QSR. Brief mention will be made of some of the initiatives introduced by the United Kingdom to assist the work of the Task Force.

Relationship to OSPARCOM and ICES

The Oslo and Paris Commissions and ICES were requested in the Ministerial Declaration of the London Conference to consider the best means of establishing a Task Force to undertake the work identified in Annex G of the Declaration. The Commissions and ICES responding in a very positive way have ratified the work of the Task Force and developed new mechanisms to improve co-operation and co-ordination between their Working Groups to prevent duplication and facilitate the work of the Task Force. Many existing structures already exist to research and monitor the state of health of the North Sea within the Commissions and ICES such as the Joint Monitoring Programme (JMP) of OSPARCOM, the Nutrients Working Group of the Paris Commission and the Advisory Committee on Marine Pollution of ICES. The Task Force will work with and make use of these existing programmes harmonizing and co-ordinating their work as necessary to produce the final QSR.

It has been agreed that the NSTF will be responsible for:

1. Advising on research, field programmes and resources needed to undertake work towards an assessment.
2. Planning, developing and putting into action a monitoring programme with appropriate associated quality control.
3. Identifying and supervising work to be contracted to ICES and OSPARCOM working-groups.
4. Developing the format and coverage for the next QSR.
5. Approval and Peer review of the contents of the QSR.

Aspects of the work in the first three categories may require approval by the Commissions or the Council of ICES.

In the past certain countries have not complied with their obligations to the Commissions and other International Organizations. It is hoped that the positive and strong backing given by Ministers to the Task Force will overcome these past problems as it is essential that the North Sea is adequately sampled in all areas within a harmonized programme and using standard methodologies to enable a holistic QSR to be produced. If one or more countries fail to comply with this programme then the value of the whole assessment may be in jeopardy.

Objectives of the Task Force

At the first meeting the role to be played by the Task Force was discussed and the following objectives were agreed, here rearranged in order to reflect progression towards the next QSR.

1. To provide an organizational framework for discussion and exchange of views between policy-makers and scientists, with the aim of attaining the respective aims of the two groups,
2. To prepare interim reports on selected subjects as and when necessary to the Commissions, to ICES, and to the North Sea Conference. Nine gaps in scientific knowledge were identified under objective 4 and are listed in Table 1. New programmes of research on the North Sea in the United Kingdom are being developed to address the subjects identified in this Table.
3. To screen and co-ordinate the scientific work carried out within the framework of OSPARCOM and ICES,
4. To fill gaps in knowledge identified by the previous QSR and the London Declaration in 1987.
5. To produce a new assessment of the North Sea (QSR) in 1993.

NSTF five-year plan

For the NSTF to fulfil assigned tasks, and the above objectives in an ordered manner and to develop a time-scale for this work a five-year plan has been developed. The plan provides a structure on which to build the co-ordination of the relevant existing activities of OSPARCOM and ICES, to assess when new programmes are needed and to evaluate the future budgetary and manpower resources that will need to be deployed by North Sea states. The plan published as North Sea Environment Report No. 1[6] has five interrelated tasks:

Task 1: Prepare new Quality Status Report of the North Sea.
Task 2: North Sea co-ordinated monitoring.
Task 3: North Sea co-ordinated modelling.
Task 4: Co-ordination of North Sea research effort.
Task 5: Specific projects.

[6] "North Sea Task Force Five-Year Plan, 1989–1993", *North Sea Environment Report*, No. 1, North Sea Task Force, OSPARCOM and ICES, London, 1989.

TABLE 1
Gaps in Scientific Knowledge of the North Sea

1. A need for better quality input data.
2. An improved understanding of nutrient dynamics and in particular their relationship to the currency of exceptional algal bloom.
3. More epidemiological information and a greater understanding of the factors causing diseases in marine organisms, including fish, birds and mammals.
4. An increased knowledge of the different ways in which classes of contaminants behave in the North Sea and their sources and fates.
5. An assessment of the critical load of nutrients and persistent bio-accumulatable toxic substances (metals and organic compounds).
6. More information on the levels of contaminants in the marine environment obtained on an internationally comparable basis.
7. More knowledge of general ecosystem effects on plankton, on benthos, birds, fish and mammals, and especially on North Sea seal stock.
8. An increased emphasis on quality assurance of mathematical models used in North Sea assessments.
9. Other specific problems: for example the problem of estimated inputs of contaminants to coastal waters from estuaries, the significance of sediment movements in the context of contaminant transport.

Source: From Table 1 of the "North Sea Task Force Five-Year Plan 1989–1993" which is published in *North Sea Environment Report*, No. 1, North Sea Task Force, OSPARCOM and ICES, London, 1989.

The NSTF Quality Status Report

The production of a new QSR will involve a rigorous review of all available data to determine the nature and severity of environmental disturbances and trends resulting from anthropogenic activity. For the first time, the data used in the assessment will be based on internationally comparable methodologies and will make use of the latest research and the sophisticated mathematical models that are now being used or developed for the North Sea. In synthesizing this information the document will aim to trace the links between human activities/inputs—concentrations, fates, effects—a sequence which was highlighted in the last QSR as poorly understood. The QSR will provide a means of assessing the adequacy of existing environmental controls, ensuring that resources and amenities continue to remain viable and preventing irreversible changes to habitats and biota. It must be emphasized, however, that the assessment is a scientific study which is independent of any measures adopted in response to the Precautionary Principle.

The Task Force has adopted the revised guidelines for the preparation of regional environmental assessments drawn up by ICES. They recommend that the contents of the resulting report should be uniform, brief and succinct, and readily readable by policy-makers and the public so that the document can be used in the formulation of policy on environmental protection. The "Overall Assessment" should be structured to review the evidence of environmental effects stating clearly where there is or is no cause for concern so that appropriate action can be initiated.

Sub-regional and North Sea-wide (holistic) assessments will be undertaken in parallel with lead countries to co-ordinate the sub-regional studies. In this way assessments of waters adjacent to each country will be available to Ministers as well as an outline of the whole North Sea system. This approach allows the considerable hydrographic, biological, etc. variability in different areas of the North Sea to be taken into account as well as recognizing that many measurements such as atmospheric inputs can only be taken on a North Sea-wide scale. A three-pronged approach will be used to produce the holistic QSR as:

1. Inputs on a national basis transmitted via the Paris Commission.
2. Relevant environmental data on a North Sea-wide scale submitted by ICES.
3. The results of sub-regional assessments.

A map of the area to be included in the QSR and the breakdown into sub-regions is given in Figure 1. The sub-regions are based to a large extent on the areas identified in the ICES Flushing Group Report.[7] A co-ordinating lead responsibility has been undertaken by the United Kingdom for three areas, the area influenced by the Orkney Shetland Current (2a, b), the East coast (3a, b), an area of the central North Sea (7b) with joint leadership with France on the Channel (9).

Monitoring master plan

Perhaps the most significant outcome of the 1987 QSR was the realization that the number of measurements of contaminants in the North Sea with respect to numbers of determinands, medium/substance used, and spatial and temporal coverage was very limited. When compounded by the poor results of inter-comparison exercises between laboratories because of differing methodologies it was impossible to make an unequivocal statement on the extent to which the North Sea is contaminated or the rate at which changes have taken place. An urgent need to address these problems was included in the Minister's remit to the Task Force.

Within the existing Joint Monitoring Programme (JMP) of OSPARCOM monitoring may have four different purposes:

1. Measurements to determine possible hazards to or effects on humans.
2. Biological Effects' Monitoring to establish the bio-availability of pollutants and integrate the effects of multiple or long-term exposure, possibly at low concentrations.
3. Monitoring the existing levels and distribution of contaminants.
4. Monitoring trends of contaminant levels.

ICES adopts a similar classification, but at present without purpose 2. This system is contaminant orientated and does not consider monitoring the biota for example for changes which may be due to climatic variability.

Given the short time for the production of the next QSR the main effort of the Task Force will be concentrated on improving existing monitoring schemes of the

[7] *Flushing Times of the North Sea*, Co-operative Research Report No. 123. ICES, Charlottenlund, Denmark, 1983.

NSTF SUBREGIONS OF THE NORTH SEA

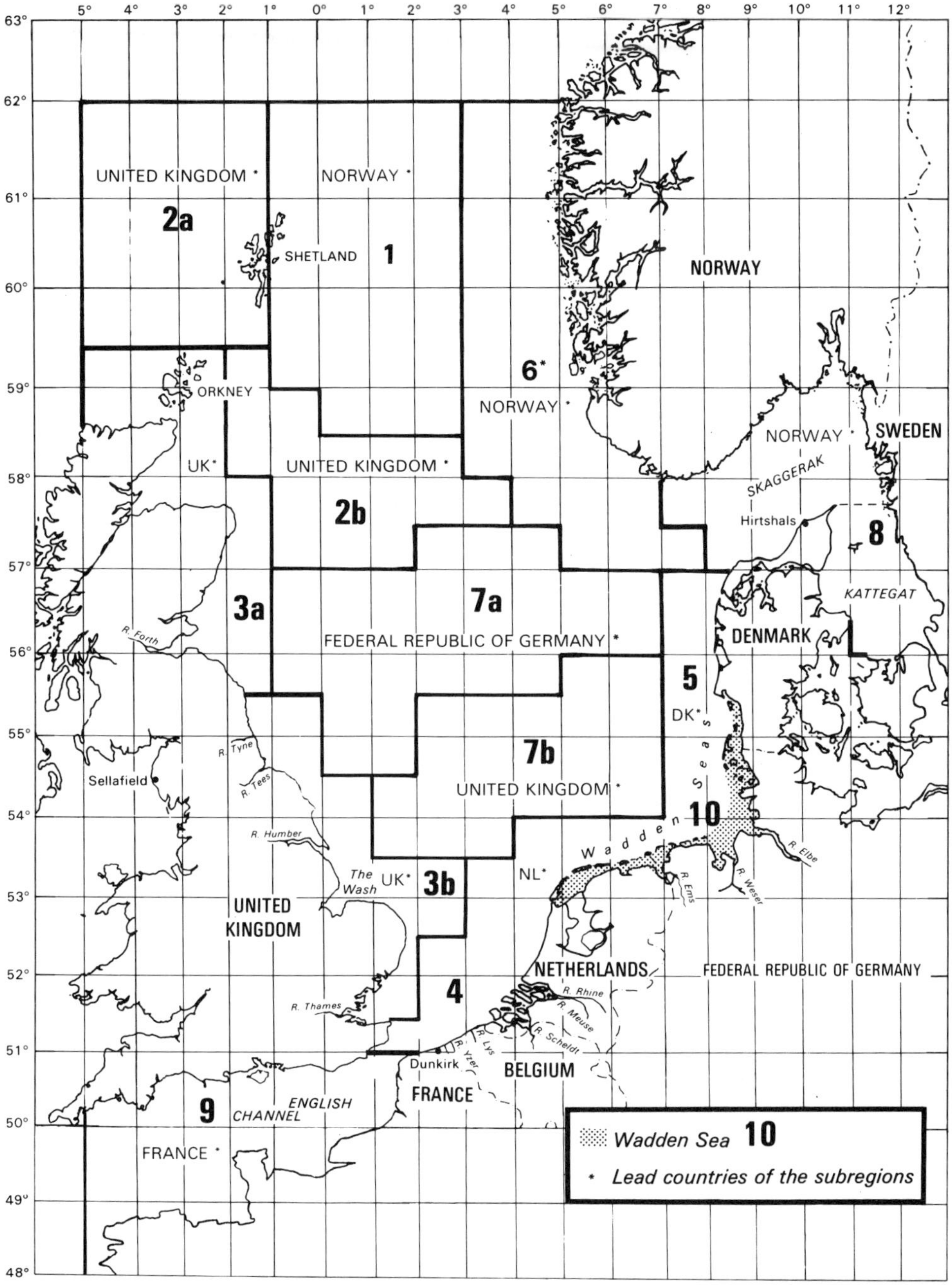

Figure 1

JMP under purpose 3. To achieve this aim a suite of new offshore sampling stations which are representative of the sub-regions are to be set up to enable estuarine/offshore gradients to be established. The Master Plan will start with a measurement campaign in 1990/91 which will include a range of mandatory heavy metal and organic substances plus nutrients with a second tier of recommended substances. Selected Biological Effects Techniques will also form an integral part of the programme.

Modelling

An evaluation of the usefulness of mathematical models for water quality and ecosystem management and for assessing the effectiveness of existing or planned controls on inputs is being produced by the Task Force. As a first initiative a questionnaire has been circulated to North Sea states asking for details of relevant existing models to include their application, scope and limitations. Three general areas of modelling are being examined: hydrodynamics, transport/dispersion/sedimentation, and ecological. A workshop is planned for the spring of 1990 to assess the questionnaires. This meeting will also identify the questions that models may be able to answer, prepare advice on future model development, discuss validation and question what is needed to improve their reliability for assessment and incorporation in the next QSR.

North Sea research

Special projects

Two types of project come under this heading, short-term tasks such as reports to the Third Ministerial Conference and longer-term goals of particular relevance to the North Sea such as the behaviour of nutrients. The Task Force is working closely with the Nutrients Working Group of the Paris Commission on the latter. Reports have been submitted to the Third Conference on "the ecological effects of algal blooms in the North Sea", "the epidemic deaths of seals in the North Sea", and areas in response to scientific research and the opinion of the public and Ministers which are of concern as "sensitive issues". Four issues have been identified as of particular concern. These are:

1. The impact of the fishing industry on the North Sea ecosystem.
2. Surveillance for chemicals not usually covered in routine monitoring programmes.
3. The environmental impact of persistent chemicals.
4. The role of atmospheric input as a source of contaminants to the North Sea.[6]

Research in the United Kingdom

Major programmes covering fishery assessment and environmental protection of the North Sea are carried out by the Fishery Departments (MAFF[8], DAFS[9]). This

[8] *Research into Fisheries and the Marine Environment 1987–88, The report of the Director*, MAFF Directorate of Fisheries Research, Lowestoft, 1989.

[9] *Marine Laboratory Aberdeen Annual Review 1987–88*, Department of Agriculture and Fisheries for Scotland, Aberdeen, 1989.

work was complemented in 1988/89 by a detailed fifteen-month study of the southern North Sea, involving biweekly alternating process and survey cruises of *RRS Challenger*, forming the North Sea Project of the Environment Research Council (NERC).[10] To the above can be added a sizeable new research programme funded by DOE to address the gaps in knowledge identified by the Task Force. Included in this programme are, for example, studies of immunosuppression and contaminants in marine mammals, projects on nutrients,[11] the coastal margin and algal blooms, an atlas of satellite imagery[12] research on estuarine plumes and sandeels in the Shetlands and measurements of fluxes of contaminants through the Dover Straits.

Research database and directory

As an initiative to help the work of the Task Force, the United Kingdom has developed a database of North Sea research in progress. This system will be used as a model for other national schemes with the eventual aim of combining all together. The database is PC orientated so that it can be widely distributed and freely accessible to scientists, administrators and the wider community interested in North Sea affairs. Project descriptions form the core of the system linked to contact information for project leaders and institutes. Sophisticated software is being developed to access the database, including a facility for keyword searches. Information from all national directories will be used to produce a printed directory of all North Sea Research projects. A second and parallel initiative is the compilation of a Research Bibliography, which again will be accessible on PCs.

United Kingdom liaison group

To ensure good communication between Government Departments represented on the Task Force (at present DOE, DAFS, MAFF) and the wider research, scientific, industrial and NGO community, a UK Shadow Group for the North Sea Task Force has been established. This group will provide a forum for discussion, enable issues to be raised with the UK delegation and give opportunities for presentation of updates on progress. Further details of the liaison group can be obtained from DOE, room A213, Romney House, 43 Marsham Street, London SW1P 3PY.

Conclusions

The Task Force is a new and possibly unique structure in international collaboration; formed under the auspices of both ICES and the Oslo and Paris Commissions with a clear and urgent mandate from North Sea ministers (Annex G, London Declaration) to enhance scientific knowledge and understanding by bringing

[10] *North Sea Project Progress Report April 1989*, NERC Marine Sciences Directorate, Proudman Laboratory, Bidston, 1989.

[11] Hydes, D.J. and Edmunds, H., *NERC North Sea Community Research Programme: Qualitative assessment of nutrient measurements, September 1988–August 1989*, Institute of Oceanographic Sciences Deacon Laboratory, Report No. 269, 1989.

[12] Holligan, P.M., Aarup, T. and Groom S.B., *The North Sea Satellite Colour Atlas*, Continental Shelf Research *9*, 667–765, 1989.

together in a co-ordinated way the diverse organizations which at present have responsibilities for and interests in the "quality" of the North Sea. The parent organizations—ICES and OSPARCOM—have responsibility for a wider geographical area than the North Sea, and the Task Force provides the mechanism to focus their respective expertise and that of other organizations on a regional sea with possibly the densest population and industrial hinterland and the greatest riverine input and seagoing traffic of any sea area in the world.

Although many of the topics identified by the Ministers in their Declaration as requiring further study are already part of the ICES AND OSPARCOM work programme through the many Working Groups sponsored by these organizations (see Annex 3 of reference 6), there are serious gaps in coverage. The Task Force was established to fill these gaps and provide a neccessary overview.

Where possible the Task Force will work with existing Working Groups asking them to provide appropriate advice; for areas not covered the Task Force may recognize that new programmes be established or may develop or bring together appropriate expertise for advice from other sources. A clearly defined working plan has already been put into action by the Task Force, providing a structure on which to assess interaction with existing Working Groups. The first actions in these plans have already been completed by submitting papers to the next Ministerial Conference in 1990 on Task Force progress on important issues, such as alagal blooms, the 1988 seal epidemic and listing new areas of concern.

Outside existing international organizations the Task Force is also unique in providing a forum for debate between scientist and policy-makers from the North Sea states and the EC, to help develop a coherent and co-ordinated plan for the long-term sustainable management of North Sea resources. At present, each country has its own North Sea programmes with different emphases and/or scientific methodologies. The Task Force provides a means to ensure the eventual harmonization and co-ordination of these different approaches.

At the national level the Task Force is a stimulus for developing new ideas on North Sea matters, whether on research policy, monitoring or management and new programmes are being developed in a co-ordinated way to help answer outstanding problems identified under the Task Force structure. Co-ordination of existing programmes is being developed through new initiatives like the United Kingdom database. Finally, in the United Kingdom via the liaison group NGOs and industry are kept informed of Task Force progress and have opportunities to input their views via national delegates.

Part II
Perspectives on Existing Frameworks

Chapter 8

The Oslo and Paris Commissions

Peter Hayward

The Convention for the Prevention of Marine Pollution by Dumping from Ships and Aircraft, commonly called the Oslo Convention, was opened for signature in 1972 and entered into force in 1974. Its geographical area of application covers the whole North East Atlantic Ocean, including the North Sea. All the maritime states of Western Europe have ratified the Convention and are therefore members of the Oslo Commission, which is the body created by the Convention to regulate activities of dumping and incineration at sea within the Convention area.

The Convention for the Prevention of Marine Pollution from Land-Based Sources, commonly called the Paris Convention, was opened for signature in 1974 and entered into force in 1978. Its area of application is broadly the same as that of the Oslo Convention, except that the Paris Convention extends up to the freshwater limit and therefore includes the internal waters of Contracting Parties. The same maritime states have ratified the Convention (with the exception of Finland which is an observer), but an important additional member is the EC. The role of the Paris Convention is more dynamic than that of the Oslo Convention in that Contracting Parties have undertaken to draw up "programmes and measures" to "eliminate pollution" by blacklist substances and to "strictly limit" pollution by grey list substances. The scope for programmes and measures is broad: these can include discharge limits, environmental quality standards, as well as regulations governing the composition and use of substances and products.

Given the existence of these two international organizations, to which all North Sea riparian states are members, an obvious question is immediately raised.

Why is there a need for the North Sea conferences?

The role of the Oslo and Paris Commissions is to provide the international legal framework, at regional level, for the control of dumping at sea (including incineration) and the regulation of discharges, whether to air or water, from both point and diffuse sources. These are the fundamental objectives although the meetings of the Commissions and their working groups provide a useful forum for the exchange of information on marine pollution issues and, more importantly, for the discussion of policy objectives at the regional level.

However, although by comparison with the global conventions the work of the Commissions is clearly regional, the geographical extent is such that it could be argued that the Commissions work at a "super regional level". The thread which binds the Contracting Parties together is the fact that they all share an Atlantic coastline. Beyond that, the differences emerge: these were revealed very clearly in the book which was published to mark the Commissions' tenth anniversary in 1984[1] and which clearly described the different industrial bases of the member countries, the waste problems to which they gave rise and the different priorities and options for their solution. More importantly, the marine waters which the Contracting Parties have pledged themselves to protect are markedly different: the Atlantic deeps off the coast of Portugal, for example, do not necessarily require the same management decisions as for the shallow ecosystem of the North Sea.

The fact that the North Sea ecosystem is a clearly identifiable region within the wider Convention area is, of course, one reason for the justification of INSCs at the scientific level. The fact that the North Sea is bounded by eight riparian states means that all potentially contribute to the ecosystem's problems and all have a role to play in ensuring its protection. The problems need discussion at international level, but not necessarily within the Commissions since not all the problems (e.g. nutrient inputs) are Convention-wide.

But although there is a scientific and management case for the discussion of North Sea problems, the primary reason for the initiation and continuation of INSCs is the political motivation. The 1984 Bremen Conference was the Federal Republic's answer to the high-level scientific study of the North Sea carried out in 1980. It was also a political response to the growing "green movement" in the Federal Republic and in Europe generally.

The question could still be asked as to why this response was not channelled through the framework of the existing regional organizations. Apart from the fact that there is no regional body at the North Sea ecosystem level, the political statements coming out of a free-standing Ministerial conference are arguably more powerful than if they were watered down within the framework of an international organization. Furthermore, the "independence" of the INSCs enables Ministers to direct questions and give political impetus to the work carried on within the relevant international organizations, not only the Oslo and Paris Commissions but also other bodies such as IMO, the Bonn Agreement and the Memorandum of Understanding on Port State Control.

Do the INSCs need OSPARCOM?

At this point it is worth examining the differences in role between the Commissions and the INSCs although the significance of the latter from the legal viewpoint is dealt with more thoroughly elsewhere.

[1] "The Oslo and Paris Commissions: The First Decade" (1984), pp. 377.

It has already been suggested that the main *raison d'être* of the INSCs is political. This is evident from the form which the Ministerial Declarations take. After the preambular paragraphs of the Bremen Declaration, the Ministers "declare their firm determination" to do certain things. At London in 1987 the Ministers "agreed" to undertake certain actions.

The INSCs are not held within the framework of any internationally ratified convention or treaty. They are meetings of Ministers with common responsibilities, similar problems and shared goals. Their statements represent a political commitment rather than a legal obligation. This is not in any way to belittle the impact or importance of the Conferences, but it is important to be clear about the nature of their "decisions".

Within the framework of the Oslo and Paris Commissions (OSPARCOM), it is the goal to move towards the adoption of Decisions which bind Contracting Parties or Recommendations for action which they are morally obliged to carry out, unless in both cases they have specifically entered reservations. It is not possible for the Commissions to bind a Contracting Party unwillingly.

Following both the Bremen and London Conferences, the Commissions have examined the Ministerial Declarations with a view to assessing the implications for their own work. In many cases the Ministers give encouragement and impetus to work already going on within the Commissions' framework. In some cases the Ministerial request for action leads, after discussion within appropriate expert groups, to the adoption of Decisions or Recommendations, e.g. the Paris Commission's Decision 88/1 of 17 June 1988 on the Use of Oil-Based Muds[2] taken in response to the invitation to tighten the criteria for the use of oil-based muds (London Conference Declaration, para. XVI. 34). In other cases, the Ministers may agree upon certain principles which the Commissions feel it appropriate to adopt in the context of their work, e.g. PARCOM Recommendation 89/1 of 22 June 1989 on the Principle of Precautionary Action.[3]

The value of the Commissions' adopting Decisions and Recommendations, either in furtherance of broad Ministerial objectives (as in the case of oil-based muds) or to consolidate politically agreed concepts, is that they give the Conference Declarations a firmer footing in international law. The work of the Commissions is therefore valuable, indeed essential, to transfer the political commitments entered into by Ministers into legal obligations incumbent on Contracting Parties under international law.

In the case of the Oslo and Paris Commissions the transfer of INSC Declarations into OSCOM and PARCOM Decisions and Recommendations has wider implications in that other states are involved. Consequently, at their meetings in 1988, the Commissions agreed on certain principles, namely that they should continue to work towards common goals for protecting the marine environment to be reached by consensus among all Contracting Parties, that agreements within the Commissions, especially as reflected in Decisions and Recommendations, should, where necessary,

[2] *Tenth Annual Report of the Paris Commission* (1988), p. 95.

[3] "Summary Record of the Eleventh Meeting of the Paris Commission" (PARCOM 11/9/1, Annex 5).

reflect the fact that different routes and different timetables for compliance may be acceptable in other parts of the Convention area from those pertaining to the North Sea, and that other parts of the convention area may have different needs from the North Sea owing to geographical, hydrographic and ecological circumstances, and that consequently they may require different measures.[4]

How did the Commissions respond to the Bremen Declaration?

The Commissions were not invited to participate in the preparatory work for the Bremen Conference, although they attended the Conference itself as observers. Nevertheless, references to the Oslo and Paris Commissions are liberally sprinkled throughout the Bremen Declaration. In many cases the Conference Declaration uses language like "work will be intensified without delay" in the framework of the Commissions. How has this been translated in reality?

It is not the purpose of this chapter to assess, on a point-by-point basis, to what extent the Oslo and Paris Commissions have fulfilled the mandate laid upon them by the INSCs. Rather is it my intention to provide a brief qualitative assessment of how the Commissions have responded. What can be said is that the pace of the Commissions' decision-making has quickened, although it must be admitted that the results are patchy.

The Bremen Declaration, with its 35 preambular paragraphs, 75 paragraphs of substance and its accompanying Annex, divided into 16 sections, can be likened to a scatter-gun approach to the problems of the North Sea. Nevertheless, from this all-embracing outlook, it is possible to identify a number of issues where the Ministers expected to see intensified action: on the black- and grey-list substances, the Commissions have taken further Decisions, notably on mercury, cadmium, organotin compounds; on new synthetic substances, reports on environmental concentrations are examined by the Commissions' Joint Monitoring Group; on atmospheric inputs, a protocol amending the Paris Convention has been signed and is now in force, a comprehensive measurement campaign has been established and proposals for reduction measures have been made; on phasing out the use of PCBs, the Paris Commission led the way in prohibiting the use of PCBs in new applications but little headway has been made in agreeing an international deadline for phasing out the vast quantities of PCBs in current use; on dumping, especially sewage sludge, further measures to restrict dumping have been agreed within the framework of the Oslo Commission but the dumping of sewage sludge *per se* is still permitted; on platforms, the Paris Commission has adopted stringent conditions on the use of oil-based muds and has firmed up the controls on effluents; on the development of the Joint Monitoring Programme, further substances have been added to the list of measured parameters—but perhaps not enough.

[4] *Thirteenth Annual Report of the Oslo Commission*, p. 5 and *Tenth Annual Report of the Paris Commission*, p. 4.

What was the impact of the London Conference?

The United Kingdom set out with the intention that the London Conference should be science based. To that end, a Scientific and Technical Working Group (STWG) was established, one of whose chief roles was to draw up a North Sea Quality Status Report (QSR). The QSR was a particularly valuable document in that it drew together, for the first time, all available knowledge on inputs to the North Sea, concentration levels and effects. Much of the information was, indeed, already available in published reports (e.g. those of the Oslo and Paris Commissions), but the value of the QSR was its synthetic approach which will be a valuable model for the second QSR to be prepared by the North Sea Task Force in 1993. The work of the STWG and the QSR were also valuable in that they identified certain gaps in knowledge of the North Sea which will be addressed by the North Sea Task Force established by the Commissions and the International Council for the Exploration of the Sea (ICES) in response to the London Conference Declaration.

But although the Conference may have been science based, the agenda was effectively settled by the Policy Working Group (PWG). Here the focus was essentially determined by the political priorities of the North Sea states.

The Commissions, in the persons of the Secretariat, were actively involved in the work of the London Conference from the outset. This was beneficial for the preparatory work of the Conference in that the Commissions' information on inputs and monitoring could be brought in to the work of STWG. At policy level, the status of work within the Commissions could be brought to the attention of PWG so that the Ministerial Declaration could focus on those areas where further Ministerial impetus could be valuable.

It is probably the case that the impact of the London Conference has been greater on North Sea states and on the Commissions than was the Bremen Conference. This is partly because the Ministerial Declaration focused on fewer issues, and no doubt also because of the follow up Conference which will be held in the Netherlands in March 1990.

It may be helpful to recap briefly the areas in which the Commissions have made significant progress since the London Conference: on inputs via rivers and estuaries, the Paris Commission has adopted Recommendations on the precautionary principle and on the use of "best available technology" (BAT), has established a comprehensive programme to measure direct inputs and riverine inputs in 1990, and has established an Industrial Sectors Working Group to review BAT in 10 industrial branches with a view to proposing process-based discharge standards; the Paris Commission Working Group on Nutrients is playing a pivotal role in directing (through the adoption of Recommendations and Decisions) and evaluating the effectiveness of North Sea states' plans for reducing nutrient inputs; as already mentioned, the work on atmospheric inputs is proceeding along the lines laid down in the Ministerial Declaration; the Oslo Commission has adopted legally binding Decisions on phasing out incineration at sea and on the reduction and cessation of dumping; the Paris Commission has adopted a Decision tightening the rules on the use and discharge of oil-based muds as well as reviewing the use of chemicals used offshore; the Paris Commission has adopted further Recommendations on the discharge of radioactive wastes in line with the London Conference Declaration; and the Commissions and ICES jointly have established a North Sea Task Force charged with filling the gaps in scientific knowledge identified by the 1987 QSR. From this inventory of actions it would seem that the Ministers' wishes expressed in 1984 that "work will be intensified without delay" is at least beginning to be fulfilled.

The way to get things done

There is a symbiotic relationship between the INSCs and the Oslo and Paris Commissions. Neither works in a vacuum. For example, a comparison of the future strategy document prepared by the Commissions in June 1984,[5] on the then important principle of the compatible aims of the EQO and UES systems, with the wording of the Bremen Declaration in November 1984 on the same subject shows the influence of the Commissions' thinking. This is but one example and, of course, there are areas (see section below) where the INSCs have influenced the Commissions' work.

The fact would seem to be that, at least during the 1980s, both frameworks needed each other—and the North Sea environment has probably benefited more by being the focus of two "regulatory" bodies.

The INSCs on their own would probably not be sufficient. Ministers can agree upon the broad principles to be followed but in many cases they have specifically left the working out of detailed implementation to the established regulatory bodies, such as the Commissions. Two examples will suffice. The 1987 Conference encouraged the Paris Commission to establish a comprehensive, long-term monitoring programme for measuring inputs of pollutants via the atmosphere. It is only within the framework of the Commissions' expert group that the details of such a programme can be worked out on an international scientific basis. Secondly, Ministers at London agreed that

> "no material should be dumped in the North Sea unless there are no practical alternatives on land and it can be shown to the competent international organizations that the materials pose no risk to the marine environment".

It is the Oslo Commission, as the competent international organization concerned, which has elaborated a so-called "prior justification procedure" which a North Sea state must follow if it proposes to issue dumping permits because (a) there are no practical alternatives on land and (b) the materials pose no risk to the marine environment. Thus the Commissions can be seen as the implementing arm of the INSCs.

In other instances, discussions within the Commissions provide the basis for political decisions at the INSCs. For example, it was agreed in principle back in 1981 that the Oslo Commission would decide before 1 January 1990 on a termination date for incineration at sea. It then embarked upon an extensive review of land-based disposal provision in order to establish a realistic termination date. Although the scientific information was available for the Commission in June 1987, it was not possible to reach

[5] *Sixth Annual Report of the Paris Commission*, p. 105.

agreement at that meeting, although the indications pointed to a termination date of 1995. It was politically necessary for Ministers to decide upon the termination date at the London Conference in November 1987 before the Oslo Commission could formally determine a termination date (which incidentally applies to all Contracting Parties and throughout the Convention area) at its subsequent meeting in June 1988.

Have the INSCs influenced the work of the Commissions?

This may seem a facile question in that it is obvious that the Conferences influence the Commissions' work in the sense that the Ministerial Declarations give further impetus to work already in hand or specifically request the Commissions to undertake certain new tasks. But there are also more subtle—and far-reaching—ways in which the INSCs exert great influence.

For example, the Oslo Convention on dumping was drawn up in 1972. Since then much has changed, particularly in the last five years. Scientific knowledge and assessment have developed but, more significantly, what the public perceives as acceptable has changed and this is reflected in changes in government policies. Consequently in 1985 the Oslo Commission's scientific body (SACSA) began to review the wastes currently dumped at sea and also to question the Convention's ground-rules for permitting dumping. SACSA recognized, however, that more than scientific issues were at stake and called for policy guidance from the Commission. Because of the political significance of decisions on dumping, the issue was placed firmly on the agenda of the 1987 INSC. The principles contained in what ultimately became paragraphs 21 and 22 of the London Conference Declaration were worked out at the highest level. The principles represent a significant shift in policy regarding dumping, which incidentally have subsequently been adopted by all members of the Oslo Commission.[6] Whereas the 1972 Oslo Convention provided a framework in which dumping could take place according to certain rules designed to ensure that there was no harm to the marine environment, now the onus is on a Contracting Party to satisfy the Commission on two grounds (see section above) before the dumping of industrial wastes can take place.

The same end may well have been achieved within the Oslo Commission in the longer run. However, it is almost certainly true that the Ministers' political agreement paved the way for the subsequent Oslo Commission Decision on the reduction and cessation of dumping.

Modus operandi

The ultimate goal of all INSCs is to draw up what is essentially a political "declaration of intent" that all participating Ministers can feel happy to sign. For this to be the case, there must be some real substance to the Ministers' statement, not just a repetition of pious platitudes. The preparation of such a document requires a period of concentrated activity, some 12 to 18 meetings in as many months. During the course of the preparatory meetings, the issues are refined and, more importantly, the precise

[6] *Fifteenth Meeting of the Oslo Commission* (OSCOM 15/11/1, Annex 6).

language is elaborated leaving the contentious issues to be resolved by Ministers themselves. This is the procedure which was first followed at Bremen, was refined in the preparations for the London Conference and is being used again in the preparations for The Hague.

The Commissions' organizational structure is different reflecting the different role and objectives. The Commissions themselves meet once a year; the details are first discussed in depth by a number of subject-orientated expert groups whose recommendations are vetted by the Commissions' standing scientific and technical bodies before being approved (or not, as the case may be) by the Commissions at their annual meetings. The Commissions' work is not geared directly to achieving a political result, although discussions within the Commissions' framework are certainly influenced by discussions in the North Sea context. This organizational framework seems to work effectively in ensuring that proposals coming before the Commissions for adoption as binding Decisions or Recommendations are soundly based on the latest state of the art in science and technology. At Commission level, broadly socio-economic considerations play their part, as do the political implications of what is proposed.

The Commissions' organizational structure also seems to be an effective mechanism for ensuring that issues of concern are brought to the Commissions at the earliest notice. For example, the problems arising from the use of organotin compounds in anti-fouling paints were first drawn to the attention of the Joint Monitoring Group, on the basis of which the Paris Commission's Technical Working Group was advised that restrictions on the use of such compounds were appropriate for action at international level. As a consequence, the Commission has adopted two Recommendations urging the restriction of the use of organotin compounds and has formally drawn the attention of IMO to the wider implications for international shipping.

The different structures which have been developed serve the two bodies well, given their different objectives. There are, however, important consequences arising from the fact that there are two international frameworks dealing with essentially the same problems.

First, the two Secretariats need to work in close co-operation in order to ensure that there is no counter-productive "competition" and that the outcome of discussions is pushed forward in the most effective way. The OSPARCOM Secretariat was not involved at all with the Bremen Conference. It worked closely with the British authorities in the preparations for the London Conference and it is working even more closely with the Dutch Secretariat in the preparations for the meeting at The Hague. For this last meeting, the Ministers will receive updated reports on, for example, inputs to the North Sea where the data will come largely from the Commissions' reporting procedures. In order to avoid unnecessary duplication of work, the PARCOM Secretariat has worked closely with the Dutch in evaluating the measures to reduce nutrient inputs.

The second consequence is that there is, inevitably, some duplication of effort. Although the INSC Secretariats have striven to avoid establishing duplicate working groups, there are inevitably some issues which are discussed both in the OSPARCOM framework and in the preparations for the Ministerial Conferences. This places a considerable burden on the personnel—and financial—resources of North Sea states who have to send representatives to cover the issues in both fora. Is it worth it?

1990 and beyond

The answer to that last question will presumably be answered during the 1990s. The Third INSC in March 1990 will be essentially a policy-based conference. Its primary purpose is to review progress on the measures contained in the London Declaration. However, in order to justify ministerial involvement, there will have to be more in The Hague Conference than the opportunity of mutual self-congratulation on progress achieved and planned. There will have to be some new issues for Ministers to resolve.

It is also inevitable that there will be at least a Fourth INSC, if for no other reason than to review the final outcome of the 1985–1995 reduction programmes.

But before the Fourth INSC (whenever that may be) there will be a Ministerial-level meeting of the Oslo and Paris Commissions in 1992. Such a high level meeting would probably have been convened earlier if it had not been for the German initiative to host the Bremen Conference restricted to North Sea matters in 1984. The agenda for the Ministerial meeting in 1992 has yet to be worked out: preparatory work will start in earnest in April 1990! But it is already clear that the Ministerial-level meeting must come forward with two outcomes if it is to be deemed successful:

- to set out the broad (and not so broad) policy direction of the Commissions in the 1990s and beyond;
- to come forward with further binding Decisions which can be expected to make a real impact on eliminating or avoiding marine pollution in the Convention area.

The meeting should be beneficial to the Commissions' activities in that it will undoubtedly raise the profile of their work. It will also broaden Ministerial involvement in marine pollution affairs to a wider political circle than only the North Sea riparian states. It will also serve to keep marine pollution issues firmly on the political agenda. There is, of course, no reason why the Ministerial-level meeting should not also deal with purely North Sea issues if this were considered by the states concerned to be appropriate; the North Sea is, after all, part of the wider Convention area.

A North Sea forum?

What then is the future for the management of the North Sea? It has long been mooted that the North Sea would be better served by a single administrative body covering all relevant issues: dumping and incineration, land-based source pollution, counter pollution activities (Bonn Agreement), shipping and transport (IMO interests), mineral extraction, fisheries resource management, sea-use planning. The list is long.

From the viewpoint of pollution prevention, it could be feasible to update the Convention texts which were drawn up almost 20 years ago. The opportunity could also be taken to rationalize the organizational structure and to create a new body for all marine pollution interests along the same lines as the Helsinki Convention. This *could* be a useful exercise provided that it was not carried out at the expense of continuing work under the existing legal regimes.

A second question which may be posed is whether North Sea pollution activities are sufficiently different or, sufficiently serious, to justify a separate convention of their own.

I see no evidence to suggest that the North Sea interests would gain significantly from such a hiving off. It is true that there are marine pollution issues which are primarily North Sea orientated, for example, at the present time nutrients. However, there is no evidence to suggest that progress on North Sea issues has been hampered by the present structures. On the other hand, it is clear that where action has been taken to protect the particular North Sea environment, this has had implications for the wider Convention area, albeit sometimes on a protracted time-scale.

Conclusions

These remarks relate solely to the pollution issues. The question of a North Sea forum dealing with all North Sea management issues is a separate matter covered in another chapter. The issues surrounding the emotive and politically sensitive field of marine pollution are not as easily solved as some would have us believe. The record of individual North Sea states, of the effectiveness of the INSCs themselves, and the international bodies specifically created for the protection of the marine environment, including the North Sea environment, may not be as exemplary as one would wish. Specifically, some may consider that the Commissions should have taken stronger measures, or acted more quickly than they have done.

There is always room for improvement, but in acknowledging past deficiencies it would be churlish to overlook past achievements—and these have been very real. Nor should it be forgotten that the Commissions are only as strong—or as weak—as their constituent Member States. The Conventions do not allow for the Commissions imposing majority decisions on their Contracting Parties. The present structures may seem rather cumbersome, perhaps inefficient. It could be tempting, therefore, to throw out the present structures and start afresh. However, the reality is that one would still be dealing with the same states, the same officials, the same need to resolve policy differences among members. If more is needed, then rearrangement of the organizational structures would be simply a distraction. What is necessary for the protection of the North Sea, as for the marine environment generally, is the political will to take the necessary measures in accordance with commonly agreed principles, which now include the precautionary principle. Secondly, there is a need to follow through the political directives with detailed implementation at the appropriate international level. These do not require new structures but, in some cases, changes in attitudes. As we move from the 1980s to the 1990s, there is increasing evidence that this is happening.

Chapter 9

The Role and Activities of the European Communities in the Protection and the Preservation of the Marine Environment of the North Sea

J.-L. Prat

Introduction

Of the eight countries that border the North Sea, six—Belgium, Denmark, France, the Federal Republic of Germany, The Netherlands, the United Kingdom—are members of the European Economic Communities (EC). Only Norway and Sweden are not.

This situation certainly has unavoidable repercussions for the development of marine environmental legislation for the North Sea. The EC is empowered to act in the environmental field in general[1] and therefore in the field of marine environmental protection.[2] The EC is empowered to take such action under article 130 R and subsequent articles of the revised Treaty of Rome,[3] which refer to the common

[1] See J. P. Jacqué, "L'Acte unique européen et la protection de l'environnement", *Environmental Policy and Law*, 16/3/4 (1986), pp. 122–124; L. Krämer, "L'Acte unique européen et la protection de l'environnement: Réflexions sur quelques nouvelles dispositions du droit communautaire", *Revue Juridique de l'Environnement 1987*, pp. 449–474; "Commentaire de l'acte unique européen en matière d'environnement", Rapporteur: Mme. P. Kromarek, *Revue Juridique de l'Environnement 1988*, pp. 75–92.

[2] See P. W. Birnie, "The European Community's Environmental Policy", in E. D. Brown and R. R. Churchill (eds.), *The UN Convention on the Law of the Sea: Impact and Implementation*, Cardiff, The Law of the Sea Institute, 1987, pp. 527–556; D. Le Morvan, "Les Communautés européennes et la protection de l'environnement marin", unpub. Ph.D. thesis (Université de Bretagne Occidentale, Brest, 1984); *id.*, "La Politique communautaire de protection de l'environnement marin", *Société française pour le droit de l'environnement—droit de l'environnement marin, developpements récents*, *Economica* (1989), pp. 103–132; P. Daillier, "Droit communautaire et protection de l'environnement marin", *Annuaire de droit maritime et aérien*, vi (Paris: Pédone, 1982), pp. 267–298; *id.*, "Les Fondements de la compétence de la C.E.E. dans le domaine maritime" (forthcoming) *Economica* (1990).

[3] The Single European Act was published in Bulletin of the European Communities, S. 2/86.

environmental policy. Use can also be made of Article 100 A on the internal market, which permits measures relating, on the one hand, to the approximation of provisions laid down by law, regulation or administrative action in Member States, and on the other hand, to a high level of environmental protection. Note also that environmental measures taken in the context of other policies—the transport policy for example—can be based on other articles in the Treaty of Rome. This can be deduced from Article 130 R.2 which indicates that environmental protection requirements shall be a component of the Community's other policies. In short the Community is legally equipped to participate in protecting the marine environment of the North Sea.

Having been made conscious at a political level of the pollution the North Sea suffers (*below*), the EC is already participating in its protection in several ways (*below*). Attaining this goal raises, however, a number of problems and questions due notably to the specific character of the system created by the Treaty of Rome (*below*).

A certain political awareness

This awareness is shown in positions taken by the Council of Ministers, the European Parliament and the European Council.

The Council of Ministers

An examination of the European Community Action Programmes in environmental matters shows that neither the First[4] nor the Second[5] refer directly to the North Sea. The Third Programme, however, shows a certain awareness in indicating that the EC will take steps towards better co-ordinated approaches to problems of the North Sea.[6]

This interest in the North Sea is further strengthened in the Fourth Programme. The Council resolution relating to this Programme of 19 October 1987 considers the fight against sea water pollution from either point or diffuse sources as a priority.[7]

In order to achieve this objective, a general improvement of the aquatic environment, notably of the North Sea, is to be sought. The Programme also provides for the implementation of the decisions taken at the First International Conference on the Protection of the North Sea and makes active participation at the Second Conference a main objective of future EC action.

More recently, the Council has shown an increased and more specific interest in the North Sea by adopting, on 28 June 1988, a resolution on its protection.[8] This resolution is motivated by the proliferation of algal bloom in May and June 1988,

[4] OJEC, C 112, 20 December 1973.
[5] OJEC, C 139, 13 June 1977.
[6] OJEC, C 46, 17 February 1983.
[7] OJEC, C 328, 7 December 1987.
[8] And that of other Community waters: OJEC, C 209, 9 August 1988.

the seal epidemic and the excessive quantities of fertilizer in the North Sea. Its general objective is to call for the strengthening of the fight against aquatic pollution. More precisely, the Commission is requested to make proposals relating to the reduction of fertilizer coming from diffuse sources, particularly agriculture. The Commission is also requested, given the specific problems of the different community regions, to present proposals for the new measures necessary at the community level for domestic and industrial sewage treatment. This resolution is part of the general programme of implementation of the conclusions reached at the Second International Conference on the Protection of the North Sea.

It operates in combination with two other policy decisions also taken in June 1988. On the one hand, it joins the conclusions of the Hanover summit in which the leaders of the Member States reiterated their concern for environmental protection in general and called for the Commission to reinforce its action in this field. It also joins the conclusions of the Ministerial Seminar on the future common water policy. Both these documents stressed the necessity of establishing guidelines for overall water management, of making simultaneous and complementary use of quality objectives and emission standards in treating dangerous substances, and of adopting measures on waste water treatment and the reduction of diffuse pollution sources.

These examples show the political awareness created by the fight against pollution during the recent period. A survey of the European Parliament's work confirms the existence of this awareness.

The European Parliament

The European Parliament regularly discusses North Sea problems. In January 1984 an important resolution was adopted on combating pollution in the North Sea.[9] This resolution made the first global approach to the specific problems of this zone's marine environment. It had the additional advantage of pointing out the multiple deficiencies of actions previously undertaken. It also showed the considerable complexity of the management of the North Sea, but in many ways it appeared excessively ambitious and poorly drafted.

Besides this resolution, the European Parliament has brought up aspects of North Sea pollution in several other resolutions.[10] Concrete effects of these resolutions are limited, however, given the characteristics of community procedure and the competences of the European Parliament.

[9] OJEC, C 46, 20 February 1984. See J. Maij-Weggen, *Report on the Combating of Pollution in the North Sea*, European Parliament Document 1–1173/83, 1983. Cf. G. Peet, "The 1984 North Sea Conference: A Preview", (1984) 8 *Marine Policy* 259–270; *id.*, "Sea-Use Management for the North Sea", in E. D. Brown and R. R. Churchill (eds.), *The UN Convention on the Law of the Sea*, pp. 430–440.

[10] See e.g. OJEC, C 274, 15 October 1984, p. 36; OJEC, C 315, 26 November 1984, p. 91; OJEC, C 315, 26 November 1984, p. 93; OJEC, C 318, 30 November 1987, p. 119; OJEC, C 49, 22 February 1988, p. 4.

The European Council

Lastly, the European Council, meeting in Rhodes in December 1988, adopted an important declaration on the environment.[11] In this declaration the Council pointed out that particular attention must be given to *seas* and *coastal regions* of Member States which are of primary importance from an economic and ecological point of view. The areas mainly concerned are the Mediterranean region, the North Sea and the Irish Sea.

The EC's political interest in the North Sea is also shown—obviously—by the Commission's participation in international conferences on the North Sea. Besides taking these policy positions, the EC has developed specific protective measures concerning the North Sea.

The main EC protective actions

Internal policy

The effective contribution of the EC to the North Sea's protection is already significant. This is manifest first of all through environmental directives in force: directives on discharges of dangerous substances,[12] directives on polluting industries on the coast,[13] directives on uses of marine waters.[14]

These directives are not expressly aimed at the North Sea. But their geographical scope being the same as that of the EC treaty, they necessarily apply to all areas where the Member States exercise their sovereignty or jurisdiction.[15] From a practical point of view the geographical scope of these Directives is variable. Some deal with coastal waters in general.[16] Others apply to the waters of the territorial sea.[17] Still others refer generally to the "sea".[18]

[11] EC Bull. 12. 1988 point 1.1.11.

[12] Council Directive 76/464 of 4 May 1976, on pollution caused by certain dangerous substances discharged into the aquatic environment of the community, OJEC, L 129, 18 May 1976; Council Directive 82/176 of 22 March 1982 on limit-values and quality objectives for mercury discharges by the chlor-alkali electrolysis industry, OJEC, L 81, 27 March 1982; Council Directive 83/513 of 26 September 1983 on limit- values and quality objectives for cadmium discharges, OJEC, L 291, 24 October 1983; Council Directive 84/156 of 8 March 1984 on limit-values and quality objectives for mercury discharges by sectors other than the chlor-alkali electrolysis industry, OJEC, L 74, 17 March 1984; Council Directive 84/491 of 9 October 1984 on limit-values and quality objectives for discharges of hexachlorocyclohexane, OJEC, L 274, 17 October 1984; Council Directive 86/280 of 12 June 1986 on limit-values and quality objectives for discharges of certain dangerous substances included in list I of the Annex to Directive 76/464 EEC, OJEC, L 181, 4 July 1986.

[13] Council Directive 78/176 of 20 February 1978 on waste from the titanium dioxide industry, OJEC, L 54, 25 February 1978; Council Directive 82/883 of 3 December 1982 on procedures for the surveillance and monitoring of the environment concerned by waste from the titanium dioxide industry, OJEC, L 378, 31 December 1982.

[14] Council Directive 76/160 of 8 December 1975 concerning the quality of bathing-water, OJEC, L 31, 5 February 1976; Council Directive 79/923 of 30 October 1979 on the quality required of shellfish waters, OJEC, L 281, 10 December 1982.

[15] See Y. Van der Mensbrugghe, "Les Frontières maritimes de la C.E.E. (Observations à propos de la Directive 84/631 sur les transferts transfrontaliers de déchets dangereux)" (1989) *Revue du Marché Commun* 360–373.

[16] See e.g Council Directive 79/923 of 30 October 1979, n. 16.

[17] See e.g Council Directive 76/464 of 4 May 1976, n. 14.

[18] See e.g Council Directive 78/176 of 20 February 1978.

The EC contribution to the protection of the marine environment is also manifested by Council Decisions. The most notable is that which institutes a Community Information System for the control and reduction of pollution.[19] This system makes use of updated data on the characteristics of hydrocarbons and other harmful substances, as well as on localizing means at the disposal of Member States for fighting pollution.

Beyond specifically environmental acts, EC participation in the protection of the North Sea is visible in various instruments and measures relating to maritime safety.[20] Besides that, the Commission has launched, as part of the Fourth Programme of environmental research 1986/1990,[21] a combined research project on the growth of Phaeocystis Pouchetii algae in the costal zones of the southern part of the North Sea which are being enriched by nutrients.[22] It has also given financial aid from time to time to work relating to the mortality of seals.[23]

Several pending directive proposals show the Commission's desire to develop the EC's contribution to the protection of the North Sea and to put into practice the objectives outlined in the Ministerial Declarations. Article 3 of the proposed directive relating to the elimination of PCBs and PCTs[24] is directly inspired by point XVI. 24 of the 1987 London Declaration. This article indicates that Member States will take appropriate measures to prohibit incineration of PCBs on incineration vessels by 1995.

The Commission has also proposed a directive on the protection of fresh, coastal and maritime waters against nitrate pollution from diffuse sources.[25] It contributes to putting into practice points XVI. 10–15 and Annex E of the London Declaration. It focuses on agricultural sources and municipal sewage treatment plants. It aims notably at avoiding the eutrophication of surface, coastal maritime, and estuarine waters. The Member States will be requested to identify "vulnerable zones", those most affected by nitrate pollution. Steps will have to be taken in these zones. These steps will determine, at a Community level, maximum manure levels. They will also guide national authorities in fixing maximal doses of chemical fertilizers, deal with land development practices and a limitation of the nitrate level in municipal waste waters.

The proposed directive on minimum requirements for vessels transporting pack-

[19] Council Decision 86/85 of 6 March 1986, OJEC, L 77, 22 March 1986 amended by Council Decision 88/346 of 16 June 1988. See A. P. Barisich, "Coopération en Europe Occidentale en cas de pollutions marines massives", Colloque de Brest, Octobre 1988 (forthcoming) *Economica* (1990).

[20] Council Directive of 21 December 1978 on minimum requirements for certain tankers entering or leaving Community ports, OJEC, L 33, 8 February 1979 amended OJEC, L 315, 11 December 1979; Council Directive of 21 December 1978 on pilotage of vessels in the North Sea and English Channel, OJEC, L 33, 8 February 1979; COST–301 project, Council Decision of 13 December 1982, OJEC, L 378, 31 December 1982; COST–311 project.

[21] OJEC, L 159, 14 June 1986.

[22] See on this project QU 608/87, OJEC, C 42, 15 February 1988; QU. 791/88, OJEC, C 132, 29 May 1989; QU 1466/88, OJEC, C 132, 29 May 1989.

[23] See QU. 1465/88, OJEC, C 132, 29 May 1989.

[24] See COM (88)559 fin of 18 October 1988; OJEC, C 319, 12 December 88.

[25] COM 88 (708) fin; OJEC, C 54, 3 March 1989.

aged dangerous or polluting cargo entering or leaving Community ports is also part of this pursuit of greater protection.[26]

Note also that the Commission is considering simultaneous use of limit-values and quality objectives for certain hazardous wastes from industry.

External level EC policy[27]

The EC participates in international actions for the protection of the North Sea in a number of different ways. The EC is a contracting party to several regional conventions on the North Sea. It is a party to the Paris Convention on land-based pollution.[28] Hence it is also a member, along with the contracting Member States, of the Paris Commission (PARCOM). It is a party to the 1983 Bonn Agreement for co-operation in dealing with pollution of the North Sea by oil and other harmful substances.[29] The EC participates in the Meetings to this agreement. The EC is also a party to the Rhine Chemical Convention and a member of the International Rhine Commission.[30]

Although the EC is not a party to the Memorandum of Understanding on Port State Control (MOU), the Commission participates in the proceedings of the Port State Control Committee created by it. The EC actively supports the Memorandum.[31]

Lastly, the EC, which is not a contracting party to the Oslo Convention, enjoys observer status in the Oslo Commission. In addition, the Commission takes part in IMO meetings. It is the Commission's belief that actions undertaken by the Community in the field of maritime safety and the prevention of pollution should essentially support the international system set up by IMO.[32]

Evaluation of the development of EC policy

This development can be perceived from both a retrospective and a prospective point of view. From a retrospective point of view, the EC internal policy is characterized by several positive developments. The rise in awareness of environmental problems in general, and those of the North Sea in particular has been confirmed, and certain Community actions have shown encouraging results.

For example, the Commission is satisfied that, generally speaking, the putting into operation of the Community Information System has achieved the desired

[26] OJEC, C 147, 14 June 1989.

[27] See generally A. Nollkaemper, "The European Community and International Environmental Co-operation—Legal Aspects of External Community Powers", (1987) 2 *Legal Issues of European Integration* 55- 91.

[28] OJEC, L 194/5 of 25 July 1975.

[29] Cf. Council Decision of 28 June 1984, OJEC, L 188, 16 July 1984.

[30] OJEC, L 240, 19 September 1977; See also G. Kasoulides, "London North Sea Conference" (1988) 19 *Marine Pollution Bulletin* 97–99.

[31] See COM (85) 90 fin of 15 March 1985 "Towards a Common Policy of Maritime Transport", points 82–92. Cf. e.g. Clinton Davis Qu. 631/88, OJEC, C 132, 29 May 89.

[32] See COM (85) 90 fin p. 87.

results.[33] On the other hand, the 129 substances listed by the Commission[34] which are supposed to form the basis of the EC water policy[35] are far from being covered by directives. Emission values have been adopted on the basis of framework-directives 76/464 and 86/280[36] for only a few.[37] Furthermore, the proposed directive on dumping in general has not as yet been adopted.[38]

At the external level, we note first of all that although the EC is not a contracting party to the Oslo Convention, it enjoys a certain influence within the OSCOM. As the EC is a PARCOM member, the European Commission is present at the joint meetings of the two Commissions. The Commission meets with officials from OSPARCOM's head office in order to avoid duplication of efforts. Finally, the existence of directives on certain types of dumping influences the positions taken by Member States.[39] It is evident that the EC's participation in the Oslo Convention would clarify the situation.[40]

The Commission's conduct in PARCOM raises several questions.[41] First of all let us consider the issue of the extent of Community competence: when is it competent? When does competence remain with the Member States? To a formal request for clarification made to it,[42] the EC responded by a general declaration stating that the distribution of competence between the EC and its Member States is an Internal Community matter.[43] This reply, not very satisfying for third-party States, can be explained by the dynamic character of EC competences.[44]

[33] See COM (89) 1 fin. 15 March 1989.

[34] See Council Resolution of 7 February 1983 concerning the combating of water pollution OJEC, C 46, p. 17.

[35] See L. Ginjaar, "Towards a New E.C. Waterpolicy", *Environmental Policy and Law*, 1988, pp. 210–219.

[36] See *above*, n. 12.

[37] See Directive 82/176; Directive 83/513; Directive 84/156; Directive 84/4091; Directive 86/280.

[38] First proposal in 1976: see OJEC, 1976 C 40, p. 3; Second proposal in 1985: see OJEC, 1985 C 245, p. 23, amended. Cf. COM (88) 8 fin. See also L. Krämer, "Le Déversement des déchets en mer et le droit communautaire" (1988) *Revue du Marché Commun* 336–337; J. Side "The European Community and Dumping at Sea" (1986) 17 *Marine Pollution Bulletin* 294–295. It has to be noted, however, that certain directives deal with specific aspects of dumping at sea; see Directive 78/176.

[39] See T. IJlstra, "L'Action communautaire dans les commissions de Paris et d'Oslo" (forthcoming) *Economica* (1990).

[40] Para. 7.16 of the Fourth Environmental Action Programme (1987–1992) indicates "certain . . . matters . . . need to be pursued as follows: strengthening Community participation in the protection of the regional seas (in particular Community participation in . . . the Oslo Convention is necessary)." Such participation implies amendment of Art. 22 of the Convention.

[41] On the conduct of the EEC in PARCOM see T. IJlstra, "L'Action communautaire"; S. Saetevik, *Environmental Cooperation between the North Sea States* (London, Belhaven Press, 1988).

[42] See letter from the chairman of the PARCOM to the EC Commission, 18 October 1985, in Saetevik, *Environmental Cooperation between the North Sea States*, Appendix 5.

[43] See Paris Commission, Eight Annual Report on the Activities of the Paris Commission, point 13.

[44] The problem of the identification of the EC's competences in the field of the protection of the marine environment became relevant in respect of the 1982 LOS Convention. The Declaration made pursuant to Art. 2 of Annex IX to the Convention stipulates that "with regard to rules and regulations for the protection and preservation of the marine environment, the Member States have transferred to the Community competences as formulated in provisions adopted by the Community and as reflected by its participation in certain international agreements", *Law of the Sea Bulletin*, No. 4 (February 1985), p. 17.

The uniqueness of the Community system appears here as a complicating factor in proceedings. The EC Commission's influence on the outcomes of PARCOM should also be examined. To paraphrase Dr. Saetevik, is it a "brake-block" or an "accelerator"?[45] Without furnishing a complete answer, let us remark that on cadmium the EC Commission merely retarded the adoption of Decision 85/2. On the other hand, the Community specifically prevented the adoption of binding resolutions on PCB. And as Ton IJlstra has indicated, it can be said in general that the EC Commission's political weight results in a certain slowdown of PARCOM in cases where Community legislation lags behind PARCOM developments.[46] Conversely, if the political will to protect the environment gathers strength, the EC could act as an accelerator.

From the prospective point of view, a few observations should be made concerning the extension and regionalization of Community Policy on North Sea protection. In the limited framework of this article these will necessarily be of a general nature.

Given the characteristics of the Community system, its action can theoretically be extended from both a substantive and a spatial point of view.

From a substantive point of view, extension of EC actions brings up first of all the choice of the legal basis for internal Community policy: Article 100 A or Article 130 R. This is important in that the decision-making procedures for environmental regulations are different.

As for measures adopted on the basis of Article 130 S, it is to be noted that it is 130 R4 which permits EC competences to be distinguished from those of the Member States. Article 130 R4 provides that the Community shall take action relating to the environment to the extent to which the objectives, especially those concerning protection, referred to in Article 130 R1 can be attained better at Community level than at the level of individual Member States. It appears difficult to determine in *abstracto* which objectives can be attained better at a Community than at a Member State level.

Any pollution which simultaneously affects more than one Member State—as is frequently the case in the North Sea—would seem logically to fall within Community competence. But it remains a fact that politically speaking, the Council will have to decide on this issue.[47]

From a spatial point of view Community law can apply to internal waters and territorial seas of Member States. It can apply beyond that, namely, in the Exclusive Economic Zone (EEZ).[48] Within the EEZ the coastal States have jurisdiction with regard to the protection and the preservation of the marine environment.[49] They

[45] See Saetevik, *Environmental Cooperation between the North Sea States*.
[46] See IJlstra, "L'Action communautaire".
[47] In this respect see also Krämer, "L'Acte unique européen".
[48] Van der Mensbrugghe, "Les Frontières maritimes de la C.E.E.".
[49] LOS Convention, esp. Art. 56 and Part XII.

must, however, have established such a zone. For the moment, France is the only EC member to have established an EEZ in the North Sea.[50]

In any case, given the facts of geography and politics, the Community will necessarily have to co-operate with non-Member States bordering the North Sea in order to act most efficiently in the environmental field.

The regionalization of EC policy called for by certain authors[51] would consist of adopting on the Community level measures which would be differentiated according to the various degrees of pollution suffered by regional seas including the North Sea.

The essential difficulty of this approach lies in the plurality of objectives pursued by the EC. It pursues its own goal of integration. It pursues an environmental objective. In principle, the adoption of environmental rules should not bring about distortions of competition, should not create unequal competitive situations among polluting activities in the EC. Once any given activity is present throughout the Community, differences in environmental rules may create obstacles to the establishment of the internal market. The adoption of stricter rules for pollution in one sea than in another could distort conditions of competition. Not all Member States border the North Sea and positions of principle taken at the level of Ministerial Declarations would necessarily have to be discussed at the Community level by all Member States before being adopted.

The risk is that in the context of these discussions, stricter Community measures for the North Sea might not be accepted by certain Member States.[52] It is true that Article 130 T indicates that common protective measures pursuant to Article 130 S shall not prevent any Member State from maintaining or introducing more stringent protective measures compatible with the Treaty. However, the fact remains that, from an economic point of view, it is not necessarily in one state's interest to establish stronger protective measures by itself. Further, even if a state were to take such measures, for certain types of pollution, it may be asked, insofar as the North Sea is concerned, how much effect these measures would have on the environment.

This difficulty seems surmountable, however. Without pretending to deal with the totality of the question, we should note first of all that Article 130 R3 provides that in preparing its action relating to the environment, the Community shall take account of environmental conditions in the various regions of the Community.[53]

We also see that the Commission is seeking to shape the EC's participation to

[50] On this problem see T. IJlstra, "Enforcement of International Environmental Instruments in the North Sea: The Missing Link", in G. Peet (ed.), *The Status of the North Sea Environment: Reasons for Concern*, Vol. ii (Amsterdam, Stichting Werkgroep Noordzee, 1987), pp. 287–318. For more recent information, see T. IJlstra and P. Ymkers, "The Netherlands and the Establishment of the Exclusive Economic Zone" (1989) 4 IJECL 224–229; also NILOS Newsletter vols. 1 and 2 (1989).

[51] See e.g. Ginjaar, "Towards a New E.C. Waterpolicy".

[52] The risk of a "Europe of the lowest denominator". See H. G. Nagelmacker, "Aftermath of the Amoco-Cadiz: Why Must the European Community Act?" (1980) *Marine Policy* 11.

[53] According to the Single European Act the environmental policy must be adapted to the circumstances in different geographic regions of the Community. The use of the word "region" does not have an institutional meaning.

conform to the international agreements of regional scope in environmental protection to which the Community is a party.[54]

Note finally that the EC is developing "a strategy and a plan of action for environmental protection in the Mediterranean region" (MEDSPA Plan).[55]

This plan refers to the general characteristics of the Basin, to the ecological situation and the socio-economic problems in order to justify a specific action on the part of the Community.[56] Of course, the North Sea hypothetically presents different characteristics, most notably concerning socio-economic problems. We may wonder, however, if the existence of the MEDSPA plan could not establish a precedent that would justify—in spite of the differences between the North Sea region and the Mediterranean region—the elaboration, at the Community level, of a specific North Sea environmental plan.

[54] OJEC, C 324, 17 December 86. Proposal amended subsequently, see COM (88) 451 fin.

[55] This policy is based on a communication of the Commission to the Council on the protection of the environment of the Mediterranean basin, OJEC, C 133, 21 May 1984; Le Morvan, "L'Action des Communautés Européennes en matière de protection de la mer Méditerranée", in B. Vukas (ed.), *The Legal Regime of Enclosed or Semi-Enclosed Seas: The Particular Case of the Mediterranean* (Zagreb, 1988), pp. 313–345.

[56] In his critical article on the EC policy in the field of "ocean management" C. Archer considers the Mediterranean policy to be a positive development: "Supranational Ocean Management: The Case of the E.C.", in A. W. Koers and B. H. Oxman (eds.), *The 1982 Convention on the Law of the Sea*, Honolulu, The Law of the Sea Institute (Hawaii, 1984), pp. 521–541.

Chapter 10

Science and North Sea Policy-Making: Organization and Communication*

Jorgen Wettestad and Steinar Andresen

Science and North Sea policy-making: institutional aspects

At an international symposium during the autumn of 1988 in connection with the 30th anniversary of the Fridtjof Nansen Institute, the relationship between science and politics in international resource management was discussed.[1] Not surprisingly, one of the main conclusions was that the actual influence of science in the decision-making process tended to be quite marginal, especially when strong national and economic interests were involved. However, also in cases where science might have had a role to play, the scientific message was often ignored. One example which was offered was the process in connection with the writing of the report of the World Commission on Environment and Development.[2] One main reason for the lack of scientific input was the malfunctioning of the communication process between policy-makers and the scientific community.

Thus, this is part of the reason why we in our chapter find it interesting to focus the communication process between politics and natural science in the North Sea environmental regime. More specifically, being political scientists, we take a special interest in the institutional and political aspects of this communication process.

* The main background material for this article is threefold: general books and articles on North Sea environmental co-operation; archive material in the Norwegian Ministry of Environment; interviews with civil servants, scientists and environmental organizations in Norway, Denmark, The Netherlands, Belgium, the Federal Republic of Germany and Great Britain. Main background publications by the authors are: Steinar Andresen, "The Environmental North Sea Regime: A Successful Regional Approach?" (The Fridtjof Nansen Institute, 1989); Jorgen Wettestad: *Uncertain Science and Matching Policies: Science, Politics and the Organization of North Sea Cooperation* (Oslo, Fridtjof Nansen Institute, 1989).

1 "The Management of International Resources: Scientific Input and the Role of Scientific Cooperation", forthcoming in book form in Steinar Andresen and Willy Østreng (eds.), *International Resource Management: Science and Politics* (Pinter/Belhaven, September 1989).

2 Timberlake Lloyd, "The Role of Scientific Knowledge in Drawing Up the Brundtland Report", *ibid.*

Hence, we raise the following three main questions: first, what are the main necessary institutional conditions for a well-functioning dialogue between science and policy-makers in environmental policy-making? Second, how is the relationship between science and policy-makers organized in the North Sea context? Third, and most important, how well do the more fundamental institutional questions seem to have been handled in the current organizational approach?

Is it obvious, then, that scientific research can legitimately claim a major role in environmental management? According to one analyst, knowledge—in the form of theoretical understanding of cause-effect relationships as well as descriptive information about relevant variables and parameters—is a necessary condition for rational resource management.[3] Scientific research is the major—but not the only—supplier of such knowledge. However, although being a necessary input, science does not constitute a sufficient basis for rational management. Sound management policies cannot simply be derived from the findings or hypotheses of scientific research. And precautionary management may often have to proceed without any conclusive evidence. Still, unless luck is an unfailing part of management, there has to be a link between basic knowledge and political decisions. This has been clearly recognized in the different international resource regimes which have been set up; for instance in the Paris Convention it is said that "the Contracting Parties shall endeavour to improve progressively techniques for gathering . . . information which can contribute to the revision of the pollution reduction programmes drawn up . . ." (Art.17).

Before going into the institutional aspects more closely, it is probably wise to elaborate a little on the question of what is gained and what is easily lost by choosing an institutional perspective. Starting on a positive note, we feel that an explicit discussion of institutional aspects is one of the most constructive and "positive" contributions political scientists can make. It can be argued that knowledge about systems of human activities can be as critical to environmental management as is knowledge about the state and dynamics of ecological or technical systems. On the other hand, the institutional focus means that very many other important aspects and factors are more or less neglected. For instance, in connection with the question of "what persuades policy-makers of the need to change policies in more environmental protectionist directions", it is very probable that discussing and improving organizational aspects of the communication process between scientists and policy-makers are much less important than for instance the different governments' perceived economic gains and losses by policy changes. However, focusing on improving the role of knowledge, communication and organizational design may be one small piece of "political engineering" contributing to "softening"/muting some of these somehow more "fundamental" economic and political conflicts. With this caveat, we can proceed.

We propose to distinguish between four fundamental functions which are pre-

[3] Underdal Arild, "The Politics of Science in International Resource Management: A Summary", *ibid*. It should be noted that our theoretical perspective here is heavily indebted to Underdal.

conditions for an effective and productive interaction between the science and the policy-making side in an international resource management context. The first function may be termed *co-ordination*. The need for international management and co-operation stems from some kind of international environmental problem, trans-boundary or concerning a shared common resource (or both). In order to be able to assess (at least roughly) the origins and extent of this environmental problem, there is obviously a need for data and assessments of data from all (or at least most) of the co-operating countries. This points to the need for quite stringent international research co-ordination—in order to provide (comparable) parts that ideally fit together like a puzzle, and ensure that all the parts are produced.

The next function may be termed *separation*. What we are hinting at here, is that it is necessary to respect and strengthen the basic distinction between science and politics, both nationally and in connection with the institutional structure of the international co-operation. The reason for this is simple: politicized science gives decision-makers skewed signals, leading to more or less irrational policies.

Third, there is the basic *communication* factor. Science and policy-making are in many ways very different activities. Differences can be noted in time horizon, language, fundamental loyalties, peer group—to mention some of the most obvious aspects. To accentuate the matter: policy-makers want definite answers to complicated questions by the end of the week in order to satisfy superiors and calm public opinion—while scientists can deliver tentative conclusions next year, if their report is not totally "massacred" by fellow scientists in the coming issue of *Science*. Speaking in terms of organization, giving priority to communication might mean separate bodies or forums, but not necessarily. That depends to a large extent on whether there is any room left for such "transient" issues on the agenda of the existing institutions.

Fourth, there is the question of *co-optation*. By the inclusion of this concept, we wish to throw some light upon the important but difficult process of mediation and "political translation" of research findings. It is obvious that scientists themselves have a responsibility to communicate their findings, both to policy-makers and to a wider audience. However, there is no a priori correlation between a scientist's ability to solve scientific problems and his ability to communicate his findings. This points to the need for supplementary mediating actors in the game of resource politics. As a point of departure the most obvious actors here are the national and international non-governmental organizations (concerned with the environment). The amplifier will of course be the mass media and we all know that reading newspapers and watching television is sometimes more amusing than useful.

Finally, what is the relationship between these functions—is it for instance possible to maximize all of them at the same time? Yes—we think so, more or less. The most obvious apparent contradiction might be between research co-ordination and "separation". The main point here must be that co-ordination first and foremost must imply the use of positive, general incentives (for instance funding of studies covering certain areas, substances, etc.) within a broad, explicit "master-plan", and not detailed day-to-day interference from the political side. The perspective must be long-term, i.e. at least 5 to 10 years. The possibility that the pollution problems will fade away in the mean time is very unlikely, we gather. The relation between "co-optation" and "separation" may also be somewhat problematic. It is not a priori given that the NGOs provide a "neutral" and "factual" translation of science in their lobbying activity. Thus, the process of "political translation" may contribute to a blurring of the lines between science and politics.

Integrating science in policy-making: a description of the scientific-political complex in the North Sea[4]

Let us then turn to a very brief descriptive section of the scientific-political complex in the North Sea. The use of the term "scientific-political complex" is of course rather loose and unpretentious, merely meant to indicate to the reader that the described bodies and organizations are at least formally and ideally connected.

Starting at the scientific end of the institutional continuum, the basic ingredient in marine scientific research in the North Sea is of course the various national laboratories and research institutes. However, since fish migrate and ocean currents disperse pollutants over wide areas, international scientific collaboration is an absolute necessity. Such collaboration takes place within several, partly interconnected, institutional settings.

ICES—the International Council for the Exploration of the Sea—is in many ways a natural point of departure in this connection, as it is the oldest inter-governmental organization concerned with marine and fishery sciences (established in 1902). With regard to its external advisory function, the main body within the ICES structure is the Advisory Committee on Marine Pollution (ACMP). According to ICES, the ACMP is composed of "a number of scientists acting—when they work as Committee members—in their personal capacity as scientists, responsible only to the Council . . . The members do not act as national representatives".

When the Oslo Commission which deals with the regulation of dumping and the Paris Commission were established in the early 1970s, they set up their own scientific/technical programmes and institutional structures. First, a Joint Monitoring Group/Programme (JMG/JMP) was established as the main body which should provide a basis for the assessment of "the existing level of marine pollution" and "the effectiveness of measures for the reduction of marine pollution taken under the terms of the present Convention" (from Art. 11 in the Paris Convention). The Programme covers 60 areas, chosen by the participating states themselves. The reports of the work carried out in the JMG are presented at meetings of the TWG and also to the annual Joint Meeting of the Commissions.

As their name indicates, the Technical Working Groups ("Technical Working Group'—TWG—connected to the Paris Commission work; "Standing Advisory Committee for Scientific Advice'—SACSA—connected to the Oslo Commission work) were created as forums for discussion of questions concerning possible practical and technical solutions to pollution problems identified by marine scientific

[4] This is a somewhat shorter version of Wettestad, *op. cit.*, chap. 3.

research. Thus, reports from ICES and the JMG are always reviewed as part of the agenda of TWG meetings. They are intended to represent a politically neutral forum for discussions. In connection with the North Sea Conferences, specific Scientific and Technical Working Groups have been established.

Within this structure, the main political bodies are the Oslo and Paris Commission Meetings and the North Sea Conferences. Conventions, programmes and regulation measures adopted by the Commissions are legally binding on the Member States. The Commissions meet once a year. Continuity in work is guaranteed by a permanent joint Secretariat which organizes and prepares the meetings of the Commissions and other bodies, and distributes documentation.

Supplementing the work of the Commissions, two ministerial-level North Sea Conferences (INSCs) have been held: in Bremen (1984) and in London (1987). The agendas of these Conferences include major issues covered by both the Oslo and Paris Conventions. The national delegations are headed by the respective environment Ministers.

Strengths and weaknesses of the scientific-political complex

Now, then, how do we assess this emerging scientific-political "puzzle'? Let us go through our four suggested analytical "check- points". First, has adequate *co-ordination* been achieved so far? A rough yardstick in this connection is the quality of the end product: a comprehensive description and analysis of the North Sea ecosystem. If judged by the quality of the STWG report produced in connection with the Second INSC, the answer to the co-ordination question must be negative. Although the STWG report clearly was a step forward compared with earlier efforts, the report contains plenty of references to lacking and incomparable data, regarding inputs, concentrations and effects. Thus, when it comes to the final "assessment of the status of the North Sea'-section, the report notes that "problems arise because of the variable quality of scientific evidence".

However, the report should be given credit for explicitly acknowledging these flaws in the existing knowledge. Also, the compilation of these data at the regional level is in itself a start for (hopefully) later co-ordination at a "higher" level. Moreover, although deficiencies are easily detected, the "reasons for concern" in the STWG were still an important point of departure for the ensuing negotiations and the output of the Conference. Admittedly, the STWG is at some points rather crude and vague, but maybe the politicians have not yet been ready to digest and respond to more precise advice? We will return to this question in the final section of this paper.

But why such a flawed end-product? Is it only due to a lack of knowledge or are also other forces at work? In order to answer this question, we think it is necessary to look into the scientific- political system more closely, taking the national level as a point of departure. On the one hand, we would tend to argue that a well-functioning national scientific-political system is a necessary, but not a sufficient, condition for a smooth and co-ordinated international effort. On the other hand, it should be acknowledged that there is probably a kind of feed-back relationship between the national and international level also: discussions and decisions taken in international forums form some of the background and framework for national organization and co-ordination.

With regard to the question of national co-ordination, we must admit that we have only more or less scattered pieces of evidence. Nonetheless, we offer some ideas about the state of affairs in Norway. On the whole, we think it is fair to say that ocean research co- ordination in Norway seems rather haphazard. Co-ordination is high in short all-out efforts leading up to international conferences, and more dormant in the periods in between. Clearly, the INSCs have been an important impetus towards increased research effort and co-ordination in Norway. However, interest seems to fade when the necessary documents are provided.[5] Links to the international research and monitoring networks are split between the State Pollution Control Authority which participates in the Joint Monitoring Group and the Ocean Research Institute which participates in the Joint Monitoring Group—to mention some of the most important networks. Problems have been witnessed concerning the co-ordination of these external links.[6]

Our very crude impression is that co-ordination is somewhat better handled in for instance the UK and The Netherlands. But, on the whole, it is not possible for us to draw a sweeping conclusion concerning the state of national co-ordination.

With regard to the international level, it seems reasonable to distinguish between the situation concerning research (i.e. predictive hazard assessment) and the state of affairs with regard to monitoring (retrospective hazard assessment).[7] If we start with research, where our knowledge is most limited, representatives of the OSPARCOM Secretariat expressed dissatisfaction with the progress witnessed in connection with the Oslo Convention work as long ago as 1984. More recently, the call for better co-ordination of research was sounded in the policy paper on enhancement of scientific knowledge and understanding in connection with the London INSC. As far as we can see, ICES must be the primary organization to focus on in this connection. It is probably fair to say that the research emphasis within ICES so far has been more on the fishery side than on the pollution side.

With regard to monitoring and data gathering, the picture has to date been rather bleak. The OSPARCOM Joint Monitoring Programme has been characterized by experienced participants in the work of the Programme as a "complete failure". Indeed, this has recently been more or less acknowledged also by the PARCOM Secretariat.[8] Several reasons may be cited for this lack of progress: first, an experienced participant in international marine scientific co-operation has pointed to "a

[5] Interview with a Norwegian senior scientist.

[6] See Andresen and Floistad, *Overvaaking av forurensningssituasjonen i norske havomraader: vektlegging, organisasjon, samordning* (The Fridtjof Nansen Institute, 1984), esp. pp. 89–91.

[7] This distinction is taken from G. Persoone, "Hazard Prediction and Relevance of Laboratory-Scale Studies", paper 34 at the International Conference on Environmental Protection of the North Sea, London, March 1987.

[8] "Measurement Campaigns of the Oslo and Paris Commissions", paper produced by the OSPARCOM Secretariat to the first meeting of the Task Force, Hague 7–9 December 1988.

lack of an ability to encourage or coerce participants to follow internationally agreed guidelines instead of the national ones". According to this observer, states often submit data to international sampling programmes that have been collected for a totally different purpose. This might have something to do with the lack of a clear North Sea assessment mandate, as the Oslo and Paris Conventions cover far wider areas than simply the North Sea. Second, others have pointed to the fact that necessary, but time-consuming methodological discussions have dominated the agenda of the JMG. These discussions have quite understandably hampered the dynamic dimension of the group's activity.[9] Third, it must be recognized that it is not until quite recently (cf. the algae and seal "incidents") that the health of the North Sea has been alarmingly focused on, despite several years of Commission meetings and INSCs. The urgency and drive to know "what is really going on" have been lacking.

Let us now turn to the question of *separation*, and ask: has the necessary separation between the scientific and the political spheres been achieved so far? Concerning the rather sensitive and difficult question of the degree of national politicization of marine science, it has for instance been maintained in connection with the case of Great Britain that: "the study of marine pollution remains the task of under-funded scientists employed less to protect the sea than to defend existing government policy".[10] As this question is quite "touchy" we do not know how much we can rely upon answers given by those involved in the North Sea environmental regime. At face value, however, it seems that the general impression is that in most countries at least, there is no strong government pressure upon the scientists to produce "loyal" science: they are free to voice their own opinions. Although there might be exceptions, it does not seem that the politicization of science has reached the North Sea in any manner comparable to for example the International Whaling Commission or the London Dumping Convention. Another matter may be that it has been documented that similar data are interpreted quite differently by scientists from different countries.[11] It cannot be "proven" however, whether this is due to government pressure. Owing, among other things, to severe methodological problems, we leave the further "sociology of science" to the sociologists. Instead, we will focus on some more tangible aspects of the scientific preparatory work for the INSCs. To start on a positive note, a seemingly conscious separation trend concerning the overall relationship between scientific and political aspects of co-operation may be noted. With regard to the preparatory work for the Bremen Conference, the scientific status report was finished just before the Conference itself. According to Norwegian observers, this meant that some of the attention and time of the Conference had to be devoted to

[9] Interview with a Norwegian senior civil servant.

[10] Quote from Sonja Boehmer-Christiansen, "The Role of Science in the International Regulation of Pollution", in Steinar Andresen and Willy Ostreng (eds.), *International Resource Management: Science and Politics*.

[11] F. de Jong, "The Quality of the North Sea: National Points of View in Proceedings of the Second North Sea Seminar", *Reasons for Concern*, Vol. i (1987), pp. 39–54.

clarification and discussion of the scientific background material. In connection with the London Conference, things were organized differently. On the one hand, the Scientific and Technical Working Group completed its work well in advance of the Conference itself. On the other hand, a separate Policy Working Group was established, and was able to use the STWG report as a point of departure for its own clarification and mediation efforts. We find it reasonable to assume that this institutional separation may have been one reason for the comparatively "successful" course of the Conference itself. However, but not reducing the value of the above-mentioned trend, the legitimacy of the scientific report produced can be questioned somewhat. The members of the group may definitely be characterized as experienced and able participants in the previous Commission work, and also representing a considerable scientific expertise between them. Nevertheless, at least half of the group must be characterized first and foremost as civil servants and not primarily as scientists. Thus, it is not surprising that the STWG report has been characterized as "negotiated science" (an expression used in an interview). For instance, it has been maintained that "there was a measure of compromise between different views, say between British and German scientists".[12] Moreover, others have pointed out that compromises were struck first and foremost with regard to the "assessment" part of the report.

Now, several other more independent scientists and scientific institutions participated of course in the national preparatory processes. But, given that civil servants really believe in the value of independent scientific advice, it is somewhat puzzling that the contribution of the "independents" had to be filtered and controlled—as reflected in the composition of the international working group. Such a filtering procedure may be a practical routine and perfectly understandable, but a somewhat stronger position on the part of the traditional "independent" (university) scientists may be worth considering.

Third, there is the no less important question of *communication*. In a science-politics perspective, we think it is possible to regard the current structure as a kind of mediation chain or continuum. At the one end, you have the national scientists and national scientific programmes, partly connected to each other through the ICES international network. On the other (receiving) end, you have the yearly Commission meetings. In between you have potentially important mediation "agents'—and these are first and foremost the Joint Monitoring Group and the technical working groups. Now, the crucial question is: do these groups fulfil their mediating role effectively? Let us first focus on the JMG more closely. This group was initially established in order to provide a basis for the assessment of "the existing level of marine pollution" and "the effectiveness of measures for the reduction of marine pollution taken under the terms of the present Convention" (from Art. 11 in the Paris Convention). As indicated in the co-ordination section, the progress concerning studies of the level of marine pollution has not been satisfactory. More-

[12] Quote from *Daily Telegraph*, Weekend Magazine, 8 October 1988, "North Sea or Dead Sea? The Rising Tide of Pollution" (special feature).

over, this means that scientific input from JMG into the activity of the technical working groups has not functioned as assumed in the original institutional design. If we quite roughly differentiate between the action-initiating (on the advice of JMG) and the action-initiated (by the work of and decisions taken by the Commissions) role of the technical working groups, much more weight seems to have been given to the latter role than initially supposed.

More generally, it is our impression that the Commission meetings have given very little priority to more basic and long-term strategic discussions concerning scientific development, communication of existing knowledge, etc. To accentuate somewhat: even if the dynamic scientific impulse might have been more or less absent, it does not seem to have been missed much at the meetings.[13] Some of the reason for this is of course that the Commission agendas gradually—as the co-operation has developed and widened—have been filled up with necessary, but time-consuming discussions of commitments already taken on.

On the one hand, this indicates that it might be interesting to study the organizational experiences gathered in connection with the London INSC more closely. In connection with this Conference, a special Policy Working Group discussed important policy matters before the Conference, with the scientific status report as point of departure. As indicated earlier, this design probably contributed to the constructive outcome of the Conference. Despite obvious differences between the Commission and Conference approach, a similar design might have something to offer also within the Commission approach. By expanding the existing preparatory CVC-mechanism or even establishing a new Policy Group, one could either relieve Commission meetings of some of the more routine matters and allow these meetings to discuss more long-term communication issues more adequately, or let the CVC/Policy Group meetings function as a more evaluative think-tank.

On the other hand, it might be that there is something fundamentally wrong with the communication chain—in a sense, it might be "too long".[14] An indication pointing in this direction, is that the information and advice provided by the comparatively most "pure" scientific element in the system—ICES—have to pass through two "filters" mostly composed of civil servants before eventually being considered by the meeting of policy-makers. Although a "translation" and simplification is of course to some degree necessary, one might wonder if not a more direct and "pure" scientific input is not possible.

Finally, there is the question of *co-optation*.[15] Let us first formulate some more specific questions for exploration. In connection with the environmental non-governmental organizations, we think it is interesting to focus the aspects of

[13] Interview with Norwegian civil servant.

[14] Interview with Norwegian senior scientist.

[15] The question of co-optation is primarily based upon interviews with the following environmental organization in The Netherlands: Friends of the Earth, Greenpeace, IUCN, North Sea Working Group and Seas at Risk. We have also interviewed a researcher working for Greenpeace and a representative of Greenpeace, Norway. We base this section of the article on interviews with the scientists mentioned in note to chapter-title *above*, as well.

"knowledge base" and "role consciousness". With regard to knowledge base, important questions are: How do they regard the present communication with the established scientific community? Do they feel that their knowledge is adequately utilized by the policy-makers? Concerning role consciousness, interesting questions are: to what extent do they consciously regard themselves as mediating agents to the public opinion? Are they aware of the dangers of "media contortion" of attention away from less visible, but ecologically very important issues?

First to the question of knowledge base. Not surprisingly all representatives of the environmental organizations claimed that knowledge was the very basis for their work concerning the North Sea. Their main source of information was derived from science, from personal contacts with scientists or via written public scientific information. Thus, generally the environmental organizations base their work upon the same sources of information as the civil servants and the politicians. Generally, the NGOs claim that enough is known about the health of the North Sea to adopt more "strict" measures than are presently agreed upon. This hints at a communication problem between the NGOs and the habitually cautious scientists. In fact the difference in time horizon, language, etc. may be more significant between scientists and environmentalists than between scientists and politicians. It is hardly feasible to give a general answer to how communication is functioning between these two groups. They are both quite heterogeneous. As to the scientists, some are in a sense quite "élitist", shunning the media as well as "ignorant" representatives of NGOs. At the other end of the spectrum you have the scientists participating actively in political debates and/or being members of NGOs—which raises difficult questions about their scientific credibility. The majority of scientists, however, probably belongs somewhere in between these two extremes. Differences exists between environmental organizations as well. On the one hand you have the more "peacefully" lobbying groups with traditionally fairly strong ties to the scientific community. On the other hand you have the more action-orientated groups, with (seemingly) somewhat looser links to science.

There is often mutual distrust and a lack of communication, especially between action-orientated NGOs and the "élitist" scientists. It is our impression, however, that communication between "mainstream" scientists as well as "mainstream" NGOs is reasonably good, giving these NGOs an important mediating function.

As to the question of use of their knowledge by the policy-makers, the environmental organizations all feel that North Sea environmental politics is moving in the "right" direction, although many are sceptical as regards the actual implementation of the agreed principles. Generally, the environmental organizations do not seem to feel that lack of communication is the main reason for their not getting through with their suggestions but rather lack of political will on the part of the policy-makers.

The chain of communication between the NGOs and the policy-makers, however, takes different routes for the action-orientated and the lobbying environmental organizations. This brings us to the point of "role consciousness". Although direct appeals through the media to the public to some extent may be used by most environmental organizations, this seems to be the main strategy for the actionists. Through extensive use of pictures and direct actions, they often appeal very directly to people's emotions and at the same time fulfil the criteria for being defined as "good news" and thus making the headlines—knowing that the politicians realize that votes decide the next election. Although more "normal" lobbying work is also carried out by the actionists, this strategy plays second fiddle.

While the actionists, prefer "separation" from the formal decision-making process, the lobbyists rely more heavily upon "integration" in the decision-making process. They have established close contacts especially with civil servants and try to influence policy more through "silent diplomacy" than through actions.

Undoubtedly the NGOs regard themselves as mediating agents to public opinion but it is debatable whether NGOs using action as their main strategy can be seen as mediators of scientific knowledge. The degree of simplification and differences in methods and approach may be too fundamentally different. This is not to say that they do not have an important part to play within the environmental North Sea regime. However, our impression is that the media distortion dimension has been somewhat neglected in their—at least public—thinking. Everybody concerned with the environment is happy about the increased public attention directed towards this issue. However, marine ecology is a complex field and the most rational policy is not necessarily the one corresponding to the daily agenda of the national and international news media. Not least due to the environmental organizations the environment has got a prominent place on the political agenda, and rightly so. Now may be the time for at least some of these NGOs to sit down and rethink what strategies are needed in this new situation. The right strategy for getting an issue on the agenda is not necessarily identical with the right strategy for keeping it there and for contributing to solving complex problems. There might also be a need for some reallocation of resources by one of the other new key players, the media. Most countries have some very capable journalists covering the "old" high politics issues like security and economy, but in most countries there are very few "environmental" journalists, which is necessary if the media shall play a constructive role in this dialogue too.

Some concluding thoughts

As was briefly summarized above, a complex international scientific-political complex has evolved within the area of the North Sea co-operation. As witnessed in connection with the production of the STWG report before the Second INSC, this complex is capable of coming up with fairly precise and usable knowledge on the state of the North Sea. In our identification and discussion of possible institutional shortcomings and deficiencies, this achievement should not be forgotten. On the other hand, having said this, our main conclusion is of course that several institutional deficiencies can be identified: co-ordination of research and monitoring is flawed; the awareness of the importance of a clear distinction between science and politics is too low; policy-makers and scientists speak different languages and translation is sparse; the media lack the necessary expertise to involve the public in a rational way.

Implicitly, therefore, we call for more and improved knowledge—a call which is not particularly fresh or original. But is it so obvious that imperfect knowledge has been an impediment in policy-making so far—and that future improvements are really necessary? We will use the final section of the paper to look into this somehow more neglected issue more closely. It is probably useful to think in terms of stages here.[16] In the initial phase of a co-operation, the precision of information is less important. Rather crude pieces of knowledge are probably enough to warrant the formulation of general reduction programmes. Precise knowledge in this phase is necessary first and foremost with the objective of establishing a firm basis for future progress assessments. In the later, more advanced phases of co-operation, where "fine-tuning" and corrections of earlier policies are crucial, the need for precise and comprehensive knowledge for policy- making purposes is more urgent and obvious.

In the North Sea context, we think that we are right now in a transition period—having been through an initial phase and moving towards a more advanced and complicated stage. This stage may for instance imply fine-tuning of the percentage reduction aims agreed on at the Second INSC and even perhaps the development of a more sophisticated system, with the largest reductions where it counts most environmentally. Perhaps the basic rationale for an intensified research and monitoring effort is that we so far have not fully established the firm basis for progress assessments which such policy development is dependent upon—and as can be recalled, was originally called for in the Paris Convention text. In such a perspective, institutional deficiencies in the scientific-political complex might be far more crippling in the coming years than they have been up to now.

[16] We owe the general idea here to Arild Underdal.

Chapter 11

The Rhine Action Programme: A Turning-Point in the Protection of the North Sea?

A. Nollkaemper

Introduction

An essential part of the regime for land-based marine pollution consists of international rules dealing exclusively with pollution of international watercourses. Though these rules necessarily protect a much wider range of interests, they nonetheless may have direct implications for the protection of the marine environment. This can pre-eminently be seen in the case of the North Sea. The rules dealing with pollution of the North Sea by watercourses—the 1974 Paris Convention for the Prevention of Marine Pollution from Land-based Sources,[1] the 1984 and 1987 INSC Declarations,[2] and EC law—are supplemented by the regime for one of the major polluters of the North Sea, the Rhine.

The potential importance of this regime has greatly increased now that the impasse in the co-operation between the riparian states of the Rhine has been broken by the adoption of the Rhine Action Programme (RAP) in September 1987.[3] If implemented adequately, one of the effects of this non-legal and flexible instrument may be a substantial reduction of the pollution of the North Sea by the Rhine. The importance attached to the RAP was emphasized by the Ninth Ministerial Conference of the Member States of the International Rhine Commission

[1] Paris, 4 June 1974, (1974) XIII ILM 352.

[2] "*Declaration of the International Conference on the Protection of the North Sea, Bremen, 31 October–1 November 1984*" published as MEPC 21/INF.11 of 22 March 1985; "Ministerial Declaration of the Second International Conference on the Protection of the North Sea, London, 24–25 November 1987", (1988) 3 IJECL 252–265.

[3] "Rhine Action Programme, Adopted by the Eighth Ministerial Conference of the Rhine States", Strasbourg, 30 September 1987.

which noted that it should serve as an example for all watercourses flowing into the North Sea.[4]

In this contribution some observations will be made on issues that are raised by the impact of the RAP on the protection of the North Sea. After a discussion of the background and contents of the RAP attention will be paid to the relation between the RAP and other instruments dealing with the protection of the North Sea against pollution by watercourses, the possible harmonization between the RAP and these instruments, the special position of the EC, and the question whether the non-legal and flexible nature of the RAP may be regarded as a model for future instruments. The chapter closes with some concluding observations.

Background of the Rhine Action Programme

The adoption of the RAP can only be understood from the perspective of the history of co-operation between the riparian states of the Rhine. This co-operation was institutionalized in the International Rhine Commission (IRC).[5] The IRC has few independent powers—its tasks are confined to investigating into the nature, extent and origin of the pollution of the Rhine and to proposing, on the basis of these investigations, appropriate measures to the states party[6]—but it does provide a framework for co-operation. Irregularly, the Member States of the IRC meet at the Ministerial level. Since 1972 ten Ministerial Conferences have been held.

Through the years, the main issues dealt with in this framework have been pollution by chlorides, thermal pollution, and chemical pollution. Of particular relevance for the present purpose is the last form of pollution, which is covered by the 1976 Rhine Chemical Pollution Convention.[7] The main element of this Convention is the system of black- and grey-lists, intended to reduce the input of dangerous substances. It is precisely this element that has proved to be the most troublesome part of the Convention. In particular, progress in the establishment of limit-values for blacklist substances, which have to be proposed by the IRC and approved by the Member States,[8] has proceeded slowly. In view of a lack of agreement on technical aspects[9] and the considerable economic interests involved, the requirement of unanimity for their adoption[10] has proven to be a major obstacle.[11] Consequently,

[4] Communiquaa the Ninth Ministerial Conference, Bonn, 11 October 1988 (published by the Wirtschaftszentrum, Bonn), para. x. 4.

[5] Established under "Agreement on the International Commission for the Protection of the Rhine against Pollution", Berne, 29 April 1963 (1976) 994 UNTS, No. 14538, supplemented by "Supplementary Agreement", Bonn, 3 December 1976 (1977) Dutch Treaty Series, No. 31. Parties are the Federal Republic of Germany, France, Switzerland, Luxemburg, The Netherlands and the European Communities.

[6] Art. 2 of the 1963 Convention.

[7] "Convention on the Protection of the Rhine against Chemical Pollution", Bonn, 3 December 1976 (1988) XXVII ILM 625.

[8] Art. 3(1)(2) jo. art. 5.

[9] See Karen Mingst, "The Functionalist and Regime Perspectives: The Case of Rhine River Cooperation", (1981) XX *Journal of Common Market Studies*, 161–166, at 162–163.

[10] Art. 14(3).

[11] At the time of writing, proposed measures have only been adopted for mercury discharged from the chlor-alkali industry and chromium (a grey-list substance).

although in the past decade some progress has been made in the improvement of the water quality of the Rhine, it became increasingly clear that the efforts proposed to attain a significant improvement of the quality of the Rhine had become deadlocked.

Against this background the Sandoz disaster of 1 November 1986—causing major threats to the ecosystem of the Rhine[12]—was only the triggering event leading to agreement on a new approach to international water quality policy. The political need to provide an adequate answer to the Sandoz disaster was felt to be inescapable. After the incident the issue was taken up at the Ministerial level. At the Seventh Ministerial Conference of December 1986 agreement was reached on the necessity of a new instrument. This instrument is the Rhine Action Programme which was adopted at the Eighth Ministerial Conference held in Strasburg in September 1987.

Contents of the Rhine Action Programme

The RAP aims at the attainment of three objectives: species which used to live in the Rhine must become indigenous again, Rhine water must remain useful for drinking-water purposes and the sediments must be free of pollution by dangerous substances. To attain these objectives the RAP provides for a series of measures, most notably a reduction of structural pollution—encompassing pollution by diffuse sources, point sources and communal discharges—and a reduction of accidental pollution.[13]

Protection of the North Sea against pollution is not the prime concern of the RAP. Nonetheless, it may be an important side-effect of the protection of the Rhine. The measures contained in the RAP may have direct implications for the protection of the North Sea environment. The link with the North Sea has explicitly been acknowledged at the Fifty-Third Plenary Session of the IRC. In pursuance of the conclusions of the Ninth Ministerial Conference[14] the protection of the North Sea environment was added as a fourth objective to the RAP. The water quality of the North Sea must be improved so that the health of the ecosystem is guaranteed and is threatened neither by structural nor by accidental pollution.[15]

The agreement has a somewhat ambiguous character. On the one hand, the RAP is characterized by its non-legal[16] and flexible nature. The realization of its objectives is left to the national level. The RAP lays down only general aims without

[12] For a description of the incident see Andrew H. Darrell, "Killing the Rhine: Immoral, but is it Illegal?" (1989) 29 *Virginia Journal of International Law*, 421–472.

[13] RAP paras. 2.3.1 and 2.3.2.

[14] Para. x of the Communiqué of the Ninth Ministerial Conference.

[15] Cf. Art. 2 of the Rhine Chemical Pollution Convention, which mentions the quality of the marine environment as one of the elements which has to be taken into account by the taking of measures.

[16] There are no indications that the signatory states intended to create a legal document; see for the view of the Government of The Netherlands: Parliamentary Papers Lower House 1987–1988, 12872, no.39, p. 4.

stipulating in detail how reduction measures should be put into effect at the national level.[17]

On the other hand, the RAP contains two elements which have to guarantee that the agreed reductions will be realized. First, the RAP contains a time-schedule according to which these measures have to be taken. The objectives of the RAP have to be realized in three consecutive stages: a first stage, finished at the end of 1989,[18] a second one running until 1995, and a third running until 2000. Second, the RAP has been made subject to international supervision. The programme is continuously subject to modification and elaboration by the Ministerial Conferences and the IRC. At present 9 Working Groups of the IRC are entrusted with its elaboration. The implementation of the RAP is a recurring theme at the meetings of the IRC and the Ministerial Conferences. Among others things, to enhance its effectiveness a monitoring programme will be elaborated.[19]

The Rhine Action Programme amidst other instruments

The relevance of the RAP for the protection of the North Sea environment can only be assessed in the light of the protection of the North Sea against pollution by watercourses offered by other applicable instruments—most notably the 1976 Rhine Chemical Pollution Convention, the 1974 Paris Convention,[20] the 1984 and 1987 INSC Declarations,[21] and EC legislation. The question whether the Rhine Action Programme goes beyond what has already been achieved by the other instruments in particular presents itself with respect to two issues: accidental pollution and structural pollution. The RAP provides for a reduction of both forms of pollution in order to attain its fourth objective, the improvement of the water quality of the North Sea.

The issue of accidental pollution can be disposed of quickly. The issue is a greater problem for the Rhine than for the North Sea. The principal interest affected by such incidents is the supply of drinking-water. Besides, not all accidents with industrial installations on the Rhine cause serious pollution of the North Sea. Consequently, the forums dealing exclusively with the North Sea appear not to have concerned themselves with the issue. The 1987 INSC Declaration confines itself to the statement that the states shall ensure that industries using dangerous substances install appropriate facilities to prevent pollution as a result of accidents or to limit

[17] For the use of the concept of flexibility in this sense see Valticos, "The Sources of International Labour Law: Recent Trends", in W. P. Heere (ed.), *International Law and its Sources. Liber Amicorum Maarten Bos* (Deventer, 1988), pp. 179–195; F. Plate, "European Water Policy: Water Quality and Quantity Aspects in an International Setting", Speech delivered during the Twenty-third Annual Conference of the Law of the Sea Institute, Noordwijk aan Zee, 12–15 June 1989.

[18] Originally, 1988 was indicated as the end of the first stage, but this was prolonged until the end of 1989 during the Ninth Ministerial Conference of October 1988.

[19] RAP, para. 2.4.2.

[20] Art. 3(c) provides that the Paris Convention among others deals with pollution of the maritime area through watercourses.

[21] A major part of these Declarations is concerned with pollution of the North Sea through watercourses. See para.1 of the 1984 Declaration, Part C of the Conclusions of the 1984 Conference and para. 2–4 of the Annex of the 1984 Declaration; para. xiv. 1–15 of the 1987 Declaration.

the consequences thereof. Also the Paris Commission has not dealt with the issue in depth. The matter came up for discussion in the Ninth Meeting of the Paris Commission but there was no consensus whether it is appropriate for the Paris Commission to deal with the prevention of pollution of the Convention area by emergencies or accidents at industrial plants under the terms of the Convention.[22]

By contrast, accidental pollution is dealt with in detail in the RAP. This is not surprising since the RAP is primarily a political answer to the Sandoz disaster. The RAP requires industrial installations to take a number of safety-measures. In the first stage the specific measures to be taken and a time-schedule will be drafted and in the second stage these measures will have to be implemented.[23] The agreement runs to some extent parallel to the action undertaken by the EC. In both cases the Post-Seveso Directive[24] was considered to provide insufficient protection as it did not even cover the Sandoz incident.

With respect to the second issue, structural pollution, the relation between the RAP and other instruments is somewhat more complex. It is in particular the co-operation on this subject that had reached an impasse before 1986. Hence, it is here that the non-legal and flexible nature of the RAP has made it possible to go beyond measures taken in other forums by making diverging measures acceptable for the participating states and the EC.[25] The RAP distinguishes itself both by the substances it covers and by the strategy by which the input of these substances has to be reduced.

The point of departure of the RAP is the identification of a number of priority branches of industry—which will be left aside here—and priority substances. The RAP identifies 27 priority substances the input of which has to be reduced. As is shown in the Annex to this contribution, almost all of these substances have already been discussed in other forums, in particular within the IRC. A difference of principle exists with the less-detailed Annex to the 1987 INSC. Apart from this, the list of the RAP remains a far cry from the 83 and 129 substances included in respectively the IRC and the EC list of black and grey substances for which measures have to be adopted. A step forward was made at the Tenth Ministerial Conference in November 1989, where the list of priority substances was supplemented.

The RAP does distinguish itself on a substantive level, however. First, although many of the priority substances have been discussed, in relatively few cases has this resulted in meaningful obligations. With a small overstatement it can be concluded from the Annex that either the discussions have never been concluded, or they have resulted in non-committal decisions. The reduction of inputs required by the RAP goes beyond these efforts. This is, secondly, also true for the substances which are covered by stringent decisions of other forums. With respect to these substances the RAP distinguishes itself by its approach. The input of the priority sub-

22 Ninth Annual Report of the Paris Commission, 1987, para.70.
23 RAP, para. 2.3.2.
24 Directive 82/501/EEC, OJ EC 1982 No.L 230/1. After the Sandoz incident the Directive was amended by Directive 87/216/EEC, OJ EC 1987 No.L 85/36.
25 See further below p. 131.

stances has to be reduced by 50 per cent by 1995. After an inventory of existing discharges has been drawn up, the RAP provides for consultations between national authorities and individual point-dischargers. The actual reduction will have to be attained by the application of the best available technology (BAT). Basically, this approach resembles the approach of the 1987 INSC Declaration, but that is less specific and lacks the programmed character of the RAP. More important is that the approach of the RAP diverges from the strategy of the Rhine Chemical Pollution Convention, the Paris Convention and the EC, consisting of the establishment of emission or water quality standards. The general agreement on the reduction of inputs by application of BAT partly overtakes the traditional approach. Depending on the circumstances the application of BAT may imply the taking of more or of less stringent measures than those required by existing emission or water quality standards.

How these two strategies are related is not quite clear. BAT is a concept which can be interpreted in different ways and at present it cannot be foreseen how it will be filled in by the IRC. Perhaps partly due to this uncertainty it has been decided not to abandon the establishment of limit-values in the framework of the Rhine Chemical Pollution Convention. The adoption of limit-values will also harmonize the commitments of states, which in view of the discretion to attain the 50 per cent reduction may differ.[26] If indeed the two approaches will be pursued in parallel, it is arguably advantageous to establish a link between them. *Inter alia*, this may imply the adaptation of the limit-values and quality-objectives to the continuously evolving concept of BAT; only then will the distinct approaches keep pace with each other. Most instruments already provide for methods to adapt standards to new developments,[27] but to date little use has been made thereof.[28]

The issue of the relation between the application of BAT and limit-values or water quality standards is less relevant for nutrients, a specific category of the priority substances.[29] Other forums have chosen an equally flexible approach as the RAP, and have not (yet) set any specific standards.[30] The decisions of the 1987 INSC Conference and the Paris Commission on the reduction of the input of nutrients are identical to the approach of the RAP, requiring a reduction of their input by 50 per cent. The Proposal for a Council Directive aiming at the protection of the aquatic environment against pollution by nitrates from diffuse sources reflects a somewhat different, but equally general approach. As these agreements will be ela-

[26] See further sect. VII.

[27] *E.g.* Art. 14(1)(2) of the Rhine Chemical Pollution Convention; Art. 9 of Directive 75/795/EEC; Art. 6(3) of Directive 86/280/EEC.

[28] See, however, the Proposal for a Council Directive amending Directives 80/778/EEC on drinking water, 76/160/EEC on bathing-water, 75/440/EEC on surface water and 79/869/EEC on methods of measurement and frequencies of analysis of surface water of 22 December 1988, OJ EC 1989, C 13/7.

[29] In the RAP only two forms of nutrients are included—phosphates and ammonium—while the other forums deal with the broader category of nutrients—a difference that can be attributed to the fact that phosphates and ammonium are the forms of nutrients especially relevant for fresh water pollution.

[30] See Annex for references.

borated questions concerning their relation may arise, however. The Ninth Ministerial Conference of the Rhine States has agreed on limit-values for municipal waste water discharges.[31] The proposed Community Directive provides for the establishment of such standards as well, and in the Paris Commission the issue has been raised of the establishment of water-quality objectives.[32]

Thus, while the measures provided for in the RAP for the reduction of accidental and structural pollution of, among others, the North Sea in a number of respects differ from what has been attained in other forums, much depends on the way in which these measures will be elaborated and implemented in the near future. Only on that basis will it be possible to assess its value for the protection of the North Sea against pollution by watercourses.

Harmonization with North Sea co-operation

The fact that in some respects the RAP goes beyond other instruments dealing with the protection of the North Sea against pollution by watercourses is not surprising. Such differences are precisely the *raison d'être* of a specific action programme for a river. They reflect the advantages of a small and relatively homogeneous forum where the issue of transboundary water pollution is dealt with in relative isolation from other issues. Besides, regional differences between water systems can be great and require solutions geared to the specific situation.

Nonetheless, a certain harmonization between the RAP and other instruments may have advantages. First and foremost this is a matter of efficiency. Both the elaboration of new standards and the exercise of supervision through monitoring in different forums are so closely related that by adjusting them to each other overlap can be prevented. Also the objective of creating standards as uniform as possible for all rivers, which—as experience has taught —is an important incentive for co-operation, can only be attained by harmonization. And third, to deal adequately with the pollution of the North Sea by watercourses it could be argued that the relatively far-reaching approach of the RAP should be utilized for all major rivers flowing into the North Sea.

On the basis of such arguments it has been suggested that harmonization should be pursued. The ultimate aim of such harmonization between the management of different waters should, it has been proposed, be an integrated decision-making system with respect to water pollution by international commissions for, e.g., the Rhine, the Meuse, the Scheldt, the Ems, the North Sea and the Wadden Sea.[33] At present the pursuit of more moderate harmonization can be seen. Three forms can be distinguished: harmonization at the national level, adjustment of the international agreements for dealing with the Rhine to those dealing with the North Sea, and vice versa.

[31] Communiqué of the Ninth Ministerial Conference, para. iii. 1.

[32] See the Tenth Annual Report of PARCOM, Annex 17, "Future Work of the Nutrients Working Group".

[33] "Third Policy Document Water Management of the Netherlands", Parliamentary Papers Lower House 1988–1989, 21250, nos. 1–2, p. 269.

First, different commitments can be harmonized in the implementation stage. Such adjustment has been pursued by, e.g., The Netherlands by two main approaches. First, the lists of substances provided for by the RAP and the INSC Declaration have been combined. Second, national measures taken in implementing the RAP will be applied to all rivers, which *de facto* means that the measures taken to reduce all river inputs in the North Sea are covered by the agreement of the RAP.[34] Harmonization at this level of course only provides the most basic advantage: greater efficiency at the national level.

In general the second option will not be very worth while, since the agreements made with respect to the North Sea will hardly ever go beyond what is agreed for the Rhine. Nonetheless, the implementation of the fourth objective of the RAP—preservation of the ecological quality of the North Sea—will have consequences for the measures adopted, *e.g.*, for the selection of priority substances. This was foreshadowed during the Ninth Ministerial Conference. The Conference agreed on measures for nitrogen, which in general is a greater problem for the North Sea environment than for the Rhine.[35] The measures are, however, more general than those contained in the 1987 INSC Declaration and some discrepancies remain.

More relevant is the third strategy: the promotion of the approach of the RAP on a broader level. The Member States of the IRC have made some efforts to generalize the approach of the RAP to the North Sea level. These efforts are to some extent reflected in the 1987 INSC Declaration. On some issues the 1987 Declaration has generalized the approach of the RAP to all watercourses flowing into the North Sea. Consequently, the participating states have accepted a similar approach to that of the RAP. As noted, however, the 1987 INSC Declaration is less specific and less instrumentalized than the RAP. Consequently, further adjustment has been deemed to be desirable. At the Ninth Ministerial Conference it was agreed that the measures agreed upon in the RAP and the INS Conferences should be further adjusted to each other.[36]

At present two institutional developments can be witnessed which may contribute to such adjustment. To date, the IRC neither participates in the Paris Commission, nor has it participated in the first two INSC Conferences. However, the IRC has been invited to participate as an observer in the Paris Commission[37] and the Third INSC Conference.[38] Another development important for a broader application of the RAP approach is that all states responsible for pollution of the North Sea by watercourses will be involved in the North Sea forums. Switzerland will participate in the Third INSC Conference and the German Democratic Republic and Czechoslovakia will have an observer status at this Conference. All three states will be invited to participate in the Paris Commission.[39]

[34] Parliamentary Papers Lower House, 1988–1989, 12872, no. 45.
[35] Communiqué of the Ninth Ministerial Conference, para. iii. 4.
[36] *Ibid.* para. x. 2.
[37] Decided at the Eleventh Meeting of the Paris Commission, 19–22 June 1989.
[38] See RAP, para. x. 3.
[39] Decided at the Eleventh Meeting of the Paris Commission, 19–22 June 1989.

The position of the EC

As noted above, a major feature of the RAP is that it has broken the impasse in the IRC. In part, this was possible because the RAP circumvented the problems that stem from the key position that is taken by the EC in the IRC and more generally in the system of protection of the North Sea against pollution by watercourses.

One of the main reasons behind the activities of the Community in the field of water pollution was the perceived need to harmonize the obligations the Member States had undertaken, or were about to undertake in the Paris Convention, the Rhine Chemical Pollution Convention and the 1974 Draft Strasburg Convention. It aimed at a "europeanization" of fragmented attempts at water protection.[40] Such harmonization indeed fulfilled a function; it was only after the adoption of Directive 76/464 that the Rhine Chemical Pollution Convention could be concluded.[41] Since then the EC has pursued the objective of harmonization in international forums.

As is now well known, this has caused some problems. The progress made in the IRC has been determined to an important extent by the progress made within the EC. For one thing, on a number of occasions the European Commission has lacked a mandate to negotiate on a specific item, which in some cases has resulted in delays in the decision-making process. During the Ninth Ministerial Conference the Council of the EC was requested to provide the European Commission with a general mandate to negotiate on regional agreements.[42] However, in the short term a solution to this problem is not to be expected.

On a substantial level the key position of the EC has manifested itself in the fact that as a rule only those measures could be agreed within the framework of the IRC which were preceded by comparable measures of the Community. In general the Commission has objected to binding measures being taken in international forums in which one or more Member States participated in case the Community had not yet taken action on the topic concerned or in case the measures adopted in the Community were less stringent.[43] As is shown in the Annex, all measures taken since in elaborating the Rhine Chemical Pollution Convention were, at the time of their coming into force, covered by a Community directive and of the measures in force none contains standards more stringent than the Community directives. Although more stringent measures on the internal level are allowed by Community law—most EC directives in the field of water pollution are minimum directives—in

[40] Günther Hartkopf, "International Protection of the Rhine", in *Environmental Policy and Law* (1975/76), pp. 166–168, at p. 166.

[41] *Ibid.*

[42] Communiqué of the Ninth Ministerial Conference, para. vii. 2. See also "Proposal for a Council Decision Authorizing the Commission to Negotiate and Approve on Behalf of the Community Certain Measures as Part of the Implementation of International Agreements of a Regional Nature Relating to Environmental Protection to which the Community is a Party" (COM(86) 536 final of 1 December 1986).

[43] See André Nollkaemper, "The European Communities and International Environmental Cooperation, Legal Aspects of External Community Powers" (1987) *Legal Issues of European Integration*, No.2, pp. 55–91 at pp. 82 *et seq*.

the case of international agreements the European Commission has always put forward objections.[44]

The RAP has circumvented the problems ensuing from the involvement of the EC in the IRC. Since the RAP is not binding and leaves open the way in which the objectives are to be realized, the Community did not object to the adoption of the Programme although at the time of adoption of the RAP EC directives were in force (for only 9 of the priority substances).[45] Moreover, as noted, the implementation of the agreement to reduce the input of substances by 50 per cent by the application of the best technology may imply that more stringent measures are taken than those required by the EC directives.

Nonetheless, assuming that the adoption of instruments such as the RAP cannot be, and is not intended to be, a structural solution for the problems in relations between the Rhine states and the Community, these problems require another solution.[46] Three options present themselves. A first possibility is a further transfer of powers to the Community by which all water quality policy within the territory of its Member States will be co-ordinated by the Community.[47] Because of the heterogeneity of the Community this co-ordination would have to take into account regional differences. Eventually this might take the form of a regional environmental policy as provided for in Article 130R(3) of the EEC Treaty. The consequence on the external level is that the Community will have to co-operate with third states such as Switzerland. At present, there are few indications that this option is more than a theoretical possibility; regional differences within the Community are hardly recognized.[48]

The second option is in essence a continuation of the existing situation, with the difference that the effectiveness of the functioning of the Community is increased and that measures are taken at a greater speed than at present. This option carries through the harmonization the Community had in mind in 1976. The different agreements concluded among Member States and between Member States and third states would then be adjusted to each other by corresponding measures taken by the Community.[49] Here as well the prospects are meagre, although the speed of the water quality policy of the Community has somewhat improved after the adoption of the second framework directive 86/280.

A third option is that more room is left for the Member States to co-operate

[44] See J. G. Lammers, "Milieuverdragen en de externe bevoegdheden van de Europese Economische Gemeenschap, T.M.C. Asser Institute", *Europees Milieurecht. Praktische problemen bij de totstandkoming en uitvoering* (The Hague, 1987), pp. 33–53 at pp. 44 *et seq*.

[45] See the European Parliament Report of H. Maij-Weggen on the Pollution of the Rhine of 4 March 1988, PE 119.125/def.

[46] See in general: L. Ginjaar, "Towards a New EC-Waterpolicy" (1988) 18 *Environmental Policy and Law*, No. 6, pp. 210–219, at p. 213.

[47] Cf. H. U. Jessurun d'Oliveira, "De vervuiling van de Rijn: een nieuwe aflevering van het feuilleton: Sandoz en institutionele fricties tussen IRC en EEG, M.C.V. Aalders en N.S.J. Koeman", *Ontwikkelingen in het Milieurecht* (Zwolle, 1987), pp. 15–47, proposing an absorption of the IRC in the EC at pp. 36–37.

[48] See Plate, *op. cit.* 8.

[49] In this sense see Maij-Weggen *op. cit.* 21.

independently on the international level. The value of a far-reaching and comprehensive environmental policy of the Community is undisputed but would not in this option determine the international environmental policy of its Member States. A first step towards this option was set at the Ninth Ministerial Conference, which noted that neither the taking of measures by the IRC, nor their stringency is dependent upon the taking of comparable measures by the EC. But at the same time it was anticipated that the entry into force of the measures could be delayed if acceptance by the Community was not forthcoming, and in order to circumvent this problem the Member States were willing to apply those measures before their entry into force.[50] In any case this option presupposes a solution for the mandate issue.

The Rhine Action Programme: an example for future instruments?

Since the objectives of the RAP only have to be realized by 1995, at present little can be said about its effectiveness. Nonetheless, the approach of the RAP has already been regarded as a model approach for action programmes for other rivers flowing into the North Sea.[51] In The Netherlands it has been proposed that similar action programmes for the Meuse and the Scheldt be drawn up.[52] Similar proposals have been made for the Elbe and the Weser and, more in general, for all important transboundary rivers.[53] While the establishment of such action programmes would be a worthwhile undertaking, doubts can be expressed whether the success of such action programmes is dependent on the adoption of a similar non-legal and flexible form as the RAP.

In the early seventies the generality and vagueness of customary international law and the absence of specific international agreements led to the drawing up of a large number of legally binding international agreements. This was not an autonomous development, but the result of a conscious choice: formulating specific obligations and moulding these in legal forms has always been thought to have a number of advantages[54] and has often been considered to be essential for environmental protection.[55] Hence, the general character of some international rules has been severely criticized. The European Parliament Report on the implementation of water directives[56] identified as a major problem the vagueness of provisions, leaving too much room for interpretation at the national level.

Corresponding to this line of thought, the legal nature and the possibility of drawing up detailed regulations were the main rationale behind the Rhine Chemi-

[50] Communiqué of the Ninth Ministerial Conference, para. vii.
[51] *Ibid.* para. x. 4.
[52] "Environmental Policy Plan", Parliamentary Papers Lower House 1988- 1989, 21137, nos. 1–2; "Third Policy Document Water Management", *op. cit.* 269.
[53] Conclusions of the Fourth Conference on the Health of the Oceans, Karlskrona, 7–9 June 1988, repr. as Annex 18, Appendix 1 of the Tenth Annual Report of the Paris Commission.
[54] Winfried Lang, "Die Verrechtlichung des internationalen Umweltschutzes. Vom 'soft law' zum 'hard law' ", (1984) 22 *Archiv des Völkerrechts*, No. 3. pp. 214–305, at p. 303.
[55] P. C. Mayer-Tasch, "Die Internationale Umweltpolitik als Herausforderung für die Nationalstaatlichkeit", *Aus Politik und Zeitgeschichte*, B20 (1985), pp. 3–13.
[56] Report by K. Collins, 11 February 1988, PE 116.085/fin., pp. 18–20.

cal Pollution Convention in order to realize the objectives of the non-legal long-term programme of the IRC adopted in 1976.[57] The advantages of legal instruments have never been exploited, however.[58] In fact the existence of very detailed regulations has often turned out to be a major obstacle to progress. Experience has taught that the drawing up of programmes that satisfy the requirements of all national implementation mechanisms can take a long time. Now that the legal and stringent approach has, seemingly, failed resort has been taken to the RAP, which circumvents these slow procedures by its flexible approach. It is not clear whether this approach will work, and doubts have already arisen. At the Ninth Ministerial Conference it was agreed to determine whether a new legal basis was required in order to give legally binding form to the RAP.[59] Also, it has been acknowledged that elaboration of the Rhine Chemical Pollution Convention should be continued since in the long run it may be a more stable basis. The legally binding character has been considered as an important advantage which can survive changes in political preferences that can threaten political agreements.[60]

In any case it is clear that the legal nature of international instruments is only one of many variables determining their effectiveness. Practice has shown that there is not always a difference in effectiveness between legal and non-legal rules.[61] Factual consensus between states is in this respect more important than the formal legal character. It will not be possible to conclude that an enhancement of the quality of the Rhine, and thereby of the North Sea, is attributable to the form of the international instrument. Consequently, while the adoption of international instruments for other rivers flowing into the North Sea has to be pursued, it is submitted that in the final analysis the form and nature of the instrument is only of relative importance for successful co-operation in comparison to the presence of the precondition for successful co-operation—a perception of common interests.

Conclusion

The adoption of the RAP is a classic example of the inevitable incremental character of international environmental policy. The fact that the RAP has been established next to other instruments dealing with partly the same subject-matter has raised a number of questions which in this contribution could only be touched upon.

Nonetheless, the adoption of the RAP has been a major event in water quality management in Europe. It has generated political commitment and thereby given a new incentive to the slowly developing work in the framework of the Rhine Chemi-

[57] Mingst, *op. cit.* 167.

[58] On disuse of legal proceedings following pollution incidents see Darrell, *op. cit.* 453.

[59] RAP, para. vii. 6.

[60] Cf. J. G. Lammers, "The Rhine: Legal Aspects of the Management of a Transboundary River", in W. D. Verwey (ed.), *Nature Management and Sustainable Development* (Amsterdam, 1989), pp. 440–457, at p. 451; see also sect. VII.

[61] M. Bothe, "Legal and Non-legal Norms—A Meaningful Distinction in International Relations?" in (1980) 11 *Netherlands Yearbook of International Law*, 65–95 at p. 85.

cal Pollution Convention.[62] It remains to be seen whether the impulse given by the RAP will be of a permanent character or whether the IRC will—in view of the time-consuming inventorization of discharges and the elaboration of harmonized rules for their reduction—reach again the impasse that has characterized its previous work. But it seems clear that the RAP, at least indirectly, contributes to the protection of the North Sea environment. Even if not all results live up to expectations, its implications for the protection of the marine environment go beyond what has been achieved for other international rivers. In this respect the RAP has set the trend for future instruments. If the RAP indeed will be followed by comparable instruments for other rivers flowing into the North Sea, it may in retrospect be considered as a turning-point for the protection of the North Sea against pollution through watercourses.

But the RAP will not be the last word. It hardly reflects a proper balance between the flexibility required and the obvious need to obtain meaningful obligations. In addition, many issues concerning its relation with the EC and other forums remain to be settled. In this respect, the RAP does not give the lie to the statement that the choice of instruments for the conduct of international environmental policy is more often than not a leap in the dark.

[62] Plate, *op.cit.* 4.

Annex

Action on Priority Substances of the Rhine Action Programme Undertaken by the International Rhine Commission (IRC), the European Community (EC), the Paris Commission (PAR.) and the North Sea Ministerial Conferences (NMC)

Aldrin, Dieldrin, Endrin and Isodrin
IRC: IRC Decision 1978 (Annual Report 1978, p.16); IRC; Proposal 1988, not yet into force.
EC: Directive 88/347/EEC (OJ 1988 No. L 158/35)
PAR.: Agreement on the phasing out of drins, 1978 (First Annual Report, 1978, p.6).
NMC: Annex A of the 1987 North Sea Ministerial Declaration

Ammonium
EC: Proposal for a Directive (OJ 1989 No.C 54/4)
PAR.: PARCOM Recommendation 88/2 (10th Annual Report Annex 18) and PARCOM: Recommendation 89/4
NMC: Annex E of the 1987 North Sea Ministerial Declaration

Benzene
IRC: A Recommendation is in discussion in Working Group B

Cadmium
IRC: IRC: Proposal 1983, not yet in force (Annual Report 1983, Annex 1.1.2)
EC: Directive 83/513/EEC (OJ 1983 No.L 291)
PAR.: PARCOM Decision 85/2 (8th Annual Report); Strategy for a future work programme (10th Annual Report Annex 10); Proposal for a PARCOM Decision presented at the 11th Meeting (1989).
NMC: Annex A of the 1987 North Sea Ministerial Declaration

Carbontetrachloride
IRC: IRC Proposal 1986, not yet into force (Annual Report 1986, Annex 1.1.3).
EC: Directive 86/280/EEC (OJ 1986 No.L 181/16)
NMC: Annex A of the 1987 North Sea Ministerial Declaration

Chloroaniline
none

Chloroform
IRC: IRC Proposal 1988, not yet in force (Annual Report 1988).
EC: Directive 88/347/EEC (OJ 1988 No. L 158/35)

Chloronitrobenzene
IRC: A Proposal is in discussion in Working Group B

Chromium
IRC: IRC Recommendation 1982, not yet into force (Annual Report 1982, Annex 1.1.2).
EC: Proposal for a Directive (OJ 1985 No.C 351/33)

Copper, Nickel, Zinc, Lead
IRC: IRC Recommendation 1985 (Annual Report 1985, Annex 1.1.3)

Dichloroethane
IRC: A Proposal is in discussion in Working Group B
EC: Proposal for a Directive (OJ 1988 No. C 253/4)

Endosulfaan
IRC: A Proposal is in discussion in Working Group B of the IRC

Hexacloorbenzene
IRC: IRC Proposal 1988, not yet in force (Annual Report 1988).
EC: Directive 88/347/EEC (OJ 1988 No. L 158/35)

Hexaclorobutadiene
IRC: IRC Proposal 1988, not yet in force (Annual Report 1988).
EC: Directive 88/347/EEC of 16 June 1988 (OJ 1988 No. L 158/35)

Mercury
IRC: IRC Proposal 1979, in force on 1 March 1983 (Annual Report 1979, Annex 1.1.3); IRC: Proposal 1985, not yet in force (Annual Report 1985, Annex 1.1.1)
EC: Directive 82/176/EEC (OJ 1982 No.L 81/29); Directive 84/156/EEC (OJ 1984 No. L 74/49)
PAR.: PARCOM Recommendation 1981; PARCOM Decision 85/1; PARCOM Decision 89/1; PARCOM Recommendation 89/3
NMC: Annex A of the 1987 North Sea Ministerial Declaration

Parathion
IRC: A Recommendation is in discussion in Working Group B

PCBs/PCTs
IRC: IRC Recommendation 1984 (Annual Report 1984, Annex 1.1.1)
EC: Directive 76/403/EEC (OJ 1976, No.L 108); Proposal for an amended Directive (OJ 1988 No.C 319/57)

PAR.: Proposal for a PARCOM Decision, presented at the 11th Meeting of PARCOM 1988.
NMC: Annex A of the 1987 North Sea Ministerial Declaration

Pentachlorophenol
IRC: IRC Recommendation 1988 (not yet into force).
EC: Directive 86/280/EEC (OJ 1986 No.L 181/16)

Perchloroethylene
IRC: A Proposal is in discussion in Working Group B
EC Proposal for a Directive (OJ 1988 No. C 253/4)

Phosphates
EC: Proposal for a Directive (OJ 1989 No.C 54/4)
PAR.: PARCOM Recommendation 88/2 (10th Annual Report Annex 18) and PARCOM: Recommendation 89/4
NMC: Annex E of the 1987 North Sea Ministerial Declaration

Trichlorobenzene
IRC: A Proposal is in discussion in Working Group B
EC: Proposal for a Directive (OJ 1988 No. C 253/4)

Trichloroethane
IRC: A Proposal is in discussion in Working Group B

Trichloroethylene
IRC: A Proposal is in discussion in Working Group B
EC: Proposal for a Directive (OJ 1988 No. C 253/4)

Chapter 12

Environmental Quality Objectives versus Uniform Emission Standards

Dr. Sonja Boehmer-Christiansen

"Things that were dangerous (like nuclear power stations), or that stank (like sewage farms), were shoved on to the coast. They were safer that way and out of sight. The coast was regarded as a natural home for oil refineries and gas storage tanks, and there was more rubbish on the coast than in any inland dump. The coast was where you got rid of things: they were borne away and lost in the deep sinkhole of the sea."[1]

Introduction

It is argued that an effective policy for the marine environment involving a simple choice between Environmental Quality Objectives (EQO)[2] and Uniform Emission Standards (UES) is neither possible nor desirable and that both types of standards are essential ingredients of effective environmental protection. The controversy over their respective uses was never primarily technical, but political. An examination of the debate itself shows how little we know about man's impact on the marine world and how foolish it is to believe that we can know everything that is needed before a "rational" choice based on monetarized cost-benefit analysis can be made. This contribution briefly analyses the debate and its outcome so far, and emphasizes Britain's role in it. It is concluded that the EC must now be considered the major actor in the regime governing the North Sea, and that this regime will adopt a growing number of Uniform Emission Standards in spite of a commitment to a "dual" approach.

[1] Paul Theroux, in *The Kingdom by the Sea* (London, 1984).

[2] The term "Environment Quality Standards" would be preferable to "Objectives", reserving the latter term for broader, longer-term aims.

Definitions and criteria of judgement

Emission Standards (ES) are referred to in Britain as "uniform" if they apply to all emitters of the same type, for example plants in the steel industry irrespective of their geographic siting and national home. EQO may also be uniform, but the need for this is more widely accepted. Both are numerical limit-values which can be measured by mechanical or electronic devices and can be subjected to statistical analyses provided they measure identical phenomena or events in identical ways. EQO measure the presence of substances in the environment (in Germanic languages: *Immissions*), ES their concentration in the actual waste stream entering the environment (emissions). As defined by the EC, ES define concentrations over a specified time-limit, thus allowing periodic revision. The latter clearly have a much more direct impact on abatement and their measurement is less subject to scientific interpretation and evaluation.

By their very nature, numerical limits have enormous administrative and legal advantages over qualitative measures. Yet neither standard measures environmental damage as such nor the total quantity of pollutants or potential pollutants discharged over time. How then can we judge whether either of them is more likely to contribute to the protection of the marine environment?

The use of numerical standards is encouraged by the computer culture; numbers can be divided and added, quantities can be shared out among countries or individual plants. Numbers give the impression of objectivity and precision, but this is not always justified. They can be enforced with the help of measuring instruments and manipulated like all statistics. Best of all, they give direct immediate guidance to the technologist. Technology is normally entrusted with providing first the means by which "pollution" (or rather the presence of pollutants in water, sediments or tissue), is measured, and second the means by which it is reduced. ES reduce the concentration of pollutants in discharges, but not necessarily the total quantity to be disposed of.

By themselves, ES control rates of inputs, nothing else. They give industry little flexibility, and are thus often rejected on the grounds that they do not allow for cost-effective solutions, such as can be achieved, in theory at least, by emission trading.[3]

Numerical standards allow enforcement agencies to "know" precisely when a breach of the law has occurred. Quality standards, based on monitoring the environment, tell very little unless they form part of a time-series, and are fully comparable. Regulation by EQO represents first of all a scientific challenge, while ES immediately promote the skills of the engineer, and therefore attract the pollution abatement industry.

[3] Emission trading refers to firms trading pollution rights between themselves so that the firm which can cut down on emissions more cheaply buys this right from others for whom abatement would be more costly. The firm with the cheaper option would thus cut down more than required, the "dirty" firm would abate less or not at all. This has been tried with mixed results for air pollution in the USA.

The appropriateness of numerical standards for "environmental protection" is another matter entirely and cannot be discussed here. Neither standard by itself tells us much about pollution as scientifically defined, i.e. about damage effects in the environment. For this much more sophisticated biological, ecological and economic measurements and evaluations are needed. We must therefore proceed on the not unreasonable, but not always justified assumption, that there is some positive link between these numerical limits and environmental damage, and that we can prevent damage by tightening these limits. Vast amounts of knowledge are required to prove this assumption quantitatively.

Nevertheless, once the discharging of wastes into the environment is believed to be risky, the best response may well be to reduce the amount discharged, monitor the environment carefully and hope that matters will improve over time. ES clearly cut inputs more directly and do not depend on environmental monitoring for enforcement purposes.

Britain versus Europe: science versus technology?

In the 1950s and 60s Britain began cleaning up its rivers by dumping more waste, especially sewage sludge and industrial "inert" materials, into the North Sea. Munitions and radioactive wastes were first dumped into the Channel (e.g. Hurd Deep), the Irish Sea and later the deep Atlantic Ocean.[4] The Irish Sea is still used for radioactive discharges from the Sellafield nuclear complex.[5] Since many neighbouring countries did not like these practices, they challenged the British scientific community to prove that these practices were indeed environmentally safe. This presented a formidable scientific challenge to which Britain might have responded even more successfully had the scientific community been given sufficient resources and independence to do so. Instead, the "science-driven" British approach, characterized by a very direct scientific involvement in the policy-making process, was increasingly challenged by the "European" technology-driven one.

The debate over EQO and UES affected several intergovernmental forums concerned with North Sea pollution and especially the Paris/Oslo Commission[6] and the EC.[7] It has now been resolved, in principle, within the EC, but not until a consider-

[4] S. A. Boehmer-Christiansen, "An End to Nuclear Waste Dumping at Sea?" (1986) 10 *Marine Policy*.

[5] These discharges have declined significantly since the early 1980s. In response, the caesium 137 pollution has declined from about 500 milli Bequerel near UK coast in 1978, to between 20–40 milli Bequerel today.

[6] G. Wettestad, *Uncertain Science and Matching Politics* (Oslo, 1989). In the Oslo/Paris Commission the argument over quality versus emission standards arose without the pressure for uniform standards.

[7] Nigel Haigh, *EEC Environmental Policy and Britain* (1984), ENDS Ltd. (1987). Haigh describes how these directives developed and affected British law and practice. In the EEC a tradition has now emerged which makes stringent emission standards based on the best technical means available the norm for new plant only, thus allowing countries to plan their investment into pollution control technology.

able amount of negotiation had taken place in which Britain was the main proponent of the EQO approach.

Britain joined the EC late, poorly prepared for "harmonized" environmental policy-making, yet with a considerable amount of "environmental" baggage: some pieces excellent and ahead of their time, others outdated in spirit and substance. It also joined with an economy that was doing poorly with many of the older, most polluting industries in decline, a poor record of industrial investment and very little centralized or co-ordinated formal environmental regulation for the marine environment. Instead, there was a host of statutes and enabling powers spread over a large range of governmental organizations and levels. Until the mid-1980s, the British economy was also characterized by a large degree of direct government participation in industrial management. This severely discouraged "public" spending on marine pollution control because cutting this expenditure was a top priority for the Conservative government.

Also, and perhaps most significant here, Britain brought into Europe one feature in its bureaucratic structure which is not found (to my knowledge) elsewhere in Europe, namely a Scientific Civil Service hierarchy working very closely with the political and administrative decision-making apparatus on the one hand, and scientific research establishments funded by government departments, on the other. It is therefore possible, in the UK, to speak of government science and government scientists. As pointed out above, quality standards are by their very nature more attractive and rational to the scientific community.

Britain has a long tradition of using rather simple water quality standards for the control of river pollution, although this method has never been used to regulate air pollution. For water, biological oxygen demand standards were supplemented by consent conditions negotiated at the local and later regional level (Water Authority) with specific industries and often individual plants, and with relatively little interference from central government. All this is likely to change, if and when the water industry is privatized.

The sea, and especially tidal estuaries, have long been used in Britain for "land-based" industrial waste disposal. This is justified with the argument that the sea has a large capacity to absorb and render such wastes harmless. Scientists were asked to confirm this view, primarily by environmental monitoring.[8] Dilution and dispersion as methods of controlling pollution clearly suited both science and industry. Industry in particular has stoutly defended the environmental quality approach as most suitable for fast-flowing streams and well-mixed tidal waters. At least until 1985, British industry remained firmly behind this traditional philosophy and decentralized regulatory approach.[9] It supported the EQO approach, arguing that UES would remove "flexibility", lead to solutions which were not cost-effective and would not take local conditions into account. Economic theory strongly supports

[8] For a British view on the role of monitoring in pollution control, see T. E. Harvey, *The Monitoring Paradigm in Environmental Control*, IES Proceedings, 1981.

[9] Interviews and correspondence with the Confederation of British Industry.

these criticisms, but the real issue rather lies in whether UES lead to more or less innovation in the realm of environmental protection. Here the evidence from Europe suggests that only emission standards, provided they are stringent and can easily be tightened, have this effect.

Britain thus joined the EC and other intergovernmental forums concerned with marine environmental protection committed by tradition, philosophy and self-interest to a system which put great emphasis not only on scientific argumentation and evidence, but also, at that time, on cost minimization and, increasingly during the 1980s on public expenditure cuts. Not surprisingly, given the close link between science and government, the former tradition came to assist the latter objective, both as justification for less stringent standards and as rationalization of the EQO approach.

The debate over EQO and UES itself reached its peak, and partial resolution, in association with EEC Directive 76/464 on pollution caused by certain dangerous substances discharged into the aquatic environment. This was proposed by the Commission in 1974 and adopted as a framework directive for numerous daughters in 1976 (e.g. on mercury in 1982 and 1984, cadmium in 1983, lindane in 1984, DDT, etc. in 1986). The other major pollutant and industry affected by this debate revolved around the manufacture of titanium dioxide. For pollutants discharged at sea from mobile sources, the issue clearly did not arise, the only feasible control instrument being emission standards. For the quality of bathing-waters and waters used to culture shellfish the issue of emission standards also did not arise.

For all dangerous substances as defined by the Community, the proposal for Directive 76/464 wanted to fix minimum uniform emission standards for specific discharges into both rivers and the sea, and would have done so except for Britain's insistence on an alternative EQO regime. This demand had to be accepted, but at considerable cost and little apparent benefit to the UK. The alternative EQO approach now requires those member states which adopt it, to set emission standards with reference to quality objectives laid down by the Community and "conditional on the Member State proving to the Commission that the quality objectives are being met in accordance with a monitoring procedure set up by the Council".[10]

In 1986 the UK accepted UES standards for blacklist substances, i.e. the most persistent or toxic of the dangerous substances in the water directive (list I sub-

[10] Haigh, *op. cit.*, 71. This victory was a costly one and forced Britain fully to develop the quality approach. It had considerable effect on research and regulatory practice, but also caused much debate. When it was discovered that in the case of mercury EQS would in fact turn out to be more costly than UES, Britain demanded, and obtained, "equality of treatment", in 1982. This Mercury from the Chloralkali Industry Directive (82/176/EEC) lays down both concentration (micrograme per litre waste water discharged) and quantity limits (grams per tonne installed capacity and total mercury discharges per site), as well as quality limits for fish flesh (in mg/per kg), inland surface waters, estuarine waters and sea water (1.0, 0.4 and 0.3 ug/l respectively). However, the EC left the decision about the location of the area considered to be affected by discharges and the appropriateness of the choice of the QS selected from above, to the national authorities. Uniformity is therefore not complete.

stances). In Britain, however, these pollutants (as well as some others) are labelled red-list substances.

EQS and UES are Complementary and additional

It seems reasonable to assume that if the introduction of pollutants into the marine environments leads to their presence or, even worse, concentration in any part (which thereby may become "unacceptably" harmed, degraded or spoilt), then we can only discover this presence (if at all) in good time by measuring environmental quality, always providing we have the means to do so.[11] If damage or injury are observed, and authority decides to protect this part of the environment because it is suspected that the observed decline in environmental quality (e.g. the presence of too many pesticides, heavy metals, fertilizers or viruses in water, sediments or fish tissue) is causally related to this damage, then the reduction of the amount of suspect substance discharged or emitted is the quickest and most direct response.

Scientifically solvable questions arise over "how" suspect a substance is and how much reduction is needed before an acceptable level of damage is reached. To prove causal links conclusively, however, is very difficult and time-consuming. The patient may indeed be dead before we know. To base environmental policy on hard fact and proven causality surely represents a very high risk strategy which did not appeal to many European countries. The preference for quality standards can therefore also serve as a tactic for delaying decisions, or for allowing polluters to clean up voluntarily before the law requires action. Britain is widely suspected of having used this tactic.

The introduction of pollutants clearly cannot be controlled directly with the aid of quality standards, which by themselves are not an instrument of abatement. Quality standards can only define a tolerable level of pollutant concentration, tolerable or desirable for whatever use we may have for a specific body of water, estuary or stretch of coast. If we want to reduce "pollution", we must either clean up after we have "harvested" the crop (e.g. shellfish), discard what is no longer edible, change sea-use or reduce the amount of pollutants introduced in the first place to such a level that the quality once again becomes more tolerable. The choice of policy options is therefore much wider for EQO than for ES.

But why should Emission Standards be uniform? And why should there have been any dispute at all about whether to use one or the other regulatory instrument, when both are clearly needed? The answer, it is argued, lies in a combination of factors, including national waste management policy differences, national and international politics, as well as international commercial relations. The controversy over "EQO" and "UES" was therefore very much an expression of con-

[11] An interesting example of tracing quality measures back to emissions is described in *New Scientist*, April 1989, when discharges from a pesticide plant in Spain were picked up by measurements of lindane in sea water and plant tissue.

cerns which were not primarily environmental ones but related to problems and motives which could not be explicitly expressed in intergovernmental negotiations.

The broader perspective: minimizing costs versus minimizing inputs

As mentioned, UK policy on the North Sea has never been to minimize the input of wastes into the North Sea, a recent exception being the discharge of Red-list substances. Waste disposal into the sea, especially of degradable substances or those presumed to have become trapped in sediments, is considered legitimate and may well be, in the current jargon, the "best practicable environmental option". Science serves this objective by trying to show that no "unacceptable" harm takes place. Policy changes are justified only if there is evidence of such harm. The polluter is innocent until proven guilty. The underlying motive of this policy is that of minimizing overall waste management costs. This powerful economic incentive for using the absorptive capacity of the sea is further strengthened by Britain's dislike for the use of regulation to force technological change. Regulation beyond what is currently "practicable" is not considered to be a legitimate governmental activity.

The above considerations did not affect other North Sea states to the same extent. Scandinavian countries in particular found a more straightforward policy of minimizing inputs more credible and implementable, and also, in some cases, not particularly burdensome.

Certain political factors not at work in the UK may also encourage the ES approach. In the Federal Republic of Germany, for example, the wish of the Federal Government to establish a more centralized regime for ocean disposal, as well as the lack of a tradition of direct scientific involvement in environmental decision-making (replaced instead by a stronger involvement of engineers and lawyers), probably relates to the preference there for input minimization. This, it is argued, is achieved relatively quickly and with fewer administrative costs, by legally binding emission standards supplemented by restrictions on total quantities which may be discharged over a specific period of time. Stringent standards are deliberately used to "force technology" and thus to encourage and direct innovation.

Policy differences alone do not explain the pressure for uniformity, however. This came from two new directions: European industry and EC institutions.

European industry

Europe's industries, especially in its German and Scandinavian bases, have come under growing pressure to "clean themselves up" from the late 1960s onward. Because some economies faltered less than that of Britain, and probably because personal affluence there continued to rise more uniformly, these pressures became overwhelming enough to bring about political action for greater, and at times very costly, regulation, especially for industries discharging wastes into the sea and atmosphere. Having shorter coastlines or being more dependent on the sea for their livelihood meant that many countries attached a far greater value to the sea than Britain and thus pressed industry harder. In addition, environmental regulation came to be seen by the state as a way of encouraging the modernization of technology.

These expanding industries came to see British industry's ability to rely on lower standards as unfair trade and thus in breach of the Treaty of Rome, and now, also as an obstacle to the desired Internal Market. With the Commission of the EEC dedicated to the same goal, the pressure for uniformity gained in strength.

Industry alleged that "pollution" havens were being created and demanded that Britain should be made to conform. Continental Europe was assisted in this objective by the fact that the foreign polluter tends to be a more convenient target of national action than domestic ones, especially if the perception of large-scale transfrontier movements of pollutants is widespread as well as credible.[12] European industrial lobbies had an important ally in the European Commission itself. Together they argued for UES, but for reasons which have little to do with environmental protection.

The administrative and political perspective of the EC

Uniform standards are administratively more convenient especially if there is a strict division of labour and cost between legislation and implementation. The costs accruing to government from UES are probably less than those arising from the implementation and enforcement of non-uniform standards. UES also provide more persuasive evidence of "effective" policy to a public which may be clamouring for action. Non-uniformity of standards may nevertheless prevail in practice, even in the EC.[13]

European institutions, and especially the Commission, are not mere administrators, but independent actors involved in a political programme of their own. Environmental protection has gradually emerged as a major growth area by which the Commission can intensify and broaden its influence over national and Community policy. It is thus a disturbing factor for other intergovernmental forums which it tends to paralyse.[14] The Environment is a regulatory area where the responsible directorate can, at times, count on support from other, more powerful branches of the Commission, e.g. when directives promise the harmonization of standards applying to traded goods and services. This in turn supports the centralization of economic power and the development of the internal market as well as the promotion of European technological competitiveness. This applies to all standards, including environmental ones which lay down stringent emission standards which can only be achieved by "the best available technology".

[12] This is discussed for global marine pollution in S. A. Boehmer- Christiansen, "Limits to the International Control of Marine Pollution", unpublished D.Phil thesis, University of Sussex (1981).

[13] In the realm of EC air pollution legislation (for example), complex timetables for compliance, different national reduction targets and the critical load approach for NOx emissions are now used. For marine pollution a similar effect can in practice be achieved by the unequal enforcement of uniform standards.

[14] S. Saetevik, *Environmental Cooperation between the North Sea States* (London, Belhaven Press, 1988).

Political opposition: maximizing national discretion

As if the above reasons were not enough to explain British resistance to UES as international instruments for marine pollution control, another major (if now weakening) reason for this persistent opposition relates to the institutional set-up within Britain itself. For a long time, the British bureaucracy has strongly believed that environmental protection should remain a national rather than international responsibility. EQO, because of their less direct effect on emission regulation, do in fact maximize national sovereignty or discretion with respect to any ES actually set, and by whom. EQO do not directly clash with the traditional British approach to pollution control based on the philosophy of best practicable means (or best practicable environmental option) and the case-by-case approach it tends to underpin. Whitehall and the pollution Inspectorate had little to gain from a transfer of their responsibilities to Brussels, and many people in Britain share the view that the transfer of power from regional and local levels to London and then to Brussels, represents an anti-democratic development.[15]

UK Government scientists/policy-makers and their close advisors interviewed by the author during the 1970s believed firmly that Europe could learn from the British experience of pollution control and its scientific approach. This strategy of persuading Europe might have worked better if Britain had not fairly persistently opposed more stringent standards, primarily on cost grounds. This policy was, however, virtually inevitable after 1979. Crisis management rather than prevention became the hallmark of British environmental policy in the 1980s, although a change for the better may now be under way. Environmentalists in the UK (in contrast to their counterparts in West Germany, for example), tend to see Brussels as the guardian of the marine environment. Growing hope is also being placed in the political stimuli now emanating from regular North Sea Conferences bringing together all the countries sharing the North Sea.

In a speech entitled "The Marine Environment—Progress by Scientific Consensus" made in early 1987 and published in 1989 as a statement of UK environmental policy, Virginia Bottomley, Parliamentary Under-Secretary of State at the Department of the Environment, confirmed that the UK has now accepted, "in the marine environment", the precautionary approach to pollution control. This was needed "as basis for decisions which may be required to control the input of dangerous substances before a causal link has been established by absolutely clear scientific evidence".[16] The admission that a purely scientific approach is not always possible, or defensible given the uncertainties associated with scientific knowledge relating to environmental questions, is a victory for all those who have questioned the reliance on quality criteria for large water bodies.

[15] This theme is dealt with in more detail by the present author in "Marine Pollution Control in Europe: Regional Approaches 1972–80", (1984) 8 *Marine Policy* 44–55.

[16] In "Environment in Trust": The texts of policy statements made by Environment Ministers, Department of the Environment, between November 1988 and January 1989 and published by the Department of HMSO March 1989.

Outcomes and prospects

The long dispute over EQO and UES was, in retrospect unavoidable and not entirely futile. It strengthened the role of science and helped to establish the EC as a major, if not the major actor in the evolving regime for the protection of the North Sea. The debate is likely to continue as more substances are scrutinized and the recognition spreads that scientific data may remain too uncertain for the higher risk EQO strategy to be a credible option for more than a handful of pollutants. Compromise in principle has now been achieved within the EC and this necessarily affects all other forums dealing with North Sea environmental protection.

Community-wide regulation, while it gives the appearance of full "harmonization", in practice allows national traditions and preferences to continue for some considerable time so that gradual adjustments can take place. From the international relations point of view, such an outcome is to be welcomed, for it is the only alternative to reverting to purely national measures or non-binding intergovernmental information exchanges. Learning has clearly taken place, the EC Commission and Britain have both had to develop a more sophisticated system of monitoring and scientific research, if only to assure each other that the EQO approach, which Britain still believes to be of superior rationality, does indeed protect the marine environment adequately.

However, given the lack of data about the effects of abatement costs on commercial competition, the need for uniformity of ES is likely to be challenged in many cases. Some coasts and estuaries may need much tougher standards than others. European firms and most UK industrial giants are likely to demand uniformity of regulation for reasons of convenience, image and resistance to more stringent limits which may be demanded at certain regional or national levels. If air pollution is an example, industry will prefer emission standards because of their commercial implications and helpfulness to the engineer. The responsibility for monitoring and checking on environmental quality may now become the primary responsibility of individual states which must regularly review emission standards in order to check on their effectiveness. If necessary, ES must be tightened and/or supplemented by other measures especially national quotas.

Conclusion

From the environmental point of view, effectiveness cannot be measured as yet in any satisfactory way other than by making the assumption that any reduction in inputs will eventually improve environmental quality. Do UES in principle reduce more inputs faster than EQO? There can be no general answer to this question, other than the very strong impression that for the UK, the immediate implementation of UES would have had precisely this effect, at costs considered not justified by uncertain environmental benefits and with political implications undesirable from the institutional perspective. This is why the UK fought UES so hard, using "science" to justify its reluctance to change and also to gain time for adjustments in both industrial practice and institutional back-up.

Whether UES alone will ensure the health of the North Sea in the future is a very different question. They can make a contribution only if a number of other conditions are fulfilled: these numerical measures will have to become better related to EQO and to environmental impacts, there will have to be a continuing political demand for high environmental quality, the technological ability of industry to devise superior land-based waste disposal and waste minimization strategies will have to progress successfully, and Europe as a whole must remain able and willing to pay for the entire abatement effort.

It is difficult to envisage a Europe, other than a politically unified one, which is able to reach consensus on issues as complex, cost- sensitive and value-laden as sea-use planning, waste disposal, marine "health" and species protection. What we can expect and demand in the foreseeable future, however, is gradual agreement on increasingly stringent measures for the most harmful and persistent substances based on minimum UES supplemented by national quantity restrictions and supported by national as well as joint environmental monitoring and research programmes. As stated in the 1986 Single Act, countries and regions must remain free to tighten standards on the basis of their particular environmental conditions as well as their socio-economic priorities.

Chapter 13

Dangerous Substances: Chameleons in Water Policy

Jitka Vennekens-Capkova

Introduction

This article gives an outline of the International Conventions and supranational regulations which deal with the concept of dangerous substances. Furthermore the article examines a few main problems which have led to a lack of momentum of the legislative process, and it indicates a number of recent developments.

Throughout the past 19 years dangerous substances have been the subject of a number of International Conventions and supranational regulations which all aimed at releasing the aquatic environment from their harmful presence. Although the field of application differed from one Convention to another, the dangerous substances covered remained (more or less) the same, even if the colours given to the various lists of substances have changed over the years.

The changes of colour symbolize the changes in philosophy behind the principle of control of dangerous substances in the aquatic environment.

The lists of dangerous substances

The black and grey lists at International Conventions

The concept of a black list and a grey list of dangerous substances was proposed for the first time at a meeting held in The Hague in September 1971 in preparation of the Oslo Convention on the Prevention of Marine Pollution by Dumping from Ships and Aircraft (February 1972). According to the Oslo Convention the dumping of black list substances is forbidden (with a proviso for exceptional circumstances) whereas dumping of grey list substances is restricted.

At that time the concept of black and grey list substances was also adopted in other Conventions :

- the London Convention on the Prevention of Marine Pollution by Dumping of Wastes and other Matter at Sea (London Dumping Convention, November 1972).

- the Convention on Marine Pollution Arising from Land-based Sources (Paris Convention, June 1974).
- the Convention for the Protection of the Rhine against Chemical Pollution (Rhine Convention, December 1976).

The concept was also included in the proposal for the European Convention for the Protection of International Water Courses against Pollution (Strasburg Convention). This proposal has not, however, been finally adopted by the Ministers of the Council of Europe.

Lists I and II of the EC

Following the examples of the Oslo, London, Paris and Strasburg Conventions, the EC Commission incorporated the principle of a black and a grey list in their proposal of 21 October 1974 for an EC Council Directive on the reduction of pollution caused by discharges of certain dangerous substances into the aquatic environment.

In a considerably modified form this proposal was adopted by the EC Council on 8 December 1975: Directive 76/464/EC.[1]

In the Directive two different control systems are stipulated, one for List I substances and one for List II substances.

List I of the Annex contains mercury and cadmium and various families and groups of substances. The individual substances belonging to these families and groups should be identified at a later stage based on their toxicity, persistence and bioaccumulation.

Pollution through the discharge of these substances must be eliminated and the substances are subject to control at Community level by means of limit values for industrial effluents or of water quality objectives, both of which are also to be fixed in subsidiary directives at a later stage.

List II is composed of 20 heavy metals and several families and groups of substances (including those substances from List I for which limit values and quality standards have not yet been determined).

Their presence in the aquatic environment of the Community has to be reduced by means of quality objectives as formulated in national reduction programmes, that is their control has been left to the individual Member States. The harmonization of the reduction programmes can be proposed *a posteriori* by the EC Commission to the Council, if the Commission considers it necessary.

The broad character of List I of Directive 76/464/EC has given rise to lengthy discussions on the identification of individual substances belonging to this group. This problem has not yet been resolved. The use of internationally unagreed selection criteria has led to a later proliferation of selection schemes and priority Lists.

Also the establishment of limit values and quality objectives for a number of List I substances has led to tortuous negotiations. By 1984 limit values and quality standards had been agreed for only three substances.

Finally, the Directive allowed the Member States to choose between pollution

[1] OJEC, L 129/23, 18 May 1976.

control by means of either limit values or quality objectives (see chapter 12). At a later stage it appeared that regulations for diffuse sources were not well covered for those Member States who had adopted the limit-value approach.

The problems mentioned above will be shortly reviewed in the following sections.

Directive 76/464 as a framework directive

In essence EC Directive 76/464 took the form of a framework Directive which should be "worked out" by means of subsidiary directives, especially for List I substances. This is common practice in international law, and it is used even more in national legislative processes where the framework construction is chosen in order to speed up legislative work by delegation of the detailed elaboration to the competent administrations (Minister, local authorities, etc.).

In the case of this Directive, both the framework (the philosophical basis) and the elaboration had to be agreed upon by the same body (the EC Council) and with the same unanimity of votes. Moreover, the Directive itself was a political compromise obtained in almost exactly one year of discussions. It allowed two philosophies to be applied independently side by side: taking into account the best technical means available to abate dangerous substances in industrial effluents (the limit values), or controlling their presence in the aquatic environment with reference to the "safe" levels (the quality objectives, or more correctly quality standards). It betrays a certain ingenuousness—but this is an easy statement to make afterwards—that it was believed, at that time, that without agreement on a common policy, agreement on detailed elaboration would be successful.

According to the original proposal for the Directive, the EC Council would adopt subsidiary directives by qualified majority. This idea was abandoned in 1975 but recently it was reintroduced, and the EC Commission has prepared the following proposal: individual dangerous substances will be identified and agreed upon by unanimity; the limit values and the quality standards will be approved by qualified majority.

Perhaps, work would be even more facilitated if a Technical Standing Committee could act as an Advisory Board to the EC Commission on limit values and quality standards. Such a Committee could consist, for example, of two delegates per Member State, one standing member and the other being appointed according to the matter to be regulated. This construction would more actively involve the Member States in the early stage of conception of regulations, as compared with the current situation of uncommitting debate with the group of national experts.

List of 129 substances (now 132)

An ongoing problem with EC Directive 76/464/EC is the fact that List I (as do other blacklists) covers primarily families and groups of substances. In the process of identifying the relevant individual substances the EC Commission was assisted by a group of national experts, who selected 4 series of priority List I substances. Apart from mercury and cadmium, which are mentioned explicitly in List I, a number of organohalogenated compounds were selected. The number of candidates amounted to 21 substances. Parallel with the first selection of priority substances, a study was carried out which aimed at identifying those substances, from about 50,000 used for technical purposes, which by virtue of their chemical structure belong to the blacklist category. As a result, about 1,500 substances were identified. A closer analysis showed that 500 of these 1,500 substances were produced or used in quantities greater than 100 tonnes/year. These 500 substances were then examined by means of an algorithm to evaluate their risk to the aquatic environment and human health.

Later, the EC Commission held an inquiry on the 122 selected substances, on the basis of the various lists, and the Member States provided additional information on quantities discharged, produced and used. This information was examined at a meeting of national experts who then selected 108 substances out of 122. Finally, the 108 substances were added to the 21 previously selected and a complete list of 129 substances was "delivered". This list was communicated to the EC Council and published.[2]

On 7 February 1983 the EC Council confirmed that the 129 substances should be the basis for the implementation of Directive 76/464/EC. Later, three other substances were added to this List by the EC Commission. The status of the List and the foundation of the selection criteria used remains a permanent item of discussion.

List I and II current status

List I

Up to the present, the EC Council has approved limit values and quality objectives for 13 of the 129 candidate substances for List I. This began with mercury (in 1982 and 1984), cadmium (in 1983) and then hexachlorocyclohexane (in1984). Ten chlorinated organic compounds were included in 1986 and 1988. Four other chlorinated organic compounds are currently under discussion in the EC Council.

The increased progress since 1986 is the result of the adoption of the "General Application" Directive 86/280.[3] This Directive made it possible to restrict the discussions on List I substances to the technical essentials specific for individual substances: the Directive deals with the general provisions common to all List I substances; technical specifications (limit values, quality standards, time limits, methods of measurement) are provided as amendments.

List II

Progress on List II substances has been troublesome too. The Commission asked Member States to supply information on their national reduction programmes. As a consequence of the information received, the Commission made a proposal to "ensure sufficient co-ordination" in the implementation of Directive 76/464, with respect to the List II substance Chromium. The original proposal[4] contained Community quality objectives.

[2] OJEC C 179, 14 July 1982
[3] OJEC L 181/16, 4 July 1986.
[4] OJEC C 351, 31 December 1985.

This was later revised, according to the advice of the European Parliament, requiring Member States to apply both Community limit values and quality objectives. This proposal remains on the table but because of the lack of progress in previous negotiations it is unlikely to be re-discussed.

The Rhine List

Immediately after the conclusion of the Rhine Chemical Convention (December 1976), the International Rhine Commission started their programme of identifying individual blacklist substances. Their selection was based on the same inventory of 1,500 substances as considered by the EC Commission. Using a slightly different selection procedure they arrived at a list of 83 priority blacklist substances for the Rhine.

The Dutch List

In the Netherlands it is the policy to treat the substances belonging to the List of 129 as *de facto* List I substances. In principle, the emission standards imposed on individual factories are based on the use the of best available technology.

The List of 129 substances at the First and Second INSC

In the Ministerial Declaration of the First INSC (Bremen, 31 October and 1 November 1984) it is stated that for the blacklist substances as well as for problematic metals, mandatory regulations (uniform emission standards and environmental quality objectives) will be adopted rapidly and applied to new installations immediately and to existing installations as soon as possible (on a step-by-step basis).

According to the Declaration, emissions should normally be limited at source, emission standards should take into account the best technical means available and quality objectives should be fixed on the basis of the latest scientific data. Also a precautionary approach was introduced: if the state of knowledge is insufficient, a strict limitation of emission of pollutants at source should be imposed for safety reasons.

When the Second INSC was prepared, the nature was questioned of the blacklist substances to which the First INSC had addressed the use of stringent uniform emission standards, quality objectives and the precautionary approach. Some Contracting Parties to the INSC were of the opinion that the Declaration applied to the whole list of 129 substances. Others were convinced that only the most dangerous substances are involved.

Here again, different opinions about the status of the List of 129 substances and the criteria on which the selection has been based, gave rise to discussion.

The UK ("red") list

The United Kingdom has independently developed a selection scheme for the "most" dangerous substances. In their selection scheme various selection criteria were applied. Besides acute and chronic toxicity to the aquatic environment and persistence and bio-accumulation (selection criteria as in Directive 76/464/EC), production figures, sources of pollution, volatility and solubility were also considered. Aspect of cancirogenicity and the possibility of classifying metals will be included in this selection scheme at a later stage.

Applying their selection scheme to the List of 129 substances, they arrived at a priority list which was called the "red list".

The red list was announced at the Second INSC held in London on 25 and 26 November 1987. The individual red list substances (23) were made known at a later stage: 11 of the 13 substances were already covered by EC Directives, chlorinated organic compounds (mostly pesticides) and triorganotin compounds.

The EC Priority list

Urged by the Ministerial Seminar at Frankfurt (June 1988), an EC priority list was unanimously agreed upon during the meeting in July 1988 of national experts (the advisory group of the EC Commission) as being the list of substances for which a proposal for limit-values and quality standards (including time-limits for compliance and methods of measurements) will be sent to the EC Council in the near future. This list consists almost entirely of those red list substances which had not, at that time, been regulated at Community level.

The EC Commission has the intention to develop, in co-operation with the EC Member States and also non-EC Member States, a selection scheme on the basis of which further "priority" substances will be selected.

A proposal for the North Sea Priority ("bordeaux") List

The proposed—a kind of bordeaux—list is mainly compiled from red list substances, six grey lists substances and some blacklist candidates. The list contains at the moment 31 or 37 substances, but is not yet final. It will be proposed that Ministers at the Third INSC decide that, for the substances of this list, the following conclusions should be applicable:

- The "principle of precautionary action" will be adopted for these substances, that is the principle of protection of the aquatic environment by reduction of the pollution by these substances at source using the BAT and other appropriate measures, even where there is no scientific evidence to prove a causal link between emissions and effects.
- The reduction of the pollution of the aquatic environment by these substances has to be realized urgently and drastically with the aim of achieving a substantial reduction (of the order of 50 per cent) of total input before 1995. In this reduction measures with respect to diffuse sources of these substances should also be included, for example, control of production and use.
- For the industrial sector discharging these substances, the BAT should be identified and applied for new industrial installations and for existing installations when quality or emission standards are not being met. In general for existing industrial installations every effort has to be done in order to reduce the discharges of these substances.

The Technical Working Group of the Paris Commission is in the process of identifying the industrial sectors involved and the BAT for these sectors.

Conclusion: the "green" list of substances

At this moment it may sound unreal that originally black, grey, red and bordeaux lists of substances will turn into a sort of green list of substances, which are well controlled and whose levels in the aquatic environment do not represent any threat.

Nevertheless, if the intentions of the programmes of the international Conventions, the INSC, the EC Member States and the EC Commission, etc. will one day be realized and the concentration of dangerous substances in the aquatic environment will be reduced to harmless levels then it can be said that the list of those substances has indeed become green.

The substances themselves, however, will remain black (or grey).

Chapter 14

The North Sea and the Concept of Special Areas

Dr. Viktor Sebek

Introduction

Most legal instruments dealing with protection of the marine environment, including that of the North Sea, have been of a global character, especially those relating to vessel source pollution: from the abortive Washington Convention of 1926 through OILPOL 1954[1] to MARPOL.[2] The rationale for this development appeared to be eminently logical. Shipping is a global international activity. Therefore, in order to prevent legal anarchy at sea, the same rules will apply to all of the world's oceans. This rule, echoing traditional predominance of the principle of the freedom of the seas in the law of the sea, is also a reflection of the belief that the economic order was what counted most. Environmental protection was thus barely glossed over in the 1958 Geneva Conventions on the Law of the Sea.

The 1970s marked a turning-point in rendering environmental awareness an increasingly respectable cause. Once the political climate became favourable, none more so than at the 1972 Stockholm UN Conference on Environment, it was only a matter of time before the new ideas were to be enshrined in what was promising to become a more comprehensive and a more progressive legal framework than the one in force. The 1973 International Convention for the Prevention of Pollution from Ships (MARPOL) appeared to be a case in point: it was to encompass all forms of vessel source pollution, from oil to garbage.

Special areas under MARPOL

Another novelty which MARPOL introduced was the recognition that not all the seas were equally vulnerable to pollution: some, especially semi-enclosed seas,

[1] International Convention for the Prevention of Pollution of the Sea by Oil 1954 as amended.
[2] International Convention for the Prevention of Pollution from Ships 1973 as amended.

required a greater degree of environmental protection than that accorded to the world's oceans in general. The scientific explanation for this important provision was that the slow exchange of waters between semi-enclosed seas and the open oceans renders such water masses more prone to suffer from both chronic, and large-scale, accidental pollution. It is particularly interesting that in this respect the MARPOL conference found itself able to legislate ahead of its time. In all other cases, it displayed considerable caution against tampering with what was to become a comprehensive code of the public law of the sea, on which the work started earlier that year in Caracas with the opening of the Third United Nations Conference on the Law of the Sea (UNCLOS).[3]

The MARPOL Convention did not provide a definition of "special areas". It rather provided an exhaustive list which included, depending on the Annex involved, the Baltic, the Mediterranean, the Black Sea, the Red Sea and the Gulf area. It became clear during the MARPOL negotiations that there was nothing sacred and definite about the list of special areas. The inclusion of the Red Sea and the Gulf was thus agreed only at the last stages of the Conference, at the pressure of the Arab countries. Indeed, the arbitrary character of MARPOL decisions on this issue was proved by the Democratic Republic Yemen which secured, after several years of campaigning at the Marine Environment Protection Committee (MEPC) of the International Maritime Organization (IMO), the addition of the Gulf of Aden as a special area: this pocket of water, sandwiched between two special areas, the Red Sea and the Gulf, became for many years a place where tankers and other ships discharged oily ballast water. The decision was taken on in 1987[4] and it is still too early to see whether it has already resulted in a reduction of oil pollution in the area.

MARPOL did not harmonize its approach to special areas. Regulation 1 (10) of Annex I defines special areas as "a sea where for recognized technical reasons in relation to its oceanographical and ecological condition and to the particular character of its traffic the adoption of special mandatory methods for the prevention of sea pollution by oil is required". A similar definition is provided in Regulation 1(7) of Annex II and Regulation 1(3) of Annex V. However, Annexes I and V provide for the special regime for all four seas, whilst Annex II recognizes this status for the Baltic and Black Sea only.

It has been argued that the special areas regime cannot be used "in a purely preventive manner" and that the existence of all three criteria, that is oceanographical and ecological features and peculiarity of traffic must all be proven before any future marine space, however ecologically sensitive, can be declared a special area.[5] The practice is nevertheless proving that when the political will is present, IMO Member States do not interpret general definitions in a dogmatic manner.

[3] The author was a member of the UK delegation at the MARPOL Conference.

[4] The three coastal states, Democratic Yemen, Djibouti and Somalia stated that they now had the incentive to become party to MARPOL 73/78 as soon as possible, and to provide adequate reception facilities.

[5] M. Forster, "Special Areas in the Sea: Treaty and Legislative Practice", (1986) *Environmental Policy and Law* 180.

"Screening" was required, both for the Gulf of Aden, and subsequently for the Gulf of Mexico and the North Sea, but mainly in order to discourage states from claiming that their adjacent seas also merit inclusion in this category if the real motive for such a claim is merely a wish to impress public opinion.

Nevertheless, the decision-makers seem to be moving closer and closer to the "precautionary" principle, as opposed to absolute proof of irreversible damage, prior to taking legal action. This principle was enshrined in the Second INSC Declaration in November 1987. Almost exactly two years later, IMO managed to squeeze a special, one-day session of MEPC during the XVI session of the Assembly, in order to declare the North Sea a special area for the purpose of Annex V.[6]

Interpretation of the special areas concept by IMO

In order to facilitate its future work, the MEPC set up a Working Group to identify, *inter alia*, criteria for determining "special areas" under MARPOL 73/78. The Working Group concluded that the criteria are grouped into the following categories:

(a) Oceanographic conditions, which include:

- particular circulation patterns, such as convergence zones and gyres;
- long residence time caused by low flushing rates;
- ice state; and
- adverse wind conditions.

(b) Ecological conditions, that is conditions indicating that protection of the area from harmful substances is needed to protect:

- depleted, threatened or endangered marine species;
- commercially or recreationally important fisheries;
- areas of high productivity such as spawning, breeding and nursery areas; and
- rare or fragile ecosystems, such as coral reefs, mangroves and wetlands.

(c) Vessel traffic characteristics, that is that the sea area is used by ships to an extent that the discharge of harmful substances by ships, when operating in accordance with non-Special Area requirements of MARPOL, would be unacceptable in the light of oceanographic and ecological conditions that exist in the area.

The Working Group also concluded that the threat to amenities posed by the discharge of harmful substances from ships operating in accordance with MARPOL Convention requirements for non-Special Areas may strengthen the argument for designating an area as a Special Area.[7]

[6] MEPC 28/WP.1 of 17 October 1989.

[7] "Identification of Particularly Sensitive Areas, Including Development of Guidelines for Designating Special Areas under Annexes I, II and V (MEPC 26/17)", 2 June 1988. This document states that "*Generally*, in order to be designated a Special Area, one of the criteria in each category should be satisfied" (emphasis added). This wording suggests that whilst the scientific and technical basis for the designation of special areas is comprehensive and elaborate, exceptions may be made from the general rule.

Law of the Sea Convention

Following MARPOL, the United Nations Law of the Sea Convention (LOSC) provided in Article 194(5) that states shall take measures to include those "necessary to protect and preserve rare or fragile ecosystems as well as habitat of depleted, threatened or endangered species and other forms of marine life". However, unlike MARPOL which spells out oil, chemical and garbage pollution standards in special areas,[8] the umbrella Article 194(5) of LOSC does not detail what environmental standards ought to apply in "fragile" seas.

Assessment of the regulation by MARPOL

The MARPOL approach towards special areas begs a number of important questions. First, can adequate environmental protection of a "fragile" sea be given for only one aspect of vessel source pollution? In particular, will the North Sea as a whole be better off than it is at present once it becomes a special areas for the purpose of garbage pollution from ships only? Admittedly, certain North Sea states would like to see the North Sea as a special area for MARPOL Annexes I and II as well. Others, however, argue (and this view prevailed during the preparatory meeting of the first, Bremen, INSC) that full compliance with Annex I of MARPOL obviates the need for additional measures.

Secondly, MARPOL deals with vessel source pollution which is generally recognized, both in quantitative and in qualitative terms, to be the least dangerous source of marine pollution. It is the land-based pollution which presents the gravest threat. Yet, regulation through the Paris Convention remains patchy. Besides, there are no global rules on land-based pollution, apart from a general declaration in Article 207 of LOSC. If the North Sea is to be declared, wholly or partly, a special area, it is the non-MARPOL aspect which is likely to prove to be of crucial importance to the health of the environment of this sea.

Thirdly, legal measures on stricter standards in special areas cannot by themselves bring about adequate protection of their marine environment. Admittedly, MARPOL Annexes contain rules which are meant to ensure the setting up of a technical infrastructure which would enable effective compliance with strict standards in special areas. This applies especially to reception facilities for oil, chemical waste and garbage. Yet, repeated debates at MEPC and questionnaires circulated by the International Chamber of Shipping (ICS) suggest that much remains to be desired. There is a general agreement that unless, and until, adequate reception facilities are provided, there can be no proper observance of MARPOL rules. The principal problem, especially in the Mediterranean, is the lack of finances,[9] a factor which should not prove unduly difficult in the North Sea. For all these reasons, whilst gradual acceptance of the special area status of the North Sea, for the pur-

[8] Annex I, Regulation 10; Annex II, Regulations 5 and 8; Annex V, Regulation 5.

[9] See questionnaire by the ICS and its report, contained in ICS/ACOPS submission to MEPC (MEPC 26/INF.23 of 5 August 1988) to assist in the World Bank's Environmental Programme for the Mediterranean.

pose of Annexes I and II of MARPOL, cannot be excluded in the foreseeable future, such a solution should not be regarded as a panacea for the North Sea problems. What other options are available?

Future developments

The MARPOL Convention itself has proved to be capable of assimilating changes in scientific, economic, social and political perceptions of environmental problems. Not only was it amended in 1978 before it entered into force,[10] but MEPC and other IMO committees have worked since 1974 to refine it and adapt it to the changing circumstances. Also, it is possible to argue that the single most effective enforcement vehicle to MARPOL was to be found not in the provisions of the Convention itself, but in the Paris Memorandum of Understanding, and its inspection procedures, which were "hooked" on to MARPOL in 1982, ten years after it was adopted.

The INS Conferences are also proving a potential effective method for dealing with any special measures in this area.[11] Admittedly, they do not adopt binding legal rules. However, it has been proved conclusively in international practice that it is the political good will which serves as a decisive factor in legalizing or outlawing a particular practice. It can be argued that the language of ministerial declarations is sufficiently vague for any dissenting country to defend activities departing from the agreed principles. Nevertheless, the fact that the North Sea Ministers meet regularly, and that a structure has been set up to allow for technocrats and civil servants to meet even more frequently, allows for a continuous review and follow-up to take place. A great advantage of the North Sea Conferences is that they encompass the entire marine environmental framework: from land-based, to offshore pollution. Moreover, their review includes both regional conventions, applicable to the North Sea alone, and to global, for example, IMO, conventions. It is therefore possible, indeed, desirable, that the work of the INSCs, and of their intersessional meetings, should also assist the work of other structures administering the relevant agreements.

Yet another advantage, which can observed since the second ministerial meeting, is that the precautionary principle has been accepted as the general guideline in determining policies and, when necessary, initiating legal action to be taken. Some technocrats suggest that this is not a desirable development for it "politicizes" the science.

On the other hand, it has certainly given a strong boost to better environmental protection because it is no longer necessary to wait until it may be too late to take preventive, if not remedial, action. It is for this reason that action on proposals to include the North Sea as a special area for the purpose of MARPOL Annexes I and II can no longer be ruled out.

This contribution has so far been confined to an analysis of legal rules, or pro-

[10] In 1983.
[11] See for an assessment the contribution by Prof. Ehlers above, chapter 1.

posals for legal rules, which regard the entire North Sea as a special area. However, precedents already exist in international legislation and in practice for designating specific sections of a sea for special protection.

Particularly sensitive areas: regulation by IMO

IMO's Tanker Safety Pollution Prevention Conference (TSPP), which amended the MARPOL 1973 Convention, passed a resolution which invited the Organization, *inter alia*, to make an inventory of sea areas in need of special protection from ships and dumping due to their sensitivity in respect of their renewable natural resources or their importance for scientific purposes.[12] However, it was only in the last few years that MEPC set up a Working Group to carry out the necessary follow-up work. The work is still in progress, but the following trends can be noted.

(1) Particularly sensitive areas may be situated within and beyond the limits of the territorial sea.

(2) Such areas are defined as an area which needs special protection through action by IMO because of its significance for the following recognized criteria.

Ecological criteria, such as: the area has rare or fragile ecosystems and provides habitats for depleted, threatened or endangered species; its ecological processes provide essential support for species for a local or larger ecosystem; it is highly representative of ecological processes, or community or habitat types of other natural characteristics; it has a high variety of species, and a rich ecosystem; it is highly biologically productive.

Social, cultural and economic criteria, such as: the area is of particular importance to utilization of living marine resources; it has special significance for recreation and tourism; it has importance for aquaculture; it is of particular importance for the support of traditional subsistence and/or cultural needs of the local human population.

Scientific and educational criteria, such as: the area has high scientific interest; it provides suitable baseline conditions with regard to biota or environmental characteristics; it offers an opportunity to demonstrate particularly natural phenomena; it has historical and/or archaeological significance.

In addition, other factors (oceanographic and meteorological) already rendering an area vulnerable, may contribute to special protection from further stress, including from maritime activities.

(3) Special protective measures which IMO can take, having decided to accept an application as satisfying one of the above criteria, include the following: to designate the area as a Special Area in Annexes I, II and V under MARPOL 73/78 or otherwise to apply the Special Area discharge restrictions to vessels operating in the area; to adopt, under COLREG, special routeing measures near or in the area or designate the area as an "area to be

[12] Resolution 9.

avoided" or other navigational restrictions; and to establish a buffer zone around the area and restrict maritime activities in the particularly sensitive area and its buffer zone.

The current future work of MEPC will include development of a manual which could provide the basis for developing proposals on Particularly Sensitive Areas. This manual, proposed by FOEI, would also include procedures for submitting proposals to IMO, information on how protective measures would be implemented, certain case studies and inventory of areas which have been designated. It was agreed, however, to stress that a proliferation of Special Area designation should be avoided. At the proposal of Norway[13] it was pointed out that if such proliferation were to occur, it might indicate a need to consider upgrading the level of protection provided by MARPOL.[14]

In view of the wide scope of issues involved, MEPC decided to request the Group of Experts on Effects of Pollutants (GEEP) of the International Oceanographic Commission (IOC), IMO and UNEP, to comment on the criteria it was developing.

Other papers presented in this book should demonstrate whether parts of the North Sea qualify for special protection under IMO rules.[15] However, there is no doubt that such proposals will be made. If they are made through a joint action by states participating at the INSC, there is little doubt that they would be accepted.

LOSC

The current work of IMO through its MEPC, follows in part provisions of Article 211 (6) of the LOSC which stipulates that "where the international rules and standards referred to in paragraph 1[16] are inadequate to meet special circumstances and coastal states have reasonable grounds for believing that a particular, clearly defined area of their respective exclusive economic zones is an area where the adoption of special mandatory measures for the prevention of pollution from vessels is required for recognized technical reasons in relation to its oceanographical and ecological conditions, as well as its utilization for the protection of its resources and the particular character of its traffic, the coastal states, after appropriate consultations through the competent international organization with any other states concerned, may for that area, direct a communication to that organization, submitting scientific and technical evidence in support and information on necessary reception facilities". The coastal state may adopt rules and regulations on vessel source pollution, implementing appropriate international rules if the Organization

[13] MEPC 26/17/1 of 5 August 1988.

[14] MEPC 26/WP.10. See also papers submitted by Norway (MEPC 25/15/1); FRG (MEPC 25/15); Sweden (MEPC 25/15/2) and the UK (MEPC 25/15/13), all of 20 July 1987.

[15] See the contribution by G. Peet and S. Gubbay below, chapter 21.

[16] Para. 1 refers to international rules and standards to prevent, reduce and control marine pollution from vessels and promote, whenever appropriate, adoption of routeing schemes designed to minimize the threat of accidents which may cause pollution.

(that is IMO)[17] determines, 12 months after having received an appropriate communication from the coastal state, whether conditions in the application correspond to those set out in Article 211 (6a)(a).

Specially protected areas under UNEP regional seas programme

Although the North Sea is not, and is most unlikely to become, a part of UNEP's Regional Seas Programme, it is important to note that protocols to conventions adopted under this programme have incorporated detailed rules on measures to safeguard the environment of specially protected areas.

The first instrument in this series was the 1982 Geneva Protocol Concerning Mediterranean Specially Protected Areas.

This Agreement, which supplements the general provisions of the 1976 Barcelona Convention, provides for the following action.

- Contracting Parties undertake to protect areas which are important for the safeguard of the natural resources.[18] Their duties include the establishment of protected areas and taking such action as is necessary to protect them or, when necessary, to restore them.[19]
- Coastal states are given examples of measures they are expected to take, and those include the establishment of a management plan and system; prohibition of the dumping or discharge of wastes; the regulation of navigation and fishing; the prohibition of the destruction of plant or animal life, etc.
- Co-operation amongst Mediterranean countries is encouraged to seek to establish a co-ordinated network of protected areas in the Mediterranean region.[20]

The 1985 Protocol Concerning Protected Areas and Wild Fauna and Flora in the East African Region[21] not only follows the pattern of the Geneva Protocol, but also anticipates the Brundtland Report by including as a criterion for the setting up of special areas the sound and sustainable management of economically important species.[22] The same principle is incorporated in Article 4 of the Draft Protocol Concerning Specially Protected Areas and Wildlife to the Convention for the Protection and Development of the Marine Environment of the Wider Caribbean Region.[23] The Draft Protocol, which is expected to be adopted at a diplomatic conference, scheduled for Santa Marta in December 1989, incorporates a number of interesting provisions which reflect the current trends in environmental law:

planning and management regime for a protected area provides for such measures

[17] The LOS Convention refrains from naming competent organizations, but it is generally accepted that IMO will deal with all matters referring to global rules on vessel source pollution.
[18] Art. 1(1).
[19] Art. 3(1).
[20] Art. 12.
[21] The Protocol is added to the general provisions of the Nairobi Convention for the Protection, Management and Development of the Marine and Coastal Environment of the Eastern African Region.
[22] Art. 8.
[23] Cartagena Convention.

as the formulation of appropriate management guidelines; development of a management plan that specifies the legal and institutional framework and development of public awareness and educational programmes; the active involvement of local people and enterprises in the planning and management of the protected area; contingency plans for responding to incidents that could cause or threaten damage to the protected areas and their resources.[24]

environmental impact assessments are requested in the planning process leading to decisions about projects and activities that would significantly affect areas or species that have been afforded special protection under the Protocol.[25]

institutional arrangements ensure that the application of rules set under the Protocol, including raising funds, is administered.[26]

It is likely that other UNEP regional seas for which umbrella conventions exist (for example, Abidjan Convention, Jeddah Convention) or for which they are under consideration (for example, South East Asian Seas) are also likely to adopt Protocols similar to those already discussed. It is also likely that the degree of protection that is afforded to specially sensitive areas will increase to respond to an increasing public awareness of the problem.

Conclusions

Future action in this field could take one of the following forms:

(1) Request for the tightening up of MARPOL, either as a whole or of its particular annexes.

(2) Request to IMO for recognition of the special area status for the purpose of Annexes I and II.

(3) Request for recognition of maritime zones as "specially sensitive areas", in accordance with proposals currently being elaborated within MEPC, insofar as vessel source pollution is concerned; papers submitted to MEPC by various North Sea countries give an indication of which areas might qualify.[27]

(4) Suggestion, possibly under the aegis of the North Sea Ministerial Conferences, for the adoption of a Protocol or a Convention on the North Sea Protected Areas which would include protection and restoration measures that may be necessary due to a threat by, or as a result of, all forms of pollution or other environmental pressures on areas requiring special protection.

(5) Legislative action by individual North Sea states in their respective territorial seas or, subject to approval by the competent Organization, in their exclusive economic zones, in accordance with the LOSC.

Other options, such as setting up of marine protected areas, are considered in another contribution in this book.[28] It is suggested that the North Sea is in a privileged position by comparison with other seas. This is due to several factors.

[24] Art. 6.
[25] Art. 13.
[26] Art. 24.
[27] See n. 14, above.
[28] Peet and Gubbay.

First, all coastal states are industrially developed countries and in a position to provide and pay for the necessary infrastructure;[29] it is the lack of such infrastructure which has caused the lack of practical implementation of otherwise progressive rules in other parts of the world. Secondly the INSCs provide a regular opportunity for a continuous overview of the environmental health of the North Sea. Therefore, as soon as a common decision is taken that additional measures are necessary, a concerted request to IMO is almost certainly likely to result in acceptance of the North Sea as a special area, or for granting specific sectors of the North Sea the status of specially sensitive areas.

In order that an environmentally sound decision can be taken it is necessary to assess, at the earliest possible date, whether the existing legislative framework, from MARPOL to the Paris Convention, affords the necessary degree of protection. If this is not the case, the next session of the INSC could provide the opportunity for taking one of the possible options outlined in this, and other chapters in the book. Certain North Sea states with important merchant fleets may nevertheless be deterred from taking such a step in the belief that a universal acceptance of the "precautionary" principle might lead to a proliferation of requests for similar action by other countries.

[29] The Netherlands' Government informed IMO, on behalf of all the North Sea states, of the availability of adequate reception facilities in all the coastal states (MEPC 28/WP.1 of 17 October 1989).

Chapter 15

A Regional Vessel Traffic Service for the North Sea

Professor John F. Kemp and Aline F. M. De Bievre

This chapter is concerned with the role which Vessel Traffic Services (VTS) may have in minimizing ship-source pollution and, in particular, how VTS support to the cause of environmental protection of the North Sea could be enhanced through the provision of a regional traffic service.

A VTS basically functions as an information exchange and management system. It involves, to a greater or lesser extent, communication between the ship and the shore-based traffic monitoring station, thus enabling the latter to provide navigational assistance and to organize vessel movements to the benefit of safety and/or smoother traffic flows in the VTS area. A useful analogy to draw upon is the (more elaborate) system offered by Air Traffic Control (ATC). Essentially this consists of the following two elements: (i) permanent radio contact between the aircraft whilst *en route* and the ground traffic control centre; (ii) radar coverage from the ground of a clearly defined area, that is the airspace above the airport and the approaches to it.

More developed VTS schemes may operate with shore-based radar to ensure continuous monitoring of, for instance, traffic with noxious or dangerous cargoes or ship movements in navigationally difficult areas such as high-density traffic zones, narrow channels, tidal waters, environmentally sensitive seas, etc. However, this is not to say that radar-assisted surveillance of the VTS area is essential. A VTS can work effectively on the basis of communication and ship reporting alone, which can be done through VHF radiotelephone and telex, provided there is full co-operation of the vessels within the area of coverage.

In North-West Europe alone there are well over sixty VTS schemes most of which are operated by port authorities. Some of these schemes reach well beyond the immediate port area, including, for instance, the approaches to a seaport. The Port of Rotterdam's VTS system thus covers the Eurochannel, a deepwater access route to Europoort, extending some 50 nautical miles out to sea. Another example of VTS operations reaching into the open sea concerns the German Bight area, which is monitored by the river port VTSs of Bremerhaven (Weser), Wilhelmshaven (Jade) and Cuxhaven (Elbe).

In the case of a river port, the VTS may cover the narrow upper reaches of the river towards the port's docks as well as the estuarial (downstream) area. Examples of this comprehensive type of river port VTS system are the recently upgraded Antwerp (River Scheldt) and Bremerhaven traffic control systems, following completion of an additional chain of inland radar sites along the river banks.

Designated coastal VTS systems are relatively rare. The most well known one worldwide is the joint Anglo-French scheme giving radar coverage of the Dover Strait and, on the French side, also the English Channel. Another VTS specifically covering coastal, as opposed to port, waters is the scheme with radar coverage operated at Aarhus, Denmark which monitors the entrance to the Baltic Sea.

The concept of a regional VTS system is based on the principle that upon entering a particular maritime region, a ship in transit through that region and which does not intend to make a port call, needs to communicate its particulars only once, that is to the nearest VTS station. It then is the latter's responsibility to relay this information to VTS centres located further along that ship's route. Thus, a regional VTS operates primarily on the basis of a shore-to-shore, as opposed to ship-to-shore, reporting system. It has the dual advantage of minimizing interference with the ship whilst permitting the ports and coastal states concerned to have an overall picture of ship movements in areas of interest to them. Should the transiting ship decide to visit a port in the region, it would of course need to inform that port accordingly upon entering its approach but if the regional VTS operates effectively and efficiently, this report could be kept to the minimum. Similarly, upon exiting the region the ship should only have to worry about supplying basic information to the nearest reporting point.

The North Sea constitutes a particularly sensitive area in terms of its vulnerability to ship-generated pollution. This has led environmental pressure groups such as the Netherlands North Sea Working Group and the Friends of the Earth International, through their consultative status at the International Maritime Organization (IMO), to advocate the establishment of a regional VTS system. Such a system could be operated on the basis of harmonized procedures for ship-shore communication, complemented by systematic data exchange between individual VTS centres. In special circumstances such as those involving larger ships or vessels carrying dangerous cargoes, and where required for the safety of traffic, the introduction of certain mandatory VTS measures such as compulsory ship reporting requirements may be contemplated, subject to such action being in accordance with international law and taking account of financial feasibility (e.g. policing costs).

However, other interest groups, particularly shipowners, have maintained that the need for regional VTS has not been established. In their view, the results of the Europe-wide COST–301[1] studies on shore-based aids to maritime navigation have

[1] COST stands for European Co-operation in the Field of Scientific and Technical Research. The COST–301 project concerned an action research programme on Shore-based Maritime Navigation Aid Systems which was carried out over a period of three and a half years (1983–1986). Conducted with the approval of the European Community's Council of Transport Ministers, it involved fourteen European countries (i.e. all maritime states of the EC except Portugal, plus Finland, Norway, and Sweden). The final COST–301 report was formally approved by the participating maritime authorities in spring 1987.

only indicated vague possibilities in terms of such a scheme bringing additional benefits, and more research needs to be done on the economic implications for shipping efficiency in particular. Furthermore, any safety and/or efficiency increments that might be gained must be weighed up against additional costs. These may arise from the further installation of technical aids in support of the shore-to-shore data exchange function in particular.

What, then, are the main objectives of VTS, and can these be enhanced, to the benefit of improved vessel-source pollution control, by it being organized on a regional basis, as opposed to simply a local (port or coastal) one?

Main objectives of Vessel Traffic Services

According to the *IMO Guidelines on Vessel Traffic Services*,[2] in general, the establishment of a VTS in a given area has three main aims: (i) increasing safety; (ii) improving traffic efficiency; (iii) protecting the environment. The IMO Guidelines define a VTS as any service designed to meet these aims and which is "implemented by a competent authority. It may range from the provision of simple information messages to extensive management of traffic within a port or waterway."

In some cases the above-mentioned aims are complementary—for instance, a VTS measure which reduces collision risk could also improve efficiency in that ship-owners, insurers and port authorities would be put to less expense and cargo losses would be reduced. There would, in addition, be a reduction in the pollution caused.

In other cases, however, the aims may be contradictory. For instance, a VTS measure may be designed to improve traffic efficiency by allowing ships to proceed in poor visibility which, in the absence of VTS assistance, would have forced the captain to anchor until the weather cleared. This particular kind of VTS intervention, whereby a vessel relies on VTS-provided information to keep it out of trouble and which has clear economic benefits (e.g. uninterrupted passage), would not necessarily give an improvement in safety. It could even increase the risk of collision or grounding and hence also increase the risk of casualty-generated pollution.

Where conflict exists, it is important that safety and environmental protection should be given proper weighting as compared with commercial considerations. The particular VTS roles which can contribute, directly or indirectly, to environmental protection include: (i) prevention of collisions; (ii) prevention of groundings; (iii) implementation of remedial action; (iv) enforcement of regulations. These four roles are now considered in more detail.

Reduction of collision risk

The number of ships involved in collisions in the North Sea is of the order of 80 per year with about 30 per cent of these occurring at sea, about 45 per cent in restricted waters, and about 25 per cent in port.[3] Many of the collisions are of a minor nature

[2] Adopted in November 1985 (Res. A. 578(14)).

[3] Netherlands Maritime Research Institute Task Report for COST–301. Doc. COST–301/NL/MARIN/T2.23, 1985.

and only a few cause significant pollution. In the 1987 ACOPS survey of oil pollution around the coast of the United Kingdom only two spills of more than two tonnes each were recorded as being due to ship collisions, resulting in a total of 173 tonnes of spilt oil.[4]

The effectiveness of VTS in preventing ship collisions is not easy to assess since, typically, when a VTS is introduced into a sea area, other conditions are changed as well and, in particular, routeing measures or traffic separation schemes may be introduced. However, estimates have been made that a VTS which consists of VHF radio coverage with ship reporting but no radar surveillance may reduce the risk by about 40 per cent, a VTS which also includes radar surveillance may reduce the risk by about 50 per cent, and a fully automated VTS deriving information from ship-borne transponders could reduce the risk by 60 per cent.[5]

A VTS does not operate in isolation. It is one of many measures which are intended to reduce risk of collision at sea, including: (i) routeing measures such as traffic separation schemes and areas to be avoided; (ii) regulations for minimum standards of shipboard watchkeeping and training; (iii) equipment standards for ships including the carriage of radar and automatic plotting aids for prescribed classes of ship; (iv) facilities for ship-to-ship communication.

The main aim of a VTS in its anti-collision role is to reduce the number of conflicts which occur between ships by ensuring their proper use of traffic separation schemes, by scheduling their movements so that they do not meet in confined waters or at bends in channels, by establishing agreed passing strategies, and by similar procedural methods. Once a conflict has occurred, a VTS may attempt to alert either or both ships to the danger if it appears that timely action is not being taken to avoid collision. However, involvement of VTS in a tactical collision avoidance situation is not an efficient process and is even considered dangerous by some authorities. It must be treated as an emergency procedure rather than a routine operation.

Reduction of grounding risk

Groundings or strandings, for the purpose of this discussion, are defined as cases where a vessel goes aground involuntarily. A striking is a similar event but where a vessel makes involuntary contact with a fixed object other than the sea-bed.

The combined number of groundings and strikings in the North Sea is of the order of 70 per year, with about 25 per cent occurring in unrestricted waters, 40 per cent in restricted waters, and 35 per cent in port.

As in the case of collisions, many of the groundings or strikings are of a minor nature and only a few cause significant pollution. In the 1987 ACOPS survey of oil pollution along the United Kingdom's shores only one spill of more than two tonnes was recorded as being due to a grounding or striking, resulting in 129 tonnes of spilt oil. However, it must be remembered that the most destructive, large-scale

[4] *Advisory Committee on Pollution of the Sea Yearbook 1987/88*, Section 8.1.

[5] A. F. M. De Bievre and J. F. Kemp, "The Environment, COST–301 and European Coastal State Policy", in *Proceedings of COST–301 Progress Seminar, Delft* (January 1986). A summary of this paper was also published in *Journal of Navigation* (September 1986).

cases of oil pollution worldwide have been due to groundings rather than collisions, as for instance the Torrey Canyon, Argo Merchant, Amoco Cadiz, and Exxon Valdez incidents.

The effectiveness of VTS in preventing strandings is not easy to assess but it would seem likely to be less than in the case of collisions. Where a VTS consists purely of a VHF radio facility and no radar surveillance, its role in preventing collisions would seem to lie mainly in the provision of information to ships either on request or by means of regular bulletins. These could contain hydrological information (e.g. unpredicted tidal conditions) and meteorological information (e.g. poor visibility due to heavy rain or fog or snow, high winds), which could be expected to make a small contribution to the prevention of strandings. Where a VTS includes radar surveillance there is the possibility that a VTS operator could detect if a vessel was following an unusual and potentially dangerous track and alert the ship's personnel before a grounding occurred. However, in many cases, for instance, where a vessel is following a narrow channel at long range from the radar scanner, the margin between safety and danger is sufficiently small that the discrimination on the VTS radar does not allow a deviation to be detected until too late.

Estimates have been made that a VTS which consists of VHF radio with ship reporting but no radar coverage has no significant effect on stranding risk, a VTS which also includes radar surveillance may reduce the risk by about 30 per cent, and a fully automated VTS drawing information from shipboard transponders could reduce the risk by about 50 per cent.

At this point it is of interest to compare two contrasting cases. In 1978 the Al Faiah, a loaded Very Large Crude Carrier (VLCC), was detected by the Channel Navigation Information Service radars (the UK HM Coastguard-operated VTS) to be deviating from the eastbound traffic lane, going up the wrong lane on a course that was also likely to cause it to go aground. Not without some difficulty contact was established by radio and the vessel's watchkeeper was alerted to the situation, leading him to take corrective action. In 1989 the Exxon Valdez oil tanker diverted from the outbound traffic lane from Valdez into Prince William Sound but the overshoot of its proper track was not detected by the Valdez VTS. It has been suggested that the Valdez VTS establishment had been run down to the extent that it was not fully effective.[6] Even so, it should never be expected that a VTS in isolation, even when operating at full efficiency, is sufficient to prevent all groundings.

Other measures which influence risk of groundings or strikings, taken either together with or as an alternative to VTS, include: (i) routeing measures such as deep draught routes, recommended tracks and areas to be avoided; (ii) compulsory pilotage; (iii) provision of navigational aids such as buoys, lighthouses, radio position fixing systems, etc.; (iv) regulations for minimum standards of watchkeeping

[6] C. W. Koburger, "Exxon Valdez—Symbol of a Myth, End of an Era?" in *Safety At Sea International* (May 1989).

and training; (v) equipment standards for ships such as the required carriage of navigational aids and gyro compasses.

Remedial action

Although the primary function of a VTS must be to prevent shipping casualties, it can also make an important contribution to safeguarding life and property and also to preventing or containing environmental damage after an accident has taken place. This role can be assumed even in the aftermath of casualties such as fire or explosion which a VTS could not be expected to prevent. In order to be fully effective in this role, a VTS needs a reliable means of locating and identifying all of the ships operating in its coverage area.

One remedial role of VTS is the possibility of recognizing an incident at an early stage and perhaps before a message is received from the ship or ships concerned. Strandings or collisions could, for instance, often be identified from a radar display. Such recognition could be important in alerting rescue, salvage and pollution-control services, and other vessels in the vicinity sufficiently early that an accident is prevented from escalating into a disaster. Another possibility is that a VTS may receive the first message from the vessel or vessels concerned in an accident.

In both of the above situations, there will be a considerable advantage if the VTS centre is able to link the identification of the vessel or vessels concerned in an accident with a databank of information on such things as size and type of ship, whether carrying hazardous, noxious or polluting cargo, voyage particulars, address of owners, etc. All useful information can thus be passed on at the outset to the emergency services as well as to the individual ships which may be involved in remedial action.

A third remedial role for VTS is to use the infrastructure associated with it, that is equipment and staff, to provide a local co-ordination centre. The communications and surveillance facilities available at a VTS centre make it eminently suited for such a role. Also, the centre will have information on weather, tides and other meteorological or hydrological conditions, traffic patterns and other local factors in its navigational area.

Finally, a VTS may help with providing a safe passage for disabled ships so that they can be conducted to sheltered havens, ports of refuge or repair facilities instead of remaining at sea where they may represent a threat to coastlines as well as to other shipping.

Enforcement function

In addition to its direct role in promoting traffic safety and efficiency, a VTS has an indirect role which consists of ensuring that regulations concerned with safety of shipping and protection of the environment are followed. The main regulations in this respect concern: (i) manning levels and the qualifications of crews; (ii) the equipment required to be carried by ships of various classes; (iii) the way in which the ships are conducted and the equipment used for navigation.

A VTS may also detect and report apparently dangerous situations which do not necessarily involve infringement of any regulations.

The matters referred to in (i) and (ii) above are not generally matters which are directly observable by VTS operators but they may suspect deficiencies as a result of communication or lack of communication with certain vessels, or observations of irregularities in vessel behaviour which may suggest that a vessel's navigational equipment is out of order or that a chart is set out of date.

In contrast, the way in which ships are conducted is something that can be directly observed by a VTS which has a surveillance capability. This could result in the detection of cases of non-compliance of a number of regulations including

Collision Regulations (COLREGS)

One of the main functions of the Channel Navigation Information Service is the detection of vessels which do not comply with Rule 10 concerning the conduct of vessels in and near traffic separation schemes (TSSs). At least partly as a result of this activity, the number of rogue vessels which do not comply fell from forty per day in 1972 to five per day in 1988.

A report of a VTS operation in the Texel area of the southern North Sea suggests that there remains considerable scope for encouraging greater discipline in TSS areas.[7] Other COLREG provisions, such as the steering and sailing rules and the proper use of lights and signals, can also be monitored by a VTS.

Routeing provisions not covered by the COLREGS

A VTS can monitor the conduct of vessels relative to international measures such as recommended tracks, deep water routes, areas to be avoided, safety zones around offshore structures, and relative to similar regulatory measures which may be introduced on a national basis in territorial waters.

Compulsory radio listening watch rules as specified by the IMO Safety of Life At Sea Convention (SOLAS)

Another conclusion of the Texel study quoted above suggests that there are deficiencies in radio watchkeeping by certain classes of vessel. However, it does not necessarily follow that a vessel which does not respond when called has not heard the call.

Marine Pollution Convention (MARPOL)

In certain circumstances a VTS might detect and identify vessels discharging polluting substances which are illegal under MARPOL.

In order that effective action can be taken as a result of VTS detection and identification of a vessel which infringes regulations it is necessary that there should be a recognized line of communication whereby reports can be made to at least the flag state and the port state with which the vessel is concerned.

[7] J. A. A. Schreuder, *et al.*, *Evaluation Report of VTS during P3-C Drilling in Texel Traffic Separation Scheme*, Part I. Doc. COST- 301/NL/DGSM/2.49, 1985.

There may, of course, be cases of infringement of regulations or of bad seamanship which require immediate intervention by a VTS centre in order to avoid immediate danger. VHF radio calls may be an effective means of communication but reception cannot always be relied upon especially in cases where the identity of a ship is not known. Light or sound signals may be used or, if available, guardships can approach and hail the vessel or vessels concerned.

Again, as in the case of remedial action, it is important that if a VTS is to act effectively to encourage and/or enforce well-disciplined behaviour, it should have a reliable means of locating and identifying all the vessels in its area of coverage. However, information provision raises certain problems of both an operational and legal nature and these will now be briefly considered. The last section of this chapter, then, discusses the role which a regional VTS in the North Sea could play in alleviating these problems.

Information provision: for better or for worse?

In order to operate effectively and efficiently a VTS needs to have at least the following basic information about the ships within its coverage area:

- Identity of ship.
- Location of ship.
- Details of any hazardous or potentially polluting cargo on board.
- Voyage data including the port of destination and estimated time of arrival (ETA), and preferably some indication of route.
- Information on any substandard conditions on board or whether the ship is in need of special treatment for other reasons (e.g. disabled vessel).

Of particular environmental concern is the potential beneficial effect which any VTS scheme may have on reducing the work-load of ship personnel. In view of the ever-increasing commercial pressures experienced by the ship master and his crew (e.g. quick turn-around time, lower manning), it is desirable that mariners are spared as much as possible from having to provide multiple reports containing the same basic data to a number of different reporting-in points. Similarly, for safety reasons the ship's navigator must not be distracted by superfluous requests for, or excessive broadcasts of, information issued from the shore.

A useful analogy to draw in this respect is with the miller who, riding his mule to town on a hot day, began to feel sorry for it struggling along under the weight of himself and the sacks. He therefore got off the mule, put the sacks on his own back, then remounted the mule and continued his ride. Information provision systems, like VTSs, can be like this—trying to be helpful in the task at hand but in effect doing little if anything to reduce the work involved, or even adding to it.

There is some evidence from both VTS task analysis studies[8] and qualitative

[8] M. B. A. Dyer-Smith and A. F. M. De Bievre, "Easing Information Overload for Bridge Officers in Congested Waters", in *Proceedings of The Royal Institute of Navigation NAV 87 Conference on Electronics in Navigation: Data Dissemination and Display* (London, September 1987).

investigations of collisions and groundings in VTS areas[9] that "information overload" is a disturbing feature of failures in navigational safety performance, that is the VTS operator or the marine navigator does not use all the information available to him, even if it includes all the information necessary to make a correct assessment. Inappropriate data displays and misunderstanding of the man-machine interface are important contributory factors.

Much more research needs to be done, however, in order to establish whether and, if so, to what extent lack of information constitutes a core issue. Unless these questions are clarified, it remains uncertain how much benefit could be derived from the provision of additional data sources and technical aids.

The "philosophy" of ensuring that the right kind of information is made available in the right amount and at the right time to the ship's navigator/VTS operator, has been of particular concern both from the safety and the efficiency viewpoints to the regional VTS studies conducted as part of the COST–301 project.[10] These covered, in two separate studies (i) the Mediterranean region and (ii) the waters of North-West Europe reaching from Spain (north of Gibraltar) to the heart of the Baltic Sea (Finland), with the maritime boundary of those regions stretching 200 nautical miles from the coastline.

Legal aspects of Vessel Traffic Services

Whether simple or more sophisticated systems, VTS schemes have been around for a great many years and to date exist in many ports world-wide. In general, legal questions relating to the jurisdiction of existing VTS schemes in terms of their geographical coverage and regulatory and enforcement powers have been dealt with within the constraints of port laws, national legislation and international law.

The legal aspects of VTS operations have, however, come under closer scrutiny in recent years as coastal states are increasingly keen to protect their maritime interests in areas under their national jurisdiction, including those relating to ship-

[9] M. B. A. Dyer-Smith and A. F. M. De Bievre, "The Human Element in Shipping Casualties", Research Report (Phase II Draft Findings and Conclusions) to the UK Marine Directorate, Department of Transport. London (The Tavistock Institute of Human Relations, March 1988 (unpublished)).

[10] "Regional Traffic Services", in *COST–301 Main Report* (London, Easams Ltd., 1987). The core issue of the COST–301 regional studies, however, was to investigate the technologal solutions available to date for obtaining information about a vessel's identity, location, speed and course/heading independently from the ship's co-operation with the shore, i.e. by means of automated technical aids (e.g. electronic position-fixing equipment, transponders). This is important when normal ship-shore communication is not possible because the ship concerned fails to participate in the reporting requirements, e.g. due to communications equipment breakdown, or because the ship is a rogue vessel. An automated shore information system of this kind could also offer an alternative to the establishment of mandatory ship reporting systems in international waters (should this be felt desirable) as, under existing international law, coastal states have no legal powers to enforce reporting requirements beyond their territorial sea, with a few exceptions. These relate to: (i) maritime search and rescue (1979 SAR Convention); (ii) shipping casualties causing or threatening major pollution by oil or other hazardous and noxious substances (1969 Intervention Convention and its 1973 Protocol); (iii) illegal or accidental polluting discharges resulting from ship operations (Article 8 and Protocol I of 1973 MARPOL Convention); the MARPOL reporting requirements were substantially revised in 1985 and entered into force on 6 April 1987.

ping safety and the prevention and control of vessel-source pollution.[11] The discussion has taken place against the background of the general trend in favour of the extension of the territorial sea limit up to 12 nautical miles In the case of the German Bight, the Federal Republic of Germany has extended even this limit further, up to 16 nautical miles. This has enabled it to amend the COLREGS unilaterally (without prior consultation and consent of the IMO) in order to improve the safe passage, with the additional aid of the port VTSs in the area, of big tankers in the vicinity of the ecologically vulnerable Waddensea.[12] These ships are not only restricted by their draught but are also tidal as well as channel bound when approaching or leaving the German Bight ports.

In addition, the new Law of the Sea Convention ((LOSC), 1982), in spite of not yet having entered into force, has been of major influence in increasing coastal states' awareness of the new jurisdictional opportunities offered to them within a 200-nautical-mile-wide offshore area (Exclusive Economic Zone (EEZ)).

Within the context of COST–301 two legal issues in particular have been the subject of heated debate: (i) the legal base for VTS messages to have a mandatory, as opposed to non-binding, status under existing international law when they affect international shipping; (ii) the question of civil liability for loss or damage in case of a casualty where the marine navigator interacted with a VTS.

These two issues were studied by the Commission of the European Communities and the findings were submitted to COST–301 for consideration.[13] Regarding the first question, which is particularly relevant to this chapter, the following main conclusions were reached by the COST–301 participants.[14]

Coastal states cannot bypass the IMO when their regulations concerning the safety of navigation and maritime traffic, and relating to marine environmental protection, affect international shipping. Foreign flag vessels passing through their territorial sea or the coastal waters beyond it, including the EEZ which forms part of the high seas, have the right of innocent passage and, in the case of international straits coming within territorial waters, the right of transit, whilst in the EEZ such vessels enjoy freedom of navigation.

[11] For an investigation of coastal state competence and its limits see G. Kasoulides, "Jurisdiction of the Coastal State and Regulation of Shipping", in *Proceedings of the 23rd Annual Conference of the Law of the Sea Institute* (Noordwijk aan Zee, The Netherlands, June 1989). Recent international legal developments with special reference to shipping in the North Sea are discussed by T. IJlstra, "Maritime Safety Issues under the Law of the Sea Convention and their Implementation", in *Proceedings of the 23rd Annual Conference of the Law of the Sea Institute*. For a comprehensive update of international customary and convention law developments with special reference to VTS operations see G. Plant, "The International Legal Implications of Vessel Traffic Services" *Marine Policy* (January 1990).

[12] L. Gündling and J. Kokott, "Die Erweiterung der deutschen Kuestengewaesser in der Nordsee", in *Zeitschrift fuer auslaendisches oeffentliches Recht und Voelkerrecht*, 45/4 (1985); L. Gündling, "The Extension of Territorial Waters in the North Sea", (1986) 1 IJECL.

[13] A. F. M. De Bievre, *Vessel Traffic Services: Responsibilities and Liabilities*, Final Report to the Commission of the European Communities, November 1985. The Interim Report by the same author was published as "Vessel Traffic Services and the Law", *Journal of Navigation* (September 1985).

[14] "Organization for Traffic Management", in *COST–301 Main Report* (London, Easams Ltd., 1987).

With special reference to the geographical scope of application of VTS operations and whether they can have a mandatory status in international waters, it was generally felt that a VTS will not work unless it is accepted by the mariner, that is the service must not be seen as "Big Brother is Watching You". Thus, whether a VTS is legally entitled to give a binding "instruction" as opposed to simple guidance through the provision of information or advice which the ship can choose either to take on board or ignore, ought to be a non-issue in practice.

In addition, from a strict legal perspective the (customary) principle of good seamanship has been, and is, the "ultimate" authority. This rule, which in effect exempts the marine navigator from compliance with compulsory requirements under certain circumstances, has been reaffirmed with respect to VTS operations in particular by the *IMO Guidelines on Vessel Traffic Services*. Similarly, it has been embodied in advanced national maritime traffic acts that have recently been introduced and which cover VTS operations, such as the Netherlands Shipping Traffic Act which entered into force on 1 September 1988. The above-mentioned *IMO Guidelines*, in the preamble, also urge VTS authorities not to give binding directives to ships and to operate VTS on a voluntary basis outside territorial waters and port areas or their approaches.

The above conclusions might be seen as upholding the status quo, or even as evading the issue. Nevertheless, the COST–301 participants acknowledged that if benefits from additional requirements were to be identified and the need for such requirements could be established, then the adoption of a new legal instrument (or amendment to an existing instrument) should perhaps be sought but this should be done in the first instance through the IMO, as opposed to regional action.

Recent developments, both political and legal, appear to indicate that a review of the issues as described above might be considered. Public awareness of shipping casualties causing serious pollution and the continuing widespread recognition of the (albeit little understood) impact of human frailty on navigational safety have recently been spurred once again by such incidents as the Exxon Valdez disaster (March 1989) and the Humber estuary oil spill which resulted from a collision involving two tankers (September 1989). These and other events have led to renewed calls for the establishment of some kind of compulsory system for routine reporting (as opposed to reporting of incidents or casualties) to the coastal state authorities concerned by ships carrying dangerous or polluting cargoes through particularly sensitive sea areas. A similar proposal was made by the 1984 International North Sea Conference in Bremen,[15] although it did not reappear explicitly in the 1987 London Declaration.

At the legal level the most advanced proposal concerning minimum routine reporting requirements for dangerous cargo vessels concerns the EC Commission's draft Council Directive of May 24, 1989.[16] This proposes that vessels entering or leaving Community ports and which carry packages of dangerous or polluting

[15] Bremen *Declaration*, Sect. E 11.
[16] Doc. COM(89) 07 Final, pub. in *Official Journal of the European Communities*, 89/C147/03.

goods, report to the competent authorities not later than twenty-four hours (or as soon as possible for short sea voyages) before they intend to enter or sail from a port in the state concerned (draft Article 5(i)). In addition, they would be required to establish as soon as possible radiotelephone communication with the nearest coast radio or radar station in that port state and maintain such contact (draft Article 5(ii)). Where they exist, use should be made of the traffic services provided by the radar station or the local VTS (draft Article 5(iii)). Significantly, it is not proposed that these reporting requirements would apply to vessels transiting coastal waters or entering the territorial sea of a coastal state, except in case of emergency including a pollution incident or when the vessel is suffering from a safety deficiency which could threaten pollution (draft Article 6).

The case for a regional VTS in the North Sea

A possible means of providing the necessary information to VTS centres while putting the minimum load on ship personnel would be to establish some form of regional VTS. Whilst there would be some merit in having a central location for the service, there would, on the other hand, be little difficulty in operating a diversified system in which each of the coastal states would take responsibility for maintaining a picture of the traffic situation in its own sector of the North Sea.

As already mentioned, the practicality of regional VTS in North-West European waters was one of the topics studied as part of the COST–301 research programme. However, a simple information service could be of considerable benefit. Such a service would need the co-operation of all ports in the North Sea basin and there would also need to be reporting points to cover all entrances to the North Sea, augmenting the existing MAREP system which operates in the Dover Strait. Basic information, as noted above, could be supplied through ports, or reporting-in points such as coast radio stations, or VTS centres where these already exist as vessels enter the North Sea, and a real time traffic model could be maintained to estimate their positions continuously until they exit from the coverage area. Updating of the positions could be carried out as further information becomes available.

Associated with the dynamic model could be a file containing the ships' particulars, voyage data, hazardous cargo details, etc. Any VTS on the expected route of a ship could be notified of the estimated time at which it should enter the VTS coverage area and, at the same time, other relevant information concerning the ship could be supplied. Conversely, a VTS which detected an unidentified vessel entering its coverage area could interrogate the information service to establish which vessel or vessels could be expected in the observed location.

In a comprehensive form, an information service as described above could have important functions for search and rescue and for providing information to ports, in addition to its support function for local, port and coastal VTS centres. However, it would seem reasonable to introduce such a service initially only for certain classes of ships such as those carrying hazardous cargo or potential pollutants, and those which otherwise need special treatment such as substandard or disabled vessels.

An information service such as that suggested above would help existing and future VTS centres to carry out their functions more effectively and would be well within present-day communications and computing technology. It could be provided relatively cheaply, especially if it is operated as a decentralized system whereby transfer of information on a vessel's expected position from one sector to another could be made manually or automatically. A diversified regional VTS of this nature might well be more attractive politically in that it would give each coastal state an overview of what traffic was using its sector irrespective of whether it was calling at any port within that state.

Comparison may be made with the air traffic control system in Europe which still operates through mainly national flight information regions, with transitions from one centre to another as aircraft cross the regions' boundaries. The exception is the Eurocontrol system which was set up with the aim of providing air traffic control facilities over the upper airspace of the six initial Member States. However, the United Kingdom and France later decided that they would retain national control of their own airspace and the Eurocontrol system therefore has limited application.

Although comparisons between air traffic and sea traffic are not always useful, it is of interest to note that most of the existing VTS centres in the North Sea operate in port approaches and have a function comparable to airport approach control centres. However, apart from the Dover Strait, there is nothing comparable with the main air traffic control network which ensures the *en route* safety of aircraft from airport to airport. Probably there is no need for the close tracking of ships in the *en route* stage in that properly managed ships are able to conduct their own collision avoidance activities which aircraft are not.

Conclusion

The need for additional VTS centres in the North Sea, whether local (port or coastal) centres or regional VTS (centralized or diversified), has to be considered in relation to other measures which affect safety of navigation. A method of applying cost-benefit analysis techniques to assist in making decisions concerning the need for a VTS in a particular location has been developed, as part of the COST–301 project, by Goss and Halliday working at the University of Wales Institute of Science and Technology.[17] This should be of considerable help in ensuring that VTS is established as and where it can be of real benefit.

However, where a new VTS is set up, the protection of the environment should be given adequate weighting in comparison with the other aims of traffic safety and efficiency, and the design and operation of the system should take account of this.

[17] "Costs and Benefits of Vessel Traffic Services", in *COST–301 Main Report* (Easams Ltd., 1987).

Chapter 16

Paris Memorandum of Understanding: A Regional Regime of Enforcement

Dr. George Kasoulides

The first developments: the Hague memorandum

All North European countries have substantial maritime interests and deal with matters of maritime safety and navigation within the limits of the international rules relating to jurisdiction but as yet these states do not have a comprehensive treaty or commission regulating or harmonizing laws concerning pollution from various sources. Nevertheless, there are several regional conventions regulating different aspects of pollution within the framework of which, supplemented by the international legal standards, North European states continue to develop their national laws and co-operate in their implementation and enforcement.

As around 25 per cent of the world's shipping accidents occur in European waters and some catastrophic disasters have occurred there, such as the foundering of the Amoco Cadiz in March 1978, the need for more stringent measures against substandard vessels was first felt in the North Sea area. Following the proliferation of maritime treaties reaffirming the port state's concurrent powers over foreign vessels, especially the adoption of the ILO Convention No. 147 on Minimum Standards,[1] which enabled port states to inspect safety and working conditions on board all ships entering their ports, all North Sea states, as a limited first step to improve enforcement, adopted the so-called Hague Memorandum on Port State Control (PSC), which came into operation in 1978.[2] The agreement merely laid down a general surveillance procedure aimed at verifying that a number of requirements derived from various international agreements were met and that conditions on board ships were not hazardous to safety or health.

[1] Reproduced in (1976) XV ILM 1288, 1984 UKTS 22 (Cmnd 9186) (hereinafter cited as the ILO Convention No.147).

[2] Reproduced in the HC Paper 105-III (1978–1979), "Measures to Prevent Collisions and Strandings of Noxious Cargo Carriers in Waters around the United Kingdom", pp. 91–99. The parties to Hague MOU were: Belgium, Denmark, France, FRG, The Netherlands, Norway, Sweden and the United Kingdom.

Unfortunately the Hague MOU failed to have any real effect on pollution and prevention of accidents and the EC decided to launch its own proposal for an effective enforcement regime. The EC proposal was directed against substandard vessels[3] and aimed at establishing uniform enforcement procedures throughout the community. The EC initiative, however, did not proceed further as a result of a parallel action by the national maritime authorities of its Member States. A conference of European ministers responsible for maritime safety, convened in Paris in December 1980,[4] unanimously agreed that the elimination of substandard shipping should be their mutual aim, best served by preventive action. A second Ministerial Conference of 14 countries met in Paris in January 1982, and approved the draft text prepared. The new document, the so-called Paris Memorandum of Understanding,[5] was signed by the North Sea states, parties to the Hague MOU but joined also by Finland, Greece, Ireland, Italy, Portugal and Spain. The following sections examine its structure, the extent of the legal obligations created for the parties, and an attempt will be made to evaluate the effectiveness of the Memorandum and its impact in its seven years of operation.

Structure of the Paris MOU

The Paris MOU came into force in July 1982. Its membership is wider than that envisaged in the draft Directive which would have applied only to EC members, although other states could adhere to it with the consent of the community participants. The Ministerial meeting was also attended by IMO, ILO and EC representatives. IMO and ILO were accorded observer status and could participate in the work of the Port State Control Committee.

Port State Control Committee

This is the executive body of the MOU composed of representatives from each of the fourteen participating maritime authorities and a representative from the EC Commission. The Committee has the task of carrying out and promoting the specific assignments allocated to it under the MOU, including the holding of seminars for surveyors, the harmonization of procedures and practices relating to inspection, rectification, detention and the application of the so-called no more favourable treatment clause.[6]

[3] "Proposal for a Council Directive concerning the Enforcement, in Respect of Shipping using Community Ports, of International Standards for Shipping Safety and Pollution Prevention", COM(80) 360.

[4] H. E. Huibers, "Safe Transport of Dangerous Goods by Sea Promoted by Control in Port: The Reciprocal Effect of Port State Control under the Memorandum of Understanding' on the Carriage by Sea of Dangerous Goods", presented at the Ninth International Symposium on the Transport and Handling of Dangerous Goods by Sea and Inland Waters (TDG–9), Rotterdam (1987), pp. 431, 432.

[5] Reproduced in (1982) XXI ILM 1 (hereinafter cited as the Paris MOU).

[6] *Ibid.* 6.1–6.3.

Administration

Secretariat facilities are provided by the Netherlands and its functions, under the guidance of the Committee, include, *inter alia*, the preparation of meetings and reports and facilitation of the exchange of information.[7]

Computer centre

The third institution within the organizational structure under the MOU is the computer centre. It is located in France and here all inspection records are inserted into a common inspection file. Daily reports of the inspections undertaken are sent to St. Malo Computer Centre—"The Centre Administratif des Affaires Maritimes"—and this information is accessible for verification and updating by means of on-line terminals in the PSC countries.[8] At regular intervals statistics are processed from the inspection data stored in the computer. Most of the parties are connected to the computer, with on-line terminals, SIRENAC system[9] but a few still use a telex line. The aim is to develop the system in such a way that in the future surveyors in the various countries will be able to communicate from terminal to terminal on all levels and eliminate duplicate inspections.

The computer facilities are also used on an experimental basis as an "electronic mailbox". This, when finalized, will allow terminal operators throughout the region to communicate by means of messages that appear on the addressee's screen, using the CAAM computer as the mailbox.

Jurisdictional scope of the Paris MOU

The MOU's principal elements are: (a) that the chief responsibility for the effective application of standards lies with the flag state; and (b) that the rights and obligations of the participating states are supreme under any international agreement.[10] Authorities are also obliged to apply those relevant instruments which are in force and to which they are parties.[11]

At the time of the adoption of the MOU there was an implicit understanding that the PSC partners should ratify the relevant instruments to avoid "significant variations in inspection procedures and any consequent distortions of competition".[12]

The relevant instruments for the purpose of the Paris MOU are:
the 1966 International Convention on Load Lines;[13]
the 1974/78 SOLAS Convention;[14]

[7] *Ibid.* 6.4.
[8] *Ibid.* 4 Annex 4.
[9] Système d'information rélatif aux navires controlés.
[10] Paris MOU, 8.1. Emphasis added.
[11] *Ibid.* 2.3.
[12] A. V. Lowe, "A Move against Substandard Shipping" (1982) 6 *Marine Policy* 326, 327.
[13] Art. 21, 640 UNTS 133 (hereinafter cited as the 1966 Load Lines Convention).
[14] Regulation 19 of Chapter 1; Regulation 2 of Chapter 8; reproduced in (1978) XVII ILM 579; 1981 UKTS 40 (hereinafter cited as SOLAS 74/78).

the 1973/78 MARPOL Convention;[15]
the 1978 STCW Convention;[16]
the 1972 COLREG;[17]
the 1976 ILO Convention No 147.[18]

Seven years after the adoption of the MOU only Ireland has not ratified all relevant instruments.[19] This implies that vessels calling at community ports are, at large, submitted to a uniform set of inspection procedures or the same regulations and standards.

Inspection procedures

Inspection procedures are included in Annex I of the MOU, supplemented by guidelines adopted by IMO. Section 3 provides that:

> "3.3 In selecting ships for inspection, the Authorities will pay special attention to:
> a) ships which may present a special hazard, for instance oil-tankers and gas and chemical carriers;
> b) ships which have several recent deficiencies.
> 3.4 The Authorities will seek to avoid inspecting ships which have been inspected by any of the other Authorities within the previous six months, unless they have clear grounds for inspection."

An inspector must use his so-called professional judgement on these matters; the parties have explicitly decided against the use of check-lists during inspections but they organize yearly seminars, arrange for the exchange of surveyors between different maritime authorities and are planning joint training on certain aspects of the MOU.[20]

Seminars for surveyors are held on an annual basis. The aim of these seminars is to harmonize inspection procedures and to facilitate discussion of the interpretation of various requirements of the relevant instruments.

So far no uniform inspection routines have been worked out, though the PSC Committee agreed at its meeting in November 1983 to observe the IMO standards as guidelines for surveyors. Each surveyor is provided with a manual, containing, *inter alia*, references to convention provisions, sections and Articles of the MOU

[15] Art. 5(2); reproduced in (1978) XVII ILM 546; (hereinafter cited as the MARPOL 73/78).
[16] Art. 10(1); 1984 UKTS 50; (Cmnd 9266) (hereinafter cited as the 1978 STCW).
[17] "Convention for the International Regulations for Preventing Collisions at Sea", 1977 UKTS 77; reproduced in (1973) XII ILM 734.
[18] ILO Convention No. 147, Art. 4.
[19] It has yet to ratify MARPOL 73/78 and the 1976 ILO No. 147, See "1988 Annual Report of the Memorandum", Annex 1.
[20] See G. C. Kasoulides, "Paris Memorandum of Understanding: Six Years of Regional Enforcement" (1989) 20 *Marine Pollution Bulletin* 255–261; S. Maier, "Port State Control: Does it Work?" in *Money and Ships in the City* (1985), pp. 113–117 (transcript of the 13th Money and Ships Conference held at London, 1985; G. A. Dubbeld, "The Role of Port State Inspectors", presented at the INTERTANKO's Annual Meeting in Scheveningen, The Hague, on *Port State Control: Safety at Sea* (Oslo, 1984), pp. 16–24.

and Codes for the information system. The "Manual for Inspectors" is reviewed and updated annually by the PSC Committee. When the inspection is concluded the inspector provides the vessel with a document giving the results of the inspection and details of any action taken. At the same time the findings enter the computer system of the region. All other surveyors consult this database before going on board a ship.[21]

If the ship is found to be in order then in principle it should be immune from further inspections in PSC countries for the next six months.[22] However, if clear grounds are present of substandard conditions the surveyor can overrule this restriction and go ahead with a thorough and detailed inspection.

Similarly, if the required certificates are not on board or are not valid, or often in cases where all certificates are impeccable but the condition of the ship does not correspond substantially with the particulars of the certificate the inspection conducted is thorough in all fields covered by the "relevant instruments" and such inspection might establish the vessel's substandard condition.

The application of the "no more favourable treatment" formula is a standard practice in recent conventions and the MOU is no exception. Nevertheless, the relevant section of the MOU is rather ambiguous. According to it:

> "In applying a relevant instrument for the purposes of port state control, the Authorities will ensure that no more favourable treatment is given to ships entitled to fly the flag of a State which is not a Party to these instruments."[23]

This formulation could be interpreted as allowing the enforcement of standards contained in conventions even if those conventions do not include a relevant provision to this effect. This provoked a number of objections from shipowners and other states and the governments of the USSR and the German Democratic Republic, in particular. In replies to a note verbale from the United Nations Conference on Trade and Development (UNCTAD),[24] these countries insisted that inspection of vessels sailing under the flags of states not parties to the international conventions could be carried out by a port state only when control provisions were specifically provided for in such conventions. This point, however, has been clarified in repeated statements from the MOU Secretariat. The provision, according to this interpretation, has been designed in order not to put a premium on non-ratification of a convention and in practice has proved non-controversial. According to the Secretariat no complaints have been directed against the MOU concerning improper use of its jurisdiction and inspection procedures.[25] On the other hand surveyors are obliged not to impose stricter requirements on the foreign vessels than they would impose on ships flying their national flag.[26]

[21] Paris MOU, 3.10.
[22] *Ibid.* 3.4.
[23] *Ibid.* 2.4. and Annex, para. 1.3.
[24] UNCTAD, TD 623/8, 9 February 1983.
[25] Huibers, "Safe Transport of Dangerous Goods", 438.
[26] Paris MOU, 1.2.

Enforcement powers

If deficiencies are found the master will have to complete the required adjustments or repairs before the ship leaves that port. In principle, this means that most vessels can follow their schedule without unnecessary and costly delays. However, between four and six per cent of vessels inspected were delayed or detained during the first seven years of the MOU operation owing to serious deficiencies. According to the MOU:

> "In the case of deficiencies which are clearly hazardous to safety, health or the environment, the Authority will . . . ensure that the ship is not allowed to proceed to sea and for this purpose will take appropriate action, which may include detention."[27]

This is the ultimate "preventive" sanction imposed by the MOU. No penalties are imposed on the master or the crew of the vessel but it should be emphasized that a port state may impose penal sanctions and fines in compliance with its other international obligations or national requirements, a right well within its competence to enforce its legislation inside its territory.

In cases where the port lacks the appropriate facilities for repairs the authority "may allow the ship to proceed to another port subject to any appropriate conditions determined by the Authority with a view to ensuring that the ship can so proceed without unreasonable danger to safety, health or the environment."[28] The next port of call in the region, the flag state and other interested authorities should also be notified. A reason for concern is that in cases of vessels in distress or where the hazard to the port state is grave and serious a ship might be ordered into international waters without any efforts undertaken to remedy the situation and prevent an imminent disaster.

Another important element in the inspection procedures is that MOU partners regard the ships of another MOU partner as foreign ships for the purpose of their inspections. Figures released indicate that a great percentage of inspections are actually executed on ships of other PSC parties.

Inspection results

The MOU imposed on its parties a quantitative criterion. According to Section 1.3 "each Authority will achieve an annual total of inspections corresponding to 25 per cent of the estimated number of foreign merchant ships". According to the information released by the Secretariat, a number of states have not met this objective and the average percentage of inspections has stabilised at around 18 to 20 per cent.[29] The main reason for this is either a shortage of personnel in the national

[27] *Ibid.* 3.7.

[28] *Ibid.* 3.8.

[29] The MOU has introduced a new method of calculating the number of inspected vessels but according to the Secretariat the number of inspections shows a tendency to stabilize around 11,500, an approximate percentage of 70% of the ships present in the region at any moment, "Annual Report of the MOU" (1988).

inspection services or, according to some authorities, the small number of non-inspected vessels visiting their ports.[30] A handicap for the evaluation of this information is the lack of evidence on the performance of individual states since the Secretariat releases information only in relation to the region. There is no free access to the relevant data held at the computer centre and it is almost impossible to evaluate the behaviour of individual governments. The Annual Reports include statements indicating that "the summarized percentage . . . continue to equalize"[31] and that inspection efforts per Maritime Authority are "balancing out"[32] but there is no concrete information on individual performance.

During research for this study all European states were requested to supply information concerning their own national records, the percentage of inspections, deficiencies and detentions. According to the replies received no state publishes individual statistics on this matter and all declined to comment on the percentage of vessels inspected in their own national ports.

The achieved percentage is, on most accounts, a satisfactory one but the MOU partners would benefit from a more detailed and vigorous investigation of the existing information files in order to establish the emerging trends relating to the inspections by each country and, if possible, by individual ports, and the type and condition of vessels inspected in each area.

This should enable the MOU parties to pin-point its less effective sub-regions and to consider the kind of services needed and the nature of training offered. The result would be a better management and allocation of resources, individual parties might offer training facilities and improve the system of exchanging information. This need was highlighted by requests from representatives of the shipping industry for the release of more information on the seriousness of certain deficiencies and the specification of more technical details in order to assist the efforts being made to improve safety conditions.

The reply of the MOU was that its present system was focused mainly on the exchange of information on the results of inspections and the series of deficiency codes that had been developed was more directed to reduction of transmission costs than statistical purposes.

The PSC Committee, however, accepted that in order to evaluate adequately the qualitative aspects of PSC under the MOU a more detailed differentiation of deficiency aspects should be considered. This will eventually lead to an improvement of the description and the specification of the deficient item. The development of a new deficiency coding system was approved in 1987.

At the same time the PSC Committee considered and rejected the notion of an inclusive list of deficiencies graded in order of importance, their characterisation as major or minor and whether they justified delay or detention of the ship. As was pointed out by the Secretary of the MOU, "accumulation of many minor' deficiencies may justify delay or detention, while on the other hand only one "major"

[30] Huibers, "Safe Transport of Dangerous Goods", 440.
[31] "Annual Report of the MOU", 20.
[32] *Ibid.*

deficiency need not necessarily lead to detention".[33] While leaving the final decision to the professional judgement of the surveyor is the best approach, inspectors should be assisted by the gradual development of non-binding guidelines or recommendations for assessing the seriousness of particular deficiencies and their implications for the safe operation of a vessel. Such guidelines would be of assistance not only to inspectors but also to the shipping industry in implementing the necessary specifications and to the international community in establishing a harmonized system of inspections and penalties.

Statistical data on deficiencies and detentions

The Annual Reports of the MOU include a considerable amount of statistical information derived from the inspection files stored in the computer. This information includes the number of inspections carried out; number of delays and detentions; number of inspections per flag state; major categories of deficiencies, with a breakdown of most common deficiencies (i.e., in ship's certificates, life-saving appliances; fire-fighting appliances, safety in general, navigational aids, marine pollution).

In 1988 295 ships (1982/83: 271, 1983/84: 436, 1984: 476, 1985: 356, 1986: 307, 1987: 280) were detained or delayed due to serious deficiencies. This amounts to 3.52 per cent of the ships inspected—an absolute and proportionate increase compared with the 1987 figures. (2.71 per cent). A similar erratic picture appears from an examination of the range of deficiencies which shows that in 1988 the number of deficiencies per inspection amounted to 1.35 per cent (cf. 1987: 1.45 per cent, 1986: 1.34 per cent) and 1.89 per cent per individual ship (cf. 1987: 1.60 per cent, 1986: 1.80 per cent).[34]

A possible interpretation of the overall slight decline in delays and detentions or both may be that they indicate that fewer substandard vessels visit the region whereas the increase in deficiencies might be attributed to the more detailed and sophisticated inspection routine. Nevertheless, it is submitted that no firm conclusion can be drawn from an examination of these factors since, as was explained earlier, the present system of recording information on the computer is simply informative and descriptive and is not sufficiently detailed to allow comprehensive technical analysis.

A question frequently asked is whether the introduction of the MOU has had any real effect on substandard shipping and thus improved the quality of vessels visiting the European ports. The statistical data provided by the Secretariat do not produce any clear evidence of this but officials in a number of ports were satisfied that there was an apparent improvement in the condition of vessels even if this was a very slow process.

No information is disclosed on individual vessels but information is provided on the number of inspections and the flag states of the vessels concerned. Vessels from

[33] Huibers, "Safe Transport of Dangerous Goods", 439.
[34] "Annual Report of the MOU", 22.

124 flag states were inspected in 1988, predominantly those from other participating countries. Other states with a significant percentage of inspected vessels are Cyprus, Honduras, Gibraltar, Iran, Hong Kong, Japan, Liberia, Malta, Panama, Singapore, St. Vincent & Grenadines, Turkey, the USSR, Poland and Yugoslavia.[35]

Clearly, no firm conclusions can be drawn concerning countries not regularly inspected, but an encouraging factor is that a number of states evidenced a better record during the second, i.e., 1988, period (Malta 1985: 37.18 per cent, 1988: 10.35 per cent; Gibraltar 1985: 27.73 per cent, 1988: 12.12 per cent; Algeria 1985: 20 per cent, 1988: 4 per cent). On the other hand an increase was actually reported in the cases of Egypt, Honduras, Morocco, Romania and Turkey.

These figures are still not very reliable and have appeared only in the last four years but in the light of them a number of interesting observations can be made, namely,

1. The number of ships calling at European ports come from virtually all areas of the world but the greater percentage is "regional shipping", i.e. from neighbouring countries.
2. Substandard conditions and deficiencies appear in a great number of vessels from different states but serious examples of such conditions occur and recur mainly in vessels registered in developing states (including open registries).
3. Some open registries have an exceptionally good record (compared with developing states), while others evidence a percentage of detentions or delays that is fairly similar to the record of other developing states.
4. Conditions vary from year to year so that it is not possible, as yet, to evaluate the impact of the inspection results.[36]
5. There is no firm information on the movement and trends of shipping on a global basis from which it could be established whether substandard shipping is simply transferred from the European region to other less regulated areas. The confidentiality surrounding information on individual vessels also does not allow such an evaluation.

Regulation of discharges

The measures included in the MOU are supplemented by an obligation to co-operate in the detection of operational violations; this for the first time relates PSC "not to the condition of the ship but to its activities". According to Section 5:

> "The Authorities will upon the request of another Authority endeavour to secure evidence relating to suspected violations of the requirements on operational matters of Rule 10 of the International Regulations for Preventing Collisions at Sea 1972, and the International Convention for the Prevention of Pollution from Ships, 1973, as modified by the Protocol of 1978, relating

[35] This was based on the average performance during the seven years of operation of the Memorandum.

[36] i.e. the sudden appearance of Iran in the top of the detention list in 1988 could be associated to the end of the Gulf war whereas the disappearance of Lebanon could be attributed to the civil war ravaging this country.

thereto. In case of suspected violations involving the discharge of harmful substances, an Authority will, upon the request of another Authority, visit in port the ship suspected of such a violation in order to obtain information and where appropriate to take a sample of the alleged pollutant."

Three annexes of the MARPOL are now in force, Annex I on oil tankers, Annex II on chemical tankers and Annex V on prevention on pollution from garbage.

It is encouraging that participating states are willing to enhance the rudimentary provisions on discharges and co-operate in their application. This should include the adoption of a uniform system based on general principles of ship reporting systems for many purposes including search and rescue, VTS, weather forecasting and prevention of marine pollution.

The computerized information system should be also made more readily available for retrieval of information, comparison of existing data and verification of suspected violations. These facilities should be gradually made available to other states or regions on a negotiated bilateral or multilateral basis; a first step should be closer co-operation with IMO and the acceptance of an obligation undertaken on the part of the MOU partners to provide this organization with all required information on subjects within its jurisdiction.

Reaction of the shipping industry

The MOU was viewed with suspicion by some parts of the shipping industry as well as individual shipowners. The International Shipowners' Association (INSA) declared in 1982 that MOU inspections were an illegal means of delaying vessels and detrimental to the shipping interests.[37] The International Association of Independent Tanker Owners (INTERTANKO), however, wholeheartedly supported the initiative, expressing the view that "idealistically there are important reasons for working for a unified PSC world-wide."[38] The rationale behind this attitude is, according to INTERTANKO, the complete inconsistency of inspection procedures in different countries, the reporting of minor and trivial deficiencies and the conduct of double or triple inspections in the same port adding to the total workload and frustration of the crew. But INTERTANKO also considered that more surveyors should be recruited and properly trained. As long as, however, flag states shoulder their responsibilities and port states do not discriminate INTERTANKO consider that the MOU "should promote sounder competition in the tanker market."[39] It also reported that the available information did not indicate that any ship had been wrongfully delayed or detained.

Co-operation with other interested parties

The establishment of the MOU was followed closely by a number of other states interested in such an institution, especially by Australia, Canada, Japan and the

[37] L. Buchingham, "INSA Sees Inspections as Means of Illegal Delay", Lloyd's List, 25 Oct. 1982.
[38] INTERTANKO, European Port State Control (1983), p. 3.
[39] *Ibid*. 4.

United States, which exercise strict PSC in their own ports. Observers from Japan and the United States also attend the annual seminars of surveyors. This activity should be encouraged and the PSC parties should also invite observers from developing states to participate to demonstrate the effectiveness of the PSC on a national or regional level, offering at the same time an opportunity to exchange information and attend training seminars.

A keen interest in establishing formal arrangements for co-operation has been expressed by parts of the shipping industry, especially charterers and insurance companies. They have suggested to the MOU on a number of occasions that the identity of ships repeatedly categorized as substandard should be disclosed to benefit environmental protection and the image of the shipping industry. This information is available only to other parties of the MOU or the flag state of the vessel on request and payment! The PSC Committee, however, continued to maintained that publication of a "black list" could be misconstrued and interference with sovereignty would not in itself eliminate the operation of substandard vessels.

Final developments: the safe ships for clean seas conference

The Preamble to the MOU included agreement among its parties to hold a new conference in 1984 to discuss and review the MOU in the light of the experience gained. This conference, entitled "Safe Ships on Clean Seas" finally took place in April 1986. Its Final Declaration,[40] re-affirmed the importance of the implementation of international standards by flag states. The Ministers also concluded that it was increasingly difficult for a substandard vessel to operate in the region without being detected and forced to rectify any serious deficiencies. Other important decisions and conclusions included the following:

1. It was considered necessary that appropriate regulations for the prevention of marine pollution included in Annexes III, and V of MARPOL should enter into force as soon as possible.
2. The parties expressed great interest in the development of PSC in other regions and welcomed any kind of co-operation with countries aiming at improving their efficiency in the field of exchanges of views on procedures and requested the PSC Committee to develop co-operation with the maritime authorities of the United States and Japan.

The International North Sea Conferences on the Protection of the North Sea

The first INSC was convened by the government of the German Federal Republic in Bremen in October 1984. It discussed the implementation of the measures necessary for the protection of the North Sea.[41] The Final Declaration[42] of the con-

[40] The *Final Declaration* is reproduced in "Annual Report of the MOU" (1986/87), Annex 7.
[41] The conference was attended by Ministers responsible for the protection of the environment from the following North Sea states: Belgium, Denmark, France, FRG, The Netherlands, Norway, the UK and the Commissioner of the EC responsible for environmental protection.
[42] The text of the Final Act is reproduced in (1985) 14 *Environmental Policy and Law*, pp. 32–36.

ference included, *inter alia*, a comprehensive set of protective measures for the reduction of pollution at sea. According to these proposals the North Sea states will pursue the detection, prosecution and punishment of violations of anti-pollution regulations and will ensure stringent controls on ships entering their ports in accordance with the Memorandum of Understanding on PSC. Enforcement should also be strengthened through more vigorous airborne surveillance.

The Second International Conference was convened in London in November 1987.[43] The main issues discussed at the conference were dumping, incineration and land-based pollution and in the case of the MOU they agreed to

> "continue to co-operate under the Memorandum of Understanding on Port State Control so that after the detection of operational violations all reports on alleged pollution incidents are dealt with speedily and effectively, so as to ensure that ships reported in respect of an alleged pollution incident will be subject to stringent and wide-ranging inspection procedures in ports, that prosecution of a violation under MARPOL 73/78 will be facilitated, and that the documentation for prosecution of violations under MARPOL 73/78 will be improved."[44]

Airborne surveillance is also stipulated as an effective aid to enforcing anti-pollution regulations. Nevertheless no specific measures to strengthen or expand the MOU are elaborated.[45]

Conclusions

The MOU was clearly perceived by the relevant maritime administrations as a formal co-operative regime on enforcement issues but not as an international regime creating new legal rights and obligations for its parties. The preceding analysis has showed this to be the case and the regime is managed by the administrations concerned.

The Secretariat is also manned by civil servants appointed by, and funded exclusively by, The Netherlands without any interference from the other participating parties. There is no question that in its present form the MOU is less rigid than its predecessor and allows the maritime authorities to concentrate on technical and other serious topics adopting a realistic and pragmatic approach. The ratification of conventions by participants was speeded up and some of its parties improved their inspection rates to an unprecedented level.

The method of processing the information and the low cost incurred is also another incentive for administrations which demand a high return but on a very tight budget.

[43] *Second International Conference on the Protection of the North Sea, London, 24–25 November 1987, Ministerial Declaration, issued by the Department of the Environment of the United Kingdom, April 1988*; G. C. Kasoulides, "London North Sea Conference", (1988) 19 *Marine Pollution Bulletin* 97–99; (1988) 9 *Hazardous Cargo Bulletin* 16–17.

[44] *Ministerial Declaration*, para. 29.

[45] *Ibid*. paras. 46–50.

The pragmatic and conservative approach adopted also allayed the fears of the industry and the rest of the world since the application of the regional measures were well within the existing international requirements and standards and every precaution was taken not to delay vessels unnecessarily or to interfere with the internal order of a foreign vessel.

Nonetheless, it might be time for the PSC Committee and the Ministers concerned to consider an expansion of the role of the port state and the Paris regime in general. Such expansion might include the inclusion of other relevant issues such as increasing the availability of reception facilities and strengthening discharge standards included in international maritime conventions. Participating states might pursue these aims under the auspices of the IMO and encourage more regional groups to adopt a co-ordinated PSC in their own national waters.

Chapter 17

The Role of the Courts in the Enforcement of Environmental Rules

Professor E. Somers

Writing about the role of the courts in the enforcement process of environmental rules necessarily requires first of all a look, albeit in a general way, at the enforcement process in international law before moving to environmental law. One may get the impression from the title of this contribution that in the field of enforcing environmental rules the courts have a specific task to perform. Basically this is not the case. The foremost function of a court is to solve legal disputes that are brought before it, normally by applying rules and norms that constitute the law. In deciding a case the court must therefore establish what the law is, how rules and norms must be interpreted and eventually even take part in the law-creating process. In several instances the courts have transformed the existing law through creative interpretation. Furthermore, decisions, especially repetitive, similar decisions often acquire an authority influencing the formulation of legal norms in subsequent cases.[1] In some cases the judge is obliged to act as if he were a legislator when he finds a gap in the law.[2] We must nevertheless bear in mind that the authority of courts may not be as strong in some parts of the world (e.g. Eastern Europe, Asia, Africa) as in others (e.g. Western Europe and North America). In the former parts of the world it may be considered unacceptable to leave the decision of general legal questions—particularly decisions which fill gaps in the existing legal system—to a court. Environmental law might be expected to form a field of (international) law where the judiciary could express its creative capacity. Whether this is actually the case with regard to environmental rules in the field of marine pollution is, however, at first glance, doubtful.

[1] W. Levi, *Contemporary International Law: A Concise Introduction* (Boulder, Colo.: Westview Press, 1979), 53.
[2] Cf. W. Friedmann, *Law in a Changing Society* (Harmondsworth: Penguin Books, 1972), 45 ff.

Enforcement of international law in general

Under international law a state has the capacity, as a manifestation of its sovereignty, to prescribe and to enforce a rule of law. A distinction is thus drawn between prescriptive jurisdiction and enforcement jurisdiction. The latter embraces acts to enforce the results of the prescriptive jurisdiction, either by some form of administrative action or by way of judicial action through the courts.[3] It is a process by which a regulation is made effective or a process designed to compel obedience to a legal rule. Enforcement grants the state the competence to adopt reasonable measures to compel, induce compliance, or to impose sanctions for non-compliance, with applicable laws, regulations, or enforceable judgments by means of administrative or executive action, or judicial proceedings.[4] International law, however, will only be directly enforced by municipal courts in a few areas, such as the protection of property of aliens and cases of diplomatic and sovereign immunity. Most international legal rules have first to be transformed into municipal law before a municipal court will take them into consideration since the bulk of international law is not self-executing. In general, much of international law is left to states to enforce, thus operationalizing the principles expressed in law.

Enforcement of international environmental rules

Enforcement was traditionally deemed to be inherent in any rule of law. A legal rule had in itself, once enacted, a call for enforcement. The concept of enforcement with regard to marine pollution can be referred to as enforcement *sensu lato* and enforcement *sensu strictu*.[5] *Sensu lato* the concept comprises all measures or methods for the effective application of the legal rules concerning marine pollution. Most of these measures or methods are to be enacted by some governmental or administrative authority. For instance the establishment of material conditions for the application of legal rules such as the organization of inspection facilities, can be seen in this way. On the other hand, enforcement *sensu strictu* refers to the process for sanctioning violations of marine pollution regulations. It is a continuous and inseparable process that contains various stages leading to a judicial appraisal. Through the decision of the court the violated legal rule is upheld and once the judgment is enforced legal effect is given to the sanction. Nevertheless, the other stages of enforcement jurisdiction are usually not entrusted to a court. Reporting the violation and collecting all evidence and necessary material is in normal circumstances a policing task.

Furthermore, enforcement jurisdiction can be subdivided into the competence to arrest (arrest jurisdiction) and the final competence of courts to deal with alleged

[3] D. Bowett, "Jurisdiction: Changing Patterns of Authority over Activities and Resources", in R. Macdonald and D. Johnston (eds.), *The Structure and Process of International Law* (The Hague: M. Nijhoff, 1983), 555.

[4] Wang Cheng-Pang, "A Review of the Enforcement Regime for Vessel- Source Oil Pollution Control" (1986) *Ocean Development and International Law* 309.

[5] Cf. G. Gtimagenis, *International Control of Marine Pollution* (Dobbs Ferry, NY: Oceana Publications, 1980), i. 57–64.

violations of the law (judicial jurisdiction). With regard to marine pollution the problem of enforcement jurisdiction carries the heavy burden of dispersion: each stage of the enforcement process may be entrusted to a different state and under different circumstances. In connection with vessel source pollution, for instance, the enforcement jurisdiction (also the legislative jurisdiction) that a state has in respect of a particular vessel will depend on whether it is a flag state, coastal state or port state.[6]

Throughout history, enforcement has always been the weakest part of international efforts regulating marine pollution. Developments in this field have shown that traditional enforcement methods were not able to meet new phenomena, in particular the universality of environmental problems. In general the record of enforcement and compliance with international environmental legal rules has, for a considerable time, been thoroughly disappointing. Due to the deficiency of several of the above-mentioned stages (detection of violations, etc.) and often the lack of implementation of the international environmental rules in the national legal order, enforcement jurisdiction has never been fully exercised. It is therefore not at all surprising that the construction of a more impressive and effective enforcement regime became one of the major pollution issues at UNCLOS III.[7] Moreover, pleas have been made for a co-ordinated regional enforcement policy.[8] The enforcement regime with regard to marine pollution is contained in the specific marine pollution conventions and is—similarly to the regulatory system—distinguished and differentiated on the basis of the source of pollution. Prima facie, the role of the courts within this enforcement regime does not seem to be a crucial one.

Enforcement with respect to vessel-source pollution

Traditionally, enforcement powers over vessels for pollution rested primarily with the flag states, save that on a customarily law basis coastal states had enforcement jurisdiction for pollution offences occurring in their territorial sea. Considering the fact that states have sovereignty over their territorial sea this is not surprising, nothwithstanding the existence of a right of innocent passage for international navigation. Moreover the 1973 MARPOL convention requires coastal states to apply and enforce their pollution provisions against all vessels in the territorial sea (Article 4, para. 2). On a customarily law basis and based on state sovereignty, a limited concept of port state jurisdiction also developed, allowing prosecution for violations in the territorial sea and internal waters of the port state. Besides, port state inspection schemes were developed in MARPOL (Article 6, para. 2) and through the "Memorandum of Understanding on Port State Control in Implementing Agreements on Maritime Safety and Protection of the Marine Environment" providing

[6] R. Churchill and A. Lowe, *The Law of the Sea* (Manchester: Manchester University Press, 1983), 222–223.

[7] A. Boyle, "Marine Pollution Under the Law of the Sea Convention" (1985) *AJIL* 363.

[8] Cf. T. IJlstra, "Enforcement of International Environmental Instruments in the North Sea: The Missing Link", in *Reasons for Concern*, Proceedings of the Second North Sea Seminar 1986, Amsterdam, Werkgroep Noordzee, 1987, pp. 289–313.

for port state inspection in Europe.[9] The very basis of the enforcement regime, however, remained within the ambit of the flag state which was free—apart from the obligation to enforce MARPOL provisions—to choose whatever action to take, if any was to be taken at all. The deficiency of the system was proven by the showing of a consistent unwillingness of many flag states to enforce pollution regulations against their ships. Of course the deficient detection system of violations and the great difficulties proving actual violations have contributed substantially to the poor enforcement record. In fact enforcement has been the most difficult problem in protecting the marine environment because it not only involves jurisdiction but also technical regulations. Sometimes, violations of technical regulations are virtually impossible to prove.[10]

In general the role of the courts with regard to enforcement jurisdiction seems to have been rather limited. Problems with implementation of international rules in the national legal order, thus ruling out any competence of a national court, and the deficiency of the enforcement jurisdiction stages preceding judicial enforcement, prevented courts from playing fully the role they might have been expected to. It is therefore not so difficult to imagine that this system, predominantly based on flag state enforcement, was often severely criticized by coastal states as being highly ineffective.

The 1982 Law of the Sea Convention introduced an enforcement machinery which is an improvement of the existing law, rather than a radical revision of it. Although the basis is still flag state jurisdiction, the 1982 Convention reflects clearly some movement away from the primacy of flag-state enforcement jurisdiction. A universal enforcement jurisdiction of the port state is provided for and extensive powers have been attributed to the coastal state, especially in order to protect their sovereign rights in the EEZ. Flag states undertake the obligation to ensure compliance by their vessels with applicable international pollution rules and standards and with their national law adopted to protect the marine environment. To this end they shall take the necessary measures to implement such laws and regulations and they shall provide for the effective enforcement of them (Article 217, para. 1). Flag states shall, in particular, take appropriate measures to prevent substandard vessels from putting to sea (Article 217, para. 2). Furthermore, they shall ensure that their vessels obtain appropriate international certificates for seaworthiness and other requirements and are inspected regularly (Article 217, para. 3). Judicial enforcement jurisdiction is specifically provided for if a vessel commits a violation of pollution rules and standards: flag states shall conduct investigations and where appropriate institute proceedings (Article 217 paras. 4–7) and they shall make sure that penalties are adequate in severity (Article 217, para. 8). It is clear that the 1982 LOSC provides for a particular role for flag state courts in the enforcement jurisdiction machinery.

[9] Text in *World Shipping Laws*, VIII/23/CONV. The Memorandum took effect on 1 July 1982.

[10] The exceeding of the 100 ppm limit for oil discharges (OILPOL) is practically impossible to prove outside harbour waters. Automatic monitoring devices objectively to register oil discharges have a poor reliability record.

Strengthening flag state duties was not accepted as being sufficient to remedy existing inadequacies. Therefore, coastal state and port state powers are extended. Port states now possess judicial enforcement jurisdiction according to Article 218 1982 LOSC. Port states may undertake investigations and institute proceedings in respect of vessels discharging on the high seas or within jurisdictional zones of other states. With regard to high seas offences, the port state may act on its own initiative. The prosecution of violations occurring within the coastal waters of another state on the other hand is only allowed if the coastal or flag state concerned so requests. In this respect, the port state acts as an agent for the coastal state or the flag state.[11] Coastal states retain the powers to investigate, arrest and prosecute vessels that, during their navigation in the territorial sea, have violated the coastal state's pollution laws.[12] Here too, the courts are endowed with powers of prosecution, including detention of the vessel if the evidence obtained by the physical inspection of the vessel so warrants. Coastal states do not possess the same plenary enforcement competence for violation of pollution laws in the EEZ. Enforcement jurisdiction is graduated according to the degree of harm threatened and judicial jurisdiction is restricted. Whenever pollution laws have been violated in the EEZ the coastal state is allowed to require the vessel in question to give information regarding its identity, port of registry, last and next port of call (Article 220, para. 3). If the violation resulted in an substantial discharge causing or threatening significant pollution of the marine environment, physical inspection of the vessel may be undertaken by the coastal state. If the eventual discharge is causing or threatening major damage to the coastal state, that state may institute proceedings, including arrest of the ship. This system implies that, except where the coastal state is itself threatened by pollution, enforcement jurisdiction is limited to the preliminary stages of judicial jurisdiction. The actual role of the courts of the coastal state therefore will be rather limited. Even more than the port state, the coastal state acts as an agent collecting the necessary information enabling the flag state or the port state to invoke judicial enforcement jurisdiction.

The full weight of judicial enforcement jurisdiction remains with the courts of the flag state. However, there is a concurrent competence with the port state and in some cases with the coastal state.

In addition, coastal state and port state enforcement jurisdiction are being balanced by a system of safeguards against possible abuses. This safeguard system shows its particular importance with regard to the judicial jurisdiction of both coastal and port states. Indeed, Article 228 LOSC allocates a preferential judicial enforcement jurisdiction right to the flag state. Any state instituting proceedings in respect of violations occurring beyond its territorial sea shall suspend them if the

[11] Boyle, "Marine Pollution Under the Law of the Sea Convention", 365.

[12] This is subject to the right of innocent passage keeping in mind, however, that a vessel engaging in any act of wilful and serious pollution contrary to the LOS Convention is not in innocent passage (Art. 19). The preliminary problem nevertheless is to ascertain whether the pollution was wilful. Cf. Cheng-Pang, "A Review of the Enforcement Regime for Vessel-Source Oil Pollution Control", 323.

flag state takes its own proceedings to impose penalties. The flag state may exercise this right during a six-month period. This preferential right is denied when the flag state in question has repeatedly disregarded its obligation to enforce effectively the applicable international rules in respect of violations committed by its vessels. Whenever the original proceedings relate to a case of major damage to the coastal state, the preferential right is also denied.

Enforcement with respect to pollution by dumping

Controlling the pollution of the marine environment by dumping of wastes has on an international scale been regulated by one world-wide (London Dumping Convention) and several regional conventions (Oslo Convention; Helsinki Convention; Protocol to the Barcelona Convention; Kuwait and West African Conventions).[13] The leading pattern for enforcement was set up by the 1972 Oslo and London Dumping Conventions (Article 15 and Article VII respectively). As a general rule compliance with the provisions of the conventions is ensured by attributing enforcement jurisdiction to the flag state of the vessel engaged in dumping operations, the loading port state and the coastal state in whose territorial waters dumping occurs. The enforcement jurisdiction with regard to dumping implies judicial jurisdiction. It is not merely a right for the states concerned but actually a treaty obligation. The courts of the flag state are competent to institute proceedings irrespective of the place where a violation has occurred. A similar situation exists concerning states in whose ports pollutants are loaded for dumping in violation of the Convention. The obligation to ensure compliance with the Convention rests upon the coastal state with respect to ships and aircraft believed to be engaged in dumping in its territorial sea. This right and obligation is not limited by the right of innocent passage since dumping operations in the territorial sea fall outside the scope of passage. With regard to this concurring jurisdiction the general rule of *non bis in idem* should apply.

The 1982 LOSC adopts the enforcement pattern of the dumping conventions. With respect to the enforcement jurisdiction of the coastal state, however, this is no longer solely limited to the territorial sea, but now also applies to the EEZ and continental shelf. Furthermore, no state shall be obliged to institute proceedings when another state has already taken this initiative (Article 216).

Enforcement with respect to pollution from land-based sources

It is generally admitted that land-based pollution is the most important source of marine pollution. Nevertheless it is the source for which the least international interest exists. The matter has not been dealt with on a global scale, save for a couple of articles (Article 194, Article 207, and Article 213) in the 1982 LOSC. Due to the wording of these articles they are, however, unlikely to generate much effect. On a regional level, the 1974 Paris Convention, applying to the north-east Atlantic

[13] The Council of the OECD established in 1977 a Multilateral Consultation and Surveillance Mechanism for Sea Dumping of Radioactive Waste.

and the North Sea, introduces the conventional pattern with respect to this type of marine pollution. Unlike the aforementioned forms of marine pollution, enforcement strategy here is rather simple. Since land-based marine pollution is actually a national source of marine pollution, emanating from an area under the sovereignty of one state, it is only that state that can enjoy prescriptive and enforcement jurisdiction. The implementation and enforcement of the Paris Convention's provisions for instance are carried out by the national authorities of the contracting states. However, the Commission established by the Paris Convention (PARCOM) is entrusted with important tasks for the furtherance of the Convention's goals. Some of the initial enforcement jurisdiction stages (e.g. collecting evidence) are carried out by PARCOM. Actual judicial enforcement jurisdiction remains of course with the courts of the contracting states. The 1982 LOSC enforcement Article 213 only contains a very general obligation to implement and enforce laws and regulations concerning land-based pollution. The value added to the Paris Convention provisions is practically nil. Other regional instruments, namely the 1976 Mediterranean Protocol and the 1974 Helsinki Convention adopt a more or less similar approach to that of the Paris Convention.

Enforcement with respect to sea-bed activities

With respect to marine pollution resulting from sea-bed activities (offshore operations) a distinction is made between the national and the international sea-bed area. Specifically concerning enforcement jurisdiction a different legal treatment can be observed. Enforcement regulations on sea-bed activities in areas under national jurisdiction (territorial sea, continental shelf, EEZ) are to be taken by the coastal state (Article 214 1982 LOSC). Enforcement of pollution regulations in the Area outside national jurisdiction is governed by the provisions of Part XI of the 1982 LOSC. However, no specific provisions dealing with enforcement are to be found in this Part. For deep sea-bed mining operations performed by entities other than the Enterprise, enforcement shall be exercised by the state whose nationality the mining entity has. In respect of activities of the Enterprise enforcement will be by the Enterprise and the Authority. In any case residual enforcement powers are vested in the Authority.[14]

Enforcement with respect to pollution from or through the atmosphere

Atmospheric pollution is essentially a form of land-based pollution. The 1982 LOSC nevertheless treats it as a separate source of marine pollution. According to Article 222 states shall enforce their applicable regulations within the air space under their sovereignty or with regard to vessels flying their flag or aircraft of their registry. The 1979 Geneva Convention on Long-range Transboundary Air Pollution is still the most significant attempt to develop international legal rules in order to prevent and reduce air pollution. The Convention, however, only provides a

[14] Churchill and Lowe, *The Law of the Sea*, 244.

very general framework, greatly lacks precise provisions for preventing and reducing air pollution and does not contain specific enforcement rules.

Conclusions

It appears from this overview that the enforcement jurisdiction of international legal rules and standards with respect to the pollution of the marine environment has not yet attained the priority treatment it deserves. Next to the implementation problem of international rules, enforcement in general and judicial enforcement in particular is clearly a weak spot in the legal machinery developed to protect the marine environment. Except with respect to vessel-source pollution, international agreements only provide general provisions for enforcement jurisdiction in respect of flag states, coastal states and port (loading) states. Judicial enforcement and therefore the role of the courts is merely a stage in the enforcement process. It can even be doubtful whether states do want courts to play an important role within the enforcement system. States have a right and in some cases an obligation to institute proceedings when violations of marine pollution law occur. It may, however, be doubtful whether states will easily turn to a court in order to prosecute for violations that are of little or no significance for their own situation. The notable unwillingness of some flag states in this respect is generally known. It can be expected that states will only institute proceedings whenever damage is suffered on their own maritime or land territory or when their own nationals are directly involved. With regard to civil jurisdiction it is necessary that an interest is shown in order to institute civil proceedings. On this level problems may also arise. Although the competence of the courts has been addressed by most of the international environmental instruments it does not necessarily follow that courts will play a predominant role in enforcing environmental rules. Courts will try to solve specific problems which are brought before them. In doing so they will eventually rely on domestic legislation and not necessarily on international environmental rules. Most of the cases in this respect will be about liability for marine pollution and the award of damages, and the courts will have to apply their municipal liability regulations (which contain in several instances provisions based on international agreements). Of course the general scope of pollution problems brought to the courts will in some way or another be linked to environmental rules. In the bulk of the cases, however, these rules only settle the problem of the competence of the courts. The role of the courts in this matter therefore is of a rather general nature, namely, to provide for a means of a legal protection of the marine environment rather than to act specifically as an enforcing entity for international environmental rules.

Chapter 18

The Wadden Sea: A Yardstick for a Clean North Sea

Karel van der Zwiep

Location and general morphology

In the south-eastern corner of the North Sea, along the coasts of southern Denmark, Germany and the northern part of The Netherlands lies a vast wetland area of about 8,000 km^2, in which mainly natural forces, in particular the tides, determine the shape and the structure of the landscape. Most of the area is protected against the destructive action of the open sea by a belt of barrier islands and sandbanks. Deep tidal channels between the islands and sandbanks allow the sea to enter the area at every tide. Tidal flats cover about two- thirds of the area and form one of the most characteristic features of the Wadden Sea, together with salt marshes which are still inundated by the sea at high tide.

The present form of the Wadden Sea is the result both of natural forces and action by man. An important natural force is the general advance of the sea caused by a rise in sea level (transgression), tending to destroy the coast and push it landward. This destructive force is counteracted by a continuous reconstruction of the coast by sedimentation of sand and silt, due to the action of tides and waves.[1]

Biological characteristics

The area regularly under the influence of the tides abounds with animal life, most of which lives on or in the tidal flats and shallows. The density of animals (mainly invertebrates) is far higher than in most parts of the North Sea. Owing to its proportions, situation and character the Wadden Sea is one of the world's richest biologically productive border seas. It fulfils vital functions in the cycle of nature, including man, especially as an extraordinarily rich source of nutrition. Birds and

[1] J. Abrahamse, *et al.*, "De Waddenzee" in *Landelijke Vereniging tot Behoud van de Waddenzee, Vereniging tot Behoud van Natuurmonumenten in Nederland* (Harlingen 1976).

fish share a large part of the abundant invertebrate fauna available. A reduction in the size of the area, or a lowering of its productivity by pollution, would have serious consequences for the populations of birds and fish, and also for man, whose North Sea fishery depends on a healthy nursery area.

Birds, notably waders, ducks and geese, are the most conspicuous users of the area. Some of these breed in the vicinity but the majority come from breeding sites in the subarctic regions of Europe and Asia and use the area as a hibernating ground. The Wadden Sea represents about 50 per cent of the feeding area available to these birds in Europe and North Africa.

For example, about 750,000 knots overwinter along the coasts of north western Europe and West Africa. This is the whole breeding population of an area, stretching from the north-east of Canada, through Greenland and Spitsbergen to Central Siberia. More than once nearly 400,000 specimen of this species of sandpiper have been observed in the Wadden area and it is even likely that the whole population visits the Wadden Sea in search of food.

The Wadden Sea plays a vital part in the lives of about 50 different bird species from the northern hemisphere. Their total number amounts to an estimated six to twelve million.[2]

The scarcity of tidal flats (the most nutritious areas) on the migration routes makes wintering wading birds very vulnerable. Their vulnerability is intensified by the circumstance that they only can reach these hibernating areas from their breeding areas by passing through shallows lying in between. And these are becoming increasingly rare. It has been established that approximately 60 per cent of all tidal flats to be found in Europe and in North Africa, as far south as the mangrove zone, lies in the Wadden Sea. Furthermore, 20 per cent of all the salt marshes remaining in Europe are found along the Wadden Sea.

The Wadden area has a very important function for fish too. For example 80 per cent of all plaice and 50 per cent of all sole caught in the North Sea, grows up in the Wadden Sea. This nursery function gives the Wadden area great economic importance. The average yield of fish from the North Sea amounts to 110 kgs per hectare. Yearly the North Sea yields 2.6 million tons of fish. The value is about US $m 100 per year. The North Sea boasts the greatest abundancy in fish and is the most profitable sea in the world.[3]

Threats

For many centuries man has lived and worked in harmony with the natural life rhythm of the Wadden Sea. There is now a threat that this balance will be destroyed and it is indeed already considerably disturbed. Technological progress and development of modern society, especially during the last decades, have put the

[2] "The Conservation of International Flyway Populations of Waders", Wader Study Group Bulletin IWRB, special publication no. 7 (April 1987); Tussen Sahara en Siberië, Verslag van een onderzoek in de Banc d'Argain Maurentanië, Stichting WIWO (1987).

[3] "Ecology of the Wadden Sea", Wadden Sea Working Group; Stichting Veth, Leiden 1983. See also D. Symes, *below*, chapter 23.

area under heavy pressure. The natural ecological stability is seriously threatened. Already several species of plants and animals have disappeared for ever from the area as a consequence of human interference.

Those threats have been quantified, analysed and systematically discussed in many studies of international repute. They can be classified in three groups:

- loss of biotopes or habitats;
- downgrading of environmental quality;
- depletion of species.

Loss of biotopes is in many cases irreversible. This is often the result of the following activities: land reclamation, land development, urban expansion, the establishment of industries including power stations, port construction, construction of recreation areas, camping sites, hotels, marinas, airports, roads or car parks, construction of dikes and other sea defences, quarrying and dumping, laying of pipelines, mining and military activities.

Downgrading of environmental quality (deterioration of plant and animal life) is the result of effluent discharge (domestic and industrial), oil pollution, air pollution, eutrophication, side effects of pesticides, disturbance caused by traffic including air traffic, by tourists, including mudflat walking, by careless nature studies, by recreational activities, mining and similar activities and alteration of the skyline.

The loss or depletion of flora and fauna may result from the destruction of biotopes and, in addition, from the following, more direct activities: fishing, shooting, collecting of botanical specimen, use of pesticides, introduction of non-indigenous species, grazing.

The relationship between the North Sea and Wadden Sea

The North Sea and Wadden Sea are closely connected by strong ecological ties. In actual fact, they form one single ecosystem. Every tide brings a flow of North Sea water in or out of the Wadden Sea. This means that whatever happens in or on the North Sea also greatly affects the Wadden Sea. Inevitably detrimental circumstances out in the North Sea also bring their consequences and effects for this extensive coastal area. And such circumstances are indeed numerous: traffic and transport, the exploitation of oil and natural gas, the dumping and incineration of waste substances and polluted dredging spoil, etc. This is without taking into account the pollution which the great rivers bring down to the North Sea and which subsequently reaches the Wadden Sea ecosystem. In this light the North Sea can be seen as a great source of danger for the further survival of the Wadden Sea. Problems of pollution well illustrate this fact.

Each year, for instance, 70 to 80 million tons of crude oil pass the Dutch and German islands at a comparatively short distance offshore; about 11 km. via the Terschelling-Elbe route and about 60 km. via the Deep-Water-route. This means approximately 200,000 tons daily. As yet there have been no major disasters, but the effect of one upon the Wadden Sea would be incalculable. Events during the weekend of 9–10 January 1988 proved once again just how great that danger is. An illegal discharge of an estimated 300 tons of heavy stoke-oil off the south-coast of The Netherlands claimed at least 10,000 bird victims. An investigation carried out by the Inselstation Helgoland reached the conclusion that in the period 1983–1985 an estimated 30,000 to 60,000 birds were killed in the German Bight as the result of oil pollution.[4] Moreover, it reported an increase in oil pollution in that area. This is in accordance with Dutch findings . The number of ships detected as illegal dischargers of oil in the North Sea showed a sharp increase during 1987.[5]

The fact that up till now no great ecological disasters have occurred can be attributed more to good fortune than good judgement. A whole series of major and minor shipping accidents (collisions and ships run aground) proves this yet again. The accident involving the German freighter Hornbelt (in October 1986 near Cuxhaven) also demonstrates how exceptionally difficult or even impossible the fight against oil pollution is in the Wadden Sea. Even though the latest techniques for fighting oil pollution are already available, they can scarcely be used at all in this area which is largely inaccessible, except perhaps in the broader and deeper channels. Against this background it is necessary to place the emphasis on prevention and to see to it that oil, from whatever source or in whatever form, no longer enters the Wadden Sea.

A series of serious environment disasters in the Rhine in 1986, 1987 and 1988 and recently also in the Wadden Sea, heightened concern over the problem of water pollution and measures for its prevention. A very large part of the polluted Rhinewater finds its way via the North Sea to the Wadden Sea with measurable effects, along with those from the other great rivers, the Ems, Weser and Elbe. Recent studies have shown that the water quality of the North Sea and that of the Wadden Sea is worse than expected and can deteriorate. Even if adequate measures were taken at this moment, improvement would be seen only after the lapse of several decades. The increasing contribution of atmospheric pollution to overall water pollution is especially worrisome.[6]

In this context attention is drawn to the disastrous epidemic which affected the seals in 1988. More than 80 per cent of the total Wadden Sea population of around 10,000 animals died from the combined effects of a virus and contaminated water.[7]

A study-report issued recently by the Dutch Ministry of Public Works makes clear, yet again, how significant the ecological relations are. In this report the situation in the Wadden and North Seas is illustrated by what is called the "Amoebe" diagram, which relates the situation to plant and animal life. For this purpose a

[4] Informationen, Mitteilungenblad der Schutzgemeinschaft Deutsche Nordseeküste, October 1987, Dornum.

[5] Karel van der Zwiep, "Statement of Concern for the Wadden Sea III", IUCN/WWF Advisory Committee for the Wadden Sea, Harlingen 1988

[6] Susan Bedding, "Zirkulation und Schadstoffumsatz in der Nordsee", Institut für Meereskunde, University of Hamburg, 1988.

[7] Hans-Ulrich Rösner und Hartwig Kremer, "Was ist der Sache bei den Seehunden", *Wattenmeer International*, Husum 1988.

number of species have been selected and the numbers in which they are present then show how matters stand at the present time.[8]

From research it has been possible to establish what these figures were in the past, when the North Sea was considerably less polluted. (For this the year 1930 was chosen as a time-basis for calculations.) Comparison with the present-day figures then gives some insight into the changes which have taken place. To demonstrate this, all the characteristic species have been drawn up in a circle, with the distance from the central point indicating what the numbers were in the 1930 situation. When the numbers for the situation today are filled in, the so-called "Amoebe" outline takes shape (see Fig. 1). This demonstrates that more complex plant life and certain sorts of fishes and mammals have almost completely disappeared. On the other hand, algae and various sorts of shellfish and birds show a great increase in numbers. The conclusion to be drawn from this is that the reduction of the discharge of toxic and nutritive substances by a half (as agreed in London in 1987 at the second International North Sea Conference; INSC) is inadequate to safeguard life in the North and Wadden Seas. The deterioration of the marine environment is still continuing, albeit at a slower tempo.

Administrative policy

Notwithstanding the fact that the ecological systems of the North Sea and the Wadden Sea are closely interwoven, the relation between both systems has never been recognized as a point of integrated policy, nor indeed has it been explicitly brought to notice. This is true of both national and international practice. As regards The Netherlands, ever since the mid-seventies much attention has been paid to the protection and conservation of the Wadden Sea. This resulted in a complex system of legal and administrative measures which came about in 1980.[9] However, in Germany and Denmark this development took place somewhat later, partly as a result of Dutch influence. But now since 1986 these countries too have at their disposal a whole series of legal instruments for the best possible protection of the ecological assets of the Wadden Sea.[10] In addition, in 1982 the three Wadden Sea countries came together in trilateral Wadden consultations intended as a more or less permanent institution and with the object of a united approach to the problems of this area.

Completely outside these developments, a North Sea administrative policy also took shape at the beginning of the eighties. In this too The Netherlands played a certain pioneering role, presenting a series of reports and studies.[11] Thanks also to

[8] "Systematically in Search of Sustainable Development", Ministerie van Verkeer en Waterstaat, Dienst Getijdewateren; B.J.E. ten Brink, Den Haag 1989

[9] "Planologische Kernbeslissing Waddenzee", Ministerie van Volkshuisvesting, Ruimtelijke Ordening en Milieuhygiëne; Den Haag 1980.

[10] "Nationalpark Niedersachsisches Wattenmeer", Gesetz-und Verordnungsblatt H5321 A/no. 48/ 21 December 1985; "Nationalpark Schleswig-Holsteinisches Wattenmeer", Drucksache 10/1043 der Schleswig-Holsteinischen Landesregierung 22 July 1985.

[11] "Inventarisatierapport Noordzee", ICONA, Den Haag 1981. "Harmonisatie van het Noordzeebeleid", Ministerie van Verkeer en Waterstaat, The Hague, 1982.

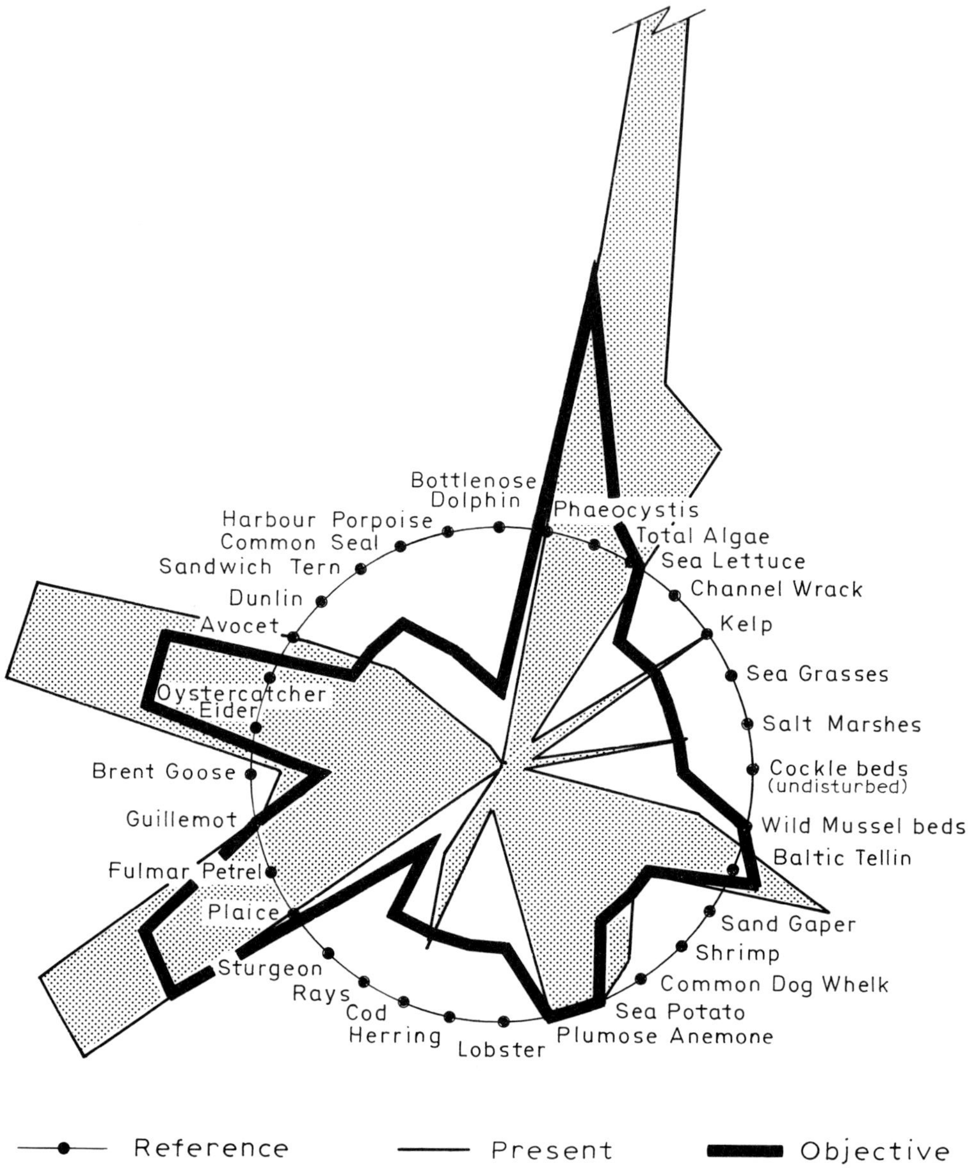

Figure 1 Amoebe diagram

German initiative this very quickly resulted in an international follow-up, the first International North Sea Conference in Bremen (1984).

In this context it is remarkable to note that the international Wadden area played no part at all in the preliminary work for this first INSC. Even more remarkable: the Wadden Sea problems were deemed totally outside the scope of the Conference since they were "matters of a national character". Together with the help of active non-governmental organizations working in this field it proved possible to forestall this resolution and the Wadden Sea now occupies a permanent place on the INSC agenda, receiving special attention to its problems. In the Final Declaration of the London INSC (1987) a separate section is devoted to this subject.[12] However, in spite of all this, we note that there is (still) no question of any explicit international co-ordination in administrative policies concerning the North Sea and the Wadden Sea. Such co-ordination does not even exist between The Netherlands, Germany and Denmark with respect to administrative policy for the Wadden Sea alone. And this is notwithstanding the fact that the (inter)national protection of the Wadden Sea goes back much further than that of the North Sea. The ecological relationships between the North Sea and Wadden Sea are so strong and important that the condition of the Wadden Sea is a measuring gauge for the quality of the North Sea. But at the same time the way in which the Wadden Sea is protected is also a yardstick for the resolution and preparedness to really overcome the problems of the North Sea.

The international Wadden Sea area

As indicated briefly above, the evolution of an administrative policy for the Wadden Sea has outgrown the stage of a national Dutch, German or Danish problem. The great natural values of the area and the many dangers threatening them impose an equally great responsibility on the three sovereign states. Each has indeed taken more or less drastic legal measures to protect its portion. Both in The Netherlands and in Denmark almost the whole area comes under nature conservation acts. In Germany two national parks have been created. Large sections have been designated as wetland of international importance in accordance with the Ramsar Convention.

Still, the fact that the Wadden is governed by three different national administrative and legal systems constitutes a major problem for its management. This has to be considered as a big omission in a territory which, from a scientific point of view, ought to be administered and managed as one ecological unit. The three responsible countries recognized this problem and declared that some kind of close, trilateral cooperation would be essential. Beginning in 1974 The Netherlands, Germany and Denmark tried to create an intergovernmental conservation mechanism for the Wadden. Until 1982 they showed little progress. That year, in Copenhagen,

[12] *Second International Conference on the Protection of the North Sea, London, 24–25 November 1987, Ministerial Declaration, issued by the Department of the Environment of the United Kingdom, April 1988*, repr. (1988) 3 IJECL 252–265.

the three countries issued a Joint Declaration.[13] The governments decided to co-operate closely in the implementation of the most important international agreements for environmental protection relevant to the Wadden Sea, namely:

- Convention on Wetlands of International Importance especially as Waterfowl Habitat (Ramsar, February 2, 1971).
- Convention on the Conservation of European Wildlife and Natural Habitats (Bern, June 1, 1982).
- Convention on the Conservation of Migratory Species of Wild Life Animals (Bonn, June 23, 1979).
- EC-Bird Directive (79/409/EC).

They also agreed to keep each other informed about their respective Wadden Sea management activities, and decided to set up a joint international Wadden Sea secretariat.[14]

However, until now the Joint Declaration has only functioned as a catalyst. It has yielded certain results for the national Wadden administration of Germany and Denmark (national parks in Germany; Ramsar assignment in Denmark) but has achieved little as an "instrument" for international co-operation. The treaties listed in the Declaration can only be implemented via the national legal codes. That means three different forms of interpretation, policy and management. Moreover, there is an absence of contact with other fields and areas of administration.

What is lacking is a well-worked-out plan with terms of reference accepted by all parties under which the three states can apply their own appropriate national regulations to safeguard the natural assets of the area. Since, as shown, the influences which affect the Wadden area also originate outside the area, an integrated system of protection must include such matters as oil discharges into the North Sea, the threat of North Sea disasters, water-pollution from the great rivers and so forth. Correlations must therefore be established with the aims and principles of North Sea policy and management.

The necessity for all this is even more urgent because the international Wadden area has a key position on important bird-migration routes. The area, as stated before, plays a vital part in the lives of 50 different bird species totalling approximately 6 to 12 million birds. These circumstances make all the more necessary good connections between this area and the one from which the birds originate (breeding areas) or are heading for (wintering areas) and the areas in between (feeding and roosting areas). If the Wadden region is to continue to fulfil its central function on the migration routes, especially the Western Palearctic Flyway, then the region's administrative policy must conform with the objectives and basic principles of the international agreements such as the Ramsar, Bonn and Bern Conventions and the EC Bird Directive. Moreover, there must come about a clear relationship with other wetlands which are inter-dependent with the Wadden region. A large

[13] *Minutes, Reports and Declarations; Third Meeting on the Protection of the Wadden Sea between The Netherlands, Germany and Denmark, Ministry of Environment, Copenhagen 1982.*

[14] Wadden Sea, National Reports; Common Wadden Sea Secretariat, Wilhelmshaven 1988.

number of countries (e.g. all the North Sea countries) are signatory to the Ramsar Convention, and the majority are also parties to those of Bonn and Bern; these include in any case, all the countries along the Western Palearctic Flyway. Therefore, in principle, "dovetailing" and co-ordination of administration and management of wetlands along this migration route is entirely possible. In this respect the concept of "wise use", borrowed from the Ramsar Convention, may offer good perspectives for the development of a joint coastal management policy along the borders of the North Sea. Seen from the aspect of "sustainable development", this would be of great advantage to the North Sea countries, both individually and collectively.

"Coastal management"

Notwithstanding many shortcomings, we can still affirm that The Netherlands, Germany and Denmark have made an important contribution to the realization of a joint international administration of the Wadden Sea. The national protective measures in the three countries offer a great number of starting-points for further development, as do also the results of long-standing other co-operation in this field. These can lead to an integrated system of conservation and protection whereby the region will be treated as a single ecological unit.[15] A healthy North Sea environment is therefore of the highest importance to The Netherlands, Germany and also Denmark: the great effort over the years to achieve this aim would otherwise have been fruitless. To put it in other words: a definite common interest has been created. A common interest which can be expressed in financial terms, for the annual practical administration costs each of the three countries many millions every year anew.

In point of fact, this common interest was also recognized at the second INSC. In the Final Declaration the participant countries affirmed "their firm intention to give high priority to the implementation of measures agreed in this declaration to have special significance for the protection of the Wadden Sea." In effect, this part of the London Declaration constitutes a political commitment by all North Sea countries, acknowledging their special responsibility for the Wadden Sea. The manner in which they implement this responsibility by performance can therefore be taken as an indication of what the measures agreed upon are really worth and also the determination and willingness to get down to real work. This, however, calls for a certain amount of doubt and some reserve.

To cite an example: with respect to nutrients (nitrogen, phosphorus) the second INSC agreed to "take effective national steps in order to reduce nutrient inputs into areas where these inputs are likely, directly or indirectly to cause pollution." Rivers and the atmosphere are the most important sources of nutrient input. The fast increase during the last decade of the amounts of nutrients entering the North Sea has caused changes in algal species composition and an increase in algal blooms and

[15] Karel van der Zwiep, "Integrated System for Conservation of Marine Environments; Pilot study on the Wadden Sea", IUCN/WWF Advisory Committee for the Wadden Sea, Harlingen 1989.

oxygen depletion in certain parts of the North Sea, e.g. the German Bight. The causes (agriculture, traffic) and the effects of eutrophication are pre-eminently international problems and can be solved only by international co-ordinated action. The INSC, however, only agreed on taking national action. Besides that, it is quite unclear which sources are responsible for negative effects in certain areas, nor have the areas been defined. Although the United Kingdom, for example, is responsible for about 50 per cent of NOx-output via the atmosphere, one can doubt from the agreement, whether the UK will reduce this amount just because it is partly responsible for environmental problems along the Dutch, German and Danish coasts.[16]

Furthermore, one can note with satisfaction that at the 2nd INSC the North Sea was declared a "special area" under Annex V of the Marpol Convention concerning discharge of litter, which is an increasing problem for the coastal areas. Ships may no longer dump their domestic garbage, packaging materials and other refuse in the North Sea so that the seashores, too, become cleaner. In this respect plastics form a special threat to the marine environment. Following the Convention of Oslo (for the Prevention of Marine Pollution by Dumping from Ships and Aircraft) it is forbidden to throw plastics into the sea. This convention has failed until now to bring about the disappearance of plastics from the marine environment. Also here, there are grounds for scepticism. If the "special area" designation is to become truly effective, adequate harbour reception facilities, efficient control and above all prosecution and punitive measures will have to be forthcoming.

One can say that in Europe, and especially so during recent years, much (political) attention has been paid to the combat against pollution of the (open) sea, e.g. the North Sea, Mediterranean and Irish Sea. The tidal and coastal regions play what amounts to a more or less subordinate role in these matters. Yet this attitude is incorrect, as is demonstrated by the situation around the North Sea and the Wadden Sea and their common relationship. The tidal areas are of vital importance for the total marine ecosystem. By and large they are the most productive parts of that system and generally they possess a great wealth of flora and fauna.

However, conservation efforts with respect to the marine environment have lagged far behind those for the terrestrial environment. And as a result, as said before, many marine areas now face loss of biotopes and habitats, downgrading of the environmental quality and depletion of species. In fact, "conflicting uses and competing users" sums up the problems facing those charged with the preservation and wise management of estuarine resources. The interests of maritime commerce, coastal fisheries, commercial coastal development, recreation and special sanctuaries often appear too divergent to reconcile. These conflicts are further complicated by multi-jurisdictional governance of coastal resources, from local to international.

Until now, even in official North Sea consultations, great attention (one might say almost exclusive attention) has been paid to pollution and above all, water pollution. The issue of nature conservation (the North Sea in its role of natural area) came up for discussion as something of only incidental importance and even then

[16] *North Sea Monitor* 87/4; Werkgroep Noordzee, Amsterdam 1988

more especially as seen in the light of the international Wadden situation. However, there are other important coastal areas on the borders of the North Sea. Recent surveys in the UK e.g. show that 80 out of 123 sites are threatened by damaging activities and the UK's estuaries hold over 30 per cent of north-west European wintering shorebird populations.[17]

Surely the various North Sea countries ought then to share a common interest in preserving and ensuring the survival of these regions in a condition that is as free from pollution and disturbance as possible. This is a responsibility which is analogous to that of The Netherlands, Germany and Denmark with respect to the Wadden Sea. The North Sea countries too have a common concern that threats from outside, from the open sea, should be averted. The advantages of this can also be expressed in financial terms and are thus of economic importance. Just how important this aspect is, was demonstrated yet again in May, 1988. A particularly devastating toxic algae bloom dominated the Skagerrak, which connects the North Sea to the Baltic Sea, killing nearly all marine life to a depth of 50 feet, including fish valued commercially at $200 million. Norway's Bergen Scientific Centre found that the bloom was caused at least in part by urban and agricultural pollution. It warns that as long as such nutrient discharges continue, similar blooms can be expected.[18]

The tidal areas lie inside the territorial boundaries and are therefore subject to the jurisdiction of each individual country. These separate countries also have clearly defined powers to protect such territories to prevent pollution and to combat deterioration of the "quality" of the area. Moreover there are numerous international instruments available which are intended to achieve these aims ultimately on a national level. The degree of ecologically motivated protection which these countries accord to their coastal areas is therefore also indicative for their readiness to co-operate effectively in action for a clean North Sea. But to achieve a cleaner North Sea of better "quality", such a well-focused and co-ordinated "coastal management" on the part of all North Sea states ("coastal" here understood as referring to all areas within the territorial limits) could probably have more effect than action concentrated exclusively upon the North Sea itself.

The establishment of sanctuaries solely is by no means the only way to insure against a further deterioration of the marine ecosystem. Nor, in isolation, are measures to protect wildlife. The trilateral agreement between The Netherlands, Germany, and Denmark on the conservation of seals in the Wadden Sea,[19] e.g., does not make any sense if nothing is done about the serious problems of water pollution coming from the mainland. Or more specifically when nothing is done to clean the home of the common seal the agreement will not help the animal to sur-

[17] A recent survey carried out by the RSPB of estuarine threat around Britain described the types of development affecting a sample of 123 estuaries. Eighty out of the 123 sites were considered by the RSPB staff to be under some degree of threat (Philip I. Rothwell, Coastal Policy Officer RSPB, August 1989)

[18] Nicholas Lenssen, "The Ocean Blues", *World Watch*, vol 2 no.4 (Washington, DC, 1989).

[19] "Agreement on the Conservation of Seals in the Wadden Sea" (Bonn, 17 November 1988) is the first (trilateral) agreement, based on the "Bonn Convention of Migratory Species of Wild Animals" (Bonn, 23 June 1979)

vive. The greatest problems lurk in the management of human activities that use or affect the marine environment. One of the most important steps in protecting the sea is for individual nations to gain better control of their waste streams. As with land-based problems, polluted seas will not become clean until less garbage is produced and the recycling of sewage and other wastes is encouraged. An administrative policy aimed at achieving this will be almost immediately reflected in the quality of the intertidal habitats.

As far as we know, The Netherlands, Germany and Denmark, have made the most headway in this respect. The evolution of the common management of the Wadden Sea worked out between these three countries could well stand as a model and form a basis for further intensification of North Sea administration. In the mean time, the Scandinavian countries too have formed a united front. At the end of 1988, the Ministers for the Environment of the Nordic Council decided to draw up a joint plan of action to combat sea pollution and also for a common environmental policy.[20] The OECD project for "sound coastal zone management" would seem to be an important initiative in this respect. This project has been designed to help reconcile economic development in coastal zones with the protection and conservation of natural resources and other environmental values. Particular attention will be paid to evaluating and recommending institutional and financial mechanisms for sound coastal zone management and to elaborating general policy initiatives for presenting and resolving conflicts arising from competing demands on the resource base.[21]

To sum up. Conservation of the North Sea begins with conservation of the coastal zones; for when one's own house is not clean and kept in good order, nothing will ever come of attempts to tackle neighbours' rubbish. This is proved yet once again and all too clearly by the scanty results of the measures agreed upon in London in 1987.

[20] *Naturopa*, newsletter 88/10 of the Council of Europe, Strasburg 1988.

[21] UNEP Regional Bulletin for Europe, December 1988.

Part III
Outstanding Issues

Chapter 19

Maritime Boundaries and Regional Co-operation

Dr. Erik Franckx

A chapter on maritime boundary delimitation in a book devoted to regional co-operation in environmental matters may appear rather awkward. Even though the exact relationship between the settlement of maritime boundaries on the one hand and enhanced regional co-operation on environmental matters on the other is not easy to ascertain, this study is based on the quite logical premiss that regional co-operation is best served by settled maritime boundaries in a particular region. This chapter, therefore, intends to analyse the North Sea and Baltic Sea practice in order to try to find out which elements enhanced the conclusion of such boundary agreements in the past, and which did not. It will also refute the commonly held belief that the North Sea stands out as a model in boundary delimitation. This might have been true in the past, but it certainly no longer corresponds with reality at present.

The Baltic Sea region has been included here to serve as point of reference. Located relatively close to the North Sea and at the same time connected with it, this regional sea has certain common features which makes a comparison worth while, especially if environmental matters are focused on: both are very much enclosed by land (which requires many maritime boundaries to be settled), median depths are well below 100 m,[1] low rate of water exchange, heavily used for shipping, surrounded by highly industrialized states, and totally divided between riparian states if 200 nautical mile (n.m.) zones are established.

A first part will focus on the problem of maritime boundaries. One section will provide a thorough survey of existing maritime boundaries and a further section, which for the purpose of this study is at least as important, will pay special attention to those boundaries which still remain to be settled. In both sections, the situation in the North Sea will be considered first, followed by a shorter picture of the situation as it exists in the Baltic in order to allow a later comparison. A second part

[1] North Sea: 80 m and Baltic Sea: 55 m.

will appraise this situation in the North Sea, and a third one will then compare it with Baltic state practice.

Maritime boundaries

This study is not only interested in the boundary agreements which are actually in force, but even more in those outstanding boundary delimitation questions which, so far, have not been settled by international agreement.

Settled maritime boundaries

North Sea

The North Sea is defined for the purpose of this study according to the definition adopted by the International Conference on the Protection of the North Sea, that is the area comprised by 62° north, Skagerrak and the English channel east of longitude 5° west.[2]

Territorial sea. Only half of the territorial sea boundaries have been negotiated so far. The oldest of them all is the boundary between Norway and Sweden in Skagerrak, which was established by a treaty of 26 October 1661, as interpreted by an Arbitral Award in 1909.[3]

Denmark and Germany fixed the limit of their territorial sea in the North Sea by an agreement of 1922,[4] which was based on the boundary provisions of the Treaty of Versailles. The boundary-line established by this agreement was based on the thalweg of the navigational channel and later amended when the actual course of this thalweg changed.[5] Apparently, the coordinates and some technical details of this boundary are currently under review.

Recently France and the United Kingdom agreed that part of their previously agreed continental shelf boundary[6] in the Straits of Dover should properly be

[2] *Addendum to the Declaration of the First International Conference on the Protection of the North Sea* (Bremen 1984).

[3] See the reply of the Swedish government to the questionnaire distributed by the Secretary-General at the request of the International Law Commission, UN Doc. A/CN 4/71/Add. 1 (12 May 1953), p. 2. For a succinct contemporary account of this arbitration, see J. Kaiser, "Grisbadarna Case", in 2 *Encyclopedia of Public International Law* (Amsterdam: North-Holland Publishing Company, 1980), pp. 124–125, where further references can be found. In 1967 both countries furthermore agreed not to extend their territorial seas without prior agreement beyond certain points in the area. See *Declaration Concerning the Territorial Sea in the North-Eastern Skagerrak* (signed 5 April 1967; entered into force 29 June 1976). Repr. in United Nations Legislative Series: *National Legislation and Treaties Relating to the Territorial Sea, the Contiguous Zone, the Continental Shelf, the High Seas and to Fishing and Conservation of the Living Resources of the Sea*, UN Doc. ST/LEG/SER.B/15, pp. 924–925 (1970).

[4] "Agreement Concerning the Demarcation of the Boundary-Lines Between the Two Countries and the Maintenance of Boundary-Markers" (signed 10 April 1922; entered into force 7 June 1922) 10 LNTS 73. See pp. 143–145 for an English translation.

[5] R. Wolfrum, "Die Küstenmeergrenzen der Bundesrepublik Deutschland in Nord und Ostsee" (1986) 24 *Archiv des Völkerrechts*, 247, 266–267.

[6] See "Agreement Relating to the Delimitation of the Continental Shelf in the Area East of 30 Minutes West of the Greenwich Meridian" (signed 24 June 1982; entered into force 4 February 1983), repr. 2 *Atlante dei Confini Sottomarini*, ed. B. Conforti, G. Francalanci, and D. Romano (Milan: Dott. A. Giuffrè Editore, 1987), pp. 13–15.

labelled as a territorial sea boundary.[7] This had of course to do with the extension by the United Kingdom of its territorial sea up to 12 n.m. in 1987.[8] It should be noted that the territorial sea delimitation around the Channel Islands remains still to be settled.[9]

Continental shelf. The North Sea has often been described as the region where the continental shelf boundary delimitation is most complete.[10] In this section the agreements are discussed chronologically according to their date of signature. If later amendments occurred these are normally discussed right afterwards unless third party settlement was relied upon.

The first agreement to be signed in the area was the one between the Federal Republic of Germany and The Netherlands.[11] In 1964, both parties delimited a short segment (26 n.m.) of their common continental shelf.

The first continental shelf agreement to enter into force, however, was agreed upon between Norway and the United Kingdom.[12] Special about this agreement is that parties totally ignored the existence of the Norwegian Trench, which is well over 200 m deep and runs parallel to the Norwegian coast in its immediate vicinity. The International Court of Justice remarked that the shelf on the other side of the trench, that is up to the equidistance line, could not be considered as adjacent continental shelf according to international law.[13] Nevertheless, the extension of this line to the north arrived at by parties in 1978,[14] that is well after this decision of the International Court of Justice, once again disregarded the particular geologic and geomorphologic features of the region. More accurate means of determining equidistance points resulted in the knowledge by parties at that time that the northern terminal point of the former agreement, even though intended by parties to be equidistant from their respective coasts, was in fact located closer to the Norwegian

[7] "Agreement Relating to the Delimitation of the Territorial Sea in the Straits of Dover" (signed 2 November 1988; entered into force 6 April 1989). Text repr. (1989) 4 IJECL 155–157.

[8] Text repr. *Law of the Sea Bulletin*, No. 10 (November 1987), pp. 12–20. With respect to the Straits of Dover this enactment repeated the geographic coordinates fixed with France in 1982 when delimiting the continental shelf. See "Agreement Relating to the Delimitation of the Continental Shelf in the Area East of 30 Minutes West of the Greenwich Meridian" (signed 24 June 1982; entered into force 4 February 1983), repr. 2 *Atlante dei Confini Sottomarini*, ed. B. Conforti, G. Francalanci, A. Labella and D. Romano (Milan: Dott. A. Giuffrè Editore, 1987), pp. 13–15.

[9] A special Order in Council is moreover necessary to extend the provision of the Territorial Sea Act 1987 to the Channel Islands. See Art. 4 (4).

[10] A detailed analysis of most of these boundaries can be found in 10 *Limits in the Seas*, revised (1974).

[11] "Agreement Concerning the Lateral Delimitation of the Continental Shelf in the Vicinity of the Coast" (signed 1 December 1964; entered into force 18 September 1965) 550 UNTS 123.

[12] "Agreement Relating to the Delimitation of the Continental Shelf Between the Two Countries" (signed 10 March 1965; entered into force 29 June 1965) 551 UNTS 214.

[13] "North Sea Continental Shelf (Federal Republic of Germany/Denmark; Federal Republic of Germany/Netherlands)", ICJ Reports (1969), pp. 3, 33 (para. 45).

[14] "Protocol Supplementary of the Agreement of 10 March 1965 Relating to the Delimitation of the Continental Shelf Between the Two Countries" (signed 22 December 1978; entered into force 20 February 1980), repr. 1 *Atlante dei Confini Sottomarini*, ed. B. Conforti and G. Francalanci (Milan: Dott. A. Giuffrè Editore, 1979), p. 30.

coast. This new agreement, of which only the initial segment south of 62° north is of importance here, rectified this flaw.[15]

Next in line was a short segment delimited between Denmark and the Federal Republic of Germany.[16] As was the case with The Netherlands, 26 n.m. of continental shelf were delimited in front of the Danish–German coast.

The Netherlands and the United Kingdom jointly established their 255 n.m. continental shelf boundary a few months afterwards.[17] Established according to the equidistance principle, those countries, together with Denmark, were of the opinion that they were the only ones whose continental shelves would reach the centre of the North Sea. A submission which the International Court of Justice later proved to be false.[18]

Denmark and Norway arrived at a common continental shelf boundary by the end of 1965.[19] This boundary agreement was amended for a first time in 1968 in order to take into account the result of a joint study by the Hydrographic Services of Denmark, Norway and Sweden, which marked the common tripoint between parties with more precision. This new tripoint was located 0.6' to the south and therefore the formerly established terminal point was changed by means of this 1968 protocol.[20] An exchange of notes of 1974 between the same parties,[21] which changed all coordinates from Norwegian to European Datum, confirmed this tripoint.

In 1966 Denmark and the United Kingdom agreed to delimit what they believed to be their common continental shelf boundary.[22] The same month, Denmark and The Netherlands entered into an agreement on the same subject.[23] The countries, as mentioned above, believed that only their continental shelves would meet in the middle of the North Sea. The International Court of Justice was to decide otherwise, however. But before addressing this procedure before the International Court of Justice, the Sweden–Norway agreement should be mentioned,[24] since the

15 A "kink" in the boundary brings the new line 331 m due west. See D. Anderson, "Maritime Delimitation: A View of British Practice" (1988) 12 *Marine Policy* 231, 234.

16 "Agreement Concerning the Delimitation, in Coastal Regions, of the Continental Shelf of the North Sea" (signed 9 June 1965; entered into force 27 May 1966) 570 UNTS 91.

17 "Agreement Relating to the Delimitation of the Continental Shelf Under the North Sea Between the Two Countries" (signed 6 October 1965; entered into force 23 December 1966) 595 UNTS 113.

18 See nn. 27–35 *below*, and accompanying text.

19 "Agreement Relating to the Delimitation of the Continental Shelf" (signed 8 December 1965; entered into force 22 June 1966) 634 UNTS 71.

20 "Exchange of Notes Constituting an Agreement Amending the Agreement of 8 December 1965 Concerning the Delimitation of the Continental Shelf" (signed 24 April 1968; entered into force 24 April 1968) 643 UNTS 414.

21 "Exchange of Notes Constituting an Agreement Amending the Agreement of 8 December 1965" (signed 4 June 1974; entered into force 4 June 1974). Repr. in United Nations, *The Law of the Sea: Maritime Boundary Agreements (1970–1984)* (New York: United Nations, 1987), pp. 13–14.

22 "Agreement Relating to the Delimitation of the Continental Shelf Between the Two Countries" (signed 3 March 1966; entered into force 6 February 1967) 592 UNTS 209.

23 "Agreement Concerning the Delimitation of the Continental Shelf Under the North Sea" (signed 31 March 1960; entered into force 1 August 1967) 604 UNTS 209.

24 "Agreement Concerning the Delimitation of the Continental Shelf" (signed 24 July 1968; entered into force 18 March 1969) 968 UNTS 235.

Skagerrak forms part of the North Sea as defined for the purpose of this study. The Norwegian Trough was once more disregarded when concluding this agreement.[25] This agreement, moreover, was concluded right after the consultations held between the Hydrographic offices of Denmark, Norway and Sweden and included therefore the newly established tripoint.[26]

On 2 February 1967 an agreement had been signed between Denmark and the Federal Republic of Germany in order to submit their maritime delimitation dispute to the International Court of Justice. On the same day, the Federal Republic of Germany and The Netherlands had signed an exactly similar agreement. In simple terms the problem centred around the particular physical geography of the area: Denmark and The Netherlands possessed convex coastlines, whereas that of the Federal Republic of Germany, located in between, had a concave form. The result was that the former two countries favoured the application of the equidistance principle. The Federal Republic of Germany, on the other hand, pretended that its continental shelf extended to the centre of the North Sea. The Court's decision of 20 February 1969 satisfied this basic German contention. But since it was not asked to draw the actual boundary-line, parties still had to conclude separate agreements on this point. This was done on 28 January 1971, when both Denmark[27] and The Netherlands[28] concluded an agreement with the Federal Republic of Germany delimiting the remaining[29] parts of their continental shelves in the North Sea. The latter was based on the principles enunciated by the decision of the International Court of Justice, but the actual boundary-line was very much influenced by pragmatic considerations[30] resulting in the so-called "Entenschnabel". On 25 November 1973, moreover, Denmark,[31] The Netherlands[32] and the

[25] See "North Sea Continental Shelf (Federal Republic of Germany/Denmark; Federal Republic of Germany/Netherlands)" and "Protocol Supplementary of the Agreement of 10 March 1965 Relating to the Delimitation of the Continental Shelf Between the Two Countries", and accompanying text.

[26] See "Exchange of Notes Constituting an Agreement Amending the Agreement of 8 December 1965 Concerning the Delimitation of the Continental Shelf", and accompanying text.

[27] "Agreement Concerning the Delimitation of the Continental Shelf Under the North Sea" (signed 28 January 1971; entered into force 7 December 1972) 857 UNTS 109.

[28] "Agreement Concerning the Delimitation of the Continental Shelf Under the North Sea" (signed 28 January 1971; entered into force 7 December 1972) 857 UNTS 130.

[29] See "Agreement Concerning the Delimitation, in Coastal Regions, of the Continental Shelf of the North Sea" and "Agreement Concerning the Lateral Delimitation of the Continental Shelf in the Vicinity of the Coast", respectively.

[30] Areas where licences had already been delivered by a particular government, remained as much as possible under the jurisdiction of that state.

[31] "Agreement Relating to the Delimitation of the Continental Shelf Between the Two Countries" (signed 25 November 1971; entered into force 7 December 1972) United Nations Legislative Series: National Legislation and Treaties Relating to the Law of the Sea (ST/LEG/SER.B/16), p. 431 (1974).

[32] "Protocol Amending the Agreement of 6 October 1965 Relating to the Delimitation of the Continental Shelf Under the North Sea Between the Two Countries" (signed 25 November 1971; entered into force 7 December 1972) United Nations Legislative Series: National Legislation and Treaties Relating to the Law of the Sea (ST/LEG/SER.B/16), p. 430 (1974).

Federal Republic of Germany[33] entered into an agreement with the United Kingdom in order to settle the maritime boundaries in the centre of the North Sea, taking into account the rightful claim of the Federal Republic of Germany.[34] In order to do so, Denmark, The Netherlands and the United Kingdom all had to change the content of formerly concluded treaties *inter se* in this respect.[35]

Another example of third-party dispute settlement occurred soon afterwards. France and the United Kingdom, although in agreement on the principle to be applied in the eastern sector of their common maritime frontier,[36] could not agree as to the delimitation of the continental shelf west of 0° 30' west of Greenwich. The latter part of the boundary, parties agreed, would be settled by arbitration. The Court of Arbitration, which was also requested to draw the boundary-line, delivered its judgment on 30 June 1977.[37] Of the three different areas to be distinguished, namely, the south-western Approaches, the mid- and eastern Channel, only the last two relate to the area comprised by the definition of the North Sea. The equidistance-line was mainly followed, but the Channel Islands were not taken into account. Instead, these islands were enclosed by a 12 n.m. enclave boundary.

Finally, during the early 1980s France and the United Kingdom further completed their maritime boundary delimitation by applying the same equidistance method east of 0° 30' west.[38] The delimitation-line provided by this agreement, it should be noted, stops short of the trijunction point with Belgium. This contrasts sharply with most other tripoints in the North Sea which were first established by way of bilateral treaties.

Baltic Sea

If one compares these findings with the situation in the Baltic Sea, the following salient features can be noted. In the Baltic all territorial sea boundaries have been

33 "Agreement Relating to the Delimitation of the Continental Shelf Under the North Sea Between the Two Countries" (signed 25 November 1971; entered into force 7 December 1972) 880 UNTS 185.

34 The Federal Republic of Germany has a 9.4 n.m. continental shelf boundary with the United Kingdom.

35 Denmark and The Netherlands (see "Agreement Concerning the Delimitation of the Continental Shelf Under the North Sea" (signed on 31 March 1960))—both countries no longer possessed a common boundary; Denmark and the United Kingdom (see "Agreement Relating to the Delimitation of the Continental Shelf Between the Two Countries" (signed on 3 March 1966))—new agreement; The Netherlands and the United Kingdom (see "Agreement Relating to the Delimitation of the Continental Shelf Under the North Sea Between the Two Countries" (signed on 6 October 1965))—amending protocol.

36 As expressed in the preamble of the "Arbitration Agreement Concerning the Delimitation of the Continental Shelf" (signed 10 July 1975; entered into force 10 July 1975). Repr. (1980) 8 *New Directions in the Law of the Sea*, London, Oceana Publications, Inc., 287–290.

37 The parts describing the boundary line were moreover reprinted in 1 *Atlante dei Confini Sottomarini*, ed. B. Conforti and G. Francalanci (Milan: Dott. A. Giuffrè Editore, 1979), p. 61–67.

38 "Agreement Relating to the Delimitation of the Continental Shelf in the Area East of 30 Minutes West of the Greenwich Meridian" (signed 24 June 1982; entered into force 4 February 1983), repr. 2 *Atlante dei Confini Sottomarini*, ed. B. Conforti, G. Francalanci, A. Labella and D. Romano (Milan: Dott. A. Giuffrè Editore, 1987), pp. 13–15.

agreed upon, at least if one takes the most recent agreement between the German Democratic Republic and Poland into account.[39]

In about half of these territorial sea delimitation agreements, navigational interests played a determinant role when fixing the boundary-line. This certainly must have burdened negotiations.

In the vast majority of cases it is not necessary in the Baltic to distinguish between continental shelf and fishery/economic zone boundaries, for single maritime boundaries have been agreed upon.

Maritime boundaries still to be settled

North Sea

Territorial sea. Half of the territorial sea boundaries still remain to be settled in the North Sea. Belgium and The Netherlands stand out in this respect as countries which did not so far delimit either of their lateral territorial sea boundaries. This results in three outstanding boundary delimitations: Belgium–France, Belgium–The Netherlands, and the Federal Republic of Germany–The Netherlands.

As far as the Belgian boundary with France is concerned, it would seem an easy task for cartographers to draw an equidistance line in the area. But the presence of many low-tide elevations in the area, combined with the adherence by both countries to a different definition of their low-water mark,[40] results in a multitude of possible lateral boundary-lines.[41]

Similar technical problems do arise with respect to the territorial sea boundary between Belgium and The Netherlands,[42] namely different low-water standards[43] and the presence of low-tide elevations. But other issues, deeply embedded in history, complicate a possible settlement even further. Examples here are the possible closing line of the river Scheldt[44] and the old Wielingen problem,[45] which still surfaces today.[46]

[39] "Agreement Concerning the Delimitation of the Sea Areas in the Oder Bight" (signed 22 May 1989). At the time of writing, this agreement has not yet entered into force. An article commenting on this agreement by the present author has appeared in (1989) 4 IJECL 237–251, to which a translation of the agreement is annexed.

[40] The French low-water line is about 30 cm lower than the one adhered to by Belgium.

[41] For a more detailed elaboration of this aspect, see E. Franckx, "Belgium Extends its Territorial Sea up to 12 Nautical Miles" (1987) 20 *Revue Belge de Droit International* 64–65 and especially pp. 68–69.

[42] *Ibid.* 64–65 and especially pp. 69–71.

[43] Even though both countries adhere to the mean lower low-water spring, more accurate calculations by the Dutch result in a difference of about 20 cm.

[44] The Netherlands claim they always applied a bay-regime to the West Scheldt.

[45] The Wielingen constitutes a major access route to the river Scheldt. Although located off the Belgian coast, The Netherlands claim the Wielingen as part of the Dutch territorial sea, based on historic rights.

[46] Good examples are the following recent articles: E. Somers, *The Problem of the Wielingen: The Delimitation of the Belgian Territorial Sea with Respect to The Netherlands* (1988) 3 IJECL 19–36 and D. Roos, "Zeeuws Territoriaal Water en de Wielingen-kwestie in Historisch Perspecticf" (1985) 4 *Zeeuws Tijdschrift* 124–132.

Also, between the Federal Republic of Germany and The Netherlands a century-old boundary dispute exists concerning the Ems-Dollard region.[47] The difference here is that formal treaties have been concluded between parties on the subject. All of them, however, were pragmatic agreements which left the crucial problem of the boundary issue unresolved.[48] The extension of the Dutch territorial sea to 12 n.m. further complicated the issue,[49] but these problems are currently being negotiated.

In order to be complete, it could be added that the boundary between Denmark and the Federal Republic of Germany, even though settled by treaty,[50] still gives rise to discussions in practice.[51] Apparently also on this subject, discussions between the parties are under way. As mentioned above, also France has still some outstanding boundary problems with the United Kingdom.[52]

The result is that only the territorial sea between Norway and Sweden seems to be settled in a definitive manner.

Continental shelf. Notwithstanding the exceptionally high degree of continental shelf delimitation in the North Sea, there remains one country which so far has not participated in this movement, namely Belgium. Three lateral boundaries, as a consequence, are still outstanding: One with France, one with the United Kingdom and one with The Netherlands. If the former two should not, in theory, cause too much trouble, this may not be true with respect to the last. Recent articles in the Belgian press indicate that this country might well be thinking of claiming a much larger area of continental shelf to the north than the one comprised by normal equidistance lines.[53]

Fishery zones. Not one single fishery boundary has been concluded so far in the North Sea area. In the literature, this is usually explained by the fact that the Com-

[47] The Federal Republic of Germany pretends that the entire Ems estuary forms part of German territory whereas The Netherlands claim that the maritime boundary follows the thalweg of the principal navigational channel.

[48] "Agreement Concerning Arrangements for Co-operation in the Ems Estuary" (signed 8 April 1960; entered into force 1 August 1963) 509 UNTS 64; "Supplementary Agreement to the Treaty Concerning Arrangements for Co-operation in the Ems Estuary" (signed 14 May 1962; entered into force 1 August 1963) 509 UNTS 140. Recently this basic treaty of 1960 was adjusted to new circumstances: "Agreement Concerning Co-operation in the Area of the Ems and Dollard as well as in the Adjacent Regions" (signed 10 September 1984). But again, sovereignty questions were left untouched. See G. Tanja, "A New Treaty Regime for the Ems-Dollard Region" (1987) 2 IJECL 123–143, where an English translation of the agreement can be found.

[49] H. de Jong, "Extension of the Territorial Sea of the Kingdom of The Netherlands" (1983) 30 *Netherlands International Law Review* 129, 141- 142 and R. Wolfrum, "Die Küstenmeergrenzen der Bundesrepublik Deutschland in Nord und Ostsee", 258–265.

[50] "Agreement Concerning the Demarcation of the Boundary-Lines Between the Two Countries and the Maintenance of Boundary-Markers", 73.

[51] R. Wolfrum, "Die Küstenmeergrenzen der Bundesrepublik Deutschland in Nord und Ostsee", 265–267.

[52] See n. 9, *above*. The Court of Arbitration found that it was not competent under the Arbitration Agreement to decide this issue.

[53] *De Standaard* (14 April 1988) and *Het Volk* (7 April 1989).

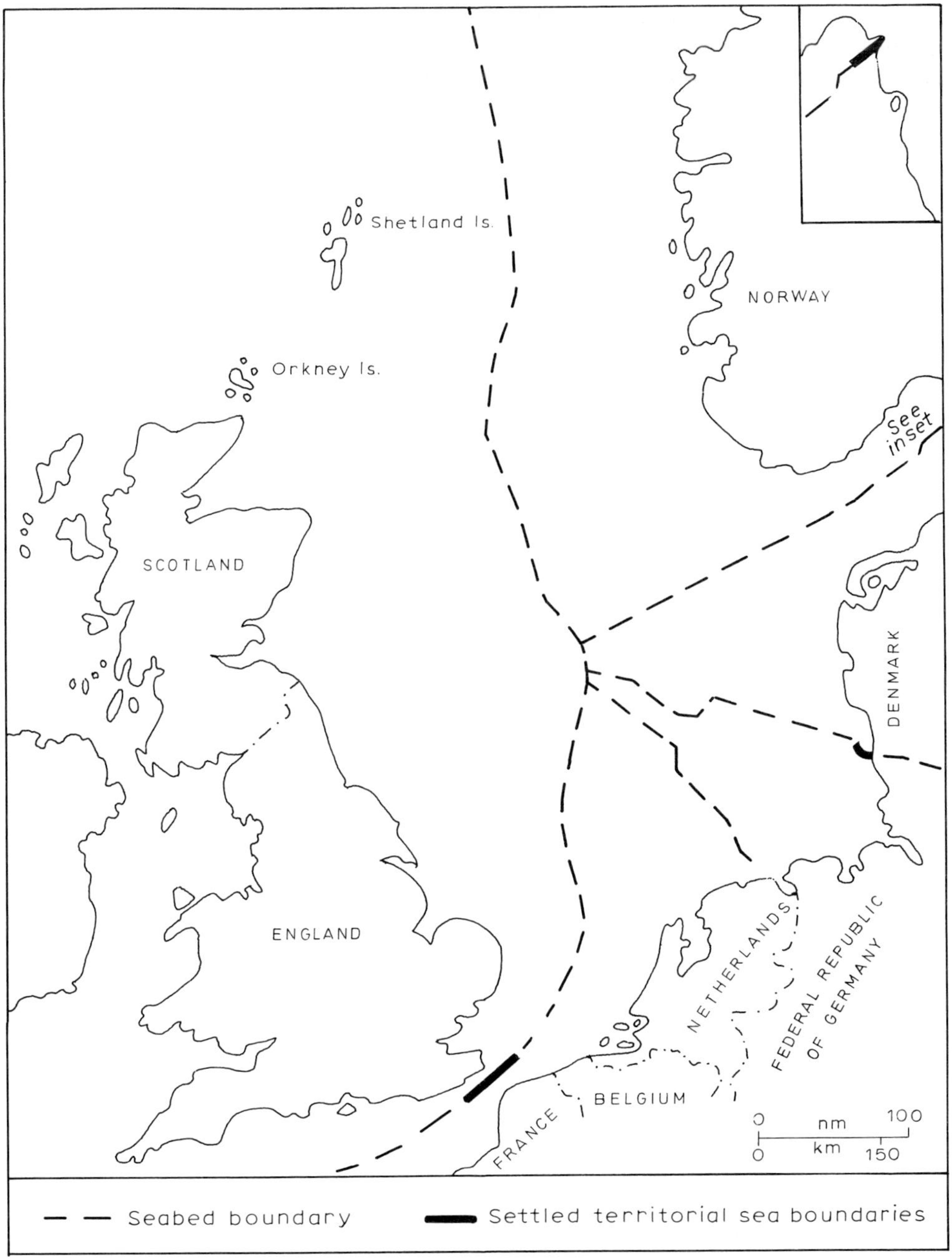

Figure 1 Maritime boundaries in the North Sea

mon Fishery Policy established by the EC in 1983[54] removed the need for negotiating common fishery boundaries. It is submitted, as elaborated later on, that this reasoning no longer applies today, but even during the 1970s, when the number of countries claiming a 200-n.m. fishery zone was on the rise,[55] this statement had to be read with care. First of all, Norway, which was a candidate member at the time of the first enlargement of the Community, had rejected this membership for several reasons, one of which was certainly the unacceptable terms concerning fisheries which were included in the treaty of accession. As a result, the entire North Sea did not become subject to the Common Fishery Policy. Second, in a zone up to 6 n.m. coastal states had exclusive fishery rights, whereas in an adjacent zone of another 6 n.m., this exclusivity was partially restricted.[56] A 12-mile zone was the result at a time when most North Sea countries still adhered to a 3 n.m. territorial sea. It suffices to look at the intricate problems encountered by the Channel Islands in this respect to understand the necessity of exact fishery limits, even within this so-called "Europond."[57]

Economic zones. France and Norway are the two only states bordering the North Sea which have so far proclaimed an Exclusive Economic Zone.[58] The government of The Netherlands stated early in 1989 that it supported the idea of establishing a Dutch EEZ, but that first of all other North Sea states had to be consulted.[59] No such boundary agreements have been concluded so far. Single maritime boundaries may be envisaged, but it should be noted that in the Federal Republic of Germany voices have been raised urging the central government to negotiate a more favourable delimitation concerning the superjacent waters than the one obtained with respect to the continental shelf.[60]

Baltic Sea

Since all territorial sea boundaries have been settled and single maritime boundaries constitute the general rule in the Baltic region, it will suffice here to note:

[54] Council Regulations 170/83, 25 January 1983, *Establishing a Community System for the Conservation and Management of Fishery Resources*, OJ 27/1/83, 26/L 24, 1–13; and of the same day 172/83, *Fixing Certain Fish Stocks and Groups of Fish Stocks Occurring in the Community's Fishing Zone, Total Allowable Catches for 1982, the Share of these Catches Available to the Community, the Allocation of that Share Between the Member States and the Conditions under which the Total Allowance Catches May be Fished*, OJ 27/1/83, 26/L 24, 30–67.

[55] Members of the EC extended their fishery zones in concert on 1 January 1977.

[56] In this zone between 6 and 12 n.m. the coastal state had to respect historic rights of fishermen of other EC countries.

[57] For a good survey article, see S. Langford, "Common Fishery Resources and Maritime Boundaries: The Case of the Channel Islands", in G. Blake (ed.), *Maritime Boundaries and Ocean Resources* (London: Croom Helm, 1987), pp. 89–116.

[58] For an English text of these enactments, see United Nations, *The Law of the Sea: National Legislation on the Exclusive Economic Zone, the Economic Zone and the Exclusive Fishery Zone* (New York: United Nations, 1986), pp. 101–103 (France) and 229–232 (Norway).

[59] T. IJlstra and P. Ymkers, "The Netherlands and the Establishment of the Exclusive Economic Zone" (1989) 4 IJECL 224–229; also (1989) 1 NILOS Newsletter No. 2, pp. 1, 4–5 and *Ocean Policy News* (March 1989), p. 2.

[60] U. Jenisch, "The North Sea—International Law of the Sea and Environmental Protection" (1989) 40 *Aussenpolitik* 76, 84.

(i) That only two segments remain to be settled, namely, the area south of Bornholm (Denmark-Poland) and the remaining part of the boundary between East and West Germany.

(ii) Only one tripoint has so far been entered into, namely where the Baltic and North Sea meet.[61] Of the remaining seven tripoints, one has recently been signed between Poland, Sweden and the USSR.[62]

North Sea: comprehensively divided area?

It is clear from this analysis that many difficult bones of contention remain between North Sea coastal states in the sphere of maritime boundary delimitation. Some of them find their roots in historical events,[63] others in the fear of certain coastal states that they might be put at a disadvantage.[64] It is therefore a commonly found misnomer to classify the North Sea as a comprehensively divided area. Such statement might have been true during the early 1970s when the North Sea states, be it with the help of the International Court of Justice, arrived at an agreed continental shelf boundary-line. Later, however, with the emergence of 200-mile fishery and especially economic zones, this submission proved to be misleading. For if the necessity of fishery boundaries could have been questioned in the North Sea because of the establishment of a Common Fishery Policy by the EC, the new trend towards EEZs in the area enhances once more the need for inter-state maritime boundaries. Indeed, it should be kept in mind that the EEZ has a multipurpose regime, which besides fisheries, also vests special rights in coastal states concerning the continental shelf, marine scientific research and environmental matters.

North Sea—Baltic Sea

In his basic work of 1985, Prescott wrote that "the construction of maritime boundaries has reached a more complete stage in the North Sea than in . . . the Baltic . . .".[65] Although correct at the time of writing, this statement no longer corresponds with reality today. The second half of the 1980s was characterized by a real inflation of boundary agreements in the Baltic: nine agreements were concluded in less than five years! Boczek writing in 1980 hoped that the negative influence of extended fishery jurisdiction which together with the ensuing delimitation problems were significantly labelled by that author as disintegrative forces of marine regionalism in the Baltic, would only be of a temporary nature.[66] These hopes, as a consequence, materialized by the late 1980s.

[61] See nn. 19–21, 24–26 *above*, and accompanying text.

[62] "Agreement Concerning the Junction Point of the Maritime Boundaries in the Baltic Sea" (signed 30 June 1989).

[63] As for instance the territorial sea boundary between The Netherlands on the one hand and Belgium and the Federal Republic of Germany on the other.

[64] Belgium's continental shelf claim and Germany's demand for a different fishery (or eventually economic zone) boundary are good examples here.

[65] V. Prescott, *The Maritime Political Boundaries of the World* (London: Methuen, 1985), p. 291.

[66] B. Boczek, "The Baltic Sea: A Study in Marine Regionalism" (1980) 23 *German Yearbook of International Law*, 196, 227–228.

As a result, the Baltic has clearly taken the lead over the North Sea in this respect. The former region, which is surrounded by states adhering to widely divergent political and economic ideas, could moreover well serve as an example in co-operation between states in the field of fisheries and pollution prevention.[67]

This contrasts sharply with the North Sea which, it should be remembered, is surrounded by countries whose basic political and economic policies are much closer to each other. Even though continental shelf boundaries are well settled if one disregards the Belgian exception, most other boundaries remain to be settled or adjusted. The present compilation moreover indicates that co-operation is still in its infancy.

The "spirit of co-operation" advanced by the above-mentioned work of Prescott in order to explain the high degree of continental shelf boundary settlement in the North Sea does not seem to be present with respect to territorial sea, fishery and economic zone delimitation problems in the area. Instead, it has to be viewed as an ad-hoc co-operation between countries with a well-defined common goal: divide the area without delay in order to allow exploratory drilling. While doing so, coastal states had no difficulty in sidestepping some very tricky legal issues, as for instance the exact impact of the Norwegian Trench. But even then, if negotiations did not succeed at an early stage, third-party settlement was agreed to. In the Baltic, on the contrary, not one single maritime boundary was arrived at by such means. Direct negotiations between parties proved to be sufficient and this in spite of the fact that the Baltic, from a theoretical point of view, appears more difficult to delimit mainly because of the many islands present, some of which are located far from the mainland.

The manner in which the tripoints were initially arrived at in the North Sea, that is by means of bilateral agreements, is evidence of a certain overconfidence in the equidistance rule. All of the tripoints established in this manner had to be revised at a later stage, either because of the non-application of the simple equidistance method to the Federal Republic of Germany[68] or because of more accurate calculations provided by the Hydrographic offices of the three countries involved.[69] The latest continental shelf agreement between France and the United Kingdom is different for it stops short of the tripoint with Belgium.[70] This last method has been followed *ab initio* in the Baltic. With the bilateral process of negotiations almost completed there, a new phase has recently been entered into with the conclusion of trilateral agreements fixing these remaining tripoints.[71] Taking into consideration the fact that the Baltic and North Sea state practice clearly demonstrate that coun-

[67] See M. Fitzmaurice-Lachs, "The Legal Regime of the Baltic Sea Fisheries" (1982) 29 NILR 174, 177 concerning fisheries and B. Boczek, "International Protection of the Baltic Sea Environment Against Pollution: A Study in Marine Regionalism" (1978) 72 AJIL 782, 812–813 concerning pollution. See also in general U. Jenisch, "Die neuere Seerechtsentwicklung in der Ostsee" (1987) 39 *Aussenpolitik* 362, 366 and by the same author, "The North Sea—International Law of the Sea and Environmental Protection", 82, where he states: "In many ways, the North Sea is less effectively protected than the Baltic Sea . . .".

[68] See nn. 31–35 *above*, and accompanying text.

[69] See nn. 20 and 21 *above*, and accompanying text.

[70] See n. 38 *above*, and accompanying text.

[71] See n. 62 *above*, and accompanying text.

tries do not like to renegotiate formerly agreed turning or terminal points, the last method is certainly to be preferred.

Conclusions

The foregoing analysis clearly demonstrates that under present circumstances the North Sea no longer stands out as a model region as far as maritime boundary delimitation is concerned.

Another misconception which should clearly be discarded is that countries with similar political and economic systems agree more easily on a particular maritime boundary. The fact that delimitation agreements in the Baltic region have reached a higher degree of completion than in the North Sea is significant in this respect.

Countries do, however, tend to resolve their lingering delimitation problems with more ease if a common goal can be identified. The exploration of the continental shelf in the North Sea is one such example, the need for safeguarding the environment and fisheries in the Baltic another one.

It can only be hoped that a similar common goal can be discerned by North Sea states in the near future. The forthcoming Third International North Sea Conference might well provide an appropriate forum in this respect.

Chapter 20

The Exclusive Economic Zone as an Instrument for Environmental Management in the North Sea Area

Dr. Uwe Jenisch

This chapter will give an international law assessment of the concept of the Exclusive Economic Zone (EEZ) as an instrument of environmental management for the specific regional purposes of the North Sea. This will require a critical examination of the innovative environmental provisions of the 1982 Law of the Sea Convention (LOSC) their degree of acceptability to the riparian states of the North Sea as well as the impact of other existing environmental conventions.

Moreover, it is highly advisable not to ignore the growing role of the European Community (EC) as a decisive factor in organizing the co-operation of states in marine areas.

The question of the establishment of EEZs for the North Sea area is of a practical nature because the forthcoming Third INSC at The Hague in March 1990 may find this issue on its agenda. On the initiative of the Dutch government the Preparatory Working Group for the Third INSC has agreed to study this question on the basis of existing working papers.[1] At this early stage it is not yet clear whether the North Sea Ministers will come to conclusions and/or recommendations. The Dutch proposal is to examine the implications and consequences of EEZs and its arguments will be dealt with in this chapter. So far, only France[2] and Norway[3] have declared EEZs while all other North Sea states exercise merely continental shelf rights in conjunction with EC fisheries rights (see Table 1, p. 346).

[1] Preparatory Working Group/Third International Conference on the Protection of the North Sea, PWG—2/7/1 of 17 February 1989.
[2] France: Law No. 76—655 of 16 July 1976.
[3] Norway: Act No. 91 of 17 December 1976.

The EEZ regime

The 1982 LOSC which is still lacking 18 of the required 60 ratifications for its entry into force cannot yet be regarded as treaty law. However, it is widely argued that this Convention, which embodies *inter alia* both the EEZ concept, and a system of environmental provisions represents the customary international law at least in these fields,[4] while the rules concerning deep sea-bed mining are still controversial. Thus, in the absence of a formal entry into force these parts generally confirm the emerging maritime law and practice and fairly balance the interests of all states. Nevertheless state practice with regard to the detailed rights of pollution control is scarce and it may be premature to maintain that the whole system of rules of the LOSC already represents customary law.[5]

According to the LOSC the EEZ is an area beyond and adjacent to the territorial sea that extends up to a maximum of 200 n.m. from the baselines from which the territorial sea is measured,[6] or up to the EEZ of adjacent and/or opposite states.[7] In this zone a coastal state is entitled to exercise sovereign rights/jurisdiction for all natural resources, for the establishment of artificial islands, for marine scientific research and for the protection and preservation of the marine environment.[8]

In view of the fact that all North Sea states already exercise continental shelf rights and, moreover, join in the EC fisheries regime, the new EEZ concept offers little additional benefits in these fields except perhaps that it constitutes an internationally accepted multi-purpose regime to cover all economically interesting uses in one system. The salient point here is the question of additional rights in the field of environmental control.

Environmental rights

A brief analysis of the environmental provisions shows an impressive and wide-ranging set of rules varying from the widely general to the highly particular. Nearly one fifth or 59 of the 320 articles and 9 annexes deal with the protection of the marine environment spread over different parts of the text. Part XII of the convention—"Protection and Preservation of the Marine Environment"—alone consists of 46 articles. Other provisions are to be found in Part II—"Territorial Sea and Contiguous Zone", in Part III -"Straits", in Part V—"EEZ", in Part VII—"High Seas", in Part IX—"Enclosed and Semi-Enclosed Seas", in Part XI—"The Area" and in Part XIII—"Marine Scientific Research", as well as in the various annexes,

[4] Louis B. Sohn, "Implications of the Law of the Sea Convention Regarding the Protection and Preservation of the Marine Environment", (1985) 18 *Law of the Sea Institute Proceedings* 105; with special regard to the EEZ *ICJ Reports* (1982), 18.
[5] L. Gündling, *Die 200 Seemeilen-Wirtschaftszone* (Berlin, 1983), p. 326.
[6] LOS Convention, Arts. 55 and 57; all articles cited hereinafter are articles of LOS Convention 1982.
[7] Art. 74.
[8] Art. 56.

thus reflecting the overriding importance of environmental protection in all marine uses.

A systematical breakdown of these provisions given by D. M. Johnston[9] reflects five groups of rules:

- Seven provisions are so generally worded as to encompass programmatic obligations or principle duties to protect the ocean environment; namely Articles 56, 58, 145, 192, 197, 237 and 240.
- Thirteen articles deal exclusively with the conservation of living resources, that is the fishing regime, namely Articles 61–67, 117–120 and 123.
- Fourteen articles are addressed to the prevention, reduction and control of marine pollution stating more or less general obligations regarding the orderly behaviour of states such as the use of adequate technologies, elaboration of contingency plans and research programmes, namely Articles 194, 195, 196, 198, 199, 200–206, 235 and 236.
- Fourteen more articles concentrate on vessel-source pollution in a more detailed "operational" way including jurisdiction, enforcement and safeguards, namely Articles 22, 23, 42, 43, 211, 217, 218, 219, 220, 221, 225, 226, 227 and 233.
- The remaining eleven articles address the environmental obligations regarding other marine activities with potential harmful effects such as mining (Articles 150, 208, 209, 214, 215), land-based sources (Articles 207 and 213), dumping (Articles 210, 216) and pollution from the atmosphere (Articles 212, 222). The LOSC is silent on the question of incineration.

While it is not possible to deal here with all provisions in detail it may suffice to focus on a few innovative aspects of this system of environmental rules:

1. The language of Part XII refers always to "states" (instead of "states parties") thus reflecting the view that these provisions are applicable to all states as customary law, irrespective of signature or ratification. Universal application is, however, subject to one exception: the settlement of disputes by means of judicial procedures under Part XV of the convention and its annexes V-VIII will only apply to states parties because no state can be compelled to international courts without its consent.[10]
2. Secondly, the environmental rules are to be applied in a very broad sense geographically and functionally in that they cover the high seas, the EEZ, the territorial sea and even ports in a system of rights of jurisdiction, enforcement and safeguards against abuse thereby striking a reasonable balance between the freedom of navigation on the one hand and the envir-

[9] S. M. Johnston, "Conservation and Management of the Marine Environment", (1985) 18 *Law of the Sea Institute Proceedings* 133.

[10] See Sohn, "Implications of the Law of the Sea Convention Regarding the Protection and Preservation of the Marine Environment", 105–108.

onmental interests of the coastal state on the other. Functionally the rights range from executive (repressive) measures to combat pollution incidents and to preventive measures such as requiring adequate standards for the design, construction and manning of ships and installations.[11]

3. Finally, unlike other previous conventions dealing with specific sources of pollution[12] the LOSC states the general rule that "states have the obligation to protect and preserve the marine environment"[13] and "shall take all measures . . . that are necessary to prevent, reduce and control pollution . . . from any source . . .".[14]

This includes the duty to adopt nationally the necessary rules and regulations, thus introducing a new and dynamic element. States are obliged to co-operate on a global or regional basis[15] through competent international organizations such as IMO to establish global and regional rules, standards and practices to be re-examined from time to time.[16] Once a rule or standard has been generally accepted, the states have the duty to enact these provisions. The combined effect of these rules is that the Convention provides a living instrument to arrive at gradually intensifying standards to be implemented automatically thereby evading the long and complicated process of ratification and entry into force of formal amendments.

This system seems to be flexible enough to keep pace with new threats to the environment as well as with new methods for remedies. However, here states are faced with a major dilemma which has been analysed in detail by several commentators:[17] the Convention uses a rather confusing variety of terms such as "laws", "rules", "standards", "regulations", "procedures" and "practices", which are characterized as "generally accepted", "international", "applicable" , "internationally agreed", "global", "regional", "relevant" and "specified".

While these terms are used throughout the Convention in different combinations there is at least some linguistic discipline to be found in those provisions which deal with the pollution from ships where the terms "generally accepted international rules and standards" are applied.[18] Since the Convention does not clarify these various terms they will have to be determined either by the states individually or, preferably, by international organizations and/or the International Law Commission, the International Court of Justice or the International Tribunal for the Law of the Sea. For the time being the implementation of these provisions remains

[11] Arts. 21.2, 194.3.b, c and d, 211.6.c, 217.2.
[12] See below the para. dealing with MARPOL.
[13] Art. 192.
[14] Art. 194.1.
[15] Art. 197.
[16] Arts. 207.4, 208.5, 210.4, 211.1, 212.3.
[17] B. Vukas, "Generally Accepted International Rules and Standards", paper presented at the 23rd Annual Conference of the Law of the Sea Institute, Noordwijk aan Zee (Netherlands), 12–15 June 1989; K. Hakapää, *Marine Pollution in International Law* (Helsinki, 1981), pp. 118; G. J. Timagenis, *International Control of Marine Pollution*, Vol. II (New York, 1980), pp. 603.
[18] Arts. 211.2, 211.5, 211.6, 226.1.a. See also Art. 21.2.

extremely difficult and ambiguous.[19] Rule-making activities of implementation which the Convention attributes to competent international organizations, that is the elaboration of rules and standards relevant for national adoption can only be legally binding after the entry into force of the Convention.[20] The result is that states simply cannot exercise sovereign rights in their EEZ in these cases unless international organizations have first taken action. National legislation adopted outside "generally accepted rules and standards" cannot be enforced on foreign states and flags.

Existing environmental protection approaches for the North Sea

In view of these ambiguities the impressive catalogue of convention rules must be analysed in the wider context of its efficiency, or in other words, its value added benefits to the existing situation. Against this background it has to be stressed again and again that North Sea pollution originates mainly inside the riparian states. According to the Quality Status Report, 1987[21] whose data coincide with the German North Sea Protection Report,[22] annual pollution is estimated at up to 1.8 million tons of pollutants with various degrees of toxicity such as nitrogen, oil, phosphorus, heavy metals and other materials. It is noteworthy that the rivers as well as direct discharges from the coast and atmospheric inputs are the main ways of pollution transport into the North Sea. At the same time other inputs like sea disposal (dumping) and incineration are at the point of being definitely banned due to the results of the Second INSC[23] and subsequent decisions of the EC Council of Ministers.[24]

The large amount of terrestrial sources of marine pollution can, in the first priority, only be reduced by national measures. Costly national programmes are needed to meet and preferably even anticipate deadlines. Only a fundamental change of industrial and agricultural methods and altered consumer attitudes along with a changed environmental consciousness of the 130 to 150 million people around the North Sea can help to overcome its pollution.[25]

Jurisdiction with respect to these sources seems to be the area of national legislation and administration to be co-ordinated and substituted, however, where

[19] International rules and standards to be implemented are to be found in, *inter alia*, Arts. 22.2, 60.3, 60.5, 208.2, 208.5, 210.2, 210.6, 211.2, 211.5, 211.6, 220. For a systematical review see T. Treves, "The Role of Universal International Organizations in Implementing the 1982 UN Law of the Sea Convention", working paper for the 23rd Annual Conference of the Law of the Sea Institute, Noordwijk aan Zee (Netherlands), 12–15 June 1989 (publication forthcoming).

[20] See T. Treves, "The Role of Universal International Organizations in Implementing the 1982 UN Law of the Sea Convention".

[21] "Quality Status of the North Sea". Summary. Second International Conference on the Protection of the North Sea, 24–25 November 1987.

[22] Deutscher Bundestag, Drucksache 11/878 of 2 October 1987.

[23] *Second International Conference on the Protection of the North Sea, London, 24–25 November 1987, Ministerial Declaration, issued by the Department of the Environment of the United Kingdom, April 1988*, repr. (1988) ILM 823 and (1988) 3 IJECL 252–265.

[24] 125th meeting of the EC Council, Luxemburg 28 June 1988 and of 24/25 November 1988 Brussels.

[25] See U. Jenisch, "The North Sea—International Law of the Sea and Environmental Protection", *Aussenpolitik / German Foreign Affairs Review* (1989), p. 92.

advisable through existing international forums such as the Paris Commission and the EC. The legal instrument of an EEZ with its purely maritime scope of applicability helps very little.

Turning now to marine pollution sources in the stricter sense of pollution at sea the existing web of specific conventions (See Table 2, pp. 346–347) has to be examined in the light of its EEZ impact

It lies in the nature of environmental protection work that the existing conventions mostly apply globally or supra-regionally[26] and often operate on a list-principle by differentiating between hazardous substances that are banned (black-list) and those that require a special permit (grey list) in some instances in conjunction with binding EC regulations.

This work is handled by differently composed government commissions, conference secretariats and/or specialized organizations and is continuously being elaborated through protocols, addenda and resolutions.

Since the aim of this contribution is to examine the potential of the EEZ regime for environmental management purposes there is no need to analyse the environmental EEZ regime in extenso. Suffice it to say that only in respect of two sources of marine pollution does the EEZ regime have a role to play, namely in the case of dumping at sea and of vessel source pollution. These two sources will be examined here.

Dumping at sea

Article 210 LOSC gives the coastal states full control over dumping operations in the EEZ because "Dumping within . . . the exclusive economic zone or on to the continental shelf shall not be carried out without the express prior approval of the coastal state". The coastal state is entitled to submit such dumping operations to licensing. In doing so the coastal state should give due consideration to the adverse consequences of dumping operations for other states. The coastal state is not only entitled to regulate dumping operations in its EEZ, but also to enforce its laws and regulations within its EEZ (Article 216 LOSC). The condition hereby is that these laws and regulations should be adopted in accordance with the LOSC and other applicable rules. In the North Sea there are two concurrent dumping regimes. Those of the Oslo and the London Dumping Conventions. Both were adopted in 1972.

Oslo Convention (1972)

The Convention for the Prevention of Marine Pollution by Dumping from Ships and Aircraft, known as the Oslo Convention, covers the same area of applicability as the Paris Convention but it applies only on the high seas and in territorial waters and regulates the deliberate dumping of waste according to the list principle with the exception of discharges relating to the operation of ships, oil platforms and aircraft. Discharge that are subject to licensing which since 1986 has included incine-

[26] *Ibid*. 85–90.

ration at sea is regulated in detail. The supervisory authority is the Oslo Commission (OSCOM).

London Dumping Convention (1972)

The Convention for the Prevention of Marine Pollution by Dumping of Wastes and Other Matter, known as the London Dumping Convention, which now applies to 61 countries (including all North Sea nations) mirrors the Oslo Convention on a world-wide scale. Its provisions are similar to those of the Oslo Convention.[27] An important exception is outlined in Article IIIc under the terms of which the disposal of waste originating directly or indirectly from research work and the exploitation or processing of sea-bed mineral resources is not subject to this Convention. This means that the North Sea oil rigs are expressly excluded from these provisions.[28] This leaves a gap in the overall environmental legislation that even the MARPOL Convention (The International Convention for the Prevention of Pollution from Ships, 1973/78) does not completely close. On the other hand, the London Convention additionally includes crude oil and oil products, highly radioactive substances and ABC weapons. The London-based IMO acts as the secretariat, thus providing a close link with the MARPOL Convention.

Shipping

Article 211 para. 1 LOSC does not explicitly mention the EEZ as such but it urges states to promote the adoption wherever appropriate of routeing systems designed to minimize the threat of accidents which might cause pollution of the marine environment, etc.

Article 211 para. 5 states that coastal states may in their EEZ adopt laws and regulations for the prevention, reduction and control of pollution from vessels. The condition hereby is that these rules have to conform to and give effect to generally accepted international rules and standards established through the competent international organization. In addition where the international rules and standards referred to are inadequate to meet special circumstances and coastal states have reasonable ground for believing that a particular clearly defined area of their respective EEZ is an area where the adoption of special mandatory measures for the prevention of pollution from vessels is required for recognized technical reasons in relation to its oceanographical and ecological conditions, as well as its utilization or the protection of its resources and the particular character of its the traffic, the coastal state may establish a special area. Conditions here are consultation and notification (see Article 211.6.a LOSC).

It seems that there are important questions that can be raised but which cannot be discussed here owing to constraints of space. A key element of course is the contents of the generally accepted international rules. One thesis is that these standards could be contained in the MARPOL 73/78 convention, insofar of course as it

[27] For details see P. Ehlers and P. Kunig, *Abfallbeseitigung auf Hoher See* (Hamburg, 1978).

[28] But (at least) the German Ratification Act of the London Convention of 11 February 1977, *BGBl* Vol. II, p. 165 provides for strict conditions and terms that must be met by oil rigs.

is in force. If this were the case not only would these rules be applicable in the EEZ in respect of vessels in that part of the North Sea but coastal states could also benefit from the combined enforcement regime as laid down in the MARPOL 73/78 convention and the enforcement regime in the LOSC. This latter regime goes far beyond the scope of the MARPOL 73/78 convention which gives only limited powers to the coastal state and the port state.

So the question is whether there is a legal basis to apply the MARPOL 73/78 regime to vessels sailing an EEZ flying a foreign flag. MARPOL has been in effect since 2 October 1983. It applies world-wide for ships under the flags of the signatory states. It is applicable in the protocol version of 1978 that now encompasses 55 countries (accounting for more than 80 per cent of global shipping tonnage) and includes all North Sea countries.

The optional Annexes III and IV have not yet received a sufficient number of ratifications.[29] But the Federal Republic of Germany ratified the Convention without excepting the optional annexes by the Act of 23 December 1981. Moreover, the North Sea countries, in accordance with the resolution adopted at the Second INSC intend to introduce Annex V—ships' garbage—for the North Sea area in the form of a special zone (see chapter 14).

The MARPOL Convention is at present the most important instrument governing pollution from shipping. The further improvement and implementation of MARPOL is the most important priority. Apart from the surveillance of shipping, it is necessary that the states concerned provide reasonably priced reception facilities for all waste disposal. This condition has been met in principle by all North Sea countries.[30] Although the MARPOL convention covers offshore oil rigs, its prohibitions and regulations apply only to the technical operation of their machinery but not to raw-materials exploration, exploitation and processing.

An important aspect is the possibility (under Regulation 10 of Annex I) of establishing special areas on a consensus principle for tighter regulations all the way to a general ban on discharges. Annex I so far covers the Baltic, the Black Sea, the Mediterranean, the Persian-Arabian Gulf and the Gulf of Oman. It does not cover the North Sea because the United Kingdom and The Netherlands have so far not been prepared to support a motion to that effect. The Gulf of Aden is to be designated a special area very soon if the bordering countries provide the necessary reception facilities.

When Annex V (ships' garbage) came into force on 31 December 1988, a general ban on the dumping of plastic waste was enacted and the dumping of other waste now requires a minimum distance from the shore of 12 n.m.[31] The entry into force of Annex V paved the way for introducing a "sectoral" special area status for the

[29] In April 1987 Annex III had been ratified by 37 states representing 48.23 % of world shipping tonnage while Annex IV received 33 ratifications or 40.61 % of tonnage.

[30] German ports have since 1983 had oil reception facilities (and since June 1988 facilities for the disposal of oil and chemicals) free of charge available to shipping under the "concept for ships' waste disposal in terms of MARPOL Annexes I and II" of May 1988.

[31] MARPOL, Annex V, Regulation 3.

whole North Sea, which the Second INSC had demanded in 1987. IMO has decided upon this proposal during its plenary meeting in autumn 1989. The entry into force may be expected in April 1991.

The IMO is in charge of the general supervision and implementation of the Convention while the North Sea countries supervise and enforce off their own shores, though effort and success vary. The rate of success is small but improving. Only a few criminal proceedings end in a conviction because causality and the responsibility of the individual polluter on board can rarely be proved. Attempts to drop the personal responsibility principle, as in Sweden, have met with constitutional reservations in the Federal Republic of Germany.[32] The demand for the introduction of "owner's liability" for shipping companies and/or masters (as in road traffic) makes eminent sense. But in any event, sea and airborne surveillance has an educational effect on environmental offenders. Here, the port state control also helps to ensure good conduct.

Port State Control (1982)

The Memorandum of Understanding on Port State Control (MOU) that has been in force since 1 June 1982 is an important practical instrument of environmental control.[33] The parties to the Memorandum are all the EC countries (except Luxemburg) plus Sweden, Norway and Finland. The Memorandum obliges the signatory states to examine in a uniform and non-discriminatory fashion at least 25 per cent of all ships to ascertain compliance with the minimum technical and social standards laid down by the IMO and the International Labour Organization (ILO). Their powers extend from a simple report on shortcomings all the way to the arrest of the ship. The successes of the instrument which has been operational for more than four years are encouraging. More than 58,000 vessels had been checked by September 1988; an annual 1,500 showed severe faults but the trend is towards improvement.

International North Sea Conferences

Regional co-ordination and co-operation and the ongoing improvement of international conventions takes place sectorally within the above-mentioned Commissions of the Paris and Oslo Conventions which collaborate with each other and with the IMO, and which in its turn is in charge of several conventions.[34]

Here we are faced with a policy of sectoral adjustment rather than one of total renewal. The diversity of existing international instruments is, fortunately, complemented by a rather unusual co-operation through sharing of secretariats, joint North Sea working groups and other means of co-operation.[35]

Above all the links between PARCOM and OSCOM are so close that a merger

[32] P. Kunig, "Nordsee" in *Handwörterbuch des Umweltrechts*, Vol. II, p. 66.

[33] G. Kasoulides, "The Port State Enforcement Regime through International Organizations", paper presented at the 23rd Annual Conference of the Law of the Sea Institute, Noordwijk aan Zee (Netherlands), 12–15 June 1989.

[34] T. IJlstra, "Regional Co-operation in the North Sea: An Inquiry" (1988) 3 IJECL 182.

[35] *Ibid*. 201.

of both would be a natural act. There are also lateral links with the EC Commission.[36] Moreover the Conferences on the protection of the North Sea in 1984 and 1987 are so far the most significant comprehensive attempts to co-ordinate all efforts for the protection of the North Sea and, in doing so, take all sources of pollution into consideration.

Particularly the results of the Second INSC must be seen in a positive light, shortcomings notwithstanding. Awareness of the importance of the marine environment has generally improved in the North Sea countries, and the present approaches of setting quality standards and deadlines, the recognition of the precautionary principle and the start of proceedings for special area status for the North Sea must be pursued without compromise.

It is also important that it be understood that the instruments in terms of maritime environmental law are available in principle and that the implementation and tightening must progress. It cannot be denied that the interplay between existing conventions, pushed ahead by recommendations of the INSCs is rapidly being intensified and the creation of some kind of a "Standing Office" could be helpful to improve day-to-day co-ordination.

The next operational steps are already set out. These are:

- Realization of the special area status for Annex V to be followed by special areas under Annexes I and II of MARPOL.
- International implementation of the other MARPOL annexes, that is III and IV.
- Reduction of the ratification shortfall for already adopted but not yet effective conventions and supplementary protocols.
- Inclusion of the Hinterland countries, Czechoslovakia, the German Democratic Republic, Switzerland and Luxemburg in the existing conventions and in the work of the International Conference, and conclusion of supplementary bilateral environmental agreements, especially an Elbe agreement with the German Democratic Republic and Czechoslovakia.

Apart from this emerging "North Sea Environmental Protection System" the wider context of integrated sea-use management must be distinguished. The significance of the EC sea—the combined 200 n.m. zones of the EC countries (as fishing or economic zones), accounting for about 75 per cent of the North Sea, is gaining in importance as the realization gradually prevails that all major tasks of the marine regime call not only for interdisciplinary but also for political and administrative co-operation.[37] Despite a number of sectoral measures on marine protection stan-

[36] Regarding the influence of the EC which is sometimes a sources of discontent, see: *ibid.* 202.

[37] U. Jenisch, "Probleme der Anwendung des Europäischen Rechts in den Meereszonen der EG-Staaten", *German Yearbook of International Law*, 1979, pp. 239–254; also see M. Michael, *L'Applicabilité du traité instituant la C.E.E. et du droit dérivé au plateau continental des états membres* (Paris, 1984), p. 237; H. R. Krämer (ed.), *Die wirtschaftliche Nutzung der Nordsee und die Europäische Gemeinschaft* (Arbeitskreis Europäische Integration, Baden-Baden, 1979); see also F. Foders and R. Wolfrum, *Meereswirtschaft in Europa* (Kieler Studien, Institut für Weltwirtschaft Kiel, Tübingen, 1989), p. 252.

dards, fishing policy and research work, efforts to provide a community regime for the EC sea are still in their infancy, notwithstanding repeated demands for an integral EC sea.

For the rest, North Sea protection is clearly shifting inland and thus towards the national lawmakers. It is against this broad background of existing marine protection conventions bound together with the help of the INSCs on the one hand and general EC policies as well as the aspect of terrestrial environmental protection on the other hand that the Dutch initiative in favour of an EEZ can be evaluated.

Conclusions

The Dutch working paper[38] to study the question of increased coastal state jurisdiction by means of an EEZ admits that the wide area of terrestrial pollution influencing the North Sea can best be handled by recommendations of the North Sea Ministers being adopted by other international forums such as the Paris Commission and national legislation. With respect to shipping, dumping and incineration, that is purely marine sources of pollution, this paper states substantial benefits of an EEZ declaration:[39]

> "With respect to shipping the most important competence that coastal states in the North Sea would attain, in addition to their existing competences as a flag state, through the establishment of EEZs are:
> • the competence to prescribe generally accepted international rules and standards as established by competent international organizations or a diplomatic conference *vis-aa-vis* all vessels in this zone; and
> • in accordance with international law:
> (a) the competence to request information from vessels when facts so warrant and thereby strengthening (amongst other things) the MOU;
> (b) the competence to enforce generally accepted international rules and standards *vis-à-vis* vessels in this zone if the situation so warrants.[40]
> With respect to dumping and incineration at sea the most important competence that coastal states in the North Sea would attain through the establishment of EEZ is:
> • the competence to regulate all dumping and incineration activities in that zone."

The Dutch working paper[41] argues that shipping decisions taken by North Sea Ministers and which are in accordance with generally accepted international rules and standards can at present only be implemented by North Sea states with respect to vessels flying their flag and vessels entering their ports. That is, North Sea coastal

[38] Preparatory Working Group / Third International Conference on the Protection of the North Sea, PWG—2/7/1 of 17 February 1989.
[39] *Ibid.* as revised in a working group meeting of 6 June 1989 at The Hague.
[40] Arts. 211.5 and 220.
[41] Preparatory Working Group / Third International Conference on the Protection of the North Sea, PWG—2/7/1 of 17 February 1989, 4.

states do not have the competence to implement such decisions with respect to foreign vessels in areas beyond their territorial seas.

Consequently the establishment of EEZs would enable each coastal state, in accordance with international law, to prescribe and, to a certain extent, enforce such decisions with respect to all vessels in its EEZ.

One could agree with this assessment in principle because the Dutch initiative rightly concentrates on enforcement rather than on prescriptive rules. But still the practical effects might be rather limited as long as "generally accepted international rules and standards" are not determined. Only if the hard work of elaborating rules and standards in IMO and other international (and regional) forums is accomplished to a high degree of consensus will the EEZ regime be efficient.

The competence to request information[42] from foreign vessels and thereby strengthening the Port State Control Memorandum is also of little practical value because inspection of the ship may take place in the ports anyway and will be done if facts so warrant.

Regretably, the Dutch working paper is silent on the question of offshore oil and gas activities which take place within the sovereign powers of coastal states.[43] The safety of offshore installations and their environmental aspects, partly covered by the Paris Convention and MARPOL, are regulated in a piecemeal approach and it is surprising that no specific North Sea action has been undertaken so far. Here the 1982 LOSC would provide a missing link.[44]

Finally, regarding dumping and incineration to be regulated in the EEZ it is true that dumping in the EEZ, irrespective of the flag state, would be subject to the rules and regulations and permission of the coastal state.[45] The relevant provisions of the LOSC follow the example of the London Dumping Convention which has been ratified by all North Sea states. When it comes to enforcement the coastal state shall enforce the relevant regulations also in its EEZ.[46] Thus the additional benefits would be that dumping activities executed by vessels under foreign flags could be prevented. Again the practical effect is minor because dumping activities by non-North Sea states seem to be very rare in the North Sea area.

Incineration on the other hand is not explicitly mentioned in the LOSC since the dumping definition[47] and the specific rules of Article 210.6 are silent in this respect. On the contrary, the Oslo and London Dumping Conventions both include incineration and are applicable to all North Sea states. An additional benefit is only conceivable if the LOSC could be amended or interpreted in a way to include incineration, which is not realistic for the time being.

To sum up one has to warn against too high expectations from the establishment of an EEZ. Compared with the current situation North Sea states would benefit

[42] Art. 220.3.
[43] T. IJlstra, "Regional Co-operation in the North Sea: An Inquiry", 196.
[44] See Arts. 208, 209 and (enforcement) Arts. 214 and 215.
[45] Art. 210.5.
[46] Art. 216.1.
[47] Art. 1.5.

only to a minor extent by acquiring broader EEZ competences. An overall solution of the problems is not to be expected from the establishment on an EEZ.[48]

Nevertheless this problem also has a political dimension in that it would not only provide a uniform umbrella regime for the progressive development of rules and standards for the North Sea as a model region, but also enhance the prospects of an anticipated entry into force of the LOSC. The EEZ regime identifies the problems and opportunities presented by the extension of marine areas under national jurisdiction and this in turn is a pre-condition for the determination of a national marine policy which is still lacking in many North Sea states. The special value in terms of the environmental protection policy of the LOSC lies in laying down a (global) mechanism and thus raising the consciousness of all those engaged in environmental protection. A fresh impetus for new initiatives is needed everywhere and above all the awareness of the importance of the marine environment in the North Sea states has to improve.

Decision-makers in all North Sea states will be left with the difficult task of evaluating whether the North Sea Conferences, which are the only existing body comprehensively to deal with North Sea pollution (albeit so far only relatively successfully), will also need the EEZ concept as another umbrella.

[48] See NILOS Newsletter, Vol. 1, no. 2, July 1989, p. 5 (letter of The Netherlands government to chairman of the Second Chamber of the National Assembly).

Chapter 21

Marine Protected Areas in the North Sea

Gerard Peet and Susan Gubbay

Introduction

The North Sea environmental debate is dominated by the attention given to the pollution of the North Sea. Relatively little attention is given to the protection of species and the protection of specific areas in the North Sea. The agendas and results of the first two International Conferences on the Protection of the North Sea bear witness to this.

There are several good reasons why priority is given to tackling pollution. Many of the most obvious signs of environmental stress in the North Sea are proven or considered to be pollution-related.[1] Both the protection of species and the protection of specific areas in the North Sea will, of course, also benefit strongly from a successful pollution prevention policy for the North Sea. The relation between reduced reproduction of harbour seals in The Netherlands part of the Wadden Sea and PCB-levels in that same region illustrates this with respect to species-protection as well as the protection of this specific part of the North Sea.

Yet, pollution is not the only threat to which species and specific areas in the North Sea are exposed. Overfishing is one of these other threats to species.[2] Coastal-defence projects, land reclamation or the destruction of the sea floor as a result of the extraction of e.g. sand or gravel are among these other threats to specific areas.[3] There are, therefore, good reasons also to consider other ways to protect

[1] J. Kuiper, "Ecotoxicological Effects of Pollution on the Ecosystems of the North Sea", in G. Peet (ed.), *The Status of the North Sea Environment: Reasons for Concern*, Vol. ii, (Amsterdam, Stichting Werkgroep Noordzee, 1987), p. 16.

[2] See e.g. *Quality Status of the North Sea, A Report by the Scientific and Technical Working Group*, Department of the Environment, London 1987, which gives little attention to fisheries but makes one very clear observation on page 2: "Virtually all important North Sea fish stocks are overfished"; a review of the current status of fish stocks was recently given by D. W. Armstrong, *et al.*, *Historical and Current State of the Major North Sea Fish Stocks*; paper presented to the North Sea 2000 Conference at the Institute of Offshore Engineering (Heriot Watt University) Edinburgh, 16–18 August 1989. See also D. Symes, Chapter 23, *below*.

[3] See e.g. a number of papers in Peet, *The Status of the North Sea Environment*, 145–192.

species and specific areas of the North Sea in addition to the attention given to pollution prevention.

Two other chapters in this issue will discuss species protection,[4] this chapter will focus its attention on the protection of specific areas, on the designation of *marine protected areas* in the North Sea.

Marine protected areas

As early as 1935, the Fort Jefferson National Monument in Florida (USA) was set up as a conservation area, covering 18,850 hectares of sea along with 35 hectares of coastal land.[5] It probably was the world's first marine protected area. In 1985 there were some 430 marine protected areas in 69 countries.[6] A more recent (1986) world-wide survey of marine protected areas listed such areas in more than 80 countries.[7]

In general, marine protected areas can be defined as "areas of inter-tidal or subtidal terrain together with their overlying waters and associated flora, fauna, historical and cultural features, which have been reserved to protect part or all of the enclosed environment."[8] Within this very general term there is a wide variety of types of marine protected areas. An indication of this variety is the number of terms used for marine protected areas such as marine sanctuary, marine reserve, marine park, protected seascape, wildlife sanctuary, and many other terms. At times different words may be used for marine protected areas which are basically similar. There are, however, different types of marine protected areas within the very general definition given above. Differences between these types can be based on such factors as location, objectives and level of protection.

Location

Most marine protected areas are located close to the shore or even in internal waters and may include land areas as well. The number of marine protected areas in open waters is very limited. Some examples of (potential) marine protected areas in open waters can be found in the United States. The Gulf of the Farallones National Marine Sanctuary near San Francisco includes a large area of open waters, the proposed National Marine Sanctuary of Cordell Bank which is to be situated directly north of the Farallon Islands Sanctuary will include open waters only. On the east coast of the United States, Stellwagen Bank, the Nantucket Sound and Shoals, Oceanographers Canyon and the Heceta-Stonewall Banks have been listed as potential marine sanctuaries which are all located in open waters.[9]

[4] See P. Birnie, Chapter 22, *below* and Symes, Chapter 23, *below*.
[5] Marine Conservation Society, *Factsheet No. 2, Marine Protected Areas*, Winter 1987/8.
[6] *Ibid.*
[7] E. Silva Maynard, *et al.*, *A Bibliographical Listing of Coastal and Marine Protected Areas: A Global Survey*, Woods Hole Oceanographic Institution (WHOI–86–11); Woods Hole, 1986.
[8] See Marine Conservation Society, *Factsheet No. 2*.
[9] Department of Commerce, National Oceanographic and Atmospheric Administration, *Announcement of National Marine Sanctuary Program Final Site Evaluation List*; pub. in Federal Register, Vol.48, no. 151, 4 August 1983.

Objectives

The existing marine protected areas have been established on the basis of a large variety of objectives. These include the protection of ecologically or biologically important areas, the protection of specific marine organisms, the protection of important geological or geomorphological processes, protection of beautiful seascapes, as well as the development of multiple use of those areas in the interest of recreation or certain forms of fisheries. In general two categories of protection can be distinguished:

- protection of an area in combination with multiple use (which may include recreation or fisheries) compatible with the protection of natural resources; and
- strict protection.

At present only very few marine protected areas do in fact provide total protection to the marine environment. Most aim at some form of multiple use management.

Level of protection

The level of protection given to specific areas is another issue which distinguishes marine protected areas. In some areas protection may be given from all activities which could cause environmental damage to such areas. In other areas protection is given only with respect to a limited number of such activities, e.g. with respect to specific fisheries activities (closed fishing zones) or to shipping (such as areas to be avoided by ships or special areas).

Some legal aspects

The question whether or not states have a right to designate marine protected areas cannot be answered easily. Firstly, there is the question of different types of jurisdiction. Secondly there are the traditional freedoms of the seas which have to be considered.

Within territorial waters coastal states have full jurisdiction (with some exceptions with respect to shipping such as the right of innocent passage). The designation of marine protected areas within territorial waters should therefore not meet substantial legal problems.

Beyond territorial waters the situation is different. In these waters the traditional freedoms of the high seas (navigation, fishing, the laying of submarine cables and pipelines, overflight and others which are recognized by international law)[10] may be applicable. Much depends, however, on the question whether or not coastal states have established extended jurisdictional zones such as Exclusive Fisheries Zones (with increased jurisdiction with respect to fisheries) or an Exclusive Economic Zone.

International law therefore limits, in different degrees, the options to protect specific marine areas. On the other hand, however, international law does not

[10] Geneva Convention on the High Seas, Art. 2 and 1982 LOSC, Art. 87.

exclude the option either. Several international conventions may be interpreted even to encourage such action where and when necessary.

The 1958 Geneva Convention on the High Seas and the 1982 United Nations Convention on the Law of the Sea contain general provisions regarding the obligations of states to protect the marine environment[11] or more specifically to protect and preserve rare or fragile ecosystems as well as the habitat of depleted, threatened or endangered species and other forms of marine life[12] or regarding the proper conservation and management of living resources.[13]

Within the framework of the International Maritime Organization international regulations have been developed which offer some options for the protection of specific sea areas such as the concept of "special areas" in the MARPOL Convention[14] and the concept of "areas to be avoided" in accordance with the General Provisions on Ships' Routeing.[15]

International Wildlife Conservation agreements also hold several elements to encourage the designation of protected areas.[16] For the North Sea the Ramsar Convention (designation of Wetlands) is of relevance as well as the Conventions of Berne (protection of European wildlife and natural habitats) and Bonn (protection of migratory species) and the Bird Directive of the European Community which all include the option of protecting specific areas essential for specific species. Within the framework of the Bonn Convention special (as yet unspecified) measures for the protection of harbour seals, bottle-nosed dolphins and harbour porpoises in the North Sea have been agreed; these could involve protecting specific areas as well.[17]

Whilst international law provides some obstacles towards protecting marine areas there are no major legal stumbling-blocks to prevent the designation of marine protected areas. This is of course no surprise given the number of existing marine protected areas some of which extend into waters beyond the territorial sea (e.g. in the USA).

Marine protected areas in the north sea

What is the current status with respect to marine protected areas in the North Sea?[18] At the international level initiatives have been taken to give (parts of) the North Sea a special protected status. At the national level, several North Sea states have already designated marine protected areas or are developing plans to do so.

[11] e.g. as in Art. 192, 1982 LOSC.
[12] Art. 194(5), 1982 LOSC.
[13] Art. 61, 1982 LOSC.
[14] *International Convention for the Prevention of Pollution from Ships*, Annex I regulations 1(10) and 10, Annex II regulations 1(7), 5(7–13) and 7(6), Annex V regulations 1(3) and 5.
[15] International Maritime Organization, *Ships' Routeing* (5th ed., including amendments nos. 6 and 7, London, 1984, 1986 and 1988).
[16] See Simon Lyster; *International Wildlife Law* (Cambridge: Grotius Publications Ltd., 1985).
[17] Peet, *Beschermde Natuurgebieden in het Noordzeegebied?* (Delft: Stichting SEA, 1987).
[18] for the purpose of this Chapter the North Sea is defined as the area south of the 62 N parallel, west of the gaps between Scotland, Orkney and Shetland, north of the Straits of Dover and including the Skagerrak in the east.

International efforts

One of the options to give the North Sea as a whole a special protected status which has been intensively discussed is the designation of the North Sea as a Special Area according to the MARPOL Convention. Pressure from environmental organizations has been high to have the North Sea designated as a Special Area according to Annexes I and II of this Convention; the North Sea states decided to have the North Sea designated as a Special Area according to Annex V instead. This issue will be discussed in another chapter in this issue.[19]

Within the framework of the International Maritime Organization the designation of "Areas to be Avoided" would be another option to protect specific areas. At present there are no "Areas to be Avoided" in the North Sea which have been designated for conservation purposes.

Within the framework of the European Communities site specific measures can be taken with respect to fisheries activities. The objective of such measures will normally be the conservation of (commercial) fish-stocks. Such measures include the closure of areas within 12 miles of the coasts of France, Belgium, The Netherlands, the Federal Republic of Germany and part of the western Danish coast for larger ships with certain fishing gears as well as the designation of special conservation zones which can extend beyond 12 miles, such as the one which has been designated around the Shetland Islands.[20]

The environmental protection of the Wadden Sea has been the subject of international co-operation between the three Wadden Sea states (Denmark, Federal Republic of Germany and The Netherlands) and has, as such, a special status within the North Sea. This too will be discussed in another article in this issue.[21]

Norway

Proposals have been developed for the Nordic region in 1984 to designate a number of sites as "valuable marine areas worthy of protection". For the Norwegian sector of the North Sea the proposed marine nature reserves were: Utvaer-Indrevaer, Lindaspollene, Framvaren and Noteroy-Tjome. These areas include either marine/littoral sites or islands and are all within Norwegian territorial waters. The proposals have not yet been implemented but it has been reported that the Norwegian Nature Conservation Act was to be used to implement these proposals.[22]

Sweden

As early as 1980 the National Swedish Environmental Protection Board published the results of a project about "Marine Reserves" with a view to selecting sites for

[19] See V. Sebek, Chapter 14, *above*.

[20] See Peet, *Beschermde Natuurgebieden in het Noordzeegebied?* pp. 5–6.

[21] See K. van der Zwiep, Chapter 18, *above*.

[22] Roger Mitchell, *Conservation of Marine Benthic Biocenoses in the North Sea and Baltic*, Nature Conservation Council, Peterborough, 1986, p. 35.

protected areas along the Swedish coast. For the Skagerrak section of the Swedish coast eight marine reserves were proposed, six of which were given a high priority. These reserves were to be established under the Swedish 1964 Nature Conservation Act.

In the proposals which were developed for the Nordic region in 1984 two Swedish sites were proposed: Vaderoarna/Tjarnoarkipelagen/Kosterarpikelagen/Kosterannan, and Gullmarsfjorden.[23] These areas too are marine/littoral sites or islands and arc all within Swedish territorial waters. Since 1984 the Gullmarsfjorden has been given protected status with special regulations with respect to discharges into the area and regarding fishing activities.[24]

Denmark

Several marine areas of Denmark have been designated for inclusion in "the List" of the Ramsar Convention[25] and the EC Bird Directive. Of relevance for the North Sea are the Nissum Fiord, the Ringkøbing Fiord and most of all the Wadden Sea. The Wadden Sea Ramsar area includes inland waters as well as a small part of the territorial waters, i.e. a small part of the North Sea up to an average of 6 metres depth and incorporates riparian and coastal zones and greater parts of the islands. The Danish part of the Wadden Sea is also classified as a Special Protection Area according to the EC Bird Directive.[26]

The entire Danish Wadden Sea is protected by the Nature Conservation Act and by the Game Act. Parts of the Wadden Sea have been declared a Wildlife Reserve by Statutory Order 1979 (rev. 1984) and a Nature Reserve by Statutory Order 1982 (rev. 1985). The Wildlife and Nature Reserve covers the state-owned sea territory, which means that areas ecologically belonging to the Wadden Sea, such as saltmarshes and parts of the islands, are not protected under Wildlife and Nature Reserve regulations.[27] In 1988 the internationally very important marsh area of Tøndersmarsken was protected by special legislation.[28]

In practice the Danish Wadden Sea has been divided into three zones: (a) areas which are closed during parts of the year or permanently, (b) areas where certain activities are prohibited (such as water sports, hunting), and (c) other areas where various regulations apply.[29]

[23] *Ibid*. 33–34.

[24] Personal communication from I. Thoresen (Swedish Society for the Conservation of Nature).

[25] *Convention on Wetlands of International Importance, especially as Waterfowl Habitat*; Art. 2.1: "Each Contracting Party shall designate suitable wetlands within its territory for inclusion in a List of Wetlands of International Importance, hereinafter referred to as the List' . . ."; Art. 3.1: "The Contracting Parties Shall Formulate and Implement their Planning so as to Promote the Conservation of the Wetlands Included in the List . . .".

[26] Fifth Trilateral Governmental Conference on the Protection of the Wadden Sea, *Conference Papers for Delegates, document TGC (88) 5–1*, Bonn, November 1988, p. 6.

[27] *Ibid*. 7.

[28] Fifth Trilateral Governmental Conference, *National Reports*, 57.

[29] As summarized in a map of the Wadden Sea and relevant conservation measures produced by the Common Wadden Sea Secretariat.

Federal Republic of Germany

The Niedersachsen part of the German part of the Wadden Sea has been designated for inclusion in the List.[30] The boundaries of this Ramsar area are the dikes and coastline on the landward side and it includes large parts of the islands and a part of the North Sea up to an average depth of 6 metres. Here too, inland waters as well as a small part of the territorial sea are included. The Schleswig-Holstein and Hamburg parts of the Wadden Sea have not yet been designated for inclusion in the List, but proposals are being prepared. The German part of the Wadden Sea has not been classified as a Special Protection Area according to the EC Bird Directive; proposals to do so are being prepared by Schleswig-Holstein.[31]

In 1982 Schleswig-Holstein established a national park in its section of the German Wadden Sea. The area includes some sandbanks in the North Sea just outside the Wadden Sea. With respect to conservation regulations it has a zoning system similar to that in Denmark.[32] In Hamburg, two nature conservation ordinances have placed the largest part of the Hamburg Wadden Sea under protection of the most stringent protection category of the Hamburg Nature Conservation Act. There are plans to proclaim a National Park for the Neuwerk and Scharhörn Wadden Sea.[33] In Bremen no protected areas were designated.[34] In 1986 Niedersachsen established its Niedersachsen Wadden Sea National Park which covers the entire Niedersachsen sector of the German Wadden Sea including the East Frisian islands.[35] It also includes a narrow strip of the North Sea directly north of the islands[36] but the Dollart as well as the waterways of the rivers Ems, Jade, Weser and Elbe are not included. In Niedersachsen too a zoning system with three different zones was developed as regards the type of conservation measures taken for the area.

Since 1981 an inter-tidal and sub-tidal area around the island of Helgoland has been given a protected status under a special ordinance with respect to the nature conservation area "Helgoländer Felssockel".[37]

The Netherlands

The Netherlands Government has developed a general policy for the protection of the Wadden Sea, the so-called Wadden Sea Key Planning Decision. This policy covers the area outside the dikes as well as those parts of the islands which are regu-

[30] See *Convention on Wetlands*.
[31] See Fifth Trilateral Governmental Conference, *Conference Papers*, 6.
[32] Der Minister für Ernährung, Landwirtschaft und Forsten des Landes Schleswig-Holstein; *Nationalpark Schleswig-Holsteinisches Wattenmeer* (English Edition), 1985.
[33] See Fifth Trilateral Governmental Conference, *National Reports*, 25.
[34] See *ibid*.
[35] See *ibid*. 26.
[36] See n. 29, *above*.
[37] Bruno P. Kremer and Klaus Janke, *Die Insel Helgoland* (A Special Edition of Seevögal), Vol. 7, 2nd ed., 1986, p. 21.

larly flooded by the sea.[38] The area protected only covers inland waters, no parts of the territorial sea have been included. On the basis of this general policy, which was not given a legal status, more specific measures were developed.

The Netherlands part of the Wadden Sea as well as two parts of this area (Boschplaat, Griend) have been designated for inclusion in the List of the Ramsar Convention.[39] The Eastern Scheldt, an estuary, has also been designated for this list.[40] These have not yet been classified as Special Protection Area according to the EC Bird Directive.[41]

The most important parts of the tidal flats, saltmarshes and islands of the Wadden Sea are nature monuments according to The Netherlands' Nature Conservation Act. A number of seal banks and feeding areas for waterfowl have not been brought under this Act.[42] Other protected areas according to Netherlands' Nature Conservation legislation are the Eastern Scheldt, and parts of the Western Scheldt (Verdronken Zwarte Polder and Verdronken Land van Saeftinge). These areas too are in inland waters.

Belgium

Belgium has designated two areas which are relevant to the North Sea for inclusion in the List of the Ramsar Convention,[43] the IJzer estuary and the Vlaamse Banken (Flemish Banks). The Flemish Banks are an area bounded by the mean high water, the 3-mile limit, the French Belgian border and a line at right angles to the coast near Ostend. Protection of this area is limited to a prohibition of hunting and of sand extraction.[44]

The Zwin near The Netherlands border has been classified as a nature reserve according to Belgian legislation. In the Belgian part of the Western Scheldt two tidal flats have been classified as nature reserve as well (Galgenschoor and Groot Buitenschoor, both just north of Antwerp).

United Kingdom

In the United Kingdom the idea of marine protected areas has been slow to develop. The first voluntary marine conservation reserve area was set up in 1977, legislation for the establishment of Marine Nature Reserves within the limits of UK territorial waters was included in the 1981 Wildlife and Countryside Act. No statutory Marine Nature Reserves have been declared yet in the North Sea. The Nature Conservancy Council has proposed one North Sea site for designation as a Marine nature Reserve: St. Abbs. Given the lack of progress with regard to statutory pro-

[38] Ministerie van Volkshuisvesting en Ruimtelijke Ordening, *De Waddenzee, deel e, tekst van de na parlementaire behandeling vastgestelde pkb*; Tweede Kamer der Staten General 13 933 no. 53, The Hague, 1980.
[39] See *Convention on Wetlands*.
[40] Personal communication from the Department of Agriculture and Fisheries.
[41] See Fifth Trilateral Governmental Conference, *Conference Papers*, 6-7.
[42] See *ibid*. 8.
[43] See *Convention on Wetlands*.
[44] Filip Volckaert, *Onze Noordzee leeft*; published in *Natuurreservaten*.

tection for marine sites, an initiative was taken to designate voluntary marine reserves. In such areas protection of the area is undertaken on a voluntary basis by the users of the area. St. Abbs was established as a voluntary marine reserve in 1984.[45]

Conclusion

From this brief (and possibly incomplete) review of the present state of affairs with respect to marine protected areas in the North Sea it is clear that the number of such areas within the North Sea proper (territorial waters and waters beyond territorial waters) is limited. None in Norway, none in Sweden. In Denmark a small part of the territorial waters east of the Wadden Sea has been given limited protection. In general the same applies to the Federal Republic of Germany. The strict protection (closed area) given to the sandbanks (Knobsande, west of Amrun) is the one exception. In The Netherlands no parts of territorial waters or waters beyond the territorial sea have been given a protected status. In Belgium the Flemish Banks have been given limited protection and in the UK the voluntary marine reserve is the only example of a marine protected area in the North Sea. Plans and proposals for additional marine protected areas have been developed in a number of North Sea states but progress appears to be slow (e.g. in Norway and the United Kingdom). This slow progress has to be set against the background of increasing pressure and threat to the marine environment of the North Sea.

Marine Protected Areas in the North Sea, future prospects

What are the future prospects as regards marine protected areas in the North Sea? Will it develop into an effective tool available for the protection of the marine environment of the North Sea? Progress is slow, yet there are some important initiatives, for example in the United Kingdom and The Netherlands.

United Kingdom initiatives

In the United Kingdom progress is being made with the task of identifying sites which should be given some form of protection for their marine nature conservation interest. In 1989 the Marine Conservation Society published a list of nearly 250 sites in UK waters worthy of consideration. Since then the Nature Conservancy Council has embarked on a Marine Nature Conservation Review which will be more comprehensive in its coverage and detail. Over the next 15 years information will be collected for this Review with the aim of describing and locating the major marine habitat types in UK waters and identifying sites of marine nature conservation interest.

Netherlands initiatives

In The Netherlands several (governmental and non-governmental) reports have discussed the option of designating protected areas within Netherlands territorial

[45] Susan Gubbay; *A Coastal Directory for Marine Nature Conservation*; World Wildlife Fund and Marine Conservation Society, 1985.

waters or even beyond territorial waters. In 1986 a study was carried out for the Ministry of Agriculture and Fisheries[46] to produce some proposals for the designation of marine protected areas in The Netherlands sector of the North Sea.[47]

The report concluded that it might be possible to designate such areas. It noted, however, that special protection of marine areas should be considered in close relation with the general environmental management of the North Sea, especially with regard to pollution as it would be useless to grant a protected status to areas which are under strong environmental pressure from pollution from sources outside the area. A policy of protecting specific areas should be accompanied by a policy regarding pollution control and environmental management in general. Such a policy has been developed in The Netherlands (in a national Water Quality Plan for the North Sea). The report also noted that knowledge about the North Sea's ecosystem was still very limited, especially as regards marine organisms which have no importance to commercial fisheries and also as regards marine mammals.

Three areas were identified which should, partly or completely, be given a protected status. It is proposed that the Ministry starts the preparation of plans and proposals on the basis of which final decisions can be made.

1. The Frisian front. An area north of the Wadden Sea, outside territorial waters with a very high biological productivity. This area, or at least part of this area, was to be protected on the basis of its ecological value, as well as for its potential value for scientific research. Protection could be achieved by a complete ban on fishing with bottom gear as well as on offshore mining activities (installations as well as pipelines).

2. Coastal waters. In the proposals for this area the question of the exact size of this area (12, 15 or 20 miles off the coast) would need to be discussed. The area needs protection because of its importance for marine organisms (nursery area for fish species, importance for sea birds, etc.) and because of the intensity of environmental stress in this area as a result of pollution and intensive use. The area could be protected by restrictions on fisheries, stricter anti-pollution measures for all sources including ships, and strict conditions for sand extraction.

3. The Voordelta. An area of newly developing sandbanks off the south-western coast of The Netherlands. This area needs protection because of the importance of the geological, geomorphological and potential ecological processes taking place in the area. The area might develop into an internationally unique area where as a result of human interference (the construction of dams, and closing of estuaries) large-scale natural processes have started to develop. The area might in the future also be important for seals, should efforts to reintroduce harbour seals in the Eastern Scheldt be successful. Protection of this area should be guaranteed by the prohibition of construction activities including offshore mining installations. Measures might also be necessary to restrict entry to the area.

[46] This ministry is responsible for nature conservation.
[47] Peet, *Beschermde Natuurgebieden in het Noordzeegebied?*

In 1989 The Netherlands Government published a draft policy document about nature conservation[48] in which further proposals with respect to conservation projects in the Voordelta, coastal waters, and Frisian Front were announced.

Conclusion

The designation of marine protected areas as a tool for environmental protection in the North Sea has been given limited attention until now. There are only a few marine protected areas in the North Sea proper, and only one of these area has strict statutory protection. The other protected areas are managed on a basis of multiple use or even on a voluntary basis.

The environmental problems of the North Sea, especially some of the non-pollution problems, and the increasing environmental pressure resulting from these problems should provide a good basis for more activity and initiatives in the field of marine protected areas.

In most, if not all, North Sea states progress in this field appears to be slow. Some promising initiatives have been taken, however, and deserve further action.

Marine protected areas are a viable option for conservation of the marine environment provided that they are considered within an overall framework which provides guidance in coastal and sea use management.

[48] *Ibid*. 156–157.

Chapter 22

Problems Concerning Conservation of Wildlife including Marine Mammals in the North Sea

Professor Patricia Birnie

Introduction

Absence of Wildlife Dimension to International North Sea Conferences

The International North Sea Conferences have so far concentrated their attention on control and prevention of pollution of the North Sea, virtually ignoring both the impact of this on living resources in this area and the numerous problems facing their conservation and management. Should the scope of future conference Declarations be extended to include these or can the problems adequately be dealt with within the existing legal regime? This regime is based on numerous international conventions, some of which establish commissions specific to their purposes, others of which are operated and administered through existing organizations, such as the European Community (EC) or the Council of Europe (CE) which themselves generate conventions or rules and recommendations. The drawback of this system is that it is not "networked" in the ordinary meaning of that term, that is the threads and notes of the conventions are not arranged in the form of a net encompassing all the problems within a single fabric.[1] They are generally addressed pragmatically, as single species-problems, despite the growing calls for an ecological approach to marine management problems, within which the inter-relationship of species themselves and with the marine environment as such would be taken into consideration.[2]

[1] "Work in which threads, wires or the like, are arranged in the form of a net", *Shorter Oxford Dictionary*, Vol. II (Oxford, OUP, 1978), p. 1398.

[2] See e.g. C. de Klemm, "Living Resources of the Oceans", in D. M. Johnston (ed), *The Environmental Law of the Sea*, IUCN Environmental Policy and Law Paper, No. 18 (1981), pp. 71–192, esp. pp. 71, 79–84.

Principles of living-resource conservation

The threefold objectives of conservation of marine living-resources have been laid down in the World Conservation Strategy;[3] namely, maintenance of ecological processes and life-support systems, the preservation of genetic diversity, and the sustainable utilization of species and ecosystems.

Only a few of the marine species in the North Sea are currently harvested. These include the various kinds of fish taken for human consumption and industrial purposes discussed in chapter 23, below. Although some marine mammals, such as various kinds of the large cetaceans and seals (phocidae) have been exploited from time to time in this area, none is currently taken in directed fisheries by North Sea states, other than Norway, which has continued to catch some minke whales. Some small cetaceans are, however, still harvested by Faroe islanders, and others (including dolphins and porpoises) are killed "incidentally" in the nets used on other fisheries. Shellfish are heavily exploited commercially and also destroyed by other activities related to the sea-bed, such as bottom trawling and commercial exploration. Birds are not harvested, but they too may be killed incidentally by activities such as gill net fishing and oil pollution. But all marine species, whether harvested or not, need to be preserved for the role they play in maintaining the complex relationships of all species and the ecosystems of the commercially harvested species. They are also valuable, to an extent as yet unknown and largely unexploited, as genetic resources which might provide new sources of food, and industrial and pharmaceutical products. The North Sea consists entirely of the continental shelves of its seven surrounding states and this is where most fisheries reside. It is thus an area presenting a large number of management problems.

Threats to the North Sea wildlife

Many scientists and involved bodies are now especially concerned by the lack of protection afforded to small cetaceans and the lack of research into and monitoring of the problems threatening their survival, particularly in the North Sea, these include: deliberate kills and incidental catching; overfishing; pollution and habitat disturbance. Information is incomplete and thus contentious but the suggested threats to these and other species of wildlife include:

Over-exploitation

Some fisheries have been over-exploited[4] including shell, demersal and pelagic fisheries but they are not threatened with extinction, since stock levels of fin fish recover fairly quickly. This is not the case with seals, whose breeding habits make them vulnerable to capture, and cetaceans, whose slow rate of reproduction may inhibit recovery if stock levels become too depleted. But fisheries may collapse to such an extent that they fail to recover their place in the ecosystem. This may result

[3] IUCN-World Conservation Strategy; IUCN, UNEP and WWF, Gland and Nairobi; 1980; see also World Charter for Nature, GAR 37/7, 9 November 1982, (1983) XXIII ILM 455–460.

[4] See D. Symes, chap. 23, *below*.

in serious ecological and economic consequences. By-catches (incidental catch) exacerbate the problem for all wildlife.

In the North Sea it is possible that the over-exploitation and collapse of the herring fishery may have caused the decline in harbour porpoise, the distribution of which follows the herring spawning. Both it and the white-beaked and white-sided dolphins may also be threatened by overfishing of sand eel, sprat and Norway pout for industrial purposes. This has already resulted in severe breeding failures in puffins and arctic tern in the Shetland Islands.

Pollution

Much of the detritus of modern industrial society is now discharged into the sea. The details of the pollutants concerned and their regulation by the relevant organizations, commissions and treaties are dealt with in other chapters herein. Marine mammals can accumulate chemical residues from pesticides and fertilisers and dumped wastes. Other less lethal substances may nonetheless become so if not subjected to controls and conditions concerning the time and place of dumping and quantity dumped. Spillage of massive quantities of oil or chemicals can occur from ship strandings or collisions, as well as deliberate discharges and wreak great havoc on seabirds.[5]

High levels of PCBs (polychlorinated biphenyls), organochlorine pesticides such as dieldrin, DDT, lindane and heptachlor and heavy metals such as mercury and cadmium have been detected in dolphins, porpoises and pilot whales in the North Sea, especially those found along the Dutch and German Wadden Sea coasts. The pollutants are absorbed by marine organisms and move up the food chain. As they are cumulative and persistent the effects may be long-term and progressive and may weaken their immune systems and their reproductive capacity, as well as those of fish. It is possible that this factor contributed to the 15,000 or so common seals that died in 1988 in the North and Baltic Seas from a virus. Small cetaceans may be among the most vulnerable to such effects. Recent algae blooms occurring along the Swedish and Danish coasts are bound to have suffocated not only fish but some dolphins and porpoises. It is notable that bottlenose dolphins that used to appear regularly in the Thames, Humber and other major English estuaries have virtually disappeared and are found only in the Moray Firth, the least polluted of the main Scottish estuaries. The harbour porpoise has also vanished from estuaries adjacent to industry (Thames, Firth of Forth, Firth of Tay, Clyde, Tyne and Tees, Mersey, Bristol Channel).

Destruction of habitat

This includes not only physical destruction, by trawling, dredging, in-filling or draining of spawning, breeding or nursery grounds of birds and mammals but the introduction of changes in the ecology that inhibit a species' continued existence; these can be brought about by pollution, warming of the water, increasing salinity, decreasing nutrients, or algae blooms that absorb all the oxygen. Until recently

[5] Advisory Committee on Pollution of the Sea (ACOPS) Annual Reports detail such incidents, and provide maps and charts of the locus of oil spills and damaged seabirds.

little research had been done on the effects of these activities on habitats, and estuaries still continue to be dammed or dredged and barrages to be contemplated, marshes drained, and harbours and piers extended on beaches round the North Sea. In particular very little research has been done on pollution levels in cetaceans in United Kingdom waters; data available were obtained 15–20 years ago and there is no information on current levels in porpoises on British North Sea Coasts and thus on regional contaminant levels; and little idea of their biological effects on cetaceans. It is suggested also that the life cycle of dolphins and porpoises in the North Sea is disturbed by shipping. Some deaths are caused by collisions and the echo-location of small cetaceans may be interfered with by sidescan sonar and echo-sounders. Exploitation of the North Sea-bed for oil, gas, sand and gravel has caused increased traffic, oil spills, oil/metal and other waste dumping and discharges, loss of hazardous cargoes and extensive use of seismic surveys generating high energy and low frequency sound waves that disrupt the habitat of small cetaceans.

Introduction of exotic, that is alien, species may also affect habitat and they may introduce new parasites and diseases.

Directed and incidental catches

Deliberate kills. These include the catching of a few bottlenose whales in the Faroe Islands and the islanders' annual kill of about 2,000 pilot whales, as well as of white-sided and white-beaked dolphins and orca. Norwegian whalers have killed orca; Iceland captures some live orca for sale to aquaria; French and Spanish fishermen kill several thousand common dolphins and other species including the bottlenose dolphin and harbour porpoises.

Incidental catches. The rapidly increased use of long-lasting monofilament nets has resulted in the drowning of many dolphin, porpoise and whale. Danish fisheries are thought to catch thousands; the Greenland salmon gill net fishing is estimated to entrap about 1,500. British driftnetters take a large by-catch of white beaked and common dolphins off the Scilly Isles and Dutch fishermen have similar (poorly documented) by-catches. It is suspected that incidental catches are far greater than hitherto supposed because data have been so lacking.

Possibilities of a multi-species approach to management?

Is it desirable and, if so, possible to manage the diversity of species involved in the North Sea on the basis of the ecological approach to conservation now advocated by some states and environmentalists. Various solutions are reviewed in a recent article by Gulland.[6] He examines the problems of over-capacity of fishing fleets; the reluctance of states to take other than economic factors into account in management—despite the co-ordinating work of ICES (the International Council for the Exploration of the Sea—the regional scientific body of which the EC is not a member). He feels that the introduction of a comprehensive multi-species approach to

[6] J. A. Gulland, "The Management of North Sea Fisheries: Looking Towards the 21st Century", (1987) 11 *Marine Policy* 259–272.

include marine mammals, and birds as well as fin and shell fisheries would make a complex situation even more complex. His conclusion is that North Sea policies are in a vicious circle; until there is pressure to reduce fishing effort there will be no substantive discussion of the forms of benefit resulting but this pressure will not arise until the benefits have been identified and in themselves exert the catalytic pressure. Gulland suggests that a new forum for scientific discussion is required, either by extending ICES's scope or establishing regional management councils of the kind instituted under the US Fishery Conservation and Management Act 1976.[7] He holds back from proposing a better way of managing North Sea fisheries since that enormous task can only be tackled once it is accepted that changes in policy are necessary. It would be best, in his view, to encourage more independent research in universities and institutes.

Gulland advocates new forums, though noting that adding another bureaucratic layer may further complicate the issue. IJlstra, in a recent article in IJECL,[8] suggested that there may now, given the growing interest in environmental issues, be an opportunity to reconsider a proposal made in 1974 by a David Davies Study Group that there should be a Standing Conference of all North Sea states, involving the EC and the CE as independent members, to co-ordinate all aspects of the North Sea Regime through various issue-specific committees.[9] IJlstra suggests that the present Ministerial Conferences could be expanded to include fisheries, conservation and management of sea-bed and other marine resources, sea and air transport, in addition to the present pollution issues, but doubts, given the widespread means for regional co-operation that now exist, that this will prove politically acceptable, however useful it may be.

The wide range of treaties and established forums relevant to North Sea environmental issues has been outlined elsewhere[10] and specific commissions, etc. are analysed in other chapters in this volume. What will be addressed here is those aspects of the regime that relate to conservation of marine wildlife in the North Sea—fisheries, marine mammals, birds—and their adequacy and aptness for resolving existing problems in relation to these species.

Legal framework for conservation and protection of North Sea wildlife

As the North Sea is only a small part of the world's oceans, we must first identify the relevant international regime. The starting-point must, therefore, be the United Nations Conventions on the Law of the Sea (UNCLOS), particularly the 1982 Convention (LOSC).

[7] Pub. Law, L 94–265, 16 USC S. 181, as amended.

[8] T. IJlstra, "Regional Co-operation in the North Sea: An Inquiry", (1988) 3 IJECL 181.

[9] M. M. Sibthorp (ed.), *The North Sea: Challenge and Opportunity* (London, Europa, 1975). See also, R. B. Clark (ed.), *The Waters Around the British Isles: Their Conflicting Uses* (Oxford, Clarendon Press, 1987) in which the David Davies Institute revised these conclusions.

[10] See P. Birnie, "The North Sea: A Challenge of Disorganised Opportunities", in D. C. Watt (ed.), *The North Sea: A New International Regime* pp. 3–29 and Clark, *The Waters Around the British Isles*.

1982 LOSC

Article 56 of the 1982 LOSC[11] provides that coastal states can exercise sovereign rights, *inter alia*, to exploit, conserve and manage the living-resources of the sea-bed and the water column in 200-mile Exclusive Economic Zones (EEZs) measured from their territorial sea baselines. Coastal states' exclusive rights over fisheries are set out in Article 63 and are subject to various conservatory duties under Article 61.

All the North Sea states have extended their fisheries jurisdiction to 200-miles either as EFZs or EEZs[12] and five of the seven North Sea states have signed but not ratified the 1982 convention.[13] Its provisions relating to fisheries were negotiated by consensus and are generally considered to have entered into customary international law through state practice (though it is not uniform in its details). The LOSC requires the coastal state to determine the catch and its own capacity to harvest it; only the surplus to this must be made available to certain other states.

Taking account of the best scientific advice, the coastal state must ensure by conservation and management measures that living resources are not endangered by over-exploitation, and must co-operate with global, regional and sub-regional international organizations to this end. Coastal states are required generally to promote optimum utilization of the living-resources in the EEZ. However, the convention adopts a species approach, under which special conditions are laid down for Highly Migratory Species (HMS, Article 64); Marine Mammals (Article 65); anadromous (e.g. salmon) and catadromous (e.g. eel) species (Articles 66 and 67 respectively). Article 68 places sedentary species under the continental shelf regime (Part VI). It also requires the states concerned, when stocks cross national boundaries or boundaries between national and international zones, to try to agree on co-ordinated conservatory measures through appropriate subregional or regional organizations.

Provisions on highly migratory species

It is important in the case of marine mammals, which are also highly migratory species, to distinguish between the requirements of Articles 64 and 65 since some marine mammals (Cetaceans: Family Physetendae, Family Balaenopteridae; Family Balaenidae; Family Esrichtiidae; Family Monodontidae; Family Ziphiidae; Family Delphididae) appear on Annex I which lists the species to which Article 64 applies. This is because in early UNCLOS drafts there was no separate article protecting marine mammals; only Article 64 on HMS. When the more conservatory Article 65 was added it was decided to leave the above cetacean families on the Article 64 Annex, even though Article 64 requires states to promote optimum utilization of the species listed, as they and dolphins can be taken incidentally in catches directed at some of the other species listed in this Annex (mackerel, pomfrets, marlins, sharks, swordfish, sail fish, sauries) and it is, therefore, appropriate to leave

[11] United Nations Convention on the Law of the Sea, 1982.

[12] The European Community co-ordinated the adoption of these by its North Sea states in 1976/77.

[13] Signatories are Belgium, Denmark, France, Netherlands, Norway.

the relevant regional tuna, etc. organizations to deal with this problem. States fishing the Annex I species in a region are required to co-operate directly or through such organizations to ensure both conservation and optimum utilization within and beyond the EEZ.

Provisions on marine mammals
These species are removed from all requirements of optimum utilization and subject to the following requirement of Article 65:

> "Nothing in this Part restricts the right of a coastal state or the competence of an international organization, as appropriate, to prohibit, limit or regulate the exploitation of marine mammals more strictly than provided for in this Part. States shall co-operate with a view to the conservation of marine mammals and in the case of cetaceans shall in particular work through the appropriate international organizations for their conservation, management and study."

North Sea states can thus in their EEZs and EFZs prohibit the taking of cetaceans and must "work through" the "appropriate" organizations for their conservation. The ambiguity of these phrases should be noted. Must states accept regulation of cetaceans by some international body? All North Sea states except Belgium are members of the International Whaling Commission but do not agree on whether it is "appropriate" for all or only some cetaceans. Is there a choice of "appropriate" bodies in this region for management of large or small cetaceans?

Available management bodies for conservation of marine mammals: their limitations

For fisheries. These are referred to in the chapter on fisheries. For our purposes the relevant bodies are as follows.

European Community
The EC concerted the adoption between 1976/77 of 200-mile fisheries zones by its North Sea members. A Common Fisheries Policy (CFP) for fishing of certain species in these zones (excluding cetaceans and seals) was concluded in 1983. Since then the Community itself has been the fishing management body. The Community and not its individual members is now a member in its own right of the relevant fisheries commissions (excluding the IWC and sealing bodies).[14] It is not clear whether whaling comes within the CFP; the Commission considered that it did and in 1979 proposed that the EC should try to become party to the International Convention for Regulation of Whaling (see below).[15] Some EC Council members disputed this and the matter was left unresolved. Thus the EC has only observer status

[14] For an excellent and exhaustive account of the EC role see R. R. Churchill, *EEC Fisheries Law* (Martinus Nijhoff, 1987).

[15] International Convention for the Regulation of Whaling, 2 December 1946; printed by direction of the Commission, January 1964, 161 UNTS 2124, p. 24.

at the International Whaling Commission (IWC) meetings but has adopted a Regulation on Common Rules for Imports of Whales and other Cetacean Products.[16] Cetaceans for this purpose include whales, porpoises and dolphins.

The EC has also by Directives banned the commercial import into EC Member States of the skins of harp and hooded seals,[17] but has played no role in regulating North Sea seals. Whether the EC, if its Council were so minded, would be the most appropriate body to manage marine mammals in the North Sea remains controversial. It has been pointed out that "the Community as a fisheries regulatory body is diffuse and multipartite",[18] which makes it difficult to communicate with, and a very bureaucratic body, which probably also reduces its efficiency since it has a relatively small and over-burdened staff. These weaknesses could, of course, be remedied were EC Member States so minded.

North East Atlantic Fisheries Commission (NEAFC)[19]

The original 1959 NEAF Convention was re-negotiated in 1980 to take account of the subsuming of a large part of the high seas area to which it related within its Member States' 200-mile zones from 1977 onwards, and entered into force in 1982. The EC is a member in its own right, replacing its individual members. Its Commission must, taking account of the best scientific advice available (to be supplied by ICES), further both conservation and optimum utilization of fisheries. However, its powers within the North Sea are very limited for within the 200-mile zones the NEAFC can only make recommendations to parties at their initiative and only if the recommendation made is voted for by the party concerned. Recommendations become binding if not objected to within a specified period.

The NEAFC provides a forum for consultation and exchange of information on the state of fisheries and on management policies. It can also co-operate with Member States concerning management of stocks that migrate between their 200-mile zones and the high seas beyond and can co-ordinate scientific research in co-operation with ICES. Enforcement is by national (or EC) means. It has not yet adopted any measures relevant to the North Sea, and like its predecessor, the new NEAFC has given no advice on marine mammals or pinnipeds, which it leaves to the IWC and ICES respectively (see below).

Its potential as a management body for these species in the North Sea seems weak but it could be given such a role if its parties so agree. The total allowable catch-limits for the Canadian harvest of hooded and harp seals, for example, are

[16] Council Regulations (EEZ) No. 348/81 of 20 January 1981 (OJ L 39/1, 12 January 1981); repr.and explained in P. Birnie, *Legal Measures for Conservation of Marine Mammals*, IUCN Environmental Policy and Law Paper No. 19 (1982), pp. 85–88. This has since been revised and extended,see Regs. 3786/81 (correction in L131/30) and L.377/42. See also N. Haigh, EEC Environmental Policy and Britain (2nd ed.) (1988).

[17] See Dir. 83/129, OJ 1983 L 91/30, as extended by Dir 85/444, OJ 1985 L259/70.

[18] Churchill, *EEC Fisheries Law*, 283.

[19] Convention on Future Multilateral Co-operation in the North West Atlantic Fisheries; text in OJ 1981 L 227/22; Cmnd 8474; its 13 parties include all North Sea states, i.e. EC and Norway.

now recommended by the Scientific Council of the North West Atlantic Fisheries Organization (NAFO), a body similar to NEAFC.

International Council for the Exploration of the Sea[20]

This includes all North Sea states amongst its members. It is not a regulatory body but a long-standing forum for scientific collaboration and debate at the regional level. Its aims are to promote research into the study of the sea, including living-resources and pollution in the North Sea and North Atlantic; to draw up programmes for this, organise the necessary research and publish the results. It has no managerial role and cannot take decisions.

ICES has a small secretariat but works through a Committee system, including about 20 fishery groups reporting to an Advisory Committee on Fishery Management. There is a similar one on Pollution. There are also many Working Groups on specific questions. It early established a subcommittee on whales that led to the conclusion of the first whaling convention in 1931.[21] It has studied, evaluated and reported on the biological effects of new uses of the sea such as oil exploitation, sand and gravel extraction, and waste disposal (including dumping and effluent discharges) and has reported on the accumulation of oceanic contaminents in marine mammals, and also on the status of some seal stocks. It has, on request, become the scientific advisory body to NEAFC and the Oslo and Paris Commissions and collaborated with bodies such as the IOC (International Oceanographic Commission), FAO, WHO, IMO and the EC. It presents the sole means in the North Sea of integrating the comprehensive advice on all fish stocks (including marine mammals) on which regulations are based and of evaluating the effect on fisheries of other activities in that area, for example sand and gravel pollution. Obviously it can and does play a very useful role in co-ordinating the research necessary for management of North Sea wildlife, if its members allow it to do so. Some are reluctant to invite it to address such sensitive issues as small cetaceans and seals but ICES has the potential to do so and is studying these questions. It already co-operates with NEAFC, FAO, UNESCO (IOC) and to a lesser extent with UNEP and is uniquely equipped to facilitate scientific co-operation on all North Sea issues but it is a link in the chain, not a comprehensive body.

Scientific advice can, of course, also be developed and co–-ordinated through other international bodies not specifically focused on the North Sea such as UNEP (United Nations Environment Programme); IUCN (International Union for Conservation of Nature); IOC (UNESCO's International Oceanographic Commission); GESAMP (Group of Experts on the Scientific Aspects of Marine Pollution).

[20] For its history, see A. Went, "70 years A-growing"; ICES 1972; for recent developments see B. Parrish, "The Future Role of ICES in the Light of Changes in Fisheries Jurisdiction" (1979) 3 *Marine Policy* 232–238.

[21] Convention for the Regulation of Whaling, signed at Geneva, 20 September 1931, LNTS CLU, No. 3586.

International Whaling Commission[22]

The large whales. This was established, primarily to regulate the catching of the great whales to enable the orderly development of the whaling industry (especially in Antarctica) by the International Convention for Regulation of Whaling (ICRW) in 1946. It now has 38 member governments, which include all North Sea states except Belgium; the majority now consists of non-whaling developing states, some of which exploit small cetaceans.

In 1982, because of the the severe depletion of all stocks, as advised by its Scientific Committee, the IWC, by a majority vote, imposed zero quotas on all stocks of whales harvested commercially, with effect from 1985 for coastal whaling and 1985/86 for pelagic operations. The whale stocks are by 1990 to be comprehensively assessed. The United Kingdom ceased whaling in 1963, The Netherlands in 1964. France and Germany have not been active in whaling for many years. Denmark is not engaged in harvesting the great whales but its Faroe Islanders still have a pilot whale hunt and take some white-sided dolphins. Norway continued to take minke whales until this year, having initially lodged an objection to the moratorium. It now controversially takes a few minke whales under special permits for scientific research which are permitted under Article VIII of the ICRW to be issued at the discretion of the states concerned even on stocks otherwise protected. In 1988, Norway instituted a 5-year programme to study and monitor minke whales in the North East Atlantic, including food selection and intake, food digestion and body composition.

Small cetaceans. There is concern that though the large whales are now protected from taking, small cetaceans are not.[23] It is common to refer to whales, porpoises and dolphins as though they were separate species.[24] The term is quite arbitrary but is often conveniently used to cover all cetaceans not yet regulated by the IWC, as it will be herein. Since the IWC does not define "whale" or "whaling", it could arguably be applied to them ad hoc if they require regulation for the purposes of conservation (Article V).

However, of the small cetaceans, the IWC currently regulates only the minke and the orca, and two species of Ziphiidae (the Arctic and Antarctic Bottlenose); the Bottlenose has for some time been a protected stock in the North Atlantic and the minke, along with all other species commercially exploited, have since 1985 been subject to zero catch-limits which are required to be reviewed upon the basis of the best scientific advice. The IWC's Scientific Committee (SC) began to examine the status of small cetaceans from 1971 onwards. It established a Subcommittee

[22] For a full description of the history of international whaling and its regulation see Birnie, *International Regulation of Whaling* (2 vols., Oceana, 1985); J. E. Scarff, "The International Management of Whales, Dolphins and Porpoises: An Interdisciplinary Assessment", (1977) 6 *Ecology Law Quarterly* 323–638; J. Tønnessen and A.Johnsen, *The History of Modern Whaling* (C. Hurst, 1982).

[23] For details of this problem see Birnie, *International Regulation of Whaling* and *id*. "Small Cetaceans", (1981) 5 *Marine Policy* 277–281, and

[24] See Nikki Meith "Saving the Small Cetaceans" (1984) XIII AMBIO 1–13 and *id*. "Small Cetaceans—The Forgotten Whales" (1989) 4 *International Whale Bulletin* (special edition).

on Small Cetaceans to keep a watch on those taken in direct catches. Member states were then required by the Schedule to keep records not on small cetaceans as such but of whales taken only in so-called "small-type whaling operations", defined as "catching operations using powered vessels with mounted harpoon guns hunting extensively for minke, bottlenose, pilot or killer whales". The IWC approved, for administrative purposes only, a list of the small cetaceans of the world.[25] Scientific papers identifying those needing protection were frequently submitted to the Subcommittee; these included the Northern Bottlenose whale and the Harbour Porpoise in the North Atlantic.

The Subcommittee indicated that some international body was required to manage stocks of all cetaceans not yet covered by the IWC, but no progress has ever been made on this.

It seems unlikely, in the writer's view, that recent proposals to consider again revision of the ICRW (initiated in the IWC in 1987 by the USSR) will meet with any greater success, whether or not the moratorium on whaling is lifted. There is thus no foreseeable prospect of any further international protection of small cetaceans by the IWC and there is no other organization exclusively concerned with this problem, though it should be noted that UNEP plans to hold a meeting on small cetaceans early in 1990 in the USSR. Should, therefore, a convention now be developed exclusively for the North Sea, through the Ministerial Conference, as it appears the United Kingdom has in mind? Or should efforts be made instead to improve the ratification and use of other wildlife conservation conventions, which whilst not specifically or exclusively focused on protection of small cetaceans (or seals, or birds) can be extended for this purpose? Before looking at these options we should, however, identify the current status of these species in the North Sea.

Cetaceans in United Kingdom waters[26]

Twenty-four species of whales and dolphins have been recorded in British and Irish waters; 12 are seen regularly, others rarely. The harbour porpoise and bottlenose dolphin are most frequently sighted because of their inshore distribution but minke, whales, white-beaked, Common and Risso's dolphins are often seen, mainly, however, off the west coast. Since 1913, reporting of stranded cetaceans has been required and this, coupled from 1973 with the Marine Mammal Society's scheme for whale sighting and reporting by a network of 750 marine biologists and volunteers, now provides the main information on whale's habits and the status of stocks in the area. There is also a harbour porpoise project in Shetland, and since 1985 one scientist has surveyed small cetacean by-catch off United Kingdom coasts, but at present there are no resources forthcoming to enhance any of these studies.

[25] Birnie, *International Regulation of Whaling*, Vol. II, p. 703; 4 Annex: "Nomenclature of Whales", The International Whaling Conference, Washington, DC 20 November–2 December 1946, Final Act.

[26] Based on presentation, "Cetaceans in U.K. Waters", given by P. E. Evans to meeting of Marine Forum, 13 June 1989; available from Marine Forum, 80 York Way, London N1 9AG. For a more extended account see *id*. "Ecological Effects of Man's Activities on Cetaceans", obtainable from the author, Department of Zoology, University of Oxford.

Action by the appropriate fishery departments is required if plans for a co-ordinated European sightings' scheme are to go ahead. Other individuals and institutes are working on particular problems.[27] Changes in status of populations have been noticed, such as widespread declines in harbour porpoises in the southernmost North Sea and Channel with declines recently indicated in the northern North Sea, and a scarcity of bottlenosed dolphins along the English Channel coast. On the other hand, more pelagic species, such as the long-finned pilot whale, sperm whale and some beaked whales, have been recorded *more* frequently.

Many of the problems besetting cetaceans in the North Sea are international ones, the solution to which requires collaboration between European states for their study and for effective controls.

In 1987, a European Cetacean Society was established, but needs EC support. The issue of how best internationally to protect these, mainly small, cetaceans, needs re-examination since, as will be seen below, present conventions and bodies are not ideally suited to this task.

Seals in United Kingdom waters (pinnipeds)

Common (harbour) seals and grey seals are those most generally found in the North Sea. Common Seals are found throughout the northern hemisphere but grey seals are found only in the North Atlantic and Baltic Sea. In the United Kingdom, the Natural Environment and Research Council (NERC), through its Sea Mammal Research Unit (SMRU), formed in 1977, is required by statute[28] to provide scientific advice on matters related to the management of seal populations; the SMRU surveys annually all major grey seal breeding colonies in Britain, the smaller ones every three to six years and common seal stocks whenever possible. As seals return to the same land sites to pup, it is possible to count or otherwise estimate, pups and these figures can be used as the basis for theoretically estimating populations.[29]

In 1982 the total size of the British grey seal population was estimated to be 84,000 animals compared to 82,500 for 1981, with the English population constant and the Scottish increasing. Common seals (generally surveyed by boat every five to six years, but annually by air in the Wash) were estimated (at a minimum) to be 20,500 animals in 1982.[30] However, by 1985, the total British grey seal population was estimated to be 92,000 animals and the common seal one to be 24,700.[31] By 1987 the figures for common seals off the United Kingdom were estimated at 25,700 (18,900 off the North Sea coast; 6,800 off the United Kingdom Atlantic coast); in North West Europe outside the United Kingdom there were thought to be 11,000; in the Wadden Sea 8,650. With the addition of 30,000 off Iceland, the total for the North East Atlantic was put at 75,350.

[27] e.g., M. Klinowska, University of Cambridge, Department of Psychology, who, *inter alia*, has produced a review of UK dolphinaria.

[28] Conservation of Seals Act 1970.

[29] See "Seal Stocks in Great Britain: Survey Conducted in 1982", 3 *NERC News* 1984, pp. 7–9.

[30] *Ibid*. 9.

[31] "Seal Stocks in Great Britain: Surveys Conducted in 1985", 1 *NERC News* 1987, pp.11–13; publication figures for 1987 forthcoming in *NERC News*.

Some stocks of grey seals were hunted until 1980/82. Since then licensed taking of grey seals has been permitted around salmon farms (4 in 1985) and off the Faroe Islands (37 in 1985) where the stocks were respectively increasing (Outer Hebrides and North Sea) or stable. Common seals were commercially hunted in the Inner and Outer Hebrides and off the West Coast of Scotland until 1981, off Orkney until 1982, and the Wash and Shetland until 1973. Since then licensed taking has been small (1 in 1985). A few scientific permits have also been issued but the total number of grey seals killed in 1985 was only 43 and only one common seal was killed. The controversial culling has ceased since the 1970s when it proved impossible scientifically to verify the need and effects of culls.

In 1988, however, at least 17,230 common seals died in North West Europe (including off the United Kingdom, The Netherlands, Danish Wadden Sea, Lower Saxony, Linfjorden, the Kattegat and Skajerrak, off Norway). The estimated die-off in the United Kingdom (2,690) is probably an underestimate. They died in an epidemic at first believed by some to be caused by a canine distemper. Its causes and effects have been studied by the SMRU, amongst others, including whether it is being transmitted to coastal otters in Europe (including in the Shetlands) and whether there is any link with pollution, to which marine mammals are particularly vulnerable as top predators, and by concentrating toxic compounds in their blubber.[32] The link has not yet been established nor do grey seals seem so vulnerable to the disease but the SMRU advised that the closed season for both species should be extended as a precaution; but the United Kingdom Parliament has not yet approved the necessary amendment to the 1970 Conservation of Seals Act. The long-term impacts of the disease on the stocks and the effects on it of pollutants is still not clear. Some DDT and PCB compounds have been found in grey seals, especially off some parts of the United Kingdom's North Sea coasts but there is no evidence of any effect of these on their survival. Higher levels found in seals from the Dutch Wadden Sea (where there is a decline in harbour seal) may have affected reproduction rates—seals in the Frisian Wadden Sea may be the most affected; harbour seals have vanished in the West Scheldt. Swedish and Danish harbour seals on the other hand have increased since hunting was banned in the mid–1960s. A European Seal Group is studying these problems, as is ICES; they cannot be resolved without collaboration at the international level. At least the epidemic has provided an opportunity to monitor the whole North Sea harbour seal population.

Birds and Seabirds[33]

Seabirds are birds relying entirely or mainly on the sea for their food. Many other species feed in estuaries around the North Sea. Many seabird colonies are located on the North Sea coastline. Birds from them and from elsewhere feed in the North Sea; the colonies are of international importance. Some seabirds (divers, grebes,

[32] "Seal Deaths—SMRU Coordinates UK Monitoring", 7 *NERC News* 1988, pp. 6–8; D. Eis, Seal Deaths in Europe, (1980) XVIII AMBIO 144.

[33] See for further details, "Vulnerable Concentrations of Birds in the North Sea", Nature Conservancy Council (1988); produced by the Seabirds at Sea Team (Mark Tasker, Michael Pienkowski), Chief Scientist Directorate NCC; and "The Conservation of Seabirds in the North Sea", NCC (1989).

seaducks, shag, cormorant, black guillemot) feed close inshore, some offshore (gulls, kittiwakes, auks, fulmars, gannets), but all dive below surface for their prey. Pollution can thus affect both birds on the surface, below it and through their food chains, especially those that feed on shellfish or crustaceans. Some feed on small fish, including sand eels, increasingly taken in industrial fisheries; overfishing of these thus reduces the birds' diet and affects breeding. All have to come to land to breed, thus destruction or degradation of habitat there can profoundly disturb breeding as well as feeding patterns. Draining of wetlands also destroys habitat.

It is only fairly recently that information on bird concentrations in the North Sea has been forthcoming; and on both natural and man-made threats to them. Pollution threats include not only oil spills but pesticides, chemicals from fertilisers and dumping, plastics, and net entanglement;[34] egg collection has also posed a hazard to survival of some species.

Relevant conventions[35]

International conventions

Convention on Trade in Endangered Species of Wild Fauna and Flora 1973 (CITES).[36] This convention, generally regarded as one of the most effective in practice for its purposes, protects species threatened by international trade in them or their products (referred to as "specimens" thereof). The EC is a party to it and has implemented it. The species are listed on three Appendices according to the degree of threat. All the large cetaceans are now given the protection of being listed on Appendix I or II but it is possible to make reservations to CITES; Japan, for example has entered a reservation on all types of whales. CITES also covers seals and birds some of which have been listed.

CITES is administered by an efficient Secretariat, which has become a repository of information on trade. It remains one of the most powerful instruments to protect traded species. At present, the few large whales straying into the North Sea are already listed on it and no small cetaceans are commercially exploited by North Sea states. The Faroese pilot whales are consumed or stored locally.

Convention on Wetlands of International Importance especially as Waterfowl Habitat 1971 (RAMSAR).[37] This convention relates to habitat protection. Wetlands, many of which are found alongside tidal estuaries provide essential sites for wildlife and plants. Wetlands in states surrounding the North Sea have been destroyed at an unprecedented and alarming rate in recent years for land reclamation, for agriculture (including afforestation) and industry. The purpose of the RAMSAR Conven-

[34] For a full account see North Sea Forum, Report 1987, chap. 17; A. Webb, *Ecological Effects of Man's Activities on Seabirds*, pp. 101- 119.

[35] For text of all these conventions, *inter alia*, and discussion, see S. Lyster, *International Wildlife Law* (1985), texts in appendices, pp. 307–461. See also Birnie, *International Regulation of Whaling*, chap. 8, , pp. 391–397; chap. 11, pp. 509–518; *id. Legal Measures for Conservation of Marine Mammals*, Pt. I, pp. 29–49; N. Meith, "Saving the Small Cetaceans", 8–9; *id.* "Small Cetaceans", 4; *id.* "The Role of Law in Protecting Marine Mammals" (1986) XV AMBIO 137–143.

[36] (1975) XII ILM 1085–1104; Lyster, *International Wildlife Law*, 384- 406.

[37] (1974) XI ILM 963.

tion, which defines wetlands in very broad terms, is to stem this tide of losses. Its parties include Denmark, West Germany, The Netherlands, Norway, the United Kingdom (not France or Belgium). Wide European participation has ensured protection of most of the Palearctic flyway, but it is not enough for the protection of North Sea birds that only North Sea states adhere to it; the widest possible number of non-European parties is also required to ensure that all migratory areas are covered. Nonetheless European listing is important. The Wadden Sea, for example, is now protected by listing by The Netherlands, the Federal Republic of Germany and Denmark.

A List of Wetlands of International Importance is maintained by the IUCN (which also provides the Bureau) under the convention; each party must designate suitable wetlands within its territory for listing, including at least one when it joins the convention. There are now over 400 wetlands on the list. Some states argue (e.g. United Kingdom, The Netherlands) that only sites already protected by national legislation should be listed. The international listing ensures the sites' full protection, for example a leaking foreign flag oil tanker was required to be removed from a United Kingdom North Sea site. Listing does not, however, entail many obligations. Parties must formulate and implement planning to "promote" conservation by "wise use", establish wardens and inform the IUCN Bureau of any changes in ecological character (the United Kingdom and Denmark have acted on this). Despite its potential weaknesses, which include a lack of both provisions for financial aid and of amendment procedures (necessitating conclusion of Protocols if changes are required) the RAMSAR convention has progressed. Amendments were made in 1987 and these (relating to financial support and establishment of a permanent Bureau and Standing Committee) are being applied even before their entry into force with beneficial effect on North Sea sites. Plans to develop some listed wetlands have been contested and have had to be abandoned (e.g. the Ouse Washes; Rhine sites, the Norfolk Broads). The Convention encourages research and exchange of data on wetlands and this has had results. Priority "Action Points" have now been laid down by the Conference of the Parties,[38] the Fourth Meeting of which will be held in 1990.

Convention Concerning the Protection of the World Cultural and Natural Heritage 1972 (World Heritage).[39] The main aim of this Convention is to protect the world's most prized cultural and natural areas of "outstanding universal value", which could include maritime sites. Its value in wildlife protection is limited since though natural habitats do contain animals and birds of interest they can be listed only if of exceptional significance. Denmark, France, the Federal Republic of Germany, Norway and the United Kingdom are parties to it, but so far no European sites, let

[38] For current progress, see Proceedings of the Third Meeting of the Contracting Parties, Regina, Saskatchewan, Canada, 27 May–5 June 1987, p. 6; RAMSAR Convention Bureau, IUCN, Gland, Switzerland.

[39] (1972) XI ILM 1358.

alone North Sea ones, have been listed and it does not seem likely that the latter will ever qualify.

Convention on the Conservation of Migratory Species of Wild Animals 1979 (Bonn Convention).[40] This Convention, which currently has 29 parties, aims to protect species "a significant proportion of whose members cyclically and predictably cross one or more jurisdictional boundaries". It does this by listing species on Appendices and requiring or encouraging Range States (that is states exercising jurisdiction over any part of the range of a particular migratory species or state whose flag vessels are engaged in taking such species beyond national jurisdiction) to take measures according to the listing. The Convention does not directly require states to take measures for listed species but requires them to conclude Agreements for their protection on the basis of guidelines laid down in the Convention. Parties are also required to promote co-operation in or support research on migratory species.

Wide ratification, essential to its success, has not been forthcoming and there are many ambiguities in the terms and definitions used in the text which require to be interpreted through state practice. Unfortunately there is very little practice under it since, despite strenuous efforts by its one woman Secretariat and concerned states and groups, not a single Agreement has yet been concluded, whether relating to the North Sea or elsewhere.

The first conference of the parties in 1985 resolved that the Secretariat should take appropriate action to develop a number of agreements on specific species including the North and Baltic Sea populations of small cetaceans but numerous problems have been encountered on these.[41]

Work on North Sea Small Cetacean Agreement.[42] A Small Cetacean Working Group has been established, drawn from the Convention's Scientific Council and outside governmental and NGO experts, which produced a draft regional Agreement for conservation of these species in the North and Baltic Sea areas. The Working Group and the Secretariat also began work on a proposal to list small cetaceans in Appendix II which was considered by the Scientific Council in 1988; irreconcilable differences of opinion were revealed on the scope and content of the agreement and no state was willing to sponsor it. The Scientific Council (SC) decided to set up its own Working Group to look at small cetaceans globally and to continue the work of identifying species that should be added to the Appendices. As Agreements can only be concluded if species are listed on Appendix II, the Scientific Council discussed a Netherlands proposal for including thereon 8 species found in the North Sea and Baltic Sea. It approved 7, phocoena phocoena; tursiops truncatos; delphinus delphinus; gramous griseus; globicephala melaena; lagenorhynchus albirostus; lagenorhynchos acutus) but deleted balaenoptera acutorostrata,

[40] (1980) XIX ILM 15, 411–427.

[41] Other failed agreements are those on palearctic waterfowl, on bats and on storks; some overlap the activities of other bodies, Lyster, *International Wildlife Law*.

[42] See M. Gibson, "The Bonn Convention and its Role in Protecting Small Cetaceans", paper presented at Marine Forum Workshop, Appendix D, from Marine Forum.

currently protected under the ICRW. The Second Conference of the Parties approved the addition of the above 7 species to Appendix II but disbanded the original regional Working Group and asked the SC to give priority to its global review, with a view to adding further species to Appendix II at the Third conference in 1991. A globally based SC Working Group on small cetaceans has been established including a broad range of scientific expertise (both the Secretary of the IWC and the Convener of its Scientific Committee's Subcommittee on Small Cetaceans are included as key participants).

The Bonn Convention is also applicable to birds and seals but they have fared no better under it than the small cetaceans since no Agreements have been concluded on either species, although a draft Agreement has been prepared for Palearctic Waterfowl, which cross the North Sea, amongst other areas.

Regional conventions

Convention on the Conservation of European Wildlife and Natural Habitats 1979 (Berne Convention).[43] This Convention, concluded under the auspices of the Council of Europe, with both the EC and individual states now party to it, aims to conserve wild flora and fauna and their natural habitats, promote co-operation between countries in their conservation effects and particularly to protect endangered and vulnerable species, including migratory species. The Convention provides in general for conservation of wildlife and habitats and for special protection for species listed in Appendices, on criteria laid down in the Convention.

Co-operation and research is also required of parties. The Convention requires parties to take the measures necessary to maintain populations of all species of animals and plants at levels corresponding to ecological, scientific and cultural requirements. Unlike the Bonn Convention, the Berne Convention requirements are binding, not hortatory. It is also backed by a substantial administration—a Standing Committee of the Parties and the Secretariat facilities of the Council of Europe itself. The Convention is not without a number of ambiguities which need to be resolved in State practice. For example, it is not clear whether the use of driftnets and gill nets which cause large incidental mortality to Appendix II marine species is prohibited under Appendix II, which prohibits deliberate capture, etc.

Eleven small cetaceans are listed as protected animals under Appendix II (Common, bottlenosed, whitebeak, white-sided, Rosso's striped and roughtooth dolphins; harbour porpoise; long-fin pilot, killer and false killer whales) but for the convention to be effective breeding grounds must be protected and therefore identified. To give proper protection, coastal areas, where these cetaceans are known to occur, should be designated as resting and breeding grounds.[44] Like the ICRW, the Convention does not address other threats such as interaction with fisheries; incidental catch; food depletion. Pollution prevention, however, could be covered

[43] European Treaty Series No.104, pp. 428–441.

[44] Greenpeace Statement to the Second Meeting of the Parties to the Bonn Convention; Geneva 11–14 October 1988: Legal Protection of Small Cetaceans in the North and Baltic Seas, p. 1. "New Life for the Action Plan", 3 *The Pilot* (April 1989), pp. 1, 16.

to the extent that it falls within the requirement that parties "have regard" for conservation implications of their activities, but there is no direct linkage to the other conventions dealing with pollution from various sources.The Convention has been partly implemented, but no party has legislation automatically protecting habitat (except for bats in the United Kingdom); such protection of habitat as exists provides for significant exceptions, for example for agriculture, industrial development (often on coasts and estuaries). Exceptions made must be reported biannually to the Standing Committee. No party has provided total protection of breeding or resting sites for Appendix II species. The IUCN reports many infractions. The United Kingdom is endeavouring to make an inventory of all important breeding and resting sites but protection of these is imperfect, despite the fact that the Wildlife and Countryside Act 1981[45] was designed to ensure this through a system of national nature reserves, marine nature reserves and sites of special scientific interest (SSSIs). The last in particular do not always receive strict protection.

Conclusions

Whilst there is a framework for protection of wildlife in the North Sea, both at the international and regional level, it is neither an integrated system nor an holistic regime for protection. Conventions have been concluded, commissions established or responsibilities allocated to existing bodies on a pragmatic basis. There is considerable overlap between bodies and conventions with no one body responsibly for taking the lead. The EC is a useful but not wholly appropriate body for this. It now has a clearer legal basis for environmental action and further development of its role in this field is contemplated, but its concerns remain primarily those of economic development, within the goal of economic integration. Moreover, Norway is not a member, while several Mediterranean states, whose concerns are different from those of North Sea states, are. Better participation in and enforcement of the existing conventions is required, and development of further measures, such as a regional convention on small cetaceans, whatever the institutional developments.

It has recently been reported that new life is being breathed into the UNEP/FAO Marine Mammals Action Plan;[46] its Planning and Co-ordinating Committee has been institutionalized, and held its first meeting in 1988; real co-ordination of its various parts is now contemplated, with better communication between all concerned commissions and secretariats, and action on the priorities set. UNEP has also, in its Regional Seas Programme, begun to add conservation protocols to its framework conventions, supplementing existing protocols on pollution prevention. It is still possible for the North Sea to be subjected to such an approach—that is a framework convention establishing a North Sea Committee, with existing conventions and bodies linked to it.

Just before the above UNEP meeting, the Director-General of IUCN convened a meeting of the Secretariats and Standing Committee members of the RAMSAR,

[45] European Treaty Series No. 104, pp. 428–441.
[46] Greenpeace Statement; "New Life for the Action Plan".

CITES, Bonn and Berne Conventions. Representatives of the World Heritage Convention and ICRW were also asked to attend but could not do so; the WWF sent an observer.[47] The participants agreed that considerable benefit would ensue from closer co-operation in programme development and activities; joint approaches to problem-solving; data matters; dovetailing meetings and developing common formats for reports. It was agreed to institutionalize meetings of the various secretariats, which IUCN would convene annually. It might be possible also to co-locate the various secretariats in the new building to be provided for IUCN by the Swiss Government. The need for greater interaction among secretariats was also stressed at a meeting of experts on biological diversity convened by UNEP in 1988.

If such moves are contemplated at the international level should not such rationalization not also be begun at the regional (or sub-regional) level of the North Sea? This is a question that should urgently be addressed by the Third INS Conference.

[47] "Co-operation among Nature Conservation Conventions", 3 RAMSAR, April 1989, p.1. See Draft Report on the Implementation of the Berne and Bonn Conventions; European Parliament Committee on the Environment, Public Health and Consumer Protection, EP DOC. 2 H536/84; 1988; and "Implementation of the Berne Convention", IUCN, Gland, 1986, which reviews relevant national legislation; Lyster, "Problems of UK Implementation of Berne"; report for Wildlife Link, London (1985).

Chapter 23

North Sea Fisheries: Trends and Management Issues

David Symes

Introduction

At a time when the world catch of marine fish has been expanding, that of the North Sea (defined as ICES Area IV) has stagnated (see Table 1). Nevertheless, the North Sea has maintained its reputation as a remarkably prolific fishery. The small, semi-enclosed sea still yields 2.5 million tonnes of fish annually, or 3 per cent of the world catch.[1]

Surrounded by some of the most densely populated and advanced industrial nations, the North Sea has endured a long history of exploitation and has been an important focus of the industrialization of fishing activity. It is just over a century since the first intimations of over-fishing, with reported reductions in catch per unit effort among British fishing smacks in the southern and central North Sea.[2]

Despite repeated crises in stock availability for several commercially important species, overall biomass has remained constant and total catches high. But the composition of the catch has changed. The range of commercially important species has widened. At the start of the century only 7 species were commercially significant;[3]

TABLE 1 Relative Change in Marine Fisheries, 1980–1986

	1980	*1981*	*1982*	*1983*	*1984*	*1985*	*1986*	*(1986) (M tonnes)*
World (a)	100	103	106	106	114	117	125	(80.3)
NE Atlantic (a)	100	99	91	95	96	96	89	(10.5)
North Sea (b)	100	86	95	94	93	94	97	(2.5)

Sources: (a) *FAO Yearbook of Fishery Statistics*, 1986; (b) *Bulletin statistique des pêches maritimes*.

[1] Except where otherwise stated all statistical data are derived from *Conseil international pour l'exploration de la mer*, *Bulletin statistique des pêches maritimes*, various dates.

[2] M. Graham, "Harvests of the Seas", in W. L. Thomas (ed.), *Man's Role in Changing the Face of the Earth* (Chicago, 1956), pp. 487–503.

[3] R. M. May, *et al.*, "Management of Multi-Species Fisheries", *Science*, 205 (1979), 267–277.

in the 1980s the number has risen to 12 out of a range of more than 40 species. More importantly, there is evidence of "trading down", in the sense that species of lower value have generally been substituted for those of higher value.

The total catch conceals a number of disturbing situations for individual species. Throughout the period 1962–1986 the most important stocks have shown themselves vulnerable to high levels of fishing effort. Catches, now largely controlled by quota restrictions, frequently fluctuate quite dramatically, usually around a declining trend. This not only creates current economic inefficiencies but also poses problems for the future planning and management of the industry.

It is almost certainly the case that, even without the intervention of fishing mortality, individual stocks would rarely achieve stability. Environmental changes are sufficient to ensure variations in the size and distribution of such stocks over time. It is, however, the contention of this chapter that, not only do the currently high levels of exploitation exacerbate the instability of stocks, but ill-judged management policies merely compound the problem and offer little hope of improvement in the future. The aims of this chapter are to review the trends in North Sea fisheries from 1962 to 1986, a period which spans an eventful and sometimes turbulent period in the political economy of North Atlantic fisheries, and to examine critically the present management strategies.

The trends, 1962–1986

Environmental background

The North Sea has been described as "one of the richest fishing grounds of all the continental shelves",[4] with a biomass of commercial and non-commercial species estimated at 9–10 million tonnes.[5] This high level of productivity is largely explained in terms of five factors: the high input of nutrients from the Atlantic, supplemented by river discharges; the recycling of nutrients in the water column through mixing by tidal streams; the shallowness of the sea which allows sunlight penetration of the water mass; vigorous spring and autumn phytoplankton blooms; and the rich benthic fauna which provides an important food supply for invertebrates and bottom-living fish.[6] The edges of the North Sea—those areas under greatest threat from pollution—provide vitally important nursery grounds and shellfish habitats.[7]

It is, however, an unstable environment, sensitive to variations in temperature, salinity and turbulence which induce changes in the phytoplankton level and so

[4] P. Korringa, "The Edge of the North Sea as Nursery Ground and Shellfish Area", in E. D. Goldberg (ed.), *North Sea Science* (Cambridge, Mass., 1973), pp. 361–382.

[5] Yang Jiming, "An Estimate of the Fish Biomass of the North Sea", *Journal du conseil international pour l'exploration de la mer*, 40 (1982), 161–172.

[6] A. J. Lee, "The North Sea—Setting the Scene", in P. J. Newman and P. R. Agg (eds.), *Environmental Protection of the North Sea* (London, Heinemann, 1988), pp. 1–24.

[7] Shellfish catches, not considered in any detail in this chapter, added a further 169,000 tonnes to the North Sea harvest in 1986.

cause alterations to the geographical and temporal patterns of stock abundance. Such changes have affected several species in recent times.[8]

The ability of the North Sea to maintain a high level of overall production suggests that most individual stocks are closely interrelated: a decline in abundance in one species can cause a vacuum to be filled by competition species.

A classic example was the remarkable change in North Sea biomass following the collapse of the herring and mackerel fisheries in the late 1960s. The 9 million tonnes biomass in 1964 was estimated to contain 6 million tonnes of herring and mackerel and 3 million tonnes of other species; by 1976 the situation had been reversed with only 2 million tonnes from herring and mackerel and 7 million tonnes from other species. Reduced stocks of herring and mackerel had resulted in less predation upon the larval and juvenile stages of other species and, thus, higher survival rates and recruitment to adult stocks.[9]

Total catches

The 1960s began a major period of growth in fishing effort in the North Sea targeted largely upon new species and with new technologies. Catches which had fluctuated between 1 and 1.5 million tonnes throughout the first half of the century,[10] were pushed to a record high of 3 to 3.5 million tonnes in the late sixties and again in the mid-seventies. But the new "equilibrium" was both short-lived and sustained only by the rapid substitution of depleted species by ones with a lower market-value.

From the mid-seventies onwards, total catch levels have fallen to around 2.5 million tonnes, still almost double those in the early part of the century. High levels of total catch obscure the underlying instability of the stocks. Only when disaggregated into major groupings do the often very severe year-to-year and longer-term fluctuations become apparent (see Figure 1). Except for pleuronectiforms (flatfish) and diadromous (freshwater) species, all groups display a greater or lesser tendency to strong, irregular fluctuations, in some cases amounting to a collapse of the principal stocks.

It is easy to seek explanations for many of these vicissitudes by reference to the dynamics of exploited fish populations but, as Lee reminds us, changes in recruitment due to variations in the abundance of parent stock, predators and competitors are the norm in marine fisheries.[11] Usually no single factor can explain such behaviour but rather a series of interactions occurring within the marine environment.[12] It is difficult to disentangle anthropogenic factors from biological ones, but in many instances the direct and indirect effects of over-fishing are important.

[8] See e.g. G. Hempel (ed.), *North Sea Fish Stocks—Recent Changes and their Causes, Rapports et procés verbaux de réunions, Conseil international pour l'exploration de la mer*, 172 (1978).

[9] May, *et al.*, "Management of Multi-Species Fisheries".

[10] M. J. Holden, "Long-term Changes in Landings of Fish from the North Sea", in G. Hempel (ed.), *North Sea Fish Stocks*, pp. 11–26.

[11] Lee, "The North Sea—Setting the Scene", 20.

[12] Hempel, *North Sea Fish Stocks*, 6.

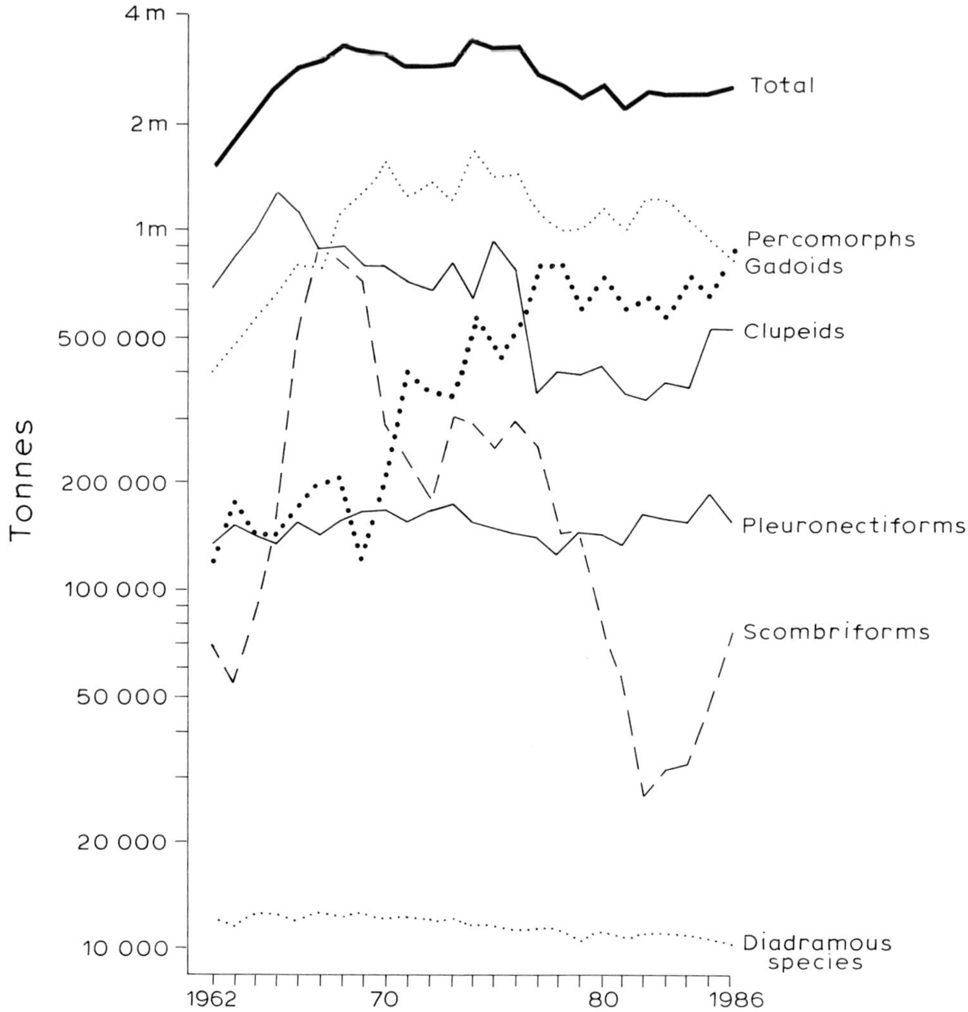

Figure 1 Stability and instability in North Sea fish populations

National trends

To appreciate the growing pressures on North Sea resources over the past 25 years, it is necessary to understand something of the changing economic structure of the area's fisheries and, in particular, the distinctive development strategies adopted by the seven coastal states surrounding the North Sea basin (see Figure 2). Not all coastal states have responded in like manner to the resource potential of the North Sea. They are, in fact, differentiated by four characteristics: the size of their North Sea fishing industry; the degree of dependence upon North Sea landings; the level of concentration upon either food or industrial fisheries; and the overall change in North Sea catches from 1962 to 1986.

TABLE 2 Participation in North Sea Fisheries by Coastal States, 1986

	North Sea Catch, 1986 (000 tonnes)	*National % Foodfish from N. Sea*	*% Herring and Mackerel*	*Industrial*	*North Sea Catch as % change 1962/6–1982/6*	
Denmark	1216	49	71	9	982	+152
Norway	503	20	28	19	4932	− 8
UK	401	16	54	75	214	+ 19
Netherlands	220	9	60	57	412	− 3
France	75	3	20	95	5−	+ 27
FRG	44	2	36	83	133	− 64
Belgium	22	1	61	98	2−	− 8
Total	2481	100	26	30	2248	+ 9

NB in 1986, North Sea catches were also recorded by Faroes (12,300 tons) and Sweden (5,900 tons)

Source: *Bulletin statistique des pêches maritimes*, 1986 and various dates.

Although most rely fairly heavily upon the North Sea as the basis of their national fishing industry and have, with the exception of FRG, increased their level of concentration on the area, the size of their North Sea fisheries varies very widely. Indeed, three countries (Denmark, Norway, UK) account for 85 per cent of all North Sea catches and only three (Denmark, France, UK) have in fact increased their North Sea catches over the period. Denmark's massive increase (+725,000 tonnes) greatly exceeds that for the region as a whole (+205,000 tonnes).

The most striking difference in the structures of the North Sea fisheries is to be found in the extent to which fishing effort is targeted upon food or industrial fisheries. A clear distinction emerges between Denmark and Norway, on the one hand, which have focused a large part of their fishing effort upon the industrial fishing (including herring and mackerel) and France, Belgium, FRG and UK, on the other, where foodfisheries predominate.

Overall, the most outstanding feature of the past 25 years has been the dramatic rise of the industrial fisheries to a point where they now account for over half the total catch (see Figure 3). One country, above all others, has been responsible for the shifting emphasis in the structure of North Sea fisheries. Denmark alone

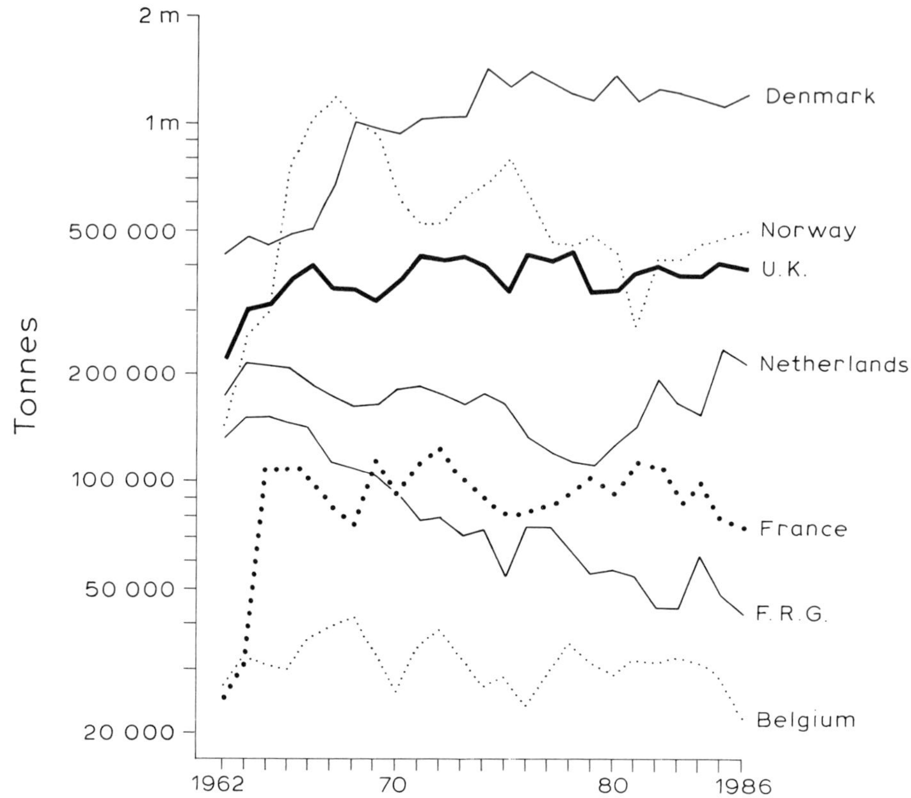

Figure 2 North Sea catches: national trends, 1962–86

accounts for 84 per cent of the industrial landings and thus for almost half the total North Sea catch.

Herring and mackerel

The most dramatic story to unfold in the sixties and seventies concerns the herring and mackerel, two of the earliest species to be targeted by the industrial fishery, though both had a previous role as food species (see Figure 4). During the first half of the century, the annual herring catch fluctuated wildly around 600,000 tonnes from an adult biomass of 2.5 million tonnes.[13] After 1950 the nature of the fishery

[13] *Ibid*. 445.

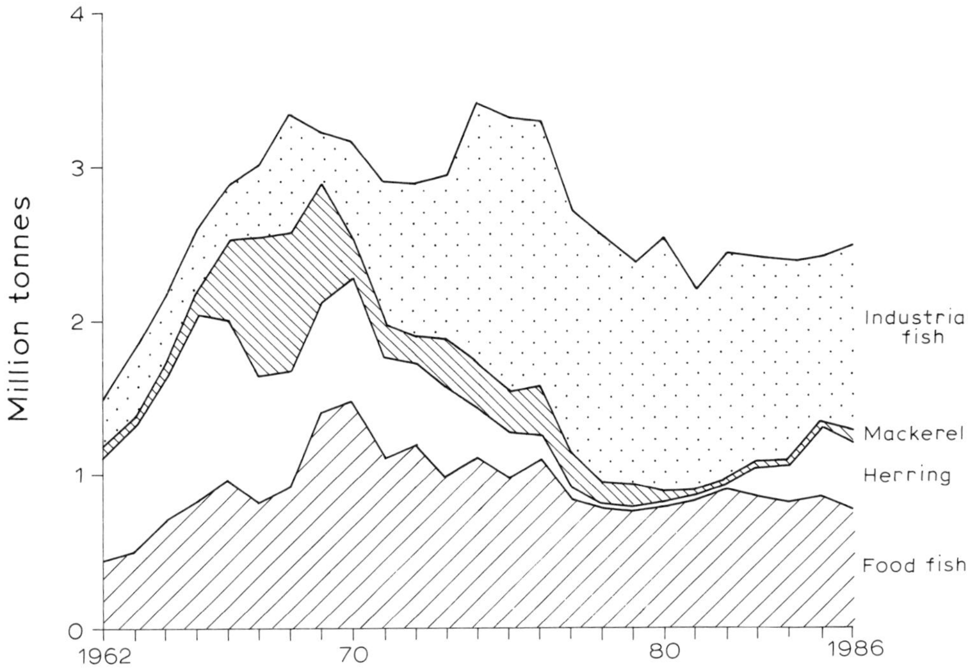

Figure 3 North Sea catches, 1962–86, by major economic groupings

altered in terms of the stocks exploited and the fishing methods used. The trawl replaced the more selective drift-net and was in turn superseded by the purse-seine.[14] As industrial fishing expanded, so the immature components of the stocks were exposed to the risk of capture. From the fifties onwards the herring fishery retreated northward in face of the early extinction of the southern North Sea stocks, which left only a declining spawning stock around Orkney and Shetland after 1965.[15] Under pressure from the Norwegian purse-seine fishery, catches were pushed to a maximum of 1.2 million tonnes in 1965 and thereafter into a steep and almost continuous decline to a point in 1976 where landings of 160,000 tonnes were extracted from an adult biomass estimated at only 250,000 tonnes.[16]

[14] C. E. Lucas, "Conservation of Fishery Resources in the North Sea", *Advancement of Science*, 27 (1971), 303–306.

[15] J. R. Coull, "The North Sea Herring Fishery in the Twentieth Century", *Ocean Yearbook*, 7 (1988), 115–131.

[16] Hempel, *North Sea Fish Stocks*, 445.

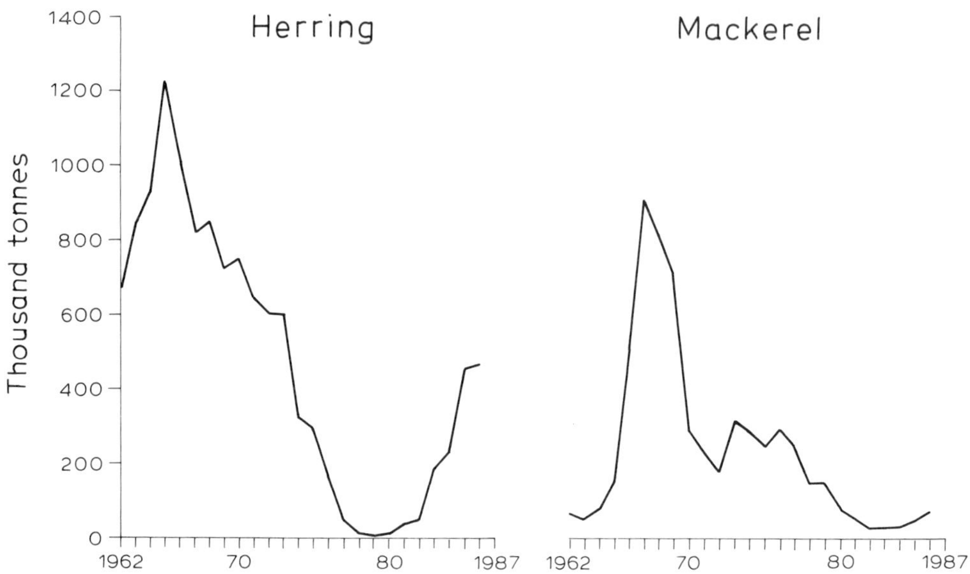

Figure 4 Herring and mackerel, 1962–86

Closure of the fishery from 1977 to 1982 allowed a partial recovery in stock size and a gradual renaissance of the herring fishery to a catch level of 466,000 tonnes in 1986, but still in excess of the Maximum Sustainable Yield (MSY).

With the onset of the decline in herring landings, the North Sea mackerel fishery emerged from relative obscurity, when annual catches in the early sixties were less than 100,000 tonnes, to supersede herring as the principal component of the North Sea catch. Maximum landings of 930,000 tonnes were recorded in 1967—again taken mainly by the Norwegian purse-seine fleet—only to fall back sharply to a level of only 42,000 tonnes in the most recent period.

Industrial species

With the eclipse of herring and mackerel stocks, their place in the industrial fishery was taken by a sequence of "new" species. As Figure 5 demonstrates each was in turn subjected to intensive fishing effort.

Initially Norway pout, a small gadoid taken mainly in the northern North Sea by the Danish and Norwegian fleets, peaked at 823,000 tonnes in 1974 and the sprat, another "opportunistic" fishery prosecuted by the Danish, Norwegian and Russian fleets in the central North Sea, reached a maximum catch of 656,000 tonnes in the following year. The latter showed the familiar "boom and bust" profile, falling rapidly to around 55,000 tonnes in the mid-80s; Norway pout landings have

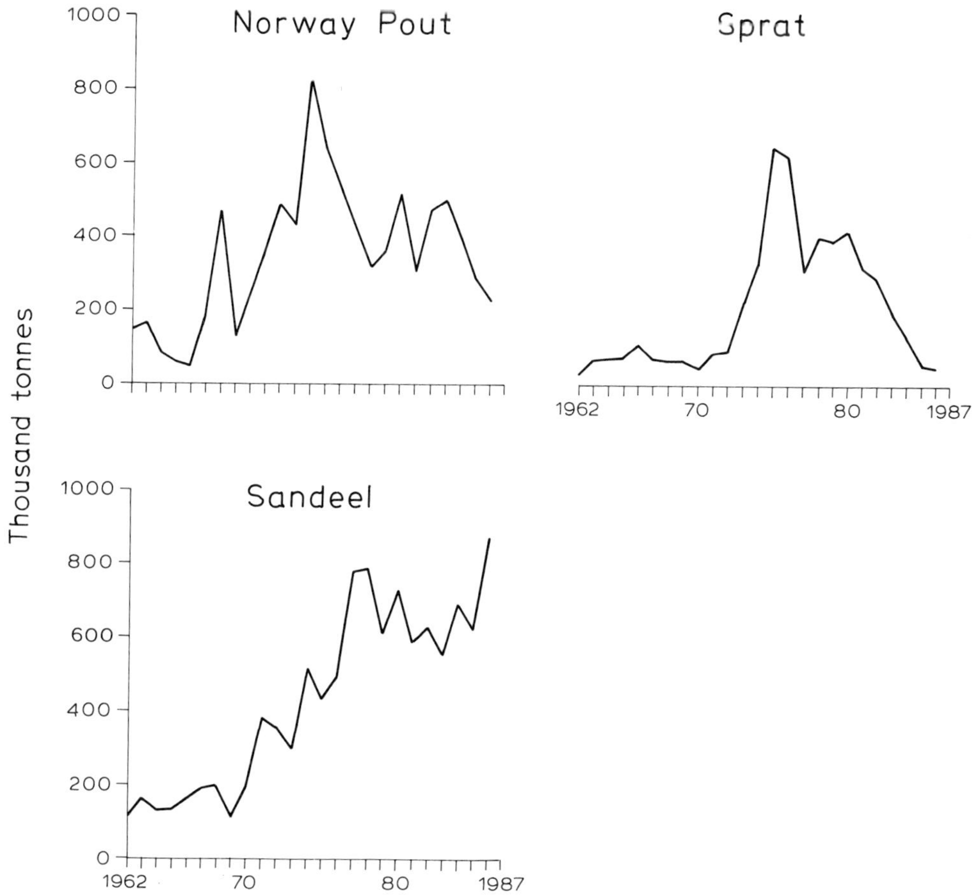

Figure 5 Industrial fisheries, 1962–86

declined more slowly and continue to provide over 20 per cent of the industrial catches in the mid-80s. The most recent recruit to the industrial catch is the sand-eel fishery in the central North Sea, dominated by the Danish industry. In 1986 peak landings of 868,000 tonnes were recorded, accounting for 73 per cent of all industrial landings from the North Sea. Blue whiting and Horse mackerel make minor contributions to the present-day industrial fishery.

Foodfish

Although none of the major industrial species offers significant potential as foodfish, their capture impinges upon the foodfish sector in two ways. First, they form an important element in the food-chains of the larger gadoid species. Second, their distributions frequently overlap the nursery and feeding-grounds of foodfish species, thus exposing the latter to the risk of significant by-catches.

Foodfish in the North Sea are made up of two main groups: the pleuronectiforms (or flat-fish) and the gadoids (members of the cod family). Taken as a whole, foodfish have been less subject to violent fluctuations in stock size and catch levels but have tended to display a gradually declining abundance over time; this is especially true in the case of the low-volume, high-value flat-fish (see Figure 6).

One remarkable exception to this general statement has been the influence of strong year classes in the late sixties and early seventies. Haddock stocks were greatly—but briefly—inflated by the presence of the very strong year class of 1967 which yielded record catches in 1969 (639,000 tonnes) and 1970 (672,000 tonnes), more than three times the average for the preceding five years. It was this, along with the less spectacular, good year classes for cod and saithe in the early and mid-70s respectively, which sustained overall foodfish catches at historically high levels in excess of 1 million tonnes throughout the first half of the 1970s.

Since that time, foodfish landings have declined to an average of 845,000 tonnes in the mid-80s (see Table 2). It is the foodfish—especially cod, haddock, whiting and plaice—which have been subjected to consistently high levels of fishing effort over the longest period of time. None of these stocks is in imminent danger of collapse, but fishing intensity remains substantially higher than that corresponding to MSY.[17]

More recently scientists have warned of increasing instability in stock levels for several major species, under the sustained pressure of high fishing effort allied to a sequence of relatively poor year classes. In the case of North Sea cod, for example, it is suggested that spawning biomass is probably at an historically low level; recruitment year classes make up disproportionately high shares of fishable stocks; and around 55 per cent of total stock is caught each year.[18] Such circumstances have led some scientists to question whether an economically viable fishery can be sustained.[19]

Management issues

Introduction

It will be clear from the preceding analysis that fishing policies and conservation plans have done little to arrest the decline in the North Sea's resource base. In fairness, it should be pointed out that an effective framework for the management of the area's fisheries has only recently emerged.

The accession of Denmark and the UK to the European Community in 1973

[17] International Council for the Exploration of the Sea, Report of Advisory Committee on Fishery Management, 1980.

[18] C. T. Macer, "North Sea Cod: Would a Closure of the Spawning Grounds Work?" *Fishing Prospects* (1987–1988), 7–12.

[19] D. Armstrong, "Cod, Haddock, Whiting and Saithe in the North Sea and to the West of Scotland", *Fishing Prospects* (1987–1988), 13–15.

Figure 6 Food fisheries, 1962–86

meant that six of the seven effective coastal states[20] were members of the Community. The declaration of a Community EFZ in 1976 virtually excluded all non-coastal states, including the increasingly powerful East European fleets which in 1975 had accounted for 10 per cent of the North Sea catch. And, after a long period of renegotiation, a revised but still controversial Common Fisheries Policy (CFP) was agreed at the start of 1983.[21]

The need for a robust resource management policy is not in doubt; the arguments surround the most appropriate measures needed to address the problems. The situation is made more complex by the fact that the North Sea is a mixed fishery and national fishing interests diverge.

Underlying the debate is a deeper set of conflicts between the longer-term goals of resource conservation and short-term economic and social expediencies. Management of North Sea fisheries has become a matter of maintaining the status quo[22] rather than a search for radical improvement of a deteriorating situation. Thus, management has been reduced to a series of essentially short-term options to protect the market and maintain the industry rather than the pursuit of a conservation strategy which could, in the longer-term, enhance the stocks of commercially important species.

The profound advice of Michael Graham in the 1930s that a reduction in fishing effort would yield long-term dividends in enhanced catch rates—and often repeated since—has never been heeded. The CFP embodies a comprehensive package of interlocking and mutually reinforcing measures to contain existing levels of fishing effort. The details, initially set out in 1983,[23] have been partially amended in 1986[24] and 1988[25] and are due for an interim revision in 1992. Broadly they combine two distinct approaches: the setting of Total Allowable Catches (TACs) and a series of technical measures mainly intended to reduce the impact of the fishery upon immature stocks.

Technical measures

The concept of "closure areas" illustrates well the problems of North Sea management. A geographically specific measure designed to protect certain foodfish species by preventing the concentration of fishing effort on vulnerable stocks at critical stages in their life cycle, it has been sparingly used because of its potentially discriminatory nature.

Only three such closures have been brought into effect (see Figure 7): the "Nor-

[20] Belgium, Denmark, FRG, France, Netherlands, UK, Norway. The Faroes' 200-mile zone (median line) also impinges on the North Sea (Area IVa): in 1986 the Faroes recorded a catch of 12,270 tonnes from the North Sea—less than 0.5 per cent of the total catch from the North Sea.

[21] For a detailed description of the renegotiation of the Common Fisheries Policy, see M. Wise, *The Common Fisheries Policy of the European Community* (London, 1984).

[22] J. A. Gulland, "The Management of North Sea Fisheries: Looking Towards the 21st Century", (1987) *Marine Policy* 259–271.

[23] Council Regulation (EEC) No. 170/83 of 25 January 1983.

[24] Council Regulation (EEC) No. 3094/86 of 7 October 1986.

[25] Council Regulation (EEC) No. 4194/88 of 21 December 1988.

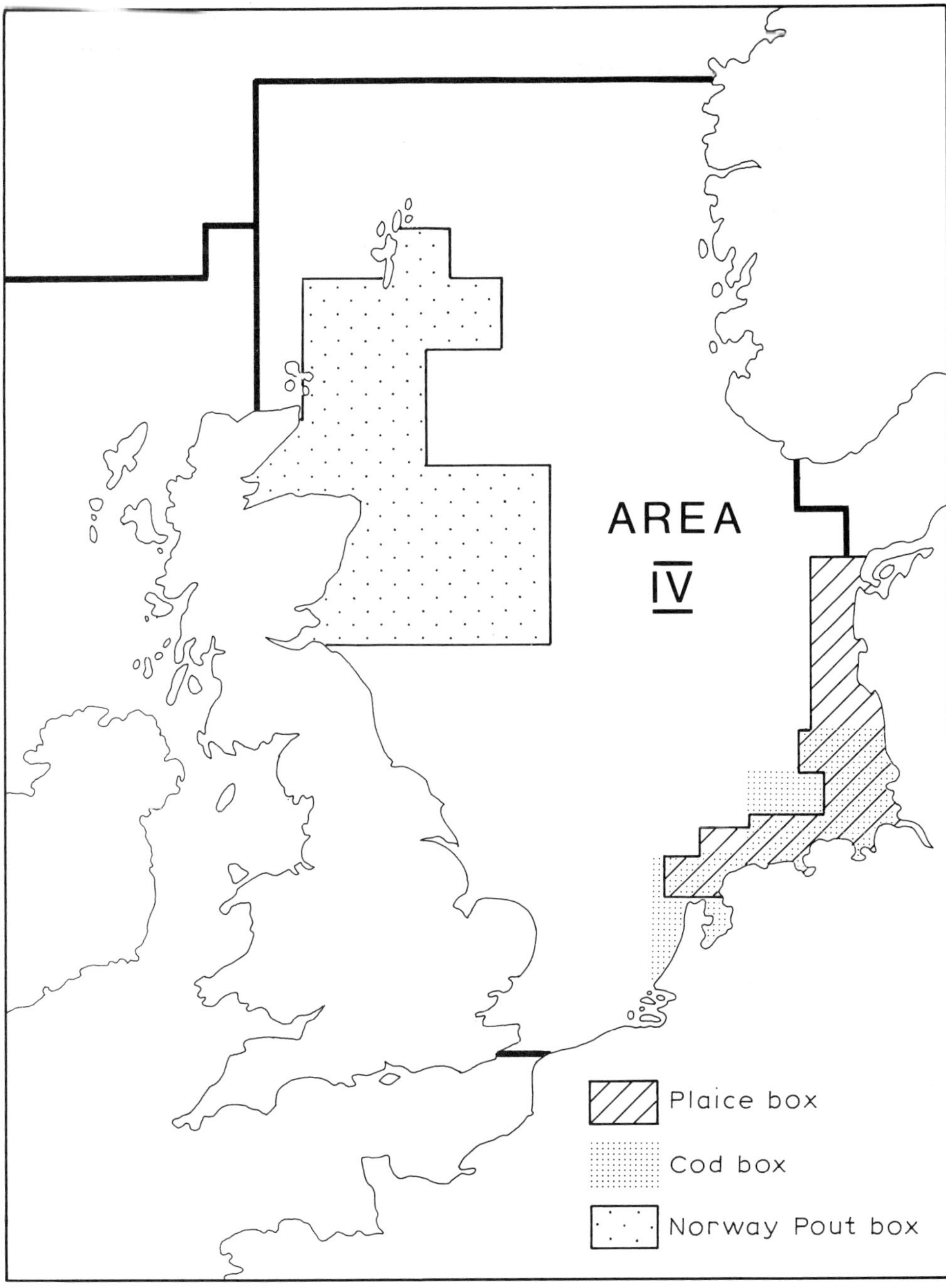

Figure 7 North Sea: closure areas, 1989

TABLE 3 Quota Regulated Stocks, North Sea, 1989

Analytical TACs			*Precautionary TACs*	
Cod Haddock Saithe Whiting European plaice Common sole	Herring Mackerel	Blue Whiting	Hake	Norway pout Horse mackerel Sprat

Source: OJ EC 1988 No. L 369, 3–37.

way pout box" off north-east Scotland to protect young haddock stocks from the industrial fishery; the "plaice box" off the Danish and Dutch coasts to impose seasonal limits on trawling by boats over 8m beyond the 12-mile zone; and, most recently, the seasonal "cod box", introduced in 1989 to ban the use of mobile gear on cod nursery grounds off the coasts of Denmark and the Netherlands.

By far the most comprehensive conservation measures are those relating to fishing gear, especially mesh sizes (see Appendix). But their effectiveness in the North Sea is to some extent limited by the need for a compromise solution in an essentially mixed fishery. In effect, two separate regimes exist: one in European Community waters, where the 90mm mesh prevails for demersal foodfish species; the other in the Norwegian sector where a mesh size of 100mm is enforced. There is growing pressure among scientists and certain fishing interests to increase the permitted mesh size to 120mm, which could enhance cod stocks by up to 26 per cent,[26] but only at the expense of catches in the fishery for the much smaller whiting.

Detailed by-catch and landing size regulations (see Appendix) are intended to reinforce the effectiveness of gear regulations in reducing the impact of fishing upon immature stocks of both target and other species. Unfortunately, their effect is partly dissipated by high discard rates at sea to ensure compliance with the regulations and also to meet the market preference for larger sizes of fish.

Total allowable catches

The system of TACs has borne the main burden of recent management policy. In theory, its aim is to limit fishing effort upon nominated species to levels which the stocks can sustain without reducing their overall size and reproductive capacity. It is, however, seriously flawed in its assumption that individual species can be analysed and treated in isolation. At present nine species in the North Sea are subject to "analytical TACs" and a further four to "precautionary TACs" (see Table 3).

Scientific recommendations from ICES form the basis for negotiating the allocation of catches between countries. But the political process of negotiation has often ended in a compromise solution, guided by the principle of "relative stability" in which safeguarding the short-term interests of the industry takes precedence over the longer-term need to conserve stocks. As a result, agreed TACs have usually been set higher than recommended TACs in years of anticipated stock

[26] Macer, "North Sea Cod: Would a Closure of the Spawning Grounds Work?"

TABLE 4 North Sea TACs for Cod and Haddock, 1985–1989

	1985	*1986*	*1987* (000 tonnes)	*1988*	*1989*
Cod	250	170	125	160	124
Haddock	207	230	140	185	68

Source: OJ, 1985, L 1; OJ, 1986, L 361; OJ, 1986, L 376; OJ, 1987, L 375; OJ, 1988, L 369.

reductions and, by way of compensation, set lower than recommended levels at times of stock abundance.

Such manipulation subverts the need for finely tuned flexibility in adjusting catch levels under conditions of unstable stocks. In effect, therefore, TACs have acted to regularize and reinforce historic pressures on particular stocks. Recently the principle of relative stability appears to have broken down with the emergence of severe year-on-year changes in cod and haddock quotas (see Table 4).

Structural reform

It may be argued that until recently TACs have exercised a conservative influence over the structure of the North Sea fishing industry, for they have tended to reflect existing over-capacity in the fishing fleet rather than point the way towards a more rational structure. Attempts to reduce fishing capacity have not met with conspicuous success. Although the gross tonnage of the combined fleets of the six Community coastal states has been cut by 17 per cent since 1983, several Member States have failed to achieve the planned reductions outlined in the 1983 programme.[27]

The latest multi-annual guidance programme seeks a further 8 per cent reduction by the end of 1991. Rationalization of fleet size and structure is bound to prove difficult in the context of unstable stocks and wildly fluctuating TACs: one year's over-capacity may be next year's under-capacity. But the urgent need to establish a new equilibrium between fishing effort and sustainable resources may require more radical action.

One possible means of accelerating the process of structural change would be to open up the licensing and quota systems to market forces by levying entry fees to quota-restricted fisheries and allowing individual vessel quotas to be bought and sold on the open market. In theory this should result in an optimal allocation of resources to the fishery,[28] providing realistic TACs are set. But there are strong moral and social objections to such a system. The right to trade in a common property resource is morally dubious and the threat to the widely established system of skipper-owners and to the smaller fishing communities under the capitalistic processes of accumulation and concentration raises familiar social issues.

[27] Journal of the European Communities, March 1988, L 62/21, L 62/27, L 62/30, L 67/14, L 67/24, L 70/21.

[28] S. Cunningham, M. R. Dunn, and D. Whitmarsh, *Fisheries Economics: An Introduction* (London, 1985), p. 169.

Conclusion

North Sea fisheries present a formidable challenge of "management under extreme uncertainty", made worse by persistently high levels of fishing effort. As stocks remain susceptible to environmental change, no conservation plan can expect to eradicate the uncertainty completely.

Some improvement can be achieved by reducing fishing effort to allow a higher proportion of the recruitment year classes to escape risk of capture and so enhance the reproductive capacity of the stock. At present the CFP offers little prospect of such improvement as the political decision-makers remain unwilling to accept a worst-case basis for planning the future development of the industry. There is little evidence, so far, of beneficial management, except in the case of the collapse of herring stocks in the 1970s which forced the closure of the North Sea fishery. Instead, the politics of compromise have led to a management policy geared towards maintaining the status quo. Strategic planning is thus hemmed in by a vicious circle in which fluctuating TACs preclude rational forward planning of fishing capacity and while fishing effort remains high so the hope of negotiating more realistic TACs remains slight.

Although the interim review of the CFP due in 1992 is unlikely to result in major changes to the overall structure of the package, it may provide an opportunity for a renewal of commitment to the fundamental aims of conservation as well as to equity in exploitation.

APPENDIX Minimum net and fish sizes for North Sea (EEC Conservation Regulation No. 3094/86, amended)

Species	*Minimum mesh size for towed nets (mm)*	*Minimum % of target species*	*Maximum % of protected species*[1]
All	90	—	100
Sole (1 Apr–31 Dec)	80	15	100[2]
Sole (vessels of 221kw or under)	75	5	100
Mackerel	32	50	10
Herring	32	50	10
Sandeel[3]	16	50	10
Sprat	16	50	10
Norway pout (except in Pout box)	16	50	10
Blue Whiting	16	50	10
Horse mackerel	16	50	10

Notes:

1 Protected species are those demersal species for which the minimum size is set plus Ling, Eel, Monkfish, Salmon and Sea Trout.
2 but not more than 20% of cod, haddock, saithe and whiting combined.
3 16mm applies 1 Nov to 28/29 Feb annually. In remaining period, meshes below 16mm may be used but not less than 50% of sandeel and not more than 10% of protected species must be taken.

Minimum fish landing sizes			
Species	*Cm*	*Species*	*Cm*
A) Flatfish		B) Gadoids	
Brill	30	Cod	35
Dab	23	Haddock	30
Flounder	25	Hake	30
Lemon sole	25	Pollack	30
Megrim	25	Saithe	35
Plaice	27	Whiting	27
Sole	24		
Turbot	30	C) Other foodfish	
Witch flounders	28	Bass	32
		Conger eel	58
		Black seabream	23
		Red seabream	25
		D) Pelagic	
		Herring	20
		Mackerel	30

Chapter 24

Atmospheric Depositions

Scott Davidson

Nature of the problem

It has long been recognized that the atmosphere is a material source of marine pollution.[1] A variety of contaminants and pollutants[2] are held in the air in gaseous or particulate form and are deposited in the sea either by rain or fall-out. Among the most common metal contaminants and pollutants produced by industry, waste disposal and motor vehicles are lead, zinc, copper, mercury, and cadmium, while carbon dioxide, carbon monoxide, methane, sulphur dioxide and nitrogen oxide comprise the major sources of gaseous inputs.[3] There are also other damaging organic compounds which are held in the atmosphere in gaseous form and deposited in the marine environment by rain. These are primarily organic—pesticides (of which the best known is DDT) and PCBs. Elements of all these metal, gaseous and chemical depositions have been identified as sources of contamination or pollution of the North Sea.[4]

While the existence of marine pollution by interaction with the atmosphere has been evident for some time, it has not, until recently, been the subject of rigorous scientific study, let alone legal regulation. In 1986, however, the Group of Experts on the Scientific Aspects of Marine Pollution (GESAMP) discussed the effects of contaminants in modification of physical, chemical and biological processes in the troposhpere and at the air and sea interface.[5] GESAMP also examined the interrelationship between carbon dioxide and the sea, especially the capacity of the

[1] See R. B. Clark, *Marine Pollution* (Oxford, Clarendon Press, 1986), pp. 6, 160–163.

[2] This dichotomy is used by ICES and GESAMP. However, the term "pollution" will be used throughout this chapter as to comprehend both concepts. On the definition of pollution see P. W. Birnie, "Pollution and Fisheries in the North Sea", in G. Ulfstein, P. Andersen and R. Churchill (eds.), *The Regulation of Fisheries: Legal, Economic and Social Aspects* (Strasbourg, Council of Europe, 1987), pp. 222–225

[3] See Paris Commission, Ninth Annual Report (1987) (hereinafter Ninth Annual Report), Annex 2.

[4] *Ibid.*

[5] Group of Experts on the Scientific Aspects of Marine Pollution (GESAMP), XVI Meeting, London, 17–21 March 1986. For a review of the proceedings and conclusions see Leif Andren (1987) 18 *Marine Pollution Bulletin* 105–106.

latter to absorb and dissipate the former. During its discussions GESAMP expressed concern on the adequacy of reliable data on the exchange of carbon dioxide and other gases between the atmosphere and the oceans.

A more recent study by the Technical Working Group (TWG) of the Paris Commission (PARCOM)[6] indicated that good progress had been made in establishing pilot projects for monitoring atmospheric depositions in Paris Convention waters, but the TWG also observed that care needed to be taken in assessing the results of such projects since no site monitored was sufficiently representative of a large area. The TWG agreed that an exercise for monitoring metals through intercomparison and intercalibration should be carried out in 1988 and that a similar exercise should take place for pesticides and mercury in 1989. It was also agreed that an inventory for selected metals, including mercury and cadmium, should be completed for important industrial sectors. This follows a clear recommendation to this effect by the London INSC of 1987.[7]

Thus, although it is accepted that atmospheric depositions are an important source of maritime pollution, it is not yet clear from the available data whether such pollution is significant. PARCOM's TWG gave the following estimates for atmospheric inputs of trace metals into the Convention area in its Ninth Annual Report (estimates are in tonnes per year):[8]

Arsenic 40–120
Cadmium 45–240
Chromium 300–900
Copper 400–1600
Mercury 10–30
Nickel 300–950
Lead 2600–7400
Zinc 4900–1100

As indicated above,[9] it is apparent that data for gaseous and pesticide residue inputs into the marine environment are extremely imprecise, since scientific research has not been carried out in a sufficiently systematic fashion to provide accurate measurements over a wide area. Furthermore, research has not yet been able to demonstrate with any degree of precision a causal connection between the presence of these pollutants in the atmosphere and the marine environment. In the absence of such data, it will be apparent that the creation of legal norms to combat

[6] Ninth Annual Report, paras. 14–28. For a summary of the report see A. D. McIntyre, (1988) 19 *Marine Pollution Bulletin* 159–161.

[7] *Second International Conference on the Protection of the North Sea, London, 24–25 November 1987, Ministerial Declaration*, para. 17. This paragraph provides: "The Conference agrees to . . . 17. Encourage the Paris Commission to develop its monitoring programmes from its present pilot phase, and to establish a comprehensive, long-term monitoring programme, making use of existing programmes where possible."

[8] See Paris Commission, Ninth Annual Report (1987) (hereinafter Ninth Annual Report), Annex 2.

[9] See *above*.

such pollution must lie in abeyance until the appropriate scientific data is available and conjoined with the political will of the North Sea states to take action

Legal regulation

There are a number of general and particular rules of international law designed to regulate pollution of the marine environment by the atmosphere. The most important of the particular rules relating to the North Sea are contained in the Convention for the Prevention of Pollution from Land-based Sources 1974 (the Paris Convention)[10] and its Protocol on Atmospheric Inputs 1986[11] and the Convention for the Prevention of Maritime Pollution by Dumping from Ships and Aircraft 1972 (the Oslo Convention)[12] and its Protocol of 1983.[13] These will be dealt with in detail later, following consideration of the wider framework of international regulation of the subject.

Customary international law

Although customary international law provides some regulation of atmospheric pollution, it is highly rudimentary and probably not apposite for application to the field of marine pollution. The International Court of Justice in the *Corfu Channel Case*[14] observed that a state was under an obligation not to allow its territory knowingly to be used to the detriment of the rights of other states. This general proposition also found approval in the *Lake Lanoux Arbitration*[15] between France and Spain in which the arbitral tribunal held that a state was not permitted to abuse its rights so as to harm the rights of other states. The *Trail Smelter Arbitration*[16] between the USA and Canada, which involved the deposition of large quantities of sulphur on US territory by a smelter operating in Canada, produced the proposition that no state has the right to use or permit the use of its territory in such a manner as to cause injury in, or to, the territory of another state. It is arguable that these customary law principles are far too general to have any meaningful effect on the regulation of sea pollution by atmospheric deposition. Nevertheless, these general propositions, when coupled with more recent examples of state practice, such as the Declaration of Principles of the 1972 Stockholm Conference on the Human Environment,[17] demonstrate that the international community has developed a rudimentary and residual system for protecting abuse of rights in the sphere of the environment.[18]

However, one of the major problems which would be encountered when

[10] UKTS 64 (1978); Cmnd 7251; (1974) XIII ILM 352.
[11] Cm 87 (Misc.).
[12] UKTS 119 (1975); Cmnd 6228; (1972) XI ILM 262.
[13] Cmnd 8942.
[14] ICJ [1949] 1.
[15] (1957) XII RIAA 281.
[16] (1941) III RIAA 1905.
[17] *Declaration of the UN Conference on the Human Environment, 16 June 1972*, UN Doc. A/Conf.48/14/Rev.1.
[18] For a thorough analysis of the customary rules in this area see B. D. Smith, *State Responsibility and the Marine Environment: The Rules of Decision* (Oxford, OUP, 1988) esp. chaps 5, 6 and 7.

attempting to apply these rudimentary customary norms to the marine environment is, exactly whose territory is the object of the injurious activity? The territorial sea of other states would appear to be the most obvious candidate for such designation, since states enjoy a totality of sovereign rights in this maritime zone.[19] It is interesting to note that Churchill and Lowe[20] have argued that the High Seas might also be embraced by customary law regulating pollution since Article 2 of the High Seas Convention of 1958 possibly incorporates such customary law by implication. They admit, however, that this "appears to be too vague to be very effective, and would certainly seem incapable of being developed."[21]

A further development of note is that the International Law Commission has suggested in Article 19 of its Draft Articles on State Responsibility[22] that where there is massive pollution of the high seas, the delinquent state should be criminally responsible at international law.[23] It should be noted, however, that this is simply progressive development, and it has not yet been established how a state can be criminally responsible for its actions in practice.[24]

General treaties

A number of treaties have been concluded to deal with the problem of atmospheric pollution of the marine environment. The UN Economic Commission for Europe's Convention on Long-range Boundary Air Pollution 1979[25] was concluded to deal with transboundary pollution resulting from acid rain. It is generally viewed as a weak instrument[26] as it is largely ambiguous and hortatory in nature and does not lay down precise guidelines for the elimination of such pollution, nor a time-scale in which it must be achieved. A 1985 Protocol[27] to the Convention which commits parties to the reduction of sulphur dioxide emissions by 30 per cent from their 1980 levels by 1993 is clearly much more precise, but it should be noted that neither the Convention nor any of its protocols are yet in force.

Part XII of the Law of the Sea Convention 1982 (LOSC),[28] which is similarly not yet in force,[29] is devoted to the protection of the marine environment. Article 212

[19] See Art. 1(1) of the Territorial Sea Convention 1958 which provides: "The sovereignty of a State extends, beyond its land territory and its internal waters, to a belt of sea adjacent to its coast, described as the territorial sea." Art. 2 of the Law of the Sea Convention 1982 (hereinafter LOSC) reproduces Art. 1(1) in almost identical terms.

[20] R. R. Churchill and A. V. Lowe, *The Law of the Sea* (Manchester, MUP, 2nd Ed., 1988) p. 245.

[21] *Ibid.*

[22] (1979) YBILC II (Pt. II) 90 and (1980) YBILC 1980 II (Pt. II) 14, 70.

[23] Art. 19(3)(a) provides: "an international crime may result, *inter alia*, from: a serious breach of an obligation of essential importance for the safeguarding and the preservation of the human environment, such as those prohibiting massive pollution of the atmosphere or of the seas."

[24] (1976) YBILC II (Pt. II) 119.

[25] (1979) XVIII ILM 1442.

[26] For discussion see A. Rosencranz, "The ECE Convention of 1979 on Long-Range Transboundary Air Pollution" (1981) 75 *AJIL* 975–982 and Birnie, "Pollution and Fisheries in the North Sea", 236.

[27] Helsinki, 8 July 1985.

[28] (1982) XXI ILM 1261.

[29] By Art. 308 LOSC will enter into force 12 months after ratification by 60 states. To date, it has been ratified by 42 states.

in particular deals with pollution of the sea from or through atmospheric inputs. Article 192 LOSC lays a general obligation on states to protect and preserve the marine environment. This is diminished somewhat by Article 193 which confirms that states have sovereign rights "to exploit their natural resources pursuant to their environmental policies and in accordance with their duty to protect and preserve the marine environment." Nevertheless, Article 194 places obligations upon states to take separate or joint action which is necessary "to prevent, reduce and control pollution of the marine environment from any source, using for this purpose the best practicable means at their disposal and in accordance with their capabilities, and they shall endeavour to harmonize their policies in this connection." Clearly the various forms of regional co-operation in the North Sea for the prevention and elimination of atmospheric pollution which impact upon the marine environment through the Oslo and Paris Conventions, the London Dumping Convention and the forms of EC coordination and legislation comply with the obligations established in the LOSC.[30]

In the present context, however, Article 212 which deals specifically with marine pollution through the atmosphere is worthy of detailed consideration. Article 212 places an obligation upon states to adopt laws and regulations to prevent, reduce and control pollution of the marine environment from or through the atmosphere applicable to the airspace under their sovereignty and to vessels flying their flag or vessels or aircraft of their registry, taking into account internationally agreed rules, standards and recommended practices and procedures and the safety of air navigation. States are also empowered to take other measures as may be necessary to prevent, reduce and control pollution, and are also placed under an obligation to take measures acting through international organizations and diplomatic conferences to establish global and regional rules. Enforcement of the rules thus established is to be achieved through flag or registry state jurisdiction.[31]

It is readily apparent that the the LOSC constitutes a *traité cadre* in which the precise nature of the obligations are to be established by states acting independently or jointly through various organizational media. There is little doubt, as observed above, that the North Sea littoral states and institutions have already made substantial progress in this field both in the forms of co-operation achieved and in the degree of regulatory activity which has been undertaken.

Convention for the Prevention of Pollution from Land-based Sources 1974 and Protocol amending the Convention 1986[32]

Under the Paris Convention the contracting parties undertake to eliminate pollution of the maritime area from land-based sources and to limit strictly pollution of

[30] See generally, S. Saetevik, *Environmental Cooperation between the North Sea States* (London, Belhaven Press, 1988); T. IJlstra, "Regional Cooperation in the North Sea: An Inquiry" (1988) 3 IJECL 181–207; Birnie, "Pollution and Fisheries in the North Sea",228–236; Clark, *Marine Pollution*, chaps. 10 and 11.

[31] Art. 217 LOSC.

[32] UKTS 64 (1978); Cmnd 7251; (1974) XIII ILM 352.

the maritime area from land-based sources.[33] Pollution from land-based sources is defined by Article 3(c) as:

"pollution of the maritime area:
(i) through watercourses,
(ii) from the coast, including introduction through underwater or other pipelines,
(iii) from man-made structures placed under the jurisdiction of a contracting party within the limits of the area to which the present Convention applies."

In accordance with Paragraph D2 of the Bremen Declaration[34] a Protocol to the Paris Convention was adopted in 1985. This Protocol is not yet in force, but when it enters into force a fourth source of land-based pollution will be added to the list contained in Article 3(c): emissions into the atmosphere from land or from man-made structures.

In order to achieve the objectives of the Convention the contracting parties agree to implement, jointly or individually, measures for the elimination of pollution from land-based sources and the reduction of pollution from land-based sources of the Annex substances.[35] Measures adopted under Article 4(2) are to include specific regulations or standards governing the quality of the environment, discharges into the maritime area, discharges into watercourses as affect the maritime area and the composition and use of substances and products. To this the Protocol has added "emissions into the atmosphere".

It should be noted that although the Protocol to the Paris Convention is not yet in force, to all intents and purposes, PARCOM, the TWG and the JMG perform their functions as if the Protocol had entered into force. This is apparent from PARCOM's Ninth (1987) Annual Report.[36] It should also be noted that the London Declaration following the Second INSC urged participating Governments to ratify the Protocol amending the Paris Convention "by the earliest practicable date".[37]

Convention for the Prevention of Marine Pollution by Dumping from Ships and Aircraft 1972, Protocol Amending the Convention 1983 and Convention on the Prevention of Marine Pollution by Dumping of Wastes and other Matter (London Convention) 1972

Neither the Oslo Convention nor the London Convention originally dealt explicitly with the question of marine pollution caused by incineration of harmful substances

[33] Art. 4.
[34] *International Conference on the Protection of the North Sea, Bremen 1984, Ministerial Declaration.*
[35] Annex A substances are classified according to the criteria of persistence, toxicity and tendency to bioaccumulation taking into account such other criteria as location and quantity of substances discharged. The substances are then further classified as Part I, II or II substances based on other specific criteria such as harm to living organisms.
[36] See Paris Commission, Ninth Annual Report (1987) (hereinafter Ninth Annual Report), Annex 2.
[37] Para. XVI.17

at sea. Both these conventions were primarily concerned with the direct dumping into the sea from ships or aircraft of waste produced on shore. While some London Dumping Convention countries argued that the Convention could be interpreted to embrace waste incineration, others argued that this was not so and that consequently incineration could continue.[38] More recent developments, however, have shown that incineration is an issue over which both London Dumping Convention and Oslo Convention states are prepared to take action.

In 1983 the Oslo Convention states adopted a Protocol to amend the original Convention to define incineration at sea as a form of dumping within the meaning of the Convention.[39] Article I provided: "Dumping means any deliberate disposal into the sea including through the medium of incineration at sea." Article I(2) further defined incineration as "any deliberate combustion of substances and materials at sea for the purposes of their thermal destruction".

The Protocol also established detailed rules for the incineration of waste at sea by limiting the kinds of substances which could be disposed of through this particular method, the technical means by which it could be disposed of and the sites at which disposal may take place. The latter, which is dealt with by Rule 9, provides that those involved in waste disposal must take into account the prevailing dispersal atmospheric characteristics of the area in order to determine the potential impact on the surrounding environment of the pollutants. They must also pay particular attention to the possibility of atmospheric transport of pollutants in fishing grounds and coastal areas. One of the main provisions, however, represents a recurring theme in the issue of waste disposal by incineration; this is that incineration should only be regarded as an interim method of waste disposal.[40]

It should be noted that although the Protocol has only just entered into force, the effects of earlier decisions taken within the framework of the London INSC of 1987 and a decision of the London Dumping Convention of June 1988 to reduce incineration by 65 per cent by 1 January 1991 and to phase out such operations by 31 December 1994, have rendered its entry into force largely irrelevant in practical terms.[41]

At present, waste disposal by incineration only takes place in the North Sea. Three incinerator vessels operate here, but they have found that it is rather more difficult to obtain disposal permits than hitherto and that the attentions of pressure groups such as Greenpeace and the Friends of the Earth are rather more difficult to avoid.[42] It would seem therefore, that given the political and the general environ-

[38] Birnie, "Pollution and Fisheries in the North Sea", 234.

[39] Cmnd 8942.

[40] See Rule 2(2) of the Protocol to then Oslo Convention and the reaffirmation of this positions by OSPARCOM at its meeting in Lisbon in June 1988. For a report of the proceedings see G. C. Kasoulides, *Marine Pollution Bulletin*, Vol. 19 (1988), p. 498. See also Para. XVI. 24 of the *Ministerial Declaration of the London Conference*.

[41] Apparently this decision was influenced by the London North Sea Conference. See G. C. Kasoulides, *Marine Pollution Bulletin*, Vol. 19 (1988), p. 648.

[42] For a recent example of such concern, see *The Times*, 13 February 1989.

mental climate that sea pollution by fall-out from the plume of incinerated waste is unlikely to be perpetuated for much longer.

The European Community

While the EC is a party to the Paris Convention[43] and takes an active role in the deliberations of, and implementation of the standards agreed by, PARCOM, it also pursues its own independent environmental policy. Inevitably elements of this policy impact upon the instant topic. While the control of various atmospheric inputs is part of the EC's general environmental policy which is aimed, *inter alia*, at improving the quality of life for Community citizens, nevertheless the regulatory activity of the EC in this field affects, albeit as a side issue, the quality of the marine environment.

While the EC has only recently acquired formal legal powers in respect of the environment with the entry into force of the Single European Act (SEA) in 1987, nevertheless, it has in the past exercised its competence in the environmental field principally through Articles 100 and 235 of the Rome Treaty.[44] In so doing, it has made a substantial impact in this area by the adoption of a considerable amount of legislation. Furthermore, it should also be noted that with the conferral of its new powers under the SEA the EC Commission has signified its intention to reorientate its approach to environmental matters. Whereas in the past the EC has proceeded on a largely pragmatic basis, it now intends to follow an holistic approach by integrating issues of environmental concern into its major policy areas such as, agriculture, free movement of goods and competition policy.[45] As yet, however, the new approach does not show signs of being consciously orientated towards the control of atmospheric emissions in order to preserve and improve the marine environment.[46] Nevertheless, there is a clear factual link between the EC's policy towards control of air pollution and the protection of the marine environment, even though the EC's decision-makers have not apparently directed their minds to such questions.

It is intended here to examine briefly the major areas of EC activity in the environmental field in order to evaluate their potential impact on the marine environment. The main areas of atmospheric pollution which will be examined are emissions from motor vehicles, industrial inputs into the atmosphere and inputs derived from energy production.

43 It is not, nor is it entitled to become, a member of the Oslo Convention.

44 For an examination of the the EC's powers under the SEA see J. P. Jaqué (1986) 16 *Environmental Policy and Law*, Nos. 3–4, pp. 122–124 and J. S. Davidson (1987) 2 IJECL 259. For a detailed examination of the EC's pre-SEA powers and achievements see E. Rehbinder and R. Stewart, *Integration through Law*, Vol. 2, *Environmental Protection Policy*, chaps. 2, 4, 6 and 8.

45 See Davidson (1987) 2 IJECL 259.

46 See e.g. A. P. Barisich, "The Protection of the Sea: A European Community Policy" (1987) 2 IJECL 1 where, significantly, there is no reference to the wider impact on marine pollution from other sectors for which the EC legislated.

Emissions from motor vehicles

There are a number of directives concerned with emissions from motor vehicles, but perhaps the most important piece of legislation affecting the marine environment is Directive 85/210[47] which governs the discharge of lead into the atmosphere through combustion by motor vehicle engines. This Directive requires Member States to reduce the content of lead in petrol from 0.40 grammes/litre (g/l) to 0.15 g/l as soon as they consider appropriate[48] and to provide for a balanced distribution of unleaded fuel within their territory by 1 October 1989.[49] Since it is thought that most of the lead content of the North Sea arises from atmospheric deposition of lead added to petrol as an anti-knock ingredient,[50] the reduction of the use of lead for this purpose will clearly have a significant effect.

Lead, however, is not the only emission from motor vehicles which have merited the attention of the EC. The Community has adopted a series of directives aimed at limiting exhaust emissions from a number of motor vehicle engines. Directive 70/220[51] sets limits for the emission of carbon monoxide and unburnt hydrocarbons from petrol engines. Directive 74/290[52] further reduced these limits and Directive 77/102[53] added limits for nitrogen oxide. Further reductions for all three sources of atmospheric pollution were legislated for in Directives 78/665[54] and 83/351.[55] The Council has also recently agreed to seek further stringent reduction of carbon monoxide, hydrocarbon and nitrogen oxide emissions by requiring the incorporation of three way catalytic converters in all motor vehicles of less than 1400 cc produced in the EC by the end of 1992.[56] It is estimated that such converters, which absorb combustion products, will reduce emissions by approximately two-thirds.[57]

Emissions from diesel-powered vehicles are also governed by EC legislation. Directive 72/306[58] sets limits to gaseous and hydrocarbon pollution from all diesel-engined vehicles except public works vehicles and tractors.[59] The latter is the subject of separate legislation by way of Directive 77/357.[60] Limits have also been set to the amount of sulphur which may be contained in the gas oil which fuels diesel vehicles. Directive 87/219[61] sets a limit of 0.3 per cent sulphur content in gas oil in most cases, although a limit of 0.2 per cent is prescribed for areas where damage is

47 OJ L 96 3 April 1985.
48 Art. 3.
49 Art. 3.
50 See Clark, *The Waters Around the British Isles: Their Conflicting Uses* (Oxford, Clarendon Press, 1987) p. 222.
51 OJ L7 6 April 1970.
52 OJ L 159 15 June 1974.
53 OJ L 32 3 February 1977.
54 OJ L 223 14 August 1978.
55 OJ L 197 20 July 1983.
56 See David Usborne, "EC Agrees to Tough Car Exhaust Controls", *Independent*, 10 June 1989.
57 *Ibid.*
58 OJ L 190 20 August 1972.
59 Art.
60 OJ L 220 29 August 1977.
61 OJ L 91 3 April 1987.

likely to be caused to the national heritage of Member States or if the geographical zone is one which is scheduled for special consideration under Article 4 of 80/779.[62] This latter Directive deals with emission limit values for smoke and sulphur dioxide from whichever source they emanate.[63]

Inputs from industry and energy production

There is a significant amount of EC legislation which is aimed at protecting and improving the quality of air in the Member States. Again, a quick perusal of the legislation indicates that the EC is primarily concerned with the effects of atmospheric pollution within the land territory of the Member States and not its relationship to maritime territory, although mention should be made of the Community's recognition of the need to take action in the prevention of transboundary air pollution (*see below*).

Directive 80/779, which has already been referred to above in the context of exhaust emissions from motor vehicles,[64] has as its overall objective the prevention of further deterioration in air quality from the emissions of smoke and sulphur dioxide from industrial plant by the use of standstill provisions,[65] and the eventual improvement of air quality by the introduction of more stringent measures by Member States.[66] Limits on the amount of smoke and sulphur dioxide in the atmosphere are expressed in microgrammes per cubic metre, and are set at different levels for different seasons of the year.[67] It is also envisaged that Member States may adopt more stringent standards for particular industrial areas and for areas of particular environmental concern.[68]

A link between Directive 80/779 and transboundary air pollution has been forged by a resolution of the Council of 15 July 1980.[69] In its resolution the Council stated:

> Taking due account of the facts and problems involved, the Member States will endeavour in accordance with the objective of Council Directive 80/779/EEC of July 1980 on air-quality limit values for sulphur dioxide and suspended particulates to limit and as far as possible gradually reduce and prevent transboundary air pollution by sulphur dioxide and suspended particulates.

It is apparent therefore, that when the Council adopted the instant directive it envisaged that the reduction of pollution by smoke and sulphur dioxide within the Member States themselves would also reduce the levels of transboundary pollution, particularly that of acid rain caused by the precipitation of sulphur dioxide held in the atmosphere.

Nitrogen dioxide which is emitted by both combustion engines and by industrial

[62] OJ L 229 30 August 1980.
[63] See *below*.
[64] OJ L 229 30 August 1980.
[65] Art. 3.
[66] *Ibid*.
[67] Annex I, Table B.
[68] Art. 4.
[69] OJ C 222 30 August 1980.

processes is also controlled by Community legislation. Directive 85/203[70] sets limit values of 200 microgrammes per cubic metre, which were to have been achieved by Member States by 1 July 1987.[71]

Although pollution from lead arises primarily from motor vehicle exhausts, it should also be noted that lead pollution occurs from a variety of industrial processes. Directive 82/884[72] therefore places limit values on the level of lead discharged into the atmosphere by such processes.

In order to combat the problem of acid rain and consequent lake and forest death, the EC adopted Directive 84/360[73] which requires Member States to authorize certain categories of industrial and energy-producing plants before they may begin or continue to operate.[74] Before authorization is given, the competent authority in each Member State must ensure that appropriate preventive measures against air pollution should be taken, using the best available technology (provided the cost is not excessive); that emissions must not cause significant air pollution and air-quality limit values should be taken into account. It should be noted that Directive 84/360 is also a framework directive in that it provides powers for the creation of further directives in this field.[75]

Conclusion

In the regulation of atmospheric depositions resulting in pollution in the North Sea area it is significant that the political impetus has superseded the majority of formal legal instruments. PARCOM treated the Protocol to the Paris Convention as if it were already in force before its actual entry into force, while the London Ministerial Meeting of 1987 and the London Dumping Convention meeting of 1988 more or less ensured the redundancy of the Protocol to the Oslo Convention. It is perhaps heartening that the littoral states of the North Sea do not consider it necessary to march down the path of legal formalism, but rather to solve these problems by way of co-operation and negotiation through the medium of international governmental and diplomatic conferences.

It is also significant that a major impact on pollution by atmospheric deposition in the North Sea has probably come from a side wind in the form of legislation adopted by the EC in pursuit of its general environmental Action Plans. Since most atmospheric pollution originates from land-based sources, it is only appropriate that the EC should take the necessary measures to curtail some of the less acceptable practices of its industrial Member States. It is suggested, however, that in its new holistic approach to issues of pollution the EC should advert specifically to the impact which air pollution has on the marine environment of the North Sea. This it

70 OJ L 87 27 March 1985.
71 Art. 3.
72 OJ L 378 31 December 1982.
73 OJ L 188 16 July 1984.
74 Art. 3. The categories of plant affected are listed in Annex I. Annex II contains a list of "the most polluting substances" covered by the directive including nitrogen oxide, sulphur dioxide, chlorine and heavy metals.
75 Art. 8.

has already done in the field of pollution from land-based sources in the unamended Paris Convention.[76] What it now needs to do is consider what effect its existing legislation on air pollution has had on the marine environment and to redefine its Action Plans to ensure that future legislation in this field clearly embraces maritime areas. This may require the EC to be rather more specific about its competences to legislate for the maritime areas of its Member States (as indeed PARCOM has requested it to do in the past),[77] but this should not prove an insuperable problem for a Community committed to the preservation and improvement of the environment.

[76] See *above*.
[77] See Saetevik, *Environmental Cooperation between the North Sea States*.

Chapter 25

Radiological Discharges

John Woodliffe

Any legal analysis and appraisal of the current practice of North Sea states concerning the discharge and disposal of liquid radioactive wastes to the marine environment must inevitably take as its main point of departure the Declaration issued at the Second International Conference on the Protection of the North Sea in 1987 (hereinafter the London Declaration). In contrast with the Bremen Declaration in 1984, the treatment of the subject is fuller and more sharply focused.

First, a prominent role is accorded to the application of the "best available technology" (BAT) as a means of reducing pollution from point sources.[1] While the broad and rather minimal objective of this approach is to "prevent any increase in pollution in the North Sea, in other sea areas, or in other parts of the environment, or any risk to the health of industrial workers or the general population", it also embraces "specific measures" in relation to, *inter alia*, "discharges and disposal of radioactive wastes".[2]

Second, the Declaration provides a framework upon which future controls on radioactive discharges will need to be based.[3]

Third, the Declaration identifies two agreed elements of that framework:

> "(1)[to] respect the relevant recommendations of competent international organizations, and to this end to apply the best available technology to minimize any pollution caused by radioactive discharges from all nuclear industries, including reprocessing plants into the marine environment. (para. 39)
> (2) the design and construction of repositories for the disposal of radioactive wastes should aim to preclude pollution of the North Sea and interference with the legitimate uses of the sea. (para. 41)"

To this end, the development of such repositories is to be reported to "the relevant international organizations and upon request to the governments of the North Sea states" (para. 42).

[1] Recital VII (a)(i).
[2] Recitals X, XI.
[3] *UK Guidance Note on the Ministerial Declaration*, Department of the Environment, 1988, para. 37.

A striking feature of these paragraphs is the acknowledgement that regulation of the discharge and disposal of radioactive waste is no longer exclusively a matter within the domain of state sovereignty. This quasi-internationalization is far removed from the view held by the nuclear industry some thirty years ago: "almost anything put in the sea is either diluted or broken down . . . or stored harmlessly on the sea-bed . . . not least of the attractions of the sea as a dumping ground has been the lack of administrative control."[4] There is a danger, however, that the undoubted advances made during this period may induce in coastal states an air of complacency. Thus in 1988 the UK announced that its "present policies (concerning radioactive discharges) already comply with the requirements of the Declaration."[5] Even so, it is evident that the paragraphs from the London Declaration, set out above, express no more than a highly generalized consensus about policy ends and means.

This chapter encompasses several interrelated aims: to document the varied institutional inputs in the formation and formulation of the above-mentioned consensus; to gauge the progress made in implementing policy goals; to identify existing and future areas of concern; and to propose ways of strengthening regional management and control of liquid radioactive discharges. By way of introduction, reference will be made to the basic scientific and geophysical background.

Radioactivity in the marine environment: sources and pathways

The normal operation of nuclear plants involves the discharge of low-level radioactive effluents directly to the environment. Liquid effluents emanate from the discharge of cooling water from plant designed to clean that water or from spent fuel storage ponds prior to reprocessing of that fuel as well as from the reprocessing operation itself. This explains why nuclear plants are mostly sited along coasts and rivers. The Quality Status Report of the North Sea (QSR),[6] in identifying the nuclear power industry as "the principal source of radiation from artificial nuclides in the North Sea",[7] produced a breakdown of the inputs of radioactivity in liquid wastes to these waters for 1984–85. This was accounted for by thirty-one nuclear establishments classified according to country of origin and to (a) their direct input to the North Sea (3); (b) inputs via rivers (20); (c) inputs from adjoining sea areas, namely, the northern inflow of Atlantic water (2), the southern inflow of water from the English Channel (5) and the eastern inflow from the Baltic Sea (2).[8] Since the QSR four more such nuclear plants have come on stream. The QSR also

[4] Quoted in J. Cook, *Red Alert* (London: New English Library), 1986, p. 182.

[5] *UK Guidance Note on the Ministerial Declaration*.

[6] For the purposes of both the *Report* and the *Declaration* the North Sea area comprises: (a) the North Sea southwards of latitude 62 N; (b) the Skagerrak, the southern limit of which is determined east of the Skaw by latitude 57 44'8'N; (c) the English Channel and its approaches eastwards of longitude 5 W. Note to Recital I. Text of *Declaration* is repr. in (1988) 3 IJECL 252.

[7] *Quality Status of the North Sea: Summary, Scientific and Working Group*, September 1987, para. 22.

[8] *Ibid.* table 7.

adduces data to show that most of the radioactivity in the North Sea comes from the Sellafield (formerly Windscale) reprocessing plant situated on the coast of north west England. The radionuclides enter the North Sea via the inflow of Atlantic water driven by tidal currents and winds around the Scottish coast[9] and are then dispersed eastward towards Norway, Denmark and Sweden.[10] Sellafield's disproportionate contribution—reportedly the largest recorded source of radioactive discharge in the world—is due to several factors. First, a reprocessing plant has a much higher rate of discharge than a nuclear reactor; second, the longevity of the plant which has been discharging by pipeline low activity effluents into the Irish Sea since 1952. This is in sharp contrast with the much lower rates of discharge from the French modern reprocessing plant at Cap de le Hague; moreover, tidal currents in the English Channel prevent any widespread dispersal of radioactive effluents from that plant.[11] Hence the emphasis in this chapter is upon UK practice and the regulation of discharges of *liquid* wastes. Nevertheless, not all of the radioactivity found in the marine environment derives from the nuclear power industry. The waters of and sediments in the North Sea contain quantities of radioactivity that are natural in origin,[12] augmented by fall-out from atmospheric testing of nuclear weapons. Quantities of radioactivity are routinely discharged to the marine environment from UK defence and naval installations and by US nuclear submarines into waters adjoining the naval base at Holy Loch, Scotland.[13] UK nuclear submarines also make routine discharges of radioactivity at sea.[14] In addition, numerous non-nuclear industrial sites on the mainland and oil installations offshore are authorized to discharge radioactive wastes to sea.[15] Over the period 1950–1982, several European states dumped containerized solid nuclear wastes in ocean sites, the largest of which is in the north-east Atlantic.[16] Lastly, uncontrolled releases can contribute to the input of radioactivity to the North Sea. Data collected in 1987 show that the Chernobyl accident in the previous year affected fish from Scottish waters and the North Sea;[17] however, the accident is expected to "only have a small and transient

[9] *Ibid.* para. 22.

[10] R. B. Clark (ed.), *The Waters Around the British Isles: Their Conflicting Uses* (Oxford, Clarendon Press, 1987), p. 18. For a map of the surface current system of the North Sea, see QSR, n. 7, para. 4 and see above, Chap. 6.

[11] Clark, *The Waters Around the British Isles*, 238.

[12] "Quality Status of the North Sea: Summary, Scientific and Working Group", para. 22.

[13] Radioactive Waste Management Advisory Committee (RWMAC), Ninth Report, 1988, Chap. 7; HC, Vol. 145, Col. 555 (24 January 1989).

[14] HC, Vol. 152, Col. 61 (2 May 1989).

[15] These are listed at: HC, Vol. 93, Col. 248 (6 March 1986). Radioactive material in the form of a sealed neutron was used in the exploration for hydrocarbons in the North Sea continental shelf; Committee A, Continental Shelf Bill, 1964, 4th sitting, Col. 145 (4 March 1964). It has also been employed in well-logging procedures and for the non-destructive testing of platform steel work (communication to the author from the Foreign and Commonwealth Office). The Civil Jurisdiction (Offshore Activities) Order 1987. S.I. 1987 Nos. 2197 and 2198 made under s. 7, Continental Shelf Act 1964, extends the Radioactive Substances Act 1960 to installations in designated areas of the UK continental shelf.

[16] *Report of the Independent Review of Disposal of Radioactive Waste in the North East Atlantic*, chairman, Prof. F. G. T. Holliday. HMSO 1984, Chap. 3 and Fig. 3.1.

[17] G. J. Hunt, *Aquatic Environment Monitoring Report No. 19: Radioactivity in Surface and Coastal Waters of the British Isles*, 1987, MAFF Directorate of Fisheries Research (1988), p. 12.

effect on radiation exposure."[18] Numerous incidents involving loss of or damage to nuclear-powered and -armed submarines at sea are well documented;[19] two such incidents involving Soviet submarines occurred in the first half of 1989 in the Norwegian Sea.[20]

Pathways to man

The two most important transfer mechanisms from the sea to man—known as radiation exposure pathways—are the consumption of fish and shellfish and external exposure to marine sediments found in estuaries and harbours. Other pathways of lower current importance are exposure by handling, of contaminated fishing-gear by fishermen and the use of *Porphyria* in the manufacture of laverbread.[21]

Principles of regulation and control

Historically, the management of liquid radioactive discharges has rested on the "dilute and disperse" principle. This sanctions discharges in amounts below authorized radiological protection limits based on recommendations of the International Commission for Radiological Protection (ICRP).[22] Underpinning the ICRP individual and collective dose limits is the guiding principle that all exposures should be kept as low as is reasonably achievable, after taking economic and social factors into account (ALARA).

Another generally accepted principle of control is that discharges are regulated by a system of authorization which is independent of plant management.[23] In respect of liquid wastes discharged to the sea from Sellafield, the current certificate of authorization granted to British Nuclear Fuels plc requires the company to, *inter alia*: use the best practicable means to limit the radioactivity of wastes discharged (BPM); adhere to controls over radionuclides which may be discharged; and maintain the pipelines in good repair.[24]

A third principle of control, invariably a condition of any authorization to discharge radioactive waste, requires the site operator to monitor and to keep records of discharges.[25] These are in turn subject to regular independent checks by the authorizing body.[26] In the UK overall responsibility for monitoring the aquatic environment is undertaken by the MAFF Directorate of Fisheries Research

[18] "Quality Status of the North Sea: Summary, Scientific and Working Group", para. 22.

[19] *Guardian*, 27 June 1989: *Naval Accidents 1945–1988* (Greenpeace).

[20] The most serious incident occurred on 7 April 1989 when a Soviet *Mike* class submarine sank in the Norwegian Sea. The Soviet Government gave assurances that there had been no leak of radioactivity; HC, Vol. 152, Col. 61 (2 May 1989).

[21] Hunt, *Aquatic Environment Monitoring Report No. 19*, 12, 23, 25.

[22] The recommendations are set out in ICRP Publication No. 26 (1977) as explained in later ICRP statements. A review of the basic recommendations and the system of dose limitation is currently under way; it is expected to be completed by 1990. (1987) 374 *Atom* 12.

[23] The system in the UK is governed by the Radioactive Substances Act 1960.

[24] The certificate is reproduced in the *Nineteenth Report of the House of Lords Select Committee on the European Communities: Radioactive Waste Management* (Session 1987–1988) HL Papers 99-i, p. 86.

[25] Certificate of Authorization, Sellafield Liquid Waste, paras. 7–9.

[26] See *Monitoring of Radioactivity in the UK Environment*, Department of the Environment, 1988.

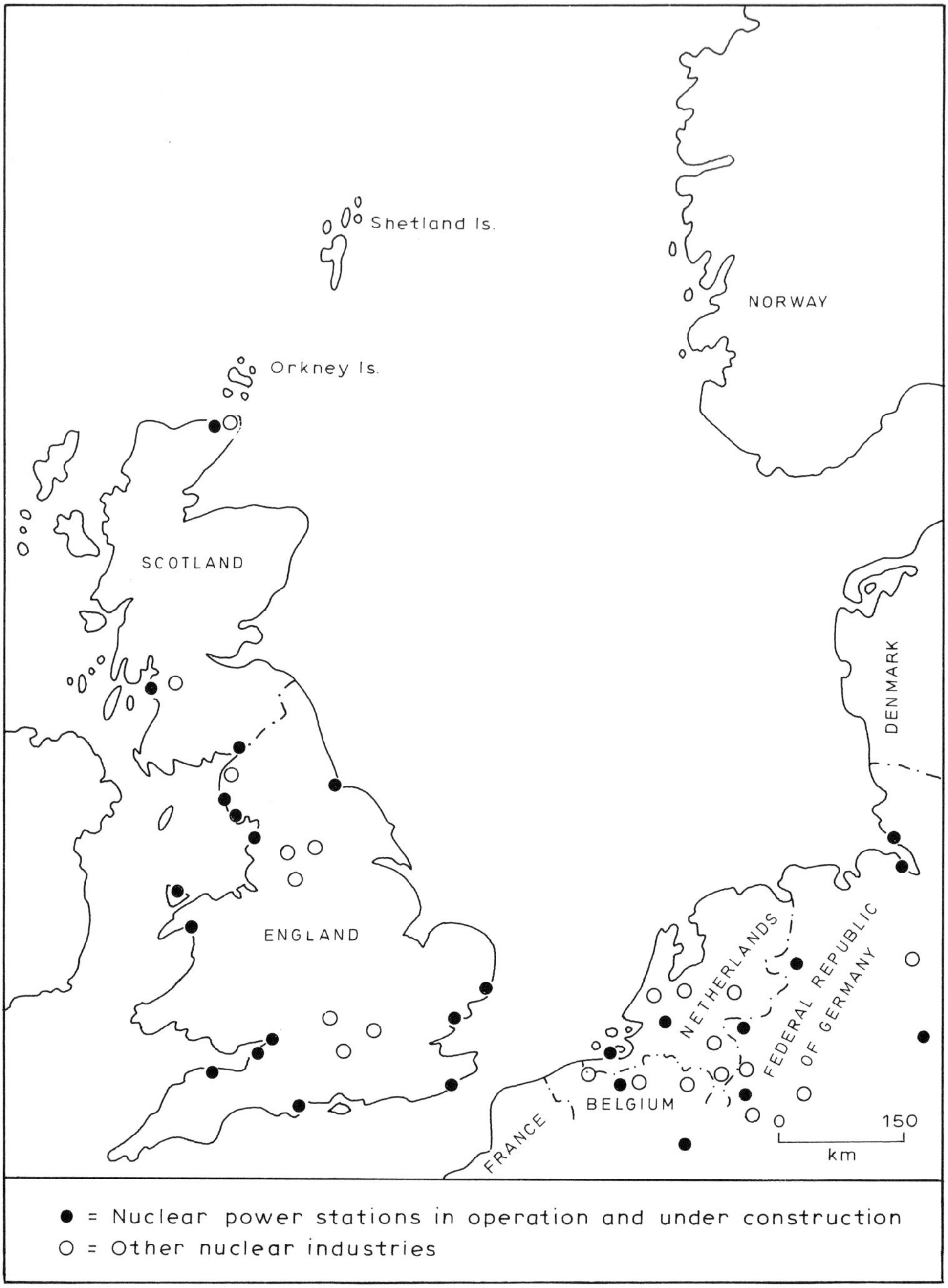
Shetland Is.
Orkney Is.
NORWAY
SCOTLAND
DENMARK
ENGLAND
NETHERLANDS
FEDERAL REPUBLIC OF GERMANY
BELGIUM
FRANCE
0 150
km
● = Nuclear power stations in operation and under construction
○ = Other nuclear industries

Figure 1

(DFR);[27] This body also carries out a number of substantial research programmes into the behaviour of radionuclides in the UK coastal environment, including the North Sea.[28] There is a limited degree of co-ordination with other North Sea states' monitoring programmes for intercomparison purposes, more especially between the UK, Denmark and the FRG.[29] North Sea coastal states also collaborate closely with the International Atomic Energy Agency's Monaco-based international laboratory of marine radioactivity, which is engaged in comparative studies of the behaviour of radionuclides in different sea areas, including the North Sea.[30]

Data on discharges from nuclear plants are published regularly both in national[31] and international forums. The European Community (EC) publishes and evaluates data on the discharge of liquid radioactive effluents from nuclear power stations and reprocessing plants located in the Community.[32] In the case of Member States of the EC the ICRP recommendations have acquired normative status.[33] Further evidence of "the essential role of international co-operation and agreed regimes, especially at regional level", noted in the London Declaration, is to be found in the activities of the Paris Commission (PARCOM) established under the Convention for the Prevention of Marine Pollution from Land-Based Sources 1974.[34] The Commission promotes action on joint measures and harmonization of policies that the Contracting parties (CPs) have pledged to adopt to combat marine pollution from land-based sources.[35] This is without prejudice to measures and programmes adopted individually by the CPs. Under the Convention, radioactive substances, including wastes, occupy a category of their own "because . . . they are already the subject of research, recommendations and in some cases, measures under the auspices of several international organizations and institutions".[36] Pursuant to the basic undertaking to "adopt measures to forestall and, as appropriate, eliminate pollution of the maritime area . . . by radioactive substances, the CPs shall take full account of the recommendations" (in particular those concerned with monitoring procedures) made by the above-mentioned bodies.[37] Despite the tentative nature

[27] Details are set out in a hitherto unpublished paper presented to a workshop organized by the Paris Commission in 1986 by two scientists at the MAFF Directorate of Fisheries Research, Lowestoft: G. J. Hunt and R. J. Pentreath, "Discharges of Liquid Radioactive Wastes into UK Coastal Waters: Control Environmental Monitoring, Radiological Impact and Research." The present writer is indebted to the authors for a pre-publication copy of their paper.

[28] Memorandum by MAFF, *Nineteenth Report of the House of Lords Select Committee*, 104.

[29] Communication to the author from G. J. Hunt, DFR, Lowestoft.

[30] See Fukai, "Report from Monaco: Waste Management and the Sea", *IAEA Bull.*, spring 1986, p. 33.

[31] See Hunt, *Aquatic Environment Monitoring Report No. 19*.

[32] F. Luykx and G. Fraser, *Radioactive Effluents from Nuclear Power Stations and Nuclear Fuel Reprocessing Plants in the European Community: Discharge Data 1976–1980*, CEC v/3267/83/EN, March 1983. A new report is currently being prepared.

[33] Dir. 80/836 EURATOM, OJECL 2446; Dir. 84/467 EURATOM, OJECL 265.

[34] Text repr.: (1974) XIII ILM 352. In force 6 May 1978; the North Sea comes within the geographical scope of the Convention, which has 12 contracting Parties; the European Community is a signatory.

[35] Art. 1.2.

[36] Annex A, Part III.

[37] Art. 5; The Nuclear Energy Agency of the OECD clearly comes within the category of international organization envisaged.

of these provisions, PARCOM has taken on an active, independent role in this sphere. PARCOM recommendations undoubtedly have been successful in putting pressure on CPs to review and improve their policies and practices on radioactive discharges; this is reinforced by CPs regularly informing the Commission of their proposals for implementing recommendations and the results achieved.[38] The recommendations also appear to have had a mutually reinforcing effect on the wording of both the Bremen and London Declarations. The most recent PARCOM recommendation, which is seen by the UK government as strengthening the 1987 London Declaration,[39] states the agreement of the Contracting Parties to:

> "respect the relevant recommendations of the competent international organizations and to apply the best available technology to minimize *and, as appropriate, eliminate* any pollution caused by radioactive discharges from all nuclear industries, including reprocessing plants, into the marine environment."[40]

Apart from the emphasized words, the text is identical to para. 39 of the London Declaration. Given that all participants in the Third North Sea Conference are members of PARCOM, there is a strong possibility that the recommendation will simply be taken as the benchmark for the 1990 Declaration.

The European Community's involvement

The major regional actor with competence over radioactive waste management is the EC. This competence, which derives from Chapter III of the 1957 EURATOM Treaty, starts from a weak base. Member States not only retain a virtually untrammelled power of decision over the siting of nuclear establishments but also are responsible for fixing and authorizing the levels of discharge of radioactive effluents from such establishments. The EC has observed that Community radiation protection norms are in no sense "emission standards for each type of plant."[41] This equally applies to plants built to the same specification and located within the same Member State: "there is no such thing as a standard environment . . . hence each plant has to be considered individually as regards its potential radiological impact."[42] Article 37 EURATOM confers on the EC Commission a limited consultative role in relation to emission levels of liquid effluents from nuclear plants that may produce transfrontier radiological effects, particularly in respect of plants sited

[38] See *Tenth Annual Report on the Activities of the Paris Commission*, London, 1989, paras. 36–42; Annex 33 contains a detailed report on discharges from nuclear installations in 1986.

[39] HC, Vol. V. 137, Col. 702 (20 July 1988).

[40] Recomm. 88/5, adopted unanimously at the Tenth Meeting of the Paris Commission, June 1988, Text reproduced *Tenth Annual Report on the Activities of the Paris Commission*, Annex 4.

[41] *EC Bull*. 7/8 1986, p. 74.

[42] Evidence of Mr. Fraser (European Commission), *Nineteenth Report of the House of Lords Select Committee*, q. 512.

alongside an international watercourse. Article 37 requires each Member State to provide the Commission with such general data relating to any plan for the disposal of radioactive waste in whatever form as will make it possible to determine whether the implementation of such a plan is liable to result in the radioactive contamination of the water, soil or airspace of another state.

The Commission must deliver its opinion within 6 months after consulting the group of experts referred to in Article 31.

The excessive vagueness of the wording is no doubt due to the fact that the article was drafted in the 24 hours preceding signature of the EURATOM Treaty.[43] The results of the experience of applying Article 37 over the past 30 years can be summarized thus.

For the purpose of the Commission's examination of disposal plans a distinction is drawn between preliminary and definitive "general data".[44] The former covers data that must be submitted by the Member State before it grants permission for the construction of a nuclear reactor or reprocessing plant; definitive general data must be submitted "whenever possible one year, but not less than 6 months, before the planned date of commencement of disposal of radioactive waste"—which the Commission interprets as connection to the national grid.[45] In the case of a plant situated on the coast a description of local and regional tides and currents must be provided, along with forecasts of discharge levels and details of the origin, composition, treatment and monitoring of radioactive effluents. The group of experts referred to in Article 37 then examines the submission and sends its report to the Commission. The Commission then draws up and approves a draft of the opinion which is communicated to the government of the Member State concerned and, where appropriate, to any neighbouring states.[46]

Opinions follow a standard format. The main issues addressed include: the distance between the power station and the nearest territory of another Member State; discharge limits for liquid effluents in the case of (a) normal operations (b) accident situations; the water body receiving the effluents; and, where appropriate, the desirability of neighbouring states concluding bilateral or multilateral agreements concerning, for example, joint regulation of the conditions governing routine discharges of radioactive waste into an international river.[47]

It is clear that the environmental gains obtained from the Article 37 procedure are not insubstantial. It is one of the few means available to the Commission for

[43] *Application of Article 37 of the EURATOM Treaty; Survey of Activities—Experiences Gained, 1959–1981*. COM (82)455 Final, p. 4.

[44] See Recommendation 82/181 of 3 February 1982 on the application of Article 37 EURATOM, OJECL 183.15.

[45] Evidence of Mr. Fraser (European Commission), *Nineteenth Report of the House of Lords Select Committee*, q. 510.

[46] *Application of Article 37 of the EURATOM Treaty; Survey of Activities—Experiences Gained, 1959–1981*. COM (82)455 Final, p. 7.

[47] See e.g. "The Franco-Belgian Convention on Radiological Protection with Regard to the Installations of the Ardennes Nuclear Power Station, 1966", 588 UNTS 227.

obtaining an up-to-date picture of the practical problems of radiological protection of the environment.[48] In addition to the harmonization of its procedural aspects, Article 37 has been strengthened in several ways.

First, since 1980, the EC Commission has prepared an annual report on the application of the Article.[49] Second, since 1986, the Commission's opinion has been published in the Official Journal.[50] Lastly, the European Court has held that the competent authorities of a Member State must receive and consider the opinion prior to authorization of the disposal of radioactive effluent by a nuclear installation.[51]

Yet very serious weaknesses in the procedure remain; above all, the opinion has no legally binding status and in practice is issued only a short time before the plant commences operations. It is, moreover, highly unusual for the opinion to conclude that the discharge limits for liquid effluents are such as to result in radioactive contamination, significant from the point of view of health, of the water, soil or airspace of another Member State.

In two recent opinions issued in the UK in respect of the nuclear power stations at Heysham (2)[52] and Torness[53] the Commission noted the view of the group of experts that the maximum envisaged discharge limits for liquid effluents appear to be unnecessarily high; it therefore recommended that these limits "be fixed at levels taking into account the as low as reasonably achievable principle". Even so, the discharge limits were not seen as posing a health hazard to Ireland, the nearest Member State. In any event, the Member State to whom the opinion is issued is under no legal obligation to react positively to it; it can decide that the conclusions in the opinion are inappropriate or are already complied with.[54] While the EC Commission clearly has power under Euratom to investigate the application of the Community's radiation exposure directives, in specific cases no legal means currently exists for formulating and enforcing a harmonized, community-wide concept of the ALARA principle, such a power is long overdue.

Two potentially hopeful developments deserve a brief mention. First, the addition of the environment to the foundation and policy of the Community effected by the Single European Act;[55] however, it appears that the view currently held by the Commission is that Euratom provides the necessary powers over health

[48] *Application of Article 37 of the EURATOM Treaty; Survey of Activities—Experiences Gained, 1959–1981*. COM (82)455 Final, p. 19.

[49] See COM(88)109 Final. This covers 1985–1986.

[50] *Ibid.* 3.

[51] Case 187/87, *Saarland* v *Ministry of Industry* (1989) 54 CMLR 529. The case arose out of the long-running dispute concerning the French nuclear power station at Cattenom, close to the borders with Luxemburg and the FRG. See Lenaerts, "Nuclear Border Installations: A Case Study" (1988) 13 *European Law Review* 158.

[52] 87/170 EURATOM, OJECL 68/33.

[53] 87/530 EURATOM, OJECL 189/42.

[54] Evidence of Mr. Fraser (European Commission), *Nineteenth Report of the House of Lords Select Committee*, q. 510.

[55] Art. 130R. For comment see Davidson (1987) 2 IJECL 259.

BNFL Establishments
UKAEA Establishments
Electricity Board Nuclear power stations
MOD establishments
Amersham International plc Establishments
Dounreay
Faslane
Rosyth
Torness
Hunterston
Chapelcross
Hartlepool
Sellafield
Heysham
Springfields
Wylfa
Capenhurst
Trawsfynydd
Sizewell
Berkeley
Harwell
Amersham
Bradwell
Cardiff
Oldbury
Aldermaston
Hinkley Point
Dungeness
Winfrith
Devonport

Figure 2

and safety matters, including the environment.[56] Second, Directive 85/337/EEC[57] on the assessment of the effects of certain public and private projects on the environment came into force in July 1988. The Directive applies, *inter alia*, to nuclear power stations and reprocessing facilities. This procedure promises to have considerable more legal clout than Article 37 in assessing the effects of nuclear installations on neigbouring Member States.[58]

Implementation of the ALARA principle

The London Declaration took note of the current downward trend of inputs of radioactivity to the North Sea (para. 40)—a development almost certainly attributable to something like a 50 per cent reduction in the collective dose in the discharges from Sellafield; this trend was expected to continue as the effect of recent reductions in inputs worked their way through the system.[59] A searching review of radioactive waste management by the House of Lords Select Committee on the European Communities recently concluded that although "discharges of radioactive effluents are acceptably low" the marked improvement in the situation at Sellafield "must be sustained".[60] The DFR laboratory report for 1987, the latest year for which figures are available, shows a continuation of this downward trend, mainly as a result of the new salt evaporator and site ion exchange effluent treatment plant.[61] Significantly, these data show that at many other UK nuclear sites the effects of discharges are still masked by discharges, past and present, attributable to Sellafield. There must come a point at which the ALARA principle, regarded by some as equivalent to ALATA (as low as is technically achievable) cannot, on cost benefit criteria, be applied further in the sense of reductions in discharges producing environmental gains. For example, the BPM requirements in the Sellafield authorization certificate expressly rule out expenditure "which is or is likely to be grossly disproportionate to the benefits to be derived from, or likely to be derived from, or the efficacy of, or likely efficacy of employing them."[62] In the UK, there are indications that the Government, independent scientific opinion and the nuclear industry see the limits of the ALARA/BPM as almost reached, the paradigm being the construction at the cost of £250 m of a new floc precipitation plant at Sellafield to save an estimated two cancer deaths over 10,000 years.[63] The notion of zero emissions of

[56] Evidence of Dr. Bennett (European Commission), *Nineteenth Report of the House of Lords Select Committee*, q. 549.

[57] OJECL 175/40, PARCOM Recomm. 88/4 adopted in June 1988, makes the construction of new nuclear reprocessing plants or any substantial increase in the capacity of existing plants, contingent on an environmental impact assessment. Text repr. *Tenth Annual Report on the Activities of the Paris Commission*, Ann. 3.

[58] See Lenaert, "Nuclear Border Installations: A Case Study", 174.

[59] "Quality Status of the North Sea: Summary, Scientific and Working Group", para. 4.1.

[60] *Nineteenth Report of the House of Lords Select Committee*, paras. 80, 199.

[61] Hunt, *Aquatic Environment Monitoring Report No. 19*, para 4.1.

[62] Certificate of Authorization, Sellafield Liquid Waste, para. 14(3)a.

[63] The example in the text is endorsed by the RWMAC Sixth Report 1985, p. 11; and by the Eighteenth Report of the *House of Lords Select Committee on the European Communities: Nuclear Power in Europe (Session 1985–1986)* HLP 227–1, paras. 83, 84.

radioactivity from nuclear plants has been said to be "impossible";[64] rather, the UK appears content to aim for discharge levels to the marine environment that are "almost zero".[65]

Conclusions and future prospects

Since the Bremen Declaration, the ALARA principle and its congeners, ALATA, BAT and BPM, have effected a constant downward pressure on discharges to the marine environment, displacing the previous heavy reliance on the "dilute and disperse" philosophy. As the QSR points out, what happens next will in part depend on "developments in the nuclear industry as well as on the standards adopted for reprocessing facilities."[66]

Several of these developments are already visible. Plans for the decommissioning of nuclear stations built in the 1950s and 1960s will gather momentum in the next decade. Some of these plants will be replaced by new facilities. Of greatest significance is the THORP reprocessing facility, expected to begin commercial operations in 1993. On the plus side, these plants will incorporate "state of the art" technology. One estimate of the impact of THORP is that it would take 10,000 years to double the present quantity of actinides in the marine environment.[67] At the same time, THORP is likely to generate a growth in the marine transportation of radioactive substances from Europe and Japan, thereby increasing the risk of collisions or other incidents. The 1990 Declaration should therefore reinstate the Bremen Declaration's reference[68]—no doubt prompted by the Mont Louis incident[69]—to the need to ensure that transportation of radioactive material is carried out in a safe way. The reported opposition of the UK Government to a draft EC Directive requiring ships carrying, *inter alia*, radioactive materials, to maintain constant contact with coastguard stations and to use a pilot when entering port,[70] is to be regretted.

The UK, while rejecting any immediate resumption of sea dumping of drummed wastes (currently the subject of a moratorium under the 1972 London Dumping Convention), appears not to have ruled out the sea disposal option in the future as regards (1) military radioactive waste arising from the decommissioning of nuclear submarines;[71] and (2) wastes and large items arising from decommissioning of civil

[64] RWMAC Fifth Report, 1984, Appendix C.
[65] HC, Vol. 106, Col. 3 (OA; 24 November 1986).
[66] "Quality Status of the North Sea: Summary, Scientific and Working Group", para. 23.
[67] RWMAC Fifth Report, 1984, para. 3.4.
[68] para. A35.
[69] Three months prior to the Bremen Declaration, a German-flag passenger-ferry collided with the *Mont Louis*, a French-flag RORO vessel which sank off the Belgian coast with the loss of 30 containers of uranium hexafluoride, all of which were salvaged. See Augustin, "The Sinking of the Mont Louis and Nuclear Safety", *IAEA Bull.* spring 1985, p. 28.
[70] *Guardian*, 10 August 1989.
[71] See *Seventh Report of the Defence Committee (Session 1988–1989): Decommissioning of Nuclear Submarines*, HC Papers 316; HC, Vol. 157, Col. 421 (25 July 1989).

nuclear power stations.[72] Another development (directly mentioned in paras. 41 and 42 of the London Declaration, above) under active consideration by several European states, is the feasibility of sub-sea-bed repositories for radioactive waste accessed either from the coast or from offshore.[73] The UK's decision, taken after extensive public consultations, not to pursue either of the sea-bed options, took note of the general concern that radioactive contamination of the sea should be avoided.[74] On the other hand, Sweden has already begun to use a specially constructed sub-sea-bed repository at Forsmark on the Swedish Baltic coast.[75]

While it would be churlish not to acknowledge the undoubted progress made in the past six years, "there remains a need to maintain steady improvement in discharge levels and to continue studies on long-term cumulative effects of discharges."[76] This call for high-quality independent scientific research and monitoring is echoed in the London Declaration (paras. 51–54) and is essential if the influence of special pleading and political expediency is to be curbed.

At an institutional level, there is considerable room for greater co-ordination and harmonization of the work of the European Community and the various organizations and other bodies who are concerned with the subject of radioactive discharges to the marine environment. This pluralism sometimes succeeds in raising standards of environmental protection but more often results in a "scattergun" approach that leaves a confused patchwork of overlapping norms, of varying weight and substance. The lessons of an important recent empirical study of the environmental co-operation between North Sea states must be digested;[77] above all, the relationship between the EC Commission (which participates in PARCOM) and the EC Member States participating in PARCOM, is in urgent need of clarification. There is compelling evidence that the EC Commission's influence in the PARCOM policy making process is a negative one.[78]

[72] HC, Vol. 139, Col. 397 (27 October 1988); *Our Common Future: A Perspective by the UK on the Report of the World Commission on Environment and Development*, 1988, para. 10.8.

[73] *The Way Forward: A Discussion Document*, UK Nirex Limited, 1987. The Paris Commission has decided that matters related to the design and construction of repositories are outside the scope of the Convention, *loc. cit.*, n. 38, para. 30.

[74] *Responses to the Way Forward*. Environmental Risk Assessment Unit, University of East Anglia, November 1988. The RWMAC also foresaw a range of practical difficulties as well as possible international repercussions. *Report of Subgroup on the Nirex Proposals for Deep Site Investigations*, HMSO 1988, para. 3.

[75] See Rippon, "Management of Intermediate and Low Level Waste", *Financial Times*, 26 July 1989.

[76] "RWMAC Ninth Annual Report 1988", para. 3.14.

[77] S. Saetevik, *Environmental Cooperation between the North Sea States* (London, Belhaven, 1988).

[78] *Ibid.* chap. 9; pp. 127 ff.; Appendix 4.

Chapter 26

Sea-Use Management and Planning in the North Sea

Dr. H. D. Smith

Introduction

The Patterns of management activities in the North Sea are intensifying and becoming more complex. This is evidenced by the development of the literature, including books on the history, science and uses of the North Sea as a whole,[1] the focus of research and development projects[2] and the North Sea Ministerial conferences.[3]

[1] E. D. Goldberg (ed.), *North Sea Science* (Cambridge, Mass., MIT Press, 1971); M. M. Sibthorp (ed.), *The North Sea: Challenge and Opportunity* (London, Europa, 1975); C. M. Mason (ed.), *The Effective Management of Resources: The International Politics of the North Sea* (London, Frances Pinter, 1979); H. van Hoorn, G. Peet, and G. M. Tiel (eds.), *The North Sea and its Environment: Uses and Conflicts* (Amsterdam, Stichting Werkgroep Noordzee, 1980); D. C. Watt (ed.), *The North Sea, A New International Regime? Proceedings of the Greenwich Forum Conference 2–4 May 1979* (Guildford, Westbury House, 1981); Der Rat von Sachverständigen für Umweltfragen, *Umweltprobleme der Nordsee* (Berlin, Verlag W. Kohlhammer, 1980); J. Sunderman and W. Lenz (eds.), *North Sea Dynamics* (Berlin, Springer Verlag, 1981); H. D. Smith and C. S. Lalwani, *The North Sea, Sea Use Management and Planning* (Cardiff, UWIST Centre for Marine Law and Policy, 1984); A. Bang-Andersen, B. Greenhill, and E. H. Grude (eds.), *The North Sea: A Highway of Economic and Cultural Exchange* (Stavanger, Norwegian University Press/London, National Maritime Museum, 1985); G. Peet (ed.), *The Status of the North Sea Environment: Reasons for Concern*, 2 vols. (Amsterdam, Stichting Werkgroep Noordzee, 1987); R. B. Clark (ed.), *The Waters Around the British Isles: Their Conflicting Uses* (Oxford, Clarendon Press, 1986); W. Salomons, B. L. Bayne, E. K. Duursma, and U. Forstner (eds.), *Pollution of the North Sea: An Assessment* (Berlin, Springer-Verlag, 1988).

[2] See Goldberg, *North Sea Science*; Sundermann and Lenz, *North Sea Dynamics*; Salomons, *et.al.*, *Pollution of the North Sea*. Also J. W. Ramster, "Development of Co-operative Research in the North Sea: The Origins, Planning and Philosophy of JONSDAP" 76 *Marine Policy* 1(4) (1977) 318–325.

[3] *Declaration of the International Conference on the Protection of the North Sea*, published by Bundesminister des Innern of the Federal Republic of Germany, 1985; Scientific and Technical Working Group, *Quality Status of the North Sea*, A Report by the Scientific and Technical Working Group (September 1987), London, Department of the Environment, 1987; *Second International Conference on the Protection of the North Sea, London, 24–25 November 1987, Ministerial Declaration,*

As a rule management activities remain primarily focused upon individual use groups in terms of both initiatives and organization, but there are significant developments towards integrated management approaches, especially in the south, which point the way towards a new type of regionally based management.

This chapter accordingly begins by reviewing key aspects in the development of uses and management, concerning both spatial organization and the marine environment as a whole. This is followed by discussion of recent developments tending towards integration including schemes relating to conflicts among uses, evolving regional frameworks of management systems and planning approaches. Finally, the evolution of North Sea management is reviewed systematically, in terms of uses and organizations, technical and general management approaches, and the validity of the North Sea as a management region.

Development of uses and management

The development of sea uses in the North Sea may be considered from two broad, interrelated perspectives in a management context. The first relates primarily to spatial organization of activities and thus to the overall regional development patterns in Europe. Included are coastal settlement, manufacturing industry and coastal engineering, together with navigation and communications, strategic uses, aspects of mineral extraction and fisheries, waste disposal and marine recreation. The second perspective is that of the environmental impact of activities, including especially rural coastal uses, mineral and energy extraction, fisheries and fish farming, waste disposal, marine science and conservation.

The central driving force in development is the coastal settlements and industrial areas grouped around the major estuaries in the south, and linked to their inland counterparts by the major rivers (Figure 1). These ultimately generate nearly all the demands for coastal and sea uses, and consist of two major regions. First is the "urban" sea of the major urban industrial areas, which is restricted in geographical extent and in which shipping and port activities, waste disposal and marine recreation are concentrated. Beyond and roughly south of an east-west transition zone through the Dogger Bank is the "metropolitan sea" characterized by intensive use by the above groups, together with fisheries, gas extraction and coastal conservation. The remainder much larger central and northern North Sea is peripheral, with fisheries, oil extraction, strategic use and a few key navigation routes as the major uses.

The management of land use and environment in the coastal zone in the south is a profound influence on adjacent waters. Major trends include the drive to clean up sewage and industrial effluent in the rivers; the regeneration of inner city port areas; and the intensification of conservation efforts along the rural coasts. Major long-term problems are the tendency towards eutrophication of inshore waters as

issued by the Department of the Environment of the United Kingdom, April 1988; Guidance Note on the Ministerial Declaration, Second International Conference on the Protection of the North Sea, London, Department of the Environment, 1988.

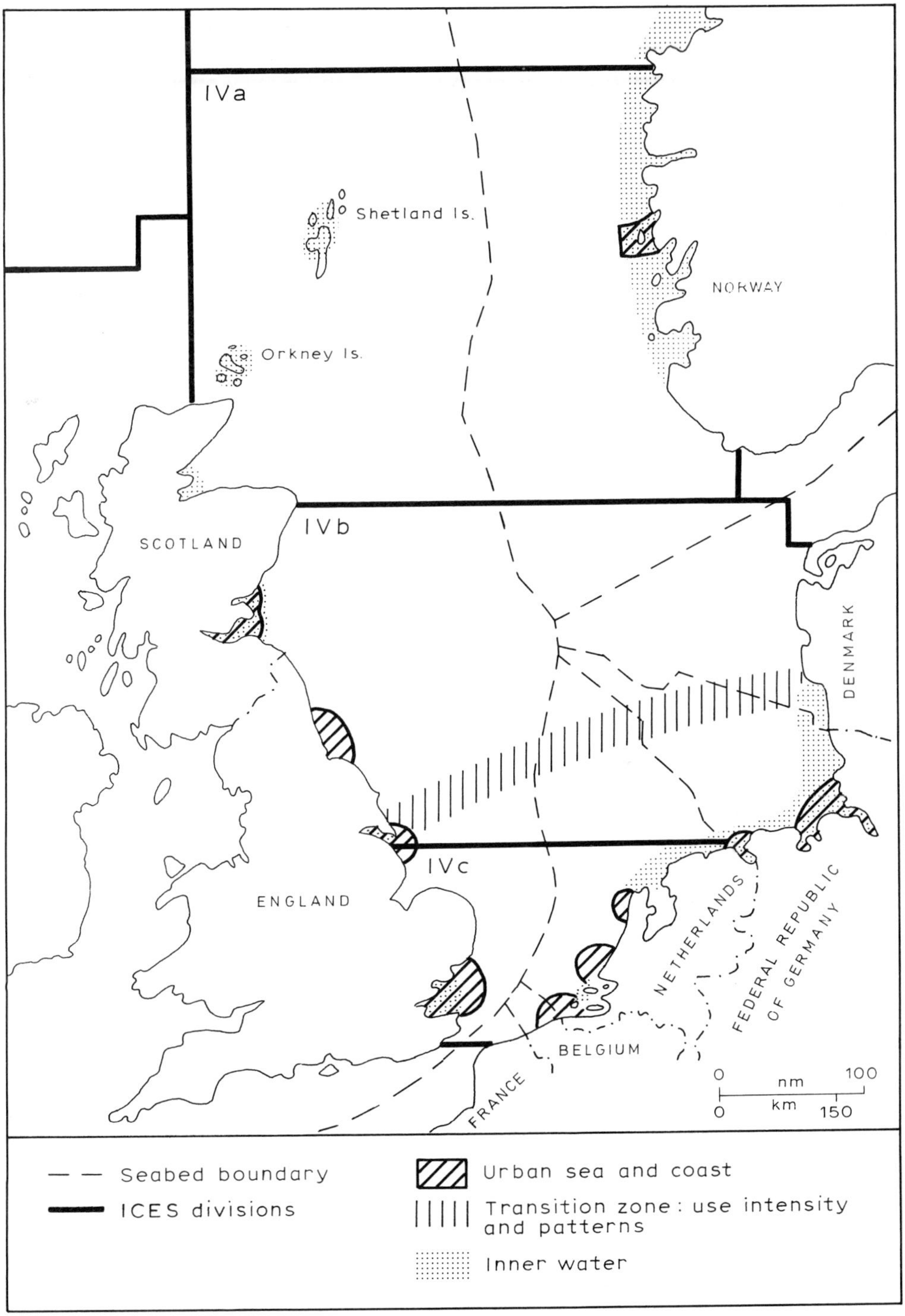
IVa
Shetland Is.
Orkney Is.
NORWAY
SCOTLAND
IVb
DENMARK
IVc
ENGLAND
NETHERLANDS
FEDERAL REPUBLIC OF GERMANY
BELGIUM
FRANCE
0 nm 100
0 km 150
Seabed boundary
ICES divisions
Urban sea and coast
Transition zone: use intensity and patterns
Inner water

Figure 1

nitrate and phosphate levels rise due to past application of fertilizers, and elaboration of coastal defences including dealing with the threat of rising sea levels and storm surges. The burden of management falls on sub-national organizations operating within national frameworks, notably river authorities and local government, with some input from port authorities. It is in these coastal waters that there is increasing pressure to extend land-use planning approaches seawards to deal with multiple-use conflicts and intense environmental impacts. The technical management tools of special importance include resource, environmental impact, and risk assessment; planning, coastal law, and social impact assessment (Figure 2).

At sea, management emphasis remains very much along the lines of individual sea-use groups. In navigation the main decision-makers are the port authorities, acting both individually and in concert through the "Memorandum on Port State Control". There are national frameworks of shipping legislation and bodies concerned with aspects of navigation management such as coastguard and navigation aids. A further important element is the International Maritime Organization (IMO) routeing scheme, and the North Sea Hydrographic Commission, both international.

Mineral and energy extraction, concerned with oil, gas and aggregates, is mainly managed at national level offshore, for example in the UK by the Department of Energy and the Crown Estate respectively. There are also inputs from the offshore operators' associations, notably in the UK. Onshore the burden falls upon local authorities concerned with planning applications for coastal installations including service bases. It is in this area that environmental impact assessment has been mainly developed, together with special planning arrangements in the case of Scotland. The oil industry has also been associated with enormous developments in related surveying and monitoring, with resource evaluation greatly complicated by fiscal considerations. Social impact assessment has also been widely carried out.

Like oil and gas, the fishing industry is managed by a combination of government and private sector producer organizations. However, in contrast to offshore oil, management is concerned with a myriad of small businesses rather than a small number of large corporations. Research and development, including fisheries laboratories, industrial development agencies together with fisheries protection are necessarily organized and funded by government. The principal objectives of management include spatial allocation of resources and areas among states, safety, research and conservation. Much emphasis has been placed on the first of these, with research (principally for conservation purposes) and conservation focused on the environment *per se*. Allocation and safety have hitherto been nationally organized and backed up by international negotiations.

In modern times the strategic use of the sea in both peacetime and wartime has been nationally organized and internationally co-ordinated latterly through the North Atlantic Treaty Organization (NATO). Much of the planning connected with this is necessarily confidential, although peacetime exercise areas have to be integrated with other uses. Oceanographic monitoring and hydrographic surveying and chart production and marine meteorology as well as coastguard-type work

SEA USE GROUPS / TECHNICAL MANAGEMENT CATEGORIES	Navigation and Communication	Strategic Uses	Mineral and Energy Resources	Biological Resources	Waste Disposal	Recreation	Research	Conservation
Monitoring								
Surveillance								
Information Technology								
Technology Assessment								
Project Development								
Resource Assessment								
Risk Assessment								
Environmental Impact Assessment								
Law: Coast and Sea								
Sea Use Planning								
Social Impact Assessment								

Figure 2 A Technical Management Matrix

including fisheries protection largely fall within the civil sphere of military operations. In the Norwegian case the civilian coastguard becomes part of the navy in wartime. Technical management is concerned with monitoring and surveillance.

Waste disposal is concentrated on the numerous point sources of the urban seas, attributable both to rivers and effluent outfalls. Technical management requirements include monitoring, surveillance and environmental impact and risk assessment. Organizational responsibilities are mainly local in the form of water and local authorities for the bulk of pollution which is land-based. The second management strand is international, notably through the Oslo and Paris Commissions.

Finally, from a spatial organization point of view is marine recreation, which is concentrated in urban seas and coasts together with certain nearshore rural areas. Management organization at the basic level is local, being the voluntary sector of the recreation organizations themselves, private sector development and local authority planning. It is also strongly linked to navigation management, and is thus a major concern of some port authorities.

For those uses where spatial organization and distribution of uses is important for the management function, there is strong emphasis on management at the local level, backed up by national and international standards. This contrasts with the environmental perspective of use development related to a combination of local and supra-national and international management associated with activities spread throughout the water column, including fisheries conservation, waste disposal and pollution control, marine science and conservation. Apart from the local organizations mentioned above and the role of the voluntary sector in conservation, key organizations are the intergovernmental International Council for the Exploration of the Sea (ICES) and the European Commission (EC) for fisheries; and the latter for coastal water quality and environmental impact control.

The development of integrated management

The increasing intensity of uses in the North Sea over the past quarter-century or so, including the increases in shipping traffic, advent of the offshore oil and gas industry, overfishing, growth of pollution and development of coastal recreation, has led to certain management developments over and above the use-based system just outlined. There are three aspects, namely, developments within the existing system; the establishment of integrated use-management approaches; and the systematic consideration of comprehensive management approaches (considered in the next section).

The developments within the existing system reflect the fundamental needs for more integrated approaches to sea-use management. These include resolution of conflicts among uses, dealing with environmental impacts, the regional dimension including problems of social impact of offshore developments, and formulation of planning approaches.

The resolution of conflicts among uses is the oldest and perhaps the most straightforward management problem. One of the earliest cases was conflicts within the fisheries, dating back to the Anglo-Dutch conflicts of the seventeenth century, which included the herring fisheries, to the trawling/inshore line fishing conflicts of the late nineteenth and early twentieth centuries. More recently a central focus has been the conflicts between the offshore oil industry and other uses, notably fisheries,[4] and the impact of this industry both offshore and on the coastal zone.

Environmental impacts generally have gained greater attention as environmental awareness has increased over the past two decades. Again, the fisheries provide the best early example through conservation efforts designed to maintain commercial stocks. In the 1980s the primary interest has been in pollution control, perhaps the major inspiration behind the ministerial conferences, and likely to result in more holistic approaches to management in the long run.[5]

Regional approaches are associated mainly with the advent of the offshore oil industry and have to do with the economic and social impact of the industry, both at national level where the emphasis has been on the impact on national economies;[6] and locally, where concern has centred round employment, income, population movement and changes in industrial structure.[7] Regional considerations have implicitly entered aspects of fisheries management, notably through negotiations aimed at obtaining favourable conditions for the Northern Isles of Scotland in the Common Fisheries Policy (CFP).[8]

It is through the CFP negotiations also that planning approaches designed to integrate all aspects of the fishing industry in particular regions can be discerned, albeit not particularly clearly. Conventional spatial planning approaches can also be seen in dealing with the onshore impact of offshore oil extraction, for example in Scotland. Special conservation arrangements have been made in some areas, most notably along the Wadden Sea coasts in the form of national parks in Lower Saxony and Schleswig-Holstein.[9]

The establishment of truly integrated use management or planning approaches

[4] University of Aberdeen, Department of Political Economy and Institute for the Study of Sparsely Populated Areas, *A Physical and Economic Evaluation of Means of Access to Fishing Grounds Due to Oil and Gas Installations in the North Sea*, for British Fishing Federation/Scottish Fishermen's Federation, 1978.

[5] *Declaration of the International Conference on the Protection of the North Sea*, published by Bundesminister des Innern of the Federal Republic of Germany, 1985; Scientific and Technical Working Group, *Quality Status of the North Sea*; *Ministerial Declaration, Second International Conference on the Protection of the North Sea, London, 24–25 November 1987*; *Guidance Note on the Ministerial Declaration, Second International Conference on the Protection of the North Sea*.

[6] D. I. MacKay and G. A. Mackay, *The Political Economy of North Sea Oil* (London, Martin Black, 1975); C. Robinson and J. Morgan, *North Sea Oil in the Future* (London, MacMillan, 1978); S. G. Hall and F. Atkinson, *Oil and the British Economy* (Beckenham, Croom Helm, 1983); O. Nøreng, *The Economics and Politics of North Sea Oil* (London, Croom Helm, 1979); C. Rowland and D. Hann, *The Economics of North Sea Oil Taxation* (London, MacMillan, 1987).

[7] MacKay and Mackay, *The Political Economy of North Sea Oil*; M. Gaskin and D. I. MacKay, *The Economic Impact of North Sea Oil on Scotland* (Edinburgh, HMSO/Scottish Office, 1978); T. M. Lewis, I. M. McNicoll, *North Sea Oil and Scotland's Economic Prospects* (London, Croom Helm, 1978).

[8] J. H. Goodlad, "Shetland Fisheries, Conservation and Development", *Marine Policy* 4(3) (1980) 244–245.

[9] R. Ronneberger, "Nationalpark Neidersachsen Wattenmeer—Human Influence on Environmental Protection and Management", Paper at IGU Commission on Marine Geography Conference, Marecont 89, Wilhelmshaven, 16–20 May 1989.

belongs to the 1970s and 1980s. There are three aspects to be considered. First is the existence of non-legislative but co- ordinated approaches dealing with conflicts among uses offshore. Perhaps the best example is the Government View procedure used in the UK by the Crown Estate to regulate the aggregate dredging industry, in which the views of government departments responsible for regulating the various sea uses are systematically taken into account before particular sea areas are licensed.[10] The second is the development of a true offshore planning system of the kind pioneered on the Dutch continental shelf. This involves both harmonization of government activities with respect to marine policies[11] through a specific co- ordinating body and development of specific spatial plans based on data acquisition and modelling of interactions among uses and related environmental impacts.[12] To the east, in the German Bight, whence came the initial impetus for the ministerial conferences, a complex navigation management system is required, and pollution prevention is an especially strong concern.

The third case is the institution of coastal zone management systems. The best examples of specific systems of this kind are on the margins of the region, in France where it is based on an Inventaire Permanent du Littoral[13] as part of a holistic approach to, coastal land and inshore management, and Sweden, where a sea-use planning system is being developed with special reference to inshore waters.[14] Elsewhere, the main emphasis is upon the conventional land-use planning, which does not extend seawards, although elements of it exist, especially in navigation management provisions within port limits.

A striking feature of both the individual use-based planning approaches (such as conservation), and the more integrated ideas, is that both inshore and offshore waters these are overwhelmingly concentrated in the extreme south—the "metropolitan" sea noted in the first section of this paper. This is to be expected, and is the response to the special problems of intense sea use and environmental impacts concentrated there. It also suggests that a uniform planning region may neither evolve nor be necessary for the North Sea as a whole.

A sea-use management and planning system

Conventional discussion on sea-use management and planning can give the impression that wholesale reorganization of the interests involved together with imposition of a full-scale spatial planning system is the solution. Such an approach neglects both the enormous investment in use-based management, and the direc-

[10] R. S. Nunny and P. C. H. Chillingworth, *Marine Dredging of Sand and Gravel*, London, Department of the Environment, 1987.

[11] H. van Hoorn, G. Peet, and K. Wieriks, "Harmonising North Sea Policy in the Netherlands" *Marine Policy* 9 (1984) 53–61.

[12] Rijkswaterstaat, Sibas, *Management Analysis North Sea*, Rijkswijk, Rijkswaterstaat, 1988.

[13] Délégation à l'aménagement du territoire et à l'action régionale, Ministère de l'environnement et du cadre de vie, Conservatoire de l'espace littoral et des rivages lacustres *Inventaire permanent du littoral, Guide*, 1980.

[14] K. Grip, "Coastal and Marine Management in Sweden", Paper at IGU Commission on Marine Geography Conference, Marecont 89, Wilhelmshaven, 16–20 May 1989.

tion of evolution of both use-based management and more novel integrated approaches. To throw all this away would be both idle and damaging to the future management of the North Sea. Rather, the objective must be to continue development of these "subsystems" while attempting to integrate these into a larger whole, so that the economic and human investment is not dissipated, but brought together in a truly integrated system of management and planning, with government and both private and voluntary sector users all working together.

The starting-point is the uses and organizations already discussed in the first part of this chapter. There are two broad directions of development discernible here. The first concerns the spatial patterns of uses, almost everywhere at its most intense in inshore waters, within territorial seas, especially adjacent to urban areas; and in the extreme south offshore, as already noted. In navigation management, aggregate dredging and the Dutch planning arrangements, together with land-use planning, there already exists an embryo spatial planning system capable of comprehensive development. It can be divided into the "urban seas" (Figure 1) adjacent to the built-up coasts, and both inshore and offshore "rural seas" still intensively used. Organizationally, in the coastal zone the focus of responsibility is at local level within national frameworks, with major roles played by the port authorities, local government and, to some extent, river basin authorities. Offshore, national agencies attached to a number of central government departments bear the main responsibilities. It may be that locally administered national planning systems are the way forward, taking into account international interests and contributions beyond the territorial seas, for example in traffic routeing provisions.

The second direction of development is environmental, focusing on ecosystems and environmental quality objectives. It covers the whole region, but becomes the primary element in management beyond coastal waters, and north of the "metropolitan" sea. In these areas fisheries, waste disposal, marine science and conservation management are the main components, with special responsibilities falling on international and supra-national agreements and agencies aimed at managing the water column. While national standards have to be set and administered both nationally and locally, precise co-ordination is required. The key organizations are the European Commission directorates concerned with the CFP, water quality and environmental impact assessment; the Oslo and Paris Commissions; ICES and the Ministerial conferences. Because Norway is not a member of the European Community, and the North Sea is connected to the Baltic, the Norwegian Government also directly plays a key role in fisheries management, and the Baltic states and Helsinki Commission activities relate to the North Sea especially in pollution control. A further key set of organizations in both the North Sea and the Baltic are the river authorities, through their responsibilities for waste management and pollution control. This is an exciting area which must take the lead in international initiatives. However, the North Sea as a whole is not really a specific management unit for any of these. Bearing in mind the use intensity patterns outlined above, it may be entirely proper that this remains so.

The second manor consideration with respect to integrated management is what may be termed technical and general management approaches[15] (Figure 2). There are three aspects to this. The first concerns management objective groups which historically may be grouped into first and second order shared among all the use groups in various permutations and combinations. The first-order groups are respectively safety, allocation, environmental control, research and regional development. These are technical management objectives, technical management being concerned with direct interactions between man and the sea. The second-order objectives consist of a variety of economic, social, political and environmental objectives indirectly operating on the overall management system. These, together with the co-ordination of technical management, form the general management objectives.

The technical management objectives are the key to effective management. The first group are scientific—monitoring of the environment, surveillance of uses, and information technology.[16] This is largely an applied science area. The key databases are governmental or inter-governmental, and include those of ICES, NATO, pure science databases of laboratories, meteorological and hydrographic databases, and private sector Lloyd's shipping data and oil companies' data, all applicable at North Sea level. Important local sets belong to local government, water and port authorities. The current state of development of information technology has opened up possibilities for networking of diverse databases, and requires intensive study to ensure economic use of data which is expensive to acquire, and in order to ensure effective planning and execution of further database projects.

The North Sea has been something of a test bed for development of the three remaining technical management areas. The first of these is technological—technology assessment and project development, both largely private sector and subject to safety regulation by government. Important examples include the development of deep water oil-extraction technology, pelagic and demersal fishing gears, coast protection, methods of waste disposal and pollution control including long sea outfalls, incineration and dumping at sea and clean-up programmes for major rivers.

The oil industry has been a central focus for the development of the remaining two categories concerned respectively with environmental and social assessment. Environmental assessment[17] consists of three components: resource, risk, and environmental impact assessment respectively. Because of the importance of the oil industry nationally, resource assessment has featured largely in its exploitation, both by companies and governments, and is an area of controversy. Risk assessment is concerned with both physical and economic temporal variations. Environmental impact assessment was widely applied to the onshore impact of offshore oil development in Scotland. It is likely to become mandatory for many coastal developments in future following upon the EC directive. Environmental assessment

[15] J. E. Halliday and H. D. Smith, "The Integration of Coastal and Sea Use Management", in *The Science and Technology of Ocean Management* (advance transcripts of the International Conference held at UWIST, Cardiff, by the Challenger Society and Society for Underwater Technology, 12–13 April 1988), pp. 22, 1–10.

[16] Smith and Lalwani, *The North Sea, Sea Use Management and Planning*.

[17] D. W. Fischer, *North Sea Oil, An Environment Interface* (Oslo, Universitetsforlaget,1982).

techniques are applied in other use areas, ranging from fishing to coastal engineering, though not necessarily termed as such.

Social assessment, the final technical management area, is concerned with law, spatial planning and social impact assessment. The North Sea was to a substantial extent the cradle of development of the public international law of the sea in the seventeenth century through the medium of the Anglo-Dutch conflicts of maritime interest. In the planning field, it has been a leading example of the settlement of maritime boundaries. Social impact assessment was extensively developed for dealing with the impact of the offshore oil industry, and has considerable potential for fisheries, recreation and other port-related developments.

In consideration of general management it is probably neither feasible nor desirable to conduct co-ordination of technical management functions via large-scale reorganization of the organizations and lines of communication involved.[18] What may rather be required is the building up or "buying in" of the full range of technical management operations required by each management agency across the spectrum of sea uses, and taking into account the multifarious interactions involved, in order that economies of scale may be applied where appropriate in both scientific input and applications.

The overall structure of management is of course based on the technical management agency, working at local, national, international and supra-national levels, together with a few private- and voluntary- sector organizations. These may indeed be largely adequate for the tasks in hand, except for the growing need for environmental agencies concerned with co-ordination and integration, such as the Dutch ICONA. This in turn focuses attention upon the second-order management objectives. Here the major innovation in the 1980s has been the ministerial conferences, concerned albeit primarily with the pollution problems of the "metropolitan" sea, whence has come the political pressure to set these up in the first instance. These require servicing by technical backup, such, as the North Sea Task Force required to co-ordinate inputs from national environment and other departments, and a possible path to long-term development of the environment agency or agencies required for integrated management.

The other remaining immediate general management issue concerns the role of the European Community. The CFP, and environmental directives indicate a trend that it may become the lead organization for the environmental management field, together with ICES on the scientific side perhaps. For example, in the case of the CFP there has even been a recent suggestion that the Community should take over full control of fisheries management from the member states.[19] Also to be taken into account at this juncture is the possible future incorporation of Norway, and

[18] For an up-to-date discussion on present regional organization and co-operation, see T. IJlstra "Regional Co-operation in the North Sea; An Inquiry" (1988) 3 IJECL 181–207.

[19] *Fishing News*, 8 September 1989. See also J. A. Gulland, "The Management of the North Sea Fisheries, Looking Towards the 21st Century" *Marine Policy* 11 (1987) 259–272; D. W. Armstrong, P. Hopkins, P. A. Kunzlik, R. Milner, "Historical and Current State of the Major North Sea Fish Stocks", Proceedings, North Sea 2000 Conference, Edinburgh, Heriot-Watt University, 16–18 August 1989.

developing political changes in the rest of Scandinavia and in eastern Europe, which brings in the Baltic interest.

These regional considerations provoke consideration of the final topic, namely, the nature of the North Sea as a sea-use management region. As already indicated, an overall regional management system is already taking shape which reflects the sum total of use-interactions and environmental impacts, and thus overall European regional development patterns in relation to the North Sea. The key elements in the system are first, the urban estuaries and other inshore waters and their associated river basins, largely locally managed, and arguably the most important part of the system despite the limited areas involved. The second region can be divided into two parts: the relatively small metropolitan south, and the remainder to the north of the Dogger Bank. The emphasis in this area is upon environmental management rather than use conflict, principally through international or EC agencies. However, at this level the North Sea is likely to remain part of wider regional responsibilities for the organizations concerned.

This wider regional context reflects both development and physical characteristics of the North East Atlantic. At both the urban and regional scales this regional context calls into question the management of the North Sea as a geographical unit *per se*. Rather, effective management will involve operation of the evolving management system at the two scales within the North Sea, simultaneously ensuring effective management of relationships within the wider regional context.

Final Perspectives

David Freestone and Ton IJlstra

It is not an easy task to draw conclusions from so many contributions on such a wide variety of issues. There is in fact a certain similarity with the task facing those responsible for the future protection of the North Sea: there are a wide variety of issues which need to be encompassed in order to be able to take a truly holistic approach. The INSCs have to date tended to concentrate on the issue of water quality, but an initiative which truly seeks to pay attention to the Protection of the North Sea—as the Ministerial meetings describe themselves—must inevitably be drawn into far wider issues of conservation and integrated management. As Jones demonstrates, this is to a large extent dictated by the very science of the problem.

We have divided the contributions into three sections—the INSCs, existing frameworks, and outstanding or neglected issues— and it might prove useful to try and pull together some of the themes that have developed within each of these sections while attempting to tease out or establish broader links and issues.

The INSCs in perspective

Ehlers shows us how the Ministerial meetings were born out of the environmental movement in Germany. He stresses (as do other contributors) the importance of the level of Ministerial co-operation which has been achieved and the high profile which these meetings have attained. There seem initially to have been problems with establishing proper links between science and policy—analysed by Andresen and Wettestad. However, the establishment of the North Sea Task Force described by Reid and the level of liaison and co-operation with existing institutions such as OSPARCOM (which as Reid and Hayward point out has now been drawn more into the preparations for the meetings) point to a much more co-ordinated scientific input. Similarly, although the Ministerial meetings themselves are short, as Reid describes, the preparation and monitoring operations have become much more sophisticated and complex. With the establishment and implementation of the Task Force programmes there is, Reid reports, a recognition of the need, identified also by Jones, for a co-ordinated and holistic approach to the science of the North Sea environment. Arguably the most important results of the INS Conferences to date have been the formal declarations issued by the participants. Van der Mensbrugghe concludes that the declarations which have emanated from the Bremen and London Meetings are not *per se* legally binding although the international law doctrine of estoppel would require that they be carried out in good faith since they announce action to be cast in legal terms "later and elsewhere", and would preclude the use of the traditional "domestic jurisdiction defence". Other lawyers among our authors (e.g. Gibson and Churchill, Gündling, Davidson) confirm this conclusion.

Ehlers suggests that the time may now have come to cast these aspirations into more traditional legal mode—by perhaps a North Sea Treaty. On the other hand a number of authors (e.g. Nollkaemper, Davidson) also point to the advantages that a declaration at a political level provides, namely a degree of flexibility and perhaps a willingness to go further down the road which a more formal approach might inhibit. This certainly is the conclusion to be drawn from Nollkaemper's analysis of the Rhine Action Plan which has tended to take that approach. Of course a number of obligations—such as the Precautionary Principle—may as Gündling demonstrates be in the process of passing into legal obligations, and the fact that both that principle and the best available technology principle have recently been adopted by the Paris Commission (as pointed out by Hayward and Gündling) demonstrates that the Declarations should not be viewed in a vacuum. Hayward explains how the Ministerial meetings can have had catalytic effects on the evolution of policy in OSPARCOM. These effects, which, like ripples, become deeper and more pronounced over time, may also overcome some of the problems of implementation which are analysed by de Jong and Gibson and Churchill. Both these wide- ranging and detailed contributions point out that it is difficult to assess the results of the Second INSC given the short period between the second and third meetings. Certainly 28 months is a short time given the administrative machinery which is needed to implement conference decisions, and it should also be borne in mind that the target date is 1993. Nevertheless, both pieces show that the implementation of a instrument is quite a different process from adopting it. It may have been that the political success of reaching agreement on a particular issue has been seen to be more important than drafting it in a way which will make it most effective. Gibson and Churchill highlight some of the debatable interpretations put upon certain provisions by the UK. This takes us back again to the issue raised above as to whether the political advantage of broad policy agreement is an acceptable price for a lack of precision, or whether, as Ehlers proposes, it is now time to crystallize these initiatives in a more formal treaty form.

Institutional perspectives

The Ministerial Meeting in The Hague in March 1990 will of course be the Third INSC. A Ministerial Meeting of OSPARCOM is scheduled for 1992, and it appears likely that the Fourth INSC will take place in Denmark (possibly in 1995). In the mean time the Task Force is preparing the updated Quality Status Report. With the ongoing work, and the preparatory meetings, they have already achieved a fairly high level of institutional development. If the INS Conferences were to develop into a more formal system, based perhaps on a legal instrument, then there would inevitably be considerable debate as to the form that system should take. The contributions in Parts II and III not only provide analysis of a number of models, but also demonstrate the existing institutional and legal frameworks which such an institution would have to absorb, work with or simply accommodate.

Prominent among the existing institutions, of which six of the eight North Sea states are members, is the European Community. From the different chapters that relate to the EC, it is apparent that the authors consider that it has become, or is becoming, a very important actor in the field of the protection and preservation of the North Sea marine environment. While not all our authors are uncritical of its role, it is certain that with the extension of its own competences, and possibly of its membership as well, it has a crucial role to play. This is of course already the case in respect of the management of the fishery resources of the North Sea through the EC Common Fisheries Policy, but EC membership of the Paris Commission is an expression of its role in the management of the water quality of the North Sea. Smith takes the view that the EC may become the lead organization in the environmental management field, together perhaps with ICES on the scientific side. In addition several authors (Nollkaemper, Davidson, Prat) point to the fact that in many related fields the EC has both the legal competence and the will to act. Although such competences relate principally to economic issues, these issues—such as air pollution (see Davidson) and product control (see de Jong)—may have important impacts on the protection of the marine environment. In other fields, such as dumping at sea and port state control, the EC might want to assume additional responsibilities. While it clearly has a growing role, some authors point out that it should not be at the expense of existing structures with proven competence, be it in science or fisheries (see Birnie), or control of radiological discharges. In the field of radiological discharges into the marine environment—a matter of increasing public concern—Woodliffe points out that the EC already has an established role under the EURATOM Treaty, but that there is considerable room for greater co-ordination and harmonization of its work with the other concerned organizations and bodies.

Symes is critical of the state of fisheries management. He convincingly demonstrates that the basic framework of the Common Fisheries Policy has deficiencies which have threatened, and are likely to continue to threaten, the effective exploitation of living resources. It seems that insufficient attention has been paid to this important issue by the Ministerial Conferences. Similarly ignored to date has been the relationship between fishery resources and the protection of wildlife. Birnie concludes that although the EC may be useful in the protection of wildlife it is not the appropriate body to take up a co-ordinating role in this area. Significantly, Reid reports that the impact of the fishing industry on the North Sea ecosystem has been identified as a matter of particular concern for the Hague meeting. There can be little doubt that plans must be made to take this into account in fishery decision-making—the EC seems to be the most obvious body to take this aboard.

Hayward assesses the role of the Oslo and Paris Commissions and their relationship with the INSCs. As a former secretary of the Commissions he is in a position to speak with considerable authority when he concludes that OSPARCOM has benefited from the initiatives taken at the INSCs. He warns, however, that there is a danger that in concentrating on new structures the momentum may be taken out of the existing bodies which work well within the constraints that their political masters impose upon them.

Nevertheless if progress is to be made towards a new institutional framework, a number of contributors put forward models that have worked in different contexts. Nollkaemper shows that non-legal instruments have had an important effect on the marine environment through the Rhine Action Plan. He concludes that any programme of this kind must be, to a greater or lesser extent, "a leap in the dark", but feels that the Rhine Action Plan, giving an impetus to the implementation of the Rhine Chemical Convention may serve as a wider model for the marine environment of the North Sea. Similarly, van der Zwiep is impressed by the co-operative management system used by the three Wadden Sea states and feels that this too "could well stand as a model and form a basis for further intensification of North Sea administration".

The Baltic is held out as an example by both Franckx and Ehlers. Franckx argues that in the area of maritime boundary delimitation—an important precondition to effective resource management—the North Sea still has a long way to go, and that it is no longer true (as it was in the 1960s) to characterize it as a front runner in this area. Indeed progress in this area over the last decade or so compares very unfavourably with the considerable effort made in the Baltic. Ehlers, who has actively participated in the INSC meetings, considers it possible that the North Sea meetings could be "legally consolidated by means of a North Sea Convention following the example of the Baltic Sea". Prat on the other hand suggests that the MEDSPA plan for the protection of the Mediterranean might well be an interesting approach for the North Sea as well.

Another theme which emerges from the discussion of existing mechanisms is dealt with by Wettestad and Andresen. They are not entirely dissatisfied with the existing international "scientific-political" complex since "it is capable of coming up with fairly precise and usable knowledge on the state of the North Sea". They conclude, however, that the co-ordination of research and monitoring is flawed in that policy-makers and scientists do not speak the same language. They feel too that the media, although responsible for generating a great deal of public interest in the environment, do not manage to "involve the public in a rational way". They too, however, echo a call by Jones for an intensified research and monitoring effort because to date no firm basis has been established for the progress assessments upon which rational policy development is dependent. They conclude with the disturbing warning that "institutional deficiencies in the scientific-political complex might be far more crippling in the coming years that they have been up to now". Boehmer-Christiansen points to similar conclusions in her contribution when she talks of the UK tradition of "government science" and of the need to ensure that there is a clear distinction between science and policy, so that, in Wettestad and Andresen's words, the policy-makers are not given "skewed" information. Boehmer-Christiansen in her discussion of the controversy over the use of environmental quality objectives and uniform emission standards points out quite correctly that this is not simply a philosophical discussion, but one with major economic consequences. Vennekens-Capkova in her chapter on the listing of dangerous substances also reinforces a point made by Nollkaemper on the need for co-ordination of scientific effort within various environmental regulatory bodies such as the Oslo, Paris, and London Dumping Conventions, the Rhine AP, the EC and now the INSCs, but seems sanguine about future prospects—although by the adoption of which model is not clear.

Several contributions deal with the enforcement of existing norms. Kasoulides, Somers and Kemp and de Bievre deal with various aspects of enforcement. Somers deals with a traditional problem of the law of the sea—the enforcement of international law norms by national courts. He must be correct to say that the basic international law of the sea system with its emphasis on flag state jurisdiction is largely deficient, but he goes further to suggest that the enforcement of international law norms by coastal state courts also has only a very limited contribution to make to a cleaner marine environment. He argues persuasively that the marine-based sources of pollution—notably vessel source pollution—do not contribute very much to total pollution loads, and that in the North Sea the main pollution source is land based—which is not subject to international control and which can only be dealt with by national courts. The same conclusion is reached by other writers, by Jenisch in his assessment of the impact of an EEZ regime on the control of marine pollution and by Sebek, who, in his assessment of the concept of Special Zones, feels that more needs to be done to afford genuine "protection" to threatened areas than to declare them special areas under IMO Conventions and looks for models in the UNEP Regional Seas treaties. Nevertheless, advances in maritime safety and the efficient enforcement of international law norms do have a part to play in an over-arching managerial strategy, and in that context Kasoulides's discussion of the Port State control system is of considerable significance among the North Sea states—even if he does show that after a convincing start the system is having difficulties expanding. He does, however, canvas the possibility of it acquiring a wider geographical scope by the possible adherence of the USA or the Eastern European States. Kemp and de Bievre plead a case for the establishment of regional vessel traffic services, not only from the point of view of maritime safety (by the prevention of accidents), and traffic efficiency, but also from the point of view of pollution prevention and law enforcement.

Neglected perspectives

The majority of contributors make suggestions for different approaches to existing problems, or for the use of different institutions. There is also a general feeling that the existing plethora of organizations with restricted competences produce what Woodliffe terms a "scattergun approach", and that some form of over-arching body adopting an holistic view is necessary. Whether or not the INS Conferences in their present or some future form will be able to meet this perceived need must remain to be seen, but as we comment above, those meetings have tended to concentrate, albeit for understandable reasons, on water quality. A truly holistic view of the protection of the North Sea would include in one way or another what we have termed "outstanding issues".

Davidson and Woodliffe focus on issues which have yet to be seriously addressed at the INS Conferences, namely atmospheric depositions and radiological discharges to the marine environment. Although these are both fields in which the EC has assumed a role, both feel that more could be done to integrate the EC approach with that of the other North Sea states. Similarly, as indicated above, Symes is critical of the EC Common Fisheries Policy, and feels that fisheries should form part of an overall resource management strategy. Significantly, atmospheric depositions and fisheries are two of four issues identified as of particular concern for the the forthcoming meeting (Reid).

The decision by the Dutch Government to raise, with its EC partners, the possibility of moving from a simple Fisheries Zone to an Exclusive Economic Zone with its enhanced pollution control competences, prompts Jenisch to consider the advantages of such a move in the North Sea (where to date only Norway and France have established such a zone on the lines of Part V, LOSC). He points out that it would confer a number of legal and procedural advantages, but (like Somers and Sebek) feels that enhanced control of vessel source pollution would not in itself address the main pollution source in the North Sea—from land. Having said this, however, it still seems important that the North Sea should be designated as a special area under MARPOL Annex I, in the same way, as Sebek reports, was recently done under Annex V. This important step against vessel source pollution is apparently under consideration. Of course one of the concepts envisaged within the EEZ by LOSC Article 211(6) is the declaration (in accordance with the specified procedure) of special areas within the EEZ for a variety of reasons including ecological conditions. Were the EEZ approach to be more widely adopted therefore, Article 211(6) could, it seems, form the legal basis for the establishment of marine protected areas. As Peet and Gubbay point out there has been some progress at a national level in the development of national protected marine areas but there is a great deal still to be done. Uncoordinated national efforts to protect habitat, etc. are not as effective within a regional ecosystem as regional efforts. An important aspect of the development of a wildlife protection regime called for by Birnie would be the development of a regional framework of protected areas.

Birnie shows vividly that there is no comprehensive legal regime for wildlife. Competences are distributed between a number of institutions and bodies, none of which can take responsibility for a full wildlife protection regime or which has felt, or been, able to take a lead in the development of such a regime. These different bodies are not even, as she says, "networked" to prevent overlaps of work or competence. Although she sees a role for UNEP and IUCN at a global level, she is convinced that work should start at a regional level and that the INSC Ministers should address this as an integral part of the overall environment to be protected.

Finally, Smith underlines the potential of the North Sea as a sea-use management regime. He takes the view that *de facto* an overall regional management system is emerging to reflect the sum total of use-interactions and environmental impacts, and thus the overall European development patterns in the North Sea. However, he pleads for a management system involving two different scales: one for coastal management—with an emphasis on use conflicts; and the second, over-arching, system concerned with water quality.

It does appear from the various contributions to this volume that there is, at least among our authors, some considerable dissatisfaction with the functioning of the present structures. It may even be that the present sectorial environmental protection institutions are beginning to reach the limits of their capacities. Environmental issues are becoming increasingly linked with other, often economic, issues. The EC, an increasingly important actor on this stage, often seems paralysed by conflicts of economic interest. The Common Agricultural Policy is only just beginning to acquire an environmental dimension; the CFP has no ecological dimension at all. The more significant that environmental protection becomes in political terms, the more it becomes a multi-disciplinary science.

It is certainly tempting to look again at the suggestion, favoured it will be remembered by the European Parliament, for an umbrella North Sea Treaty. The editors are not, however, convinced that the adoption of such a treaty would in itself solve the existing problems in the North Sea. Such a solution would only seem desirable if it represented a net increase in the competences and powers available to existing institutions. At the very least this would entail the parties acknowledging the significance of land-based sources of pollution and accepting the need for very strict measures in that field.

The basic appeal of such an over-arching convention is of course that it could possibly provide a more flexible approach to every aspect of the North Sea environment, but the list of concerns is continually growing—not only to include issues such as wildlife and marine protected areas, but also areas of land-based pollution like atmospheric depositions and riverine pollution.

Whatever the final decisions reached by the 1990 Meeting, it is clear that institutional arrangements—in whatever form—can only be as effective as the political will which directs them. There is now a very strong body of opinion—largely represented in these pages—that what is needed is an holistic view of the protection of the quality of the North Sea environment—interpreted in the widest sense. The very existence of the INS Conferences suggests that there is now some political recognition of this basic issue. In meeting the challenge which this poses, we are convinced that the next decade will be decisive.

Bibliography

Books and Theses

Advisory Commission on Pollution of the Sea Yearbooks (ACOPS Yearbooks) appear each year, the most recent version is 1987/1988.

Bates, J., *United Kingdom Marine Pollution Law* (London, Lloyd's of London Press, 1985).

Bjorndal, T., *The Optimum Management of North Sea Herring* (Vancouver, Univ. of British Columbia, 1983).

Bluston, H., *A North Sea A B C*, Bedford Energy Consultancy (1978).

Boehmer-Christiansen, S. A., "Limits to the International Control of Marine Pollution", D. Phil. thesis, Univ. of Sussex, 1981.

Bouchez, L. J., R. Y. Jennings, and G. Jaenicke, *Feasibility Study on the Development of Industrial Islands in the North Sea*; Report phase A, vol. 4, International Law Aspects, Papendrecht (Nl.), North Sea Island Group (1974).

Burgt, C. van der, *The Oslo and Paris Commissions, the First Decade* (The Chameleon Press, London, 1984).

Callow, C., *Power from the Sea: The Search for North Sea Oil and Gas* (London, Victor Gollancz, 1973).

Cameron, P., *Property Rights and Sovereign Rights: Case of North Sea Oil* (London, Academic Press, 1983).

Carson, W., *The Other Price of Britain's Oil: Safety and Control in the North Sea* (Oxford, Martin Robertson, 1982).

Churchill, R. R., *EEC Fisheries Law* (Dordrecht, Martinus Nijhoff, 1987).

Clark, R. B. (ed.), *The Waters Around the British Isles: Their Conflicting Uses* (Oxford, Clarendon Press, 1987).

Cuyvers, L., *The Strait of Dover* (Dordrecht, Martinus Nijhoff, 1986).

Dafter, R., and I. Davidson, *North Sea Oil and Gas and British Foreign Policy* (London, RIIA, 1980).

Department of the Environment, *Oil Pollution of the Sea, the Government Response to the Eighth Report of the Royal Commission on Environmental Pollution* (Pollution Paper no. 20), London, HMSO, 1983.

Department of the Environment, *Controlling Pollution: Principles and Prospects, the Governmental Response to the Tenth Report of the Royal Commission on Environmental Pollution* (Pollution Paper no. 22), London, HMSO, 1984.

Dietzman, W., N. Rafiol, and T. Ross, *The Petroleum Resources of the North Sea* (Washington, DC, Energy Information Administration, 1983).

Foders, F., and R. Wolfrum (eds.), *Meereswirtschaft in Europa* (Kieler Studien, Institut für Weltwirtschaft Kiel, Tübingen, 1989).

Grogan, W. C., *Input of Contaminants to the North Sea from the United Kingdom*, (Herriot Watt Univ., 1985).

Hartley, J. P., and R. B. Clark, *Environmental Effects of North Sea Oil and Gas Developments* (CUP, 1988).

Henderson, H. M., *Oil and Gas Law: The North Sea Exploitation* (loose-leaf New York, Oceana Publications, 1979).

Hoorn, H. van, G. Peet, and G. M. Tiel (eds.), *The North Sea and its Environment, Uses and Conflicts* (Amsterdam, Stichting Werkgroep Noordzee, 1980).

House, J. D. (ed.), *Fish v. Oil Resources and Rural Development in North Atlantic Societies*, St. Johns, Newfoundland, Institute of Social and Economic Research (1986).

International Management and Engineering Group of Britain Ltd., Study of Potential Benefits to British Industry from Offshore Oil and Gas Developments, London, HMSO, 1972.

Kane, T., North Sea Petroleum Operations in the United Kingdom and Norway: A Study (Washington, DC, Congressional Research Service, 1977).

Keto, D., *Law and Offshore Oil Development: The North Sea Experience* (New York, Praeger, 1978).

Krämer, H. R. (ed.), *Die wirtschaftliche Nutzung der Nordsee und die Europäische Gemeinschaft*, Arbeitskreis Europäische Integration, Baden-Baden, 1979.

Lewis, T. M., and I. M. McNicoll, *North Sea Oil and Scotland's Economic Prospects* (London, Croom Helm, 1978).

Macsween, I. M., *The Extension of Fishing Limits: The North Sea* (Edinburgh, White Fish Authority, 1975).

Mason, C. M. (ed.), *The Effective Management of Resources: The International Politics of the North Sea* (London, Francis Pinter, 1979).

Morvan, D. Le, "Les Communautés européennes et la protection de l'environnement marin", unpub. Ph.D. thesis, Université de Bretagne Occidentale, Brest, 1984.

Michael, M., *L'Applicabilité du traité instituant la C.E.E. et du droit derivé au plateau continental des états membres* (Pedone, Paris, 1984).

Newman, P. J., and A. R. Agg (eds.), *Environmental Protection of the North Sea* (London, Heinemann Professional, 1988).

Noreng, O., *The Oil Industry and Government Strategy in the North Sea* (London, Croom Helm, 1980).

Pearce, D. W., G. A. Mackay, R. Blackmore, and A. Stewart, *A Physical and Economic Evaluation of Loss of Access to Fishing Grounds Due to Oil and Gas Installations in the North Sea* (Univ. of Aberdeen, 1978).

Peet, G. (ed.), *The Status of the North Sea Environment: Reasons for Concern*, Vol. 2 (Amsterdam, Stichting Werkgroep Noordzee, 1987).

—— and E. Hey (eds.), *The Status of the North Sea Environment: Reasons for Concern*, Vol. 1 (Amsterdam, Stichting Werkgroep Noordzee, 1987).

Platzöder, R., *Völkerrechtliche und politische Auswirkungen der dritten seerecht Konferenz der Vereinten Nationen auf Nord und Ostsee* (Ebenhausen, Stiftung Wissenschaft und Politik, 1978).

Quality Status Report, Scientific and Technical Working Group, Quality Status of the North Sea; published as supplement no. 16 to the *Deutsche Hydrographische Zeitschrift*, Depart. of the Environment, London, 1987.

Qvale, T., *Safety and Offshore Working Conditions: The Quality of Work Life in the North Sea* (Stavanger, Norwegian Univ. Press, 1984).

Royal Commission on Environmental Pollution, *Eighth Report, Oil Pollution of the Sea*, London, HMSO, 1981.

Royal Commission on Environmental Pollution, *Tenth Report, Tackling Pollution: Experience and Prospects*, London, HMSO, 1984.

Secretariat d'Éat a l'Environnement, *Notre mer du Nord, précieux patrimoine international* (Ostende, 1986).

Saeter, M., and I. Smart, *Political Implications of North Sea Oil and Gas* (Universitetsforlaget, 1975).

Saetevik, S., *Environmental Cooperation between the North Sea States* (London Belhaven Press, 1988).

Sibthorp, M. M. (ed.), *The North Sea: Challenge and Opportunity* (London, Europa Publications, 1975).

—— and M. Unwin (eds.), *Oceanic Management: Conflicting Uses of the Celtic Sea and other Western U.K. Waters* (London, Europa Publications, 1977).

Simmonds, K. R., *Oil and Gas Law: The North Sea Exploitation* (looseleaf, New York, Oceana, 1988).

Smith, H. D., and C. S. Lalwani, *The North Sea: Sea Use Management and Planning* (Cardiff, UWIST, 1984).

Technica, *Prediction of the Proportions of Errant Vessels in Traffic Lanes on the United Kingdom Continental Shelf*, London, HMSO, 1985.

—— *The Risk of Ship/Platform Collisions in the Area of the United Kingdom Continental Shelf*, London, HMSO, 1986.

Ulfstein, G., P. Andersen, and R. Churchill (eds.), *The Regulation of Fisheries: Legal, Economic and Social Aspects* (Strasburg, Council of Europe, 1987).

Water, Two special issues of the Belgian magazine *Water* containing the contributions to a seminar on the Belgian continental Shelf: (1986), vol. 5, no. 31 and (1987), vol. 6, no. 32 (All contributions are preceded by a summary in English), V.Z.W. water, energie en leefmilieu, Bruges, 1986.

Watt, D. C. (ed.), *The North Sea: A New International Regime?* (Greenwich forum V, Greenwich, Westbury House, 1980).

Werkgroep Noordzee, *Distress signals: Signals from the Environment in Policy and Decision-making*; Proceedings of a Seminar held in Rotterdam, 1989, (Amsterdam, Stichting Werkgroep Noordzee (forthcoming) 1989).

Wettestad, J., *Uncertain Science and Matching Policies: Science, Politics and the Organization of North Sea Cooperation* (Oslo, Fridtjof Nansen Institute, 1989).

White, I., The Technology Assessment Group, Science and Public Policy Program. *North Sea Oil and Gas: Implications for Future United States Development* (Univ. of Oklahoma Press, 1973).

Wilke, H., *Abgrenzung des Festlandsockels der Nordsee: die Verträge und ihre Bedeutung für den Abbau grenzüberschreitender Lagerstätten* (Essen, Glückauf, 1980).

Young, E., and P. Fricke, *Sea Use Planning* (London, Fabian Society, 1975).

Articles

Adam, P., "Notes on the Management of North Sea Fisheries", in L. M. Alexander (ed.), *The Law of the Sea: The United Nations and Ocean Management* (Kingston, RI, Univ. of Rhode Island, 1970), pp. 256–263.

Andresen, S., "The Authorities Management of the Relation between the Oil and Fishing Industries: Coexistence or Confrontation?" (1985) *Fridtjof Nansen Institute Newsletter*, no. 4, p. 10.

—— "A Comprehensive North Sea Convention: New Approach, Old Policy?" in G. Peet (ed.), *The Status of the North Sea Environment* (Amsterdam, Stichting Werkgroep Noordzee, 1987), pp. 319–332.

—— "National and International Premises in Ocean Management: The Case of Norway", in A. W. Koers and B. H. Oxman (eds.), *The 1982 Convention on the Law of the Sea*, Honolulu (Law of the Sea Institute, Hawaii, 1984), pp. 500–520.

—— "Oil Activity and the Fishing Industry in Norway", in J. D. House (ed.), *Fish v. Oil Resources and Rural Development in North Atlantic Societies*, St. Johns, Newfoundland, Institute of Social and Economic Research (1986), pp. 78–91.

—— and B. Floistad, "Sea Use Planning in Norwegian Waters: National and International Dimensions" (1988) 16 *Coastal Management* 183–220.

Aquarone, M-C., "French Marine Policy in the 1970s and 1980s" (1988) 19 *Ocean Development and International Law* 267–285.

Archer, C., "Danish Ocean Management: A Study in Promiscuous Policy Making", Paper presented to the 23rd Annual Convention of the International Studies Association, Cincinnati.

—— "Supranational Ocean Management: The Case of the EC", in A. W. Koers and B. H. Oxman (eds.), *The 1982 Convention on the Law of the Sea*, Honolulu (Law of the Sea Institute, Hawaii, 1984), pp. 521–541.

—— "Two North Sea Policies: The Danish and Norwegian Attitudes Compared" (1977) 1 *Marine Policy* 289–300.

Armstrong, D. W., P. Hopkins, P.A. Kunzlik, and R. Milner, "Historical and Current State of the Major North Sea Fish Stocks", Paper presented at the Conference, North Sea 2000, Environment and Sea Use Planning, held in Edinburgh 16–18 August 1989, Heriot-Watt, Edinburgh.

Balogh, Lord, "The North Sea Oil Blunder" (1974) 124 *Banker* 281–288.

Barisich, A., "The Protection of the Sea: A European Community Policy" (1987) 2 IJECL 1–9.

Barrett, B., and R. Howells, "Safe Systems for Exploiting the Petroleum Resources of the North Sea" (1984) 33 *International and Comparative Law Quarterly* 811–824.

Beck, F., "Le Dispositif français contre la pollution de la mer", Societé française pour le droit de l'environnement, *Droit de l'environnement marin, développements récents* (Paris, Economica, 1989), pp. 185–200.

Becker, C., "Abfallbeseitigung auf der Nordsee, Aktuelle Praxis und Rechtslage in der Bundesrepublik Deutschland", (1985) 122 *Hansa* 315–318.

Bellamy, C., "The Military Uses of the North Sea, 1990–2000", Paper presented at the Conference North Sea 2000, Environment and Sea Use Planning, held in Edinburgh 16–18 August 1989, Heriot-Watt, Edinburgh.

Bentil, J. K., "Ensuring Control of Pollution Aspects of the EEC's Aquatic Environment" (1984) *Journal of Planning and Environmental Law* 707–721.

Bergot, G., "La Prévention et la lutte contre les pollutions par substances dangereuses", Societé française pour le droit de l'environnement, *Droit de l'environnement marin, développements récents*, 1989 pp. 219–240.

Bernhard, F., "Der Europaeische Festlandsockel", *Aspekte der Seerechtsentwicklung* (Munich, 1980), pp. 33–74.

Beukema, J., "Euthrophication: Reasons for Satisfaction or Concern", in G. Peet (ed.), *The Status of the North Sea Environment*: (Amsterdam, Stichting Werkgroep Noordzee, 1987), pp. 25–40.

Beurier, J.-P., "La Conservation des stocks halieutiques et la CEE" (1979) 22 *German Yearbook of International Law*, pp. 221–238.

Bievre, A. de, "La navigation en mer du Nord", Secretariat d'État à l'environnement, *Notre mer du nord, précieux patrimoine international* (Ostende, 1986), pp. 163–184.

—— "Shipping and the North Sea Environment: Is There a Need for Special International Regulation of Liability and Compensation for Environmental Damages Arising from the Maritime Transportation of Hazardous and Noxious Cargoes", in G. Peet (ed.), *The Status of the North Sea Environment* (Amsterdam, Stichting Werkgroep Noordzee, 1987), pp. 257–286.

Birks, J., "Oil and Gas in the North Sea", in H. van Hoorn, G. Peet, and G. M. Tiel (eds.), *The North Sea and its Environment, Uses and Conflicts* (Amsterdam, Stichting Werkgroep Noordzee, 1980), pp. 116–126.

Birnie P., "Did Failures in the North Sea Legal Regime Contribute to the Ekofisk Blow-Out?" (1978) 4 *Ocean Management* 119–135.

—— "The European Community's Environmental Policy", in E. Brown, and R. Churchill (eds.), *The UN Convention on the Law of the Sea: Impact and Implementation* (The Law of the Sea Institute, Hawaii, 1988), pp. 527–556.

—— "The Legal Regime of North Sea Oil Exploitation", in A. Meyers (ed.), *National Offshore Information Conference Papers*.

—— "The North Sea: A Challenge of Disorganized Opportunities?" in D. C. Watt (ed), *The North Sea: A New International Regime?* (Greenwich forum V. Greenwich, Westbury House, 1980), pp. 3–29.

—— "The North Sea: A Challenge of Disorganised Opportunities?", in H. van Hoorn, G. Peet, and G. M. Tiel (eds.), *The North Sea and its Environment*, (Amsterdam, Stichting Werkgroep Noordzee, 1980), pp. 75–96.

—— "The Legal Regime of the North Sea", Paper presented at the Conference North Sea 2000, Environment and Sea Use Planning, held in Edinburgh 16–18 August 1989, Heriot-Watt, Edinburgh.

—— "Pollution and Fisheries in the North Sea", in G. Ulfstein, P. Andersen, and R. Churchill (eds.), *The Regulation of Fisheries* (Strasburg, Council of Europe, 1987), pp. 219–248.

—— and C. Mason, "Oil and Gas: The International Regime", in C. Mason (ed.), *The Effective Management of Resources* (London, Francis Pinter, 1979), pp. 19–52.

Blaikley, D. R., "Environmental Protection in North Sea Exploration and Protection Operations" (1977) 1 *Marine Policy* 143–155.

Boehmer-Christiansen, S., "Marine Pollution Control in Europe: Regional Approaches 1972–80" (1984) 8 *Marine Policy* 44–55.

Bouchez, L. J., "The Netherlands and its Jurisdiction over the Continental Shelf", in H. F. Panhuys (ed.), *International Law in the Netherlands* (Alphen a/d Rijn, 1978), pp. 289–314.

Brask, G., "Blow-out in the North Sea" (1975) 3 *Lloyd's Maritime and Commercial Law Quarterly* 271–280.

Brenscheidt, M., "Petroleum Legislation in the North Sea Countries" (1976) 11 *Texas International Law Journal* 281–303.

Breuer, G., "Case Study on Technical Management of the North Sea", in L. M. Alexander (ed.), *The Law of the Sea: The United Nations and Ocean Management* (Kingston, Univ. of Rhode Island, 1970), pp. 270–276.

Broere, C., "Consequences of Implementation of Marine Environment Protection Measures for Specific Availability of Shore Reception Facilities for Oil and Chemicals for Shipping Industry", in H. van Hoorn, G. Peet, and G. M. Tiel (eds.), *The North Sea and its Environment* (Amsterdam, Stichting Werkgroep Noordzee, 1980), pp. 126–130.

Brown, C., "Forecast of North Sea Developments Well Drilling" (1976) 11 *Ocean Industry* 52–55.

Brown, E. D., "Sea Use Planning in the North Sea: The Legal Framework", in J. K. Gamble (ed.), *Law of the Sea: Neglected Issues* (Law of the Sea Institute, Hawaii, 1978), pp. 436–480.

Buchholz, H., "Die seerechtliche Regionalisierung der Nordsee" (1985) 35 *Geographische Rundschrift* 274–280.

—— "Territorialplanung zur See. Jede begrenzte Ressource bedarf der vorausschauenden Planung", *Das Beispiel Nordsee, Geographie der Küsten und Meere* (Berlin, 1985), pp. 153–168.

Burger, W., and H. D. Smith, "Sea-Use Planning in the Southern North Sea: The Shipping Background", in D. C. Watt (ed), *The North Sea: A New International Regime?* (Greenwich forum V, Greenwich, Westbury House, 1980), pp. 119–132.

Burton, T., and D. Freestone, "The Control of Pollution Act, 1974 and Tidal Waters: Problems of the Implementation of Part II" (1986) 1 IJECL 241–268.

Camphuysen, K., "Review of Seabird Mortality, 1915–1988" (1989) *North Sea Monitor*, no. 1, pp. 2–4.

—— "Seabird Mortality and Oil Pollution: Netherlands' Coast 1947–1985", in G. Peet (ed.),

The Status of the North Sea Environment (Amsterdam, Stichting Werkgroep Noordzee, 1987), pp. 63–72.

Carlberg, E. C., and K. Gripp, "Coastal Policy in Sweden: Use and Protection of Marine Resources", *Ekistics*, vol. 49, no. 293.

Churchill, R., "The Conflict between Oil and Fisheries: A Survey of Norwegian and United Kingdom Law and Practice", in G. Ulfstein, P. Andersen, and —— (eds.), *The Regulation of Fisheries: Legal, Economic and Social Aspects* (Strasburg, Council of Europe, 1987), pp. 197–210.

—— "Revision of the EEC's Common Fisheries Policy" (1980) 5 *European Law Review* 3–37 (pt. I) pp. 95–111 (pt. II).

Coenen, R., "Effects of the International Conference on the Protection of the North Sea" (1986) *North Sea Monitor*, no. 1, pp. 2–6.

Cormack, D., "Plan of the European Communities for Dealing with Pollution of the Sea by Oil and other Hazardous Substances", 3 *Oil and Chemical Pollution* 343–353.

Couper, A., and H. Smith, "The North Sea Basis for Management and Planning in a Multi-State Sea Region", in D. M. Johnston, and N. G. Letalik (eds.), *The Law of the Sea and Ocean Industry: New Opportunities and Restraints* (Law of the Sea Institute, Hawaii, 1984), pp. 63–88.

Cuyvers, L., "North Sea Planning: The Role of National Regimes", in D. C. Watt (ed.), *The North Sea: A New International Regime?* (Greenwich Forum V, Greenwich, Westbury House, 1980), pp. 30–44.

Daan, N., "Multispecies and Single Species Stock Assessment in Relation to Fisheries Management", in H. van Hoorn, and G. Peet (eds.), *The North Sea and its Environment* (Amsterdam, Stichting Werkgroep Noordzee, 1980), pp. 132–136.

Daintith, T., and I. Townsend Gault, "Oil and Gas: National Regimes", in C. Mason (ed.), *The Effective Management of Resources* (London, Francis Pinter, 1979), pp. 53–70.

Daniel, G. H., "Adaptation Clauses in North Sea Oil Supply Agreements" (1983) 2 *Journal of Energy and Natural Resources* 100–103.

Davidson, S., "The Single European Act and the Environment" (1987) 2 IJECL 259–263.

Davies, G., and J. Side, "Inputs to the North Sea", Paper presented at the Conference North Sea 2000, Environment and Sea Use Planning, held in Edinburgh 16–18 August 1989, Heriot-Watt, Edinburgh.

Davis, J., and I. Faurby, "The Paradox of Danish Offshore Policy: A Deviant Case in North Sea Oil and Gas Exploitation", in R. L. Lawrence, and M. O. Heisler (eds.), *International Energy Policy*, pp. 163–183.

Davis, P., "The Dutch Sector of the North Sea: A Concentration of Multiple Activities or Multiple Sorrows", Paper presented at the Conference North Sea 2000, Environment and Sea Use Planning, held in Edinburgh 16–18 August 1989, Heriot-Watt, Edinburgh.

Dethlefsen, V., "Marine Pollution Mismanagement: Towards the Precautionary Concept", 17 (1986) *Marine Pollution Bulletin* 54–57.

Devaraj, M., "Government Policies Concerning the Development of New Offshore Oil Provinces with Focus on India and the North Sea" (1982) 8 *Ocean Management* 251–274.

Dicke, D.-C., "Die Europaeischen Gemeinschaften und das Problem der seerechtlichen Wirtschaftszone", Gedächtnisschrift Friedrich Klein, Munich, 1977, pp. 65–85.

Dixon, T. J., and T. R. Dixon, "Marine Litter Distribution and Composition in the North Sea" (1983) 14 *Marine Pollution Bulletin* 145–148.

Dixon, T. R., and T. J. Dixon, "Marine Litter Surveillance" (1981) 12 *Marine Pollution Bulletin* pp. 289–295.

Driscoll, D., and N. McKellar, "The Changing Regime of North Sea Fisheries", in C. Mason (ed.), *The Effective Management of Resources* (London, Francis Pinter, 1979), pp. 125–167.

Dubais, B., "The Risk of Pollution Damage arising from Oil Exploration and Production in the North Sea" (1977) 5 *International Business Lawyer* 346–352.

Eisma, D., "Need for Sea-Use Planning in the North Sea", in J. K. Gamble (ed.), *Law of the Sea: Neglected Issues* pp. 425–435.

—— "The North Sea, A Summary", in H. van Hoorn and G. Peet (eds.), *The North Sea and its Environment* (Amsterdam, Stichting Werkgroep Noordzee, 1980), pp. 55–74.

—— "The North Sea: An Overview", in G. Peet, and E. Hey (eds.), *The Status of the North Sea Environment* (Amsterdam, Stichting Werkgroep Noordzee, 1987), pp. 10–28.

—— H. van Hoorn, and A. de Jong, "Concepts for Sea-Use Planning in the North Sea" (1979) 5 *Ocean Management* 295–307.

Ehlers, P., "Die erste internationale Nordseeschutz-Konferenz" (1985) *Natur und Recht*, 102–106.

—— "Wichtige Fortschritte beim Schutz der Nordsee—Bericht über die 2. internationale Nordseeschutz-Konferenz" (1988) *Natur und Recht*, 126–130.

Evans, A., "North Sea Oil and EEC Law" (1982) 6 *International Lawyer* 529–540.

—— "The United Kingdom North Sea Policy and EEC Law" (1982) 7 *European Law Review* 355–368.

Faurby, I., "Danish Offshore Policy", in D. C. Watt (ed.), *The North Sea: A New International Regime?* (Greenwich forum V, Greenwich, Westbury House, 1980), pp. 203–212.

Fitzmaurice, V. E., "Liability for North Sea Oil Pollution" (1978) 2 *Marine Policy* 105–111.

Fotheringham, P., "The Political Dimensions of North Sea Pollution Control", in H. van Hoorn, and G. Peet (eds.), *The North Sea and its Environment* (Amsterdam, Stichting Werkgroep Noordzee, 1980), pp. 156–161.

—— and P. Birnie, "Regulation of North Sea Marine Pollution", in C. Mason (ed.), *The Effective Management of Resources* (London, Francis Pinter, 1979), pp. 168–223.

Fowler, S. L., "Conservation of the Coastal and Estuarine Zones of the North Sea", Paper presented at the Conference North Sea 2000, Environment and Sea Use Planning, held in Edinburgh 16–18 August 1989, Heriot-Watt, Edinburgh.

Fox, A., "Oil and Gas Operations in the North Sea", in L. M. Alexander (ed.), *The Law of the Sea: The United Nations and Ocean Management* (Kingston, Univ. of Rhode Island, 1970), 264–269.

Franckx, E., "Belgium Extends its Territorial Sea up to 12 Nautical Miles" (1987) 20 *Revue Belge de Droit International* 41–71.

—— "Belgium Joins the Majority of Coastal States by Claiming a 12-mile Territorial Sea" (1988) 3 IJECL 155–157.

—— "Juridische aspecten van het ongeval met de Mont-Louis" (with summary in English) (1986) 31 *Water* 60–61.

Furness, R. W., "The Impact of Fisheries on Seabird Population in the North Sea", in G. Peet (ed.), *The Status of the North Sea Environment* (Amsterdam, Stichting Werkgroep Noordzee, 1987), pp. 179–194.

Gaskell, T., "Exploitation of Oil in the North Sea; Marine Technology and Law, Development of Hydrocarbon Resources and Offshore Structures", *Proceedings of the Second International Ocean Symposium*, 1977.

Glansdorp, C. C., J. F. Kemp, E. M. Goodwin, and R. Tresfon, "Quantification of Navigational Risk in European Waters" (1986) 39 *Journal of Navigation* 90–96.

Goodlad, J. H., "Fisheries and Oil: An Update of the Shetland Experience", in J. D. House (ed.), *Fish v. Oil Resources and Rural Development in North Atlantic Societies*, St. Johns, Newfoundland, Institute of Social and Economic Research (1986), pp. 62–72.

Grant, J. P., "The Conflict between the Fishing and Oil Industries in the North Sea: A Case Study" (1978) 4 *Ocean Management* 137–149.

Greenwoord, D., "Security and Policing", in C. Mason (ed.), *The Effective Management of Resources* (London, Francis Pinter, 1979), pp. 224–258.

Groot, S. de, "On the Interference between Beamtrawls and Submarine Telephone Cables in the Southern North Sea: The Way Out of the Problem" (1979) 5 *Ocean Management* 285–294.

—— "An Assessment of the Potential Environmental Impact of Large-Scale Sand Dredging for the Building of Artificial Islands in the North Sea" (1979) 5 *Ocean Management* 211–233.

—— "The Potential Environmental Impact of Marine Gravel Extraction in the North Sea" (1979) 5 *Ocean Management* 233–250.

—— "The Impact of Laying and Maintenance of Offshore Pipelines on the Marine Environment and the North Sea Fisheries" (1982) 8 *Ocean Management* 1–27.

—— "The Impact of Bottom Trawling on Benthic Fauna on the North Sea" (1984) 9 *Ocean Management* 177–190.

—— "Marine Sand and Gravel Extraction in the North Atlantic and its Potential Environmental Impact with Emphasis on the North Sea" (1986) 10 *Ocean Management* 21–36.

Gubbay, S., and P. Horsman, "Land Reclamation on the North Sea Coast of the UK", in G. Peet (ed.), *The Status of the North Sea Environment* (Amsterdam, Stichting Werkgroep Noordzee, 1987), pp. 145–154.

Gulland, J. A., "The Management of North Sea Fisheries: Looking Towards the Twenty-First Century" (1987) 11 *Marine Policy* 259–272.

Gündling, L., "The Extension of Territorial Waters in the North Sea" (1986) 1 IJECL 312–315.

—— "Rechtsprobleme der Abfallbeseitigung auf See" (1982) 4 *Natur und Recht* 41–53.

Guruswamy, L., "Environmental Management in a North Sea Coastal Zone: Law, Institutions and Policy" (1985) 1 *Natural Resources Journal* 233–247.

Hallers-Tjabbes, C.C. ten, "Signals of a Diseased Environment: A Basis for a North Sea Environmental Policy", in G. Peet (ed.), *The Status of the North Sea Environment* (Amsterdam, Stichting Werkgroep Noordzee, 1987), pp. 245–256.

Hayward, P., "Environmental Protection, Regional Approaches", (1984) 8 *Marine Policy* 106–119.

Heap, J. M., M. Elliott, and T. Rheinallt, "Marine Disposal of Municipal Waste", Paper presented at the Conference North Sea 2000, Environment and Sea Use Planning, held in Edinburgh 16–18 August 1989, Heriot-Watt, Edinburgh.

van Hoorn, H., "Industrial Islands in the North Sea? in id., G. Peet, and G. M. Tiel (eds.), *The North Sea and its Environment* (Amsterdam, Stichting Werkgroep Noordzee, 1980), pp. 137–139.

—— and K. Wieriks, "Governmental North Sea Policies into the 1990s", Presentation given at the XI Greenwich Forum Conference, Edinburgh, April 1985.

—— G. Peet, and K. Wieriks, "Harmonizing North Sea Policy in the Netherlands" (1985) 9 *Marine Policy* 53–61.

Horigan, J., "Unitization of Petroleum Reservoirs Extending across Sub-sea Boundary Lines of Bordering States in the North Sea" (1974) *Natural Resources Lawyer* 67–76.

House, J. D., "Fish is Fish and Oil is Oil: The Case for North Sea Comparisons to Atlantic Canada", in J. D. House (ed.), *Fish v. Oil Resources and Rural Development in North Atlantic Societies*, St. Johns, Newfoundland, Institute of Social and Economic Research (1986), pp. 129–140.

Huisman, H., "EIA for Offshore Activities in the Netherlands" (1988) *North Sea Monitor* 9–12.

IJlstra, T., "Enforcement of International Environmental Instruments in the North Sea: The Missing Link", in G. Peet (ed.), *The Status of the North Sea Environment* (Amsterdam, Stichting Werkgroep Noordzee, 1987), pp. 287–318.

—— "The Dutch Policy Report on Maritime Traffic in the North Sea" (1987) *North Sea Monitor* 2–5.

—— "Regional Cooperation in the North Sea: An Inquiry" (1988) 3 IJECL 181–207.

—— "L'Action communautaire dans les commissions de Paris et d'Oslo", Paper presented at the conference *La Communauté Européenne et la mer*, Brest, 6–8 October 1988 (forthcoming).

—— "The Netherlands and the Institution of the Exclusive Economic Zone" (1988) *North Sea Monitor* 2–3.

—— and F. de Jong, "The 1987 International North Sea Conference" (1988) 3 IJECL 246–265.

Ipsen, H., "EWG über See. Zur seerechtlichen Orientierung des europäischen Gemeinschaftsrechts, Recht über See", in *Festschrift Rolf Stödter* (Hamburg 1979), pp. 167–208.

—— "Die Europäische Gemeinschaft und das Meer", in *Die Plünderung der Meere* (Frankfurt-a-M., 1981), pp. 300–324.

Jacques, T. G., "Plans d'intervention des pouvoirs publics en cas de pollution grave en mer", Secretariat d'État à l'environnement, *Notre mer du Nord, précieux patrimoine international* (Ostende, 1986).

Jeannel, A., and M. Ben Allal, "Ressources pétrolières de la Mer du Nord et control des états riverains", in J. Dupuy (ed.), *Le Pétrole et la mer* (Paris, PUF, 1976), pp. 35–50.

Jeanson, P., "La Pollution tellurique en droit français", Société française pour le droit de l'environnement (Droit de l'environment marin, développements récents, 1989) pp. 241–272.

Jenisch, U., "Massnahmen zur Bekämpfung der Meeresverschmutzung in Nordsee und Ostsee" (Braunkohle, 1975), pp. 39–43.

—— "The Law of the Sea and the Maritime Interests of the Federal Republic of Germany" (1976) 27 *Aussenpolitik* 3–30.

—— "The North Sea: International Law of the Sea and Environmental Protection", 1 *Aussenpolitik* 76–93.

Jong, F. de, "The Second Ministerial Conference on the Protection of the North Sea" (1987) *North Sea Monitor*, no. 4, pp. 2–4.

—— "The Quality of the North Sea, National Points of View", in G. Peet, and E. Hey (eds.), The Status of the North Sea Environment (Amsterdam, Stichting Werkgroep Noordzee, 1987), pp. 40–54.

—— "Towards the Third North Sea Conference" (1988) *North Sea Monitor* 2–4.

—— "Policies for Effluent Waters", Proceedings of the Third North Sea Seminar", *Distress Signals: Signals from the Environment in Policy and Decision-Making* (Rotterdam, 1989).

Kasoulides, G., "London North Sea Conference" (1988) 19 *Marine Pollution Bulletin* 97–99.

Kehden, M., "Auswirkungen der Aenderung von Grenzen im europäischen Seeverkehr" (1979) 17 *Deutscher Verkehrsgerichtstag* 248–255.

Kemp, J. F., "Vessel Traffic Services in the Southern North Sea", in G. Peet (ed.), *The Status of the North Sea Environment* (Amsterdam, Stichting Werkgroep Noordzee, 1987), pp. 231–244.

Kenneth, R. G., "Offshore Petroleum Exploitation and Environmental Protection: The International and Norwegian Response" (1980) 17 *San Diego Law Review* 629–660.

Kim, C., "Optimal Management of Multi-Species North Sea Fishery Resources" 119 *Weltwirtschaftliches Archiv* 139–151.

Kiselev, V. A., "Special Areas for Preventing Pollution of the Sea" (1988) 12 *Marine Policy* 241–246.

Kleinsteuber, H., "Fisheries Management and the North Sea Ecosystem", in G. Peet (ed.), *The Status of the North Sea Environment* (Amsterdam, Stichting Werkgroep Noordzee, 1987), pp. 163–178.

Klinowska, M., "The Status of Marine Mammals in the Southern North Sea", in G. Peet (ed.), *The Status of the North Sea Environment* (Amsterdam, Stichting Werkgroep Noordzee, 1987), pp. 73–96.

Koekebakker, P., and G. Peet, "Solving the Problems at Sea is not only a Question of

Regime", in D. C. Watt (ed.), *The North Sea: A New International Regime?* (Greenwich forum V, Greenwich, Westbury House, 1980), pp. 83–90.

Koers, A., "The European Economic Community and the Sea", in L. M. Alexander (ed.), *The Law of the Sea: The United Nations and Ocean Management* (Kingston Univ. of Rhode Island, 1970), pp. 277–288.

—— "Artificial Islands in the North Sea", in J. K. Gamble, and G. Pontecorvo (eds.), *The Law of the Sea: The Emerging Regime of the Oceans* (Proceedings of the Seventh Conference of the Law of the Sea Institute, Hawaii, 1973), pp. 223–245.

—— "Dutch Offshore Policy", in D. C. Watt (ed.), *The North Sea: A New International Regime?* (Greenwich Forum V, Greenwich, Westbury House, 1980) pp. 182–191.

Koertel, G., "Ausdehnung der niederländischen Hoheitsgewässer auf Zwölf Seemeilen Breite—ein neues Ems-Dollart-Problem?" (1985) 122 *Hansa* 2272–2274.

Kokott, J., and L. Gündling, "Die Erweiterung der deutschen Küstengewässer in der Nordsee" (1985) 45 *ZaöRV* 677–693.

Koopmann, G., "Internationale Massnahmen zur Reinhaltung des Meeres—Umweltschutzbereich Nordsee", *Die wirtschaftliche Nutzung der Nordsee und die Europäische Gemeinschaft* (Baden-Baden, 1979), pp. 9–20.

Kramer, K., and M. van der Loeff, "Marine Pollution in the North Sea Area", in H. van Hoorn, and G. Peet (eds.), *The North Sea and its Environment* (Amsterdam, Stichting Werkgroep Noordzee, 1980), pp. 97–103.

Krämer, H. "Die Nordsee in der EWG" (1978) 33 *Europa-Archiv* 571–580.

—— "Die Stellung der EWG im Bereich der Ostsee" (1979) 34 *Europa-Archiv*, 221–230.

Krämer, L., "Le Déversement des déchets en mer et le droit communautaire" (1988) *Revue du Marché Commun* 328–340.

—— "Le Déversement des déchets en mer et le droit communautaire", Société française pour le droit de l'environnement (Droit de l'environment marin, développements récents, 1989), pp. 133–162.

Kuiper, J., "Effects of Oil Pollution in the North Sea" (1988) *North Sea Monitor* 4–5.

Kunig, P., "Oelverschmutzung durch Schiffe—das Verhältnis von Recht und Wirklichkeit am Beispiel der Nordsee" (1986) 8 *Natur und Recht*, 266–270.

Lagoni, R., "Einrichtungen des Marine Bergbaus und die Schiffarhtsfreiheit in Nord und Ostsee", in Bernhardt and Rudolf (eds.)

—— "The Federal Republic of Germany and the United Nations Convention on the Law of the Sea" (1987) 2 IJECL 86–96.

Ligthart, V. H. M., "An Inquiry into North Sea Navigation" (1985) 38 *Journal of Navigation* 332–346.

Lund, S., "The Danish Regime in the North Sea", in D. C. Watt (ed.), *The North Sea: A New International Regime?* (Greenwich forum V, Greenwich, Westbury House, 1980), pp. 192–202.

Mackay, G. A., "The Conflicts between the Oil and Fishing Industries in the North Sea", in J. D. House (ed.), *Fish v. Oil Resources and Rural Development in North Atlantic Societies*, St. Johns, Newfoundland, Institute of Social and Economic Research (1986), pp. 22–33.

—— and P. G. Sadler, "The Conflict between the Offshore Oil and Fishing Industries in the UK Sector of the North Sea", in H. van Hoorn, and G. Peet (eds.), *The North Sea and its Environment* (Amsterdam, Stichting Werkgroep Noordzee, 1980), pp. 150–155.

Mandl, V., "Politique communautaire de protection du milieu marin"; Secretariat d'État à l'environnement", *notre mer du Nord, précieux patrimoine international* (Ostende, 1986), pp. 111–125.

Marine Conservation Society, Control of Inputs of Dangerous Substances to Waters in the UK (1988) *North Sea Monitor* 2–7.

Marriage, P., "North Sea Petroleum Project Financing in the United Kingdom" (1977) 5 *International Business Lawyer* 207–224.

Mason, C., "Oil and Gas: The Law and Policy of the European Community", in C. Mason (ed.), *The Effective Management of Resources* (London, Francis Pinter, 1979), pp. 100–124.

Mayhew, G., "How Tax may Affect the Ideal Development of the North Sea" (1981) *Petroleum Review* 6–10.

McColl, R., "Consequences for the Fishing Industry of Oil Industry Debris" (1980) 4 *Marine Policy* 61–63.

McIntyre, A., "North Sea Conferences and Commissions" (1988) 19 *Marine Pollution Bulletin* 159–161.

McVicar, A. H., D. W. Bruno, and C. O. Fraser, "Fish Diseases in the North Sea in Relation to Sewage Sludge Dumping" (1988) 19 *Marine Pollution Bulletin* 169–173.

Milnar, P., "Petroleum Legislation and Licensing Procedures in the North Sea and some Associated International Problems" (1978) 18 *Natural Resources Journal* 545–568.

Minford, P., "North Sea Oil and the British Economy" (1977) 127 *Banker* 23–27.

Mohr, P. van der Meer, "Measures to Prevent Collisions with Offshore Installations on the Dutch Continental Shelf" (1988) 1 *Leiden Journal of International Law*, pp. 222–230.

Morvan, D. Le, "La Politique communautaire de protection de l'environnement marin", Societé française pour le droit de l'environnement (Droit de l'environment marin, développements récents, 1989), pp. 103–132.

Munch, F., "Federal Republic of Germany", in R. R. Churchill, K. R. Simmonds, and J. Welch (eds.), 3 *New Directions in the Law of the Sea*, London, British Institute of International and Comparative Law, 1973, pp. 253–256.

Murray, C., and H. Kautsky, "Plutonium and American Activities in the North Sea and German Coastal Regions" (1977) 5 *Estuarine and Coastal Marine Sciences* 319–328.

Nihoul, C., "International Cooperation", Paper given at the First International Conference on Chemical Spills and Emergency Management at Sea, Amsterdam, 1988.

—— "Dumping at Sea", Paper presented at the Conference, North Sea 2000, Environment and Sea Use Planning, held in Edinburgh 16–18 August 1989, Heriot-Watt, Edinburgh.

Odell, P., "Oil and Gas Exploitation and Exploration in the North Sea" (1978) 1 *Ocean Yearbook* 139–159.

—— "Offshore Resources: Oil and Gas", in R. P. Barston, and P. Birnie (eds.), *The Maritime Dimension* (London, George Allen & Unwin, 1980), pp. 76–107.

Park, J., "Oil and Gas: Governments and Companies", in C. Mason (ed.), *The Effective Management of Resources* (London, Francis Pinter, 1979), pp. 71–99.

Peet, G., "The 1984 North Sea Conference: A Preview" (1984) 8 *Marine Policy* 259–270.

—— "Sea Use Management for the North Sea", in E. Brown, and R. Churchill (eds.), *The UN Convention on the Law of the Sea: Impact and Implementation* (The Law of the Sea Institute, Hawaii, 1988), pp. 430–440.

—— "Protection du milieu de la mer de nord uniquement grace à une collaboration internationale", Secretariat d'État à l'environnement, *Notre mer du Nord, précieux patrimoine international* (Ostende, 1986).

—— "Environmental Pressures: The North Sea under Siege", Paper presented at the Conference North Sea 2000, Environment and Sea Use Planning, held in Edinburgh 16–18 August 1989, Heriot-Watt, Edinburgh.

Pellenbarg, N., "The Conflict between Shipping and Oil and Gas Extraction", in H. van Hoorn, and G. Peet (eds.), *The North Sea and its Environment* (Amsterdam, Stichting Werkgroep Noordzee, 1980), pp. 140–149.

Petersen, S., "Staatsrechtliche Probleme einer Erweiterung des Küstenmeeres der Bundesrepublik Deutschland" (1987) 2 *DVBl* 78–85.

Platzoeder, R., "Regional Factors in Managing Marine Resources after the Third UN Conference of the Law of the Sea: A European View", in E. Douglas, and M. Johnston (eds.), *Regionalization of the Law of the Sea*, Proceedings of the Eleventh Conference of the Law of the Sea Institute, Hawaii, 1977, pp. 63–72.

Platzöder, R., "The North Sea and Its Approaches: The Case for and against an International Regime: A German View", in D. C. Watt (ed.), *The North Sea: A New International Regime?* (Greenwich forum V, Greenwich, Westbury House, 1980), pp. 91–100.

Prat, J.-L., "Le Système spécifique de l'Europe du nord-ouest", Société française pour le droit de l'environnement (Droit de l'environnement marin, développements récents, 1989), pp. 83–102.

Pritchard, S., "The North Sea as a Special Area" (1978) 2 *Marine Policy* 65–67.

Pyman, M. A. F., P. R. Lyon, and G. Rowe May, "A Survey of Traffic Passing Offshore Installations in the North Sea" (1984) 37 *Journal of Navigation* 251–263.

Ramster, J., "Development of Cooperative Research in the North Sea: The Origins, Planning and Philosophy of the North Sea Data Acquisition Project 1976" (1977) 1 *Marine Policy* 318–325.

Ranken, M. B. F., "Preconditions for an International Offshore Regime: Administration, Management, Policing and Emergency Services", in D. C. Watt (ed.), *The North Sea: A New International Regime?* (Greenwich forum V, Greenwich, Westbury House, 1980), pp. 45–77.

Reintanz, G., "Welche Bedeutung haben die Oel- und Erdgasfunde in der Nordsee?" (1976) 21 *Aussenpolitik* 438–444.

Roggenkamp, M., "Safety on the Dutch Continental Shelf" (1988) *North Sea Monitor*, no. 3, pp. 18–19.

Roggeveen, V., "Offshore Operations, Safe or Susceptible?" (1988) *North Sea Monitor*, no. 3, pp. 19–21.

Rouw, S. C. J. de, "Harmonization of North Sea Policy in the Netherlands", in B. Vukas (ed.), *The Legal Regime of Enclosed or Semi-Enclosed Seas: The Particular Case of the Mediterranean* (Zagreb, Faculty of Law, Univ. of Zagreb, 1988), pp. 405–426.

Saetevik, S., "The EC and the Environment: Internal Factors" (1986) *Fridtjof Nansen Institute Newsletter*, no. 4, pp. 1–10.

—— "The EC and the Environment: External Performance; Effects on Policy-Outcome in the Paris Commission" (1986) *Fridtjof Nansen Institute Newsletter*, no. 4, pp. 11–18.

—— "Environmental Cooperation between the North Sea States: Success or Failure?" (1988) 8 *International Challenges* 40–47.

Schriel, R. C., "Aerial Surveillance on Pollution at Sea" (1988) *North Sea Monitor*, no. 3, pp. 16–17.

Scott, I., "The Importance of North Sea Fishery Resources", in D. C. Watt (ed.), *The North Sea: A New International Regime?* (Greenwich forum V, Greenwich, Westbury House, (1980), pp. 133–151.

Sebek, V., "Legal Regime for the North Sea", in H. van Hoorn, G. Peet, and G. M. Tiel (eds.), *The North Sea and its Environment* (Amsterdam, Stichting Werkgroep Noordzee, 1980), pp. 162–168.

Side, J., "The North Sea Conference, Bremen 1984–London 1987", (1986) 17 *Marine Pollution Bulletin* 394–399.

—— "The European Community and Dumping at Sea", (1986) 17 *Marine Pollution Bulletin* 294.

—— "North-West Europe—Clean Seas and Emergency Services" (1988) 19 *Marine Pollution Bulletin* 153–155.

Smet, A. de, "Policing on the High Sea: With Special Reference to the North Sea", in R. R. Churchill, K. R. Simmonds, and J. Welch (eds.), 3 *New Directions in the Law of the Sea* (London, British Institute of International and Comparative Law, 1973), pp. 193–205.

Smith, H., "The North Sea: Sea-Use Management and Planning", Paper presented at the Conference North Sea 2000, Environment and Sea Use Planning, held in Edinburgh 16–18 August 1989, Heriot-Watt, Edinburgh.

—— C. Lalwani, and I. Brookfield, "Sea-Use Planning and the North Sea" (1981) 5 *Marine Policy* 75–77.

Somers, E., "The Problem of the Wielingen: The Delimitation of the Belgian Territorial Sea with Respect to the Netherlands" (1988) 3 IJECL 19–36.

Squires, M. D., "Facilities for the Reception of Wastes: A Shipping Industry Review", in G. Peet (ed.), *The Status of the North Sea Environment* (Amsterdam, Stichting Werkgroep Noordzee, 1987), pp. 195–212.

Stalp, H.-G., "A German View of North Sea Mineral Development", in D. C. Watt (ed.), *The North Sea: A New International Regime?* (Greenwich forum V, Greenwich, Westbury House, 1980), pp. 78–82.

Standring, K., and T. Stowe, "Marine Oil Pollution and Birds", in H. van Hoorn, G. Peet and G. M. Tiel (eds.), *The North Sea and its Environment* (Amsterdam Stichting Werkgroep Noordzee, 1980), pp. 108–115.

Starkle, G., "Les Épaves de navires en haute mer et le droit international: le cas du 'Mont-Louis' " (1985) *Revue Belge de Droit Internation*al 496–528.

Symmons, C. R., "British Offshore Continental Shelf and Fishery Limit Boundaries: An Analysis of Overlapping Zones" (1979) 28 *International and Comparative Law Quarterly* 703–733.

Taylor, B. G. S., "Offshore Oil and Gas", Paper presented at the Conference North Sea 2000, Environment and Sea Use Planning, held in Edinburgh 16–18 August 1989, Heriot-Watt, Edinburgh.

Townsend Gault, I., "The Frigg Gasfield: Exploitation of an International Cross Boundary Petroleum Field" (1979) 3 *Marine Policy* 302–311.

—— "The Impact of Offshore Petroleum Regimes on Other Users: The North Sea and North America", in D. M. Johnston, and N. G. Letalik (eds.), *The Law of the Sea and Ocean Industry: New Opportunities and Restraints* (Law of the Sea Institute, Hawaii, 1984), pp. 411–419.

Uthoff, D., "Konfliktfeld Nordsee—Nutzungen, Nutzungsansprüche und Nutzungskonflikte" (1983) 35 *Geographische Rundschau*, 282–291.

Vauk, G. J. M., and E. Schrey, "Litter Pollution from Ships in the German Bight" (1987) 18 *Marine Pollution Bulletin* 316–319.

Vethaak, A. D., "Fish Diseases: Signals for a Diseased Environment", in G. Peet (ed.), *The Status of the North Sea Environment*, (Amsterdam, Stichting Werkgroep, Noordzee, 1987), pp. 41–62.

Vindenes, H., "The UN Conference on the Law of the Sea: The Basic Problems from a Norwegian Point of View" (1974) *Cooperation and Conflict*, nos. 2/3, pp. 69–81.

Volckaert, F., "Formulation of a National Marine Policy: The Case of Belgium" (1986) 10 *Marine Policy* 91–100.

Voogt, P. de, and B. van Hattum, "Cadmium Pollution of the North Sea: Sources, Occurrences, Effects and Control" in H. van Hoorn, G. Peet, and G. M. Tiel (eds.), *The North Sea and its Environment* (Amsterdam, Stichting Werkgroep Noordzee, 1980), pp. 104–107.

Watt, D. C., "Britain and North Sea Oil: Policies Past and Present" (1976) 47 *Political Quarterly* 377–397.

—— "Offshore Policies and Policy Making in the United Kingdom", in D. C. Watt (ed.), *The North Sea: A New International Regime?* (Greenwich forum V, Greenwich, Westbury House, 1980), pp. 165–181.

Welsch, H., "The London Dumping Convention and Sub-sea-bed Disposal of Radioactive Waste" (1985) 28 *German Yearbook of International Law*, pp. 322–354.

Wettestad, J., "The Outcome of the 1987 North Sea Conference: Science Counts, but Politics Decides?" (1988) 8 *International Challenges* 31–35.

—— "Science, Politics and Ocean Pollution: Explaining the Outcome of the 1987 North Sea Conference" (1988) 8 *International Challenges* 26–31.

—— "Science, Politics and the Organization of Environmental Cooperation in the North Sea: Moderate Science, Moderate Policies: but are 'Ecosystems Needs' looked after?"

Paper 1, "The Management of International Resources: Scientific Input and the Role of Scientific Cooperation", Oslo 10–11 October 1988.

Wilke, H., "Nutzungsregelungen für die Aufsuchung und Gewinnung von Bodenschätzen in maritimen Bereichen", (1970) 86 *Erdöl-Erdgas Zeitschrift*, 452–456.

Winter, G., "Der Schutz der Nordsee als Problem internationaler Uebereinkommen und EG-Richtlinien" (1988) 10 *Natur und Recht*, 265–272.

Woodliffe, J., "North Sea Oil and Gas: The European Community Connection" (1975) 12 *Common Market Law Review* 12.

—— "International Unitisation of an Offshore Gasfield" (1977) 26 *International Comparative Law Quarterly* 338–353.

—— "State Participation in the Development of United Kingdom Offshore Petroleum Resources" (1977) *Public Law* 249–271.

—— "The Offshore Safety Provisions of the Oil and Gas (Enterprise) Act 1982" (1983) *Journal of Energy and Natural Resources Law* no. 1, pp. 44–49.

Wrathmell, B., "The De-unitisation of a North Sea Oilfield" (1985) 3 *Journal of Energy and Natural Resources Law*, 195–199.

Zwiep, K. van der, "Reclamation and Embankment in the International Wadden Area", in G. Peet (ed.), *The Status of the North Sea Environment* (Amsterdam, Stichting Werkgroep Noordzee, 1987), pp. 155–162.

Documents relating to the North Sea Minister's Conferences

Declaration of the International Conference on the Protection of the North Sea, IMO Doc. MEPC 21/INF. 11 of 22 March 1985.

International Conference on the Protection of the North Sea, *International Conference on the Protection of the North Sea 1984, Summary Records of the Second International Conference.*

FRG, *Handover Report by the Federal Republic of Germany for the Second International Conference on the Protection of the North Sea, 15 October 1985.*

Ministerial Declaration of the Second International Conference on the Protection of the North Sea (1988) 3 IJECL 252–265; (1988) 27 ILM 835.

Department of the Environment UK, *International Conference on the Protection of the North Sea, Second Report by the Scientific and Technical Working Group.*

Department of the Environment UK, *International Conference on the Protection of the North Sea, Report of the meeting of 24/25 November 1987.*

TABLE 1
Claims of North Sea States to maritime jurisdiction

	TS	*CZ*	*Excl. fish*	*CS*	*EEZ*	*MB SIGN*
Belgium	12	—	200(b)	y	—	12/5/84
Denmark	3	4	200	200m/E	—	12/10/82
France	12	—	—	200m/E	200	12/10/82+
FRG	3/12	—	200	200m/E	—	—
Netherlands	12	—	200	y	—	12/10/82
Norway	4	10	—	200m/E	200	12/10/82
Sweden	12	—	200	200m/E	—	12/10/82+
UK	12	—	200	200m/E	—	—

b — defined by its bilateral maritime boundaries or by an equidistant line
m/E — metres/depth of exploitation
\+ — declaration made at the time of signature of the Convention

Source: Limits in the Seas, 36, National Claims to Maritime Jurisdictions (5th rev.), U.S. Dept. of State (recent data have been added).

TS — territorial sea
CZ — contiguous zone
Excl. fish — exclusive fishery zone
CS — continental shelf
EEZ — exclusive economic zone
MG SIGN — Signature of the United Nations Convention on the Law of the Sea

TABLE 2
North Sea States and the Conventions

	B	*D*	*FRG*	*F*	*NI*	*No*	*S*	*UK*	*in force*
GLOBAL									
GENERAL									
UNCLOS III[1]	s	s	–	s	s	s	s	–	——
TSC 1958[2]	x	x	–	–	x	–	–	x	1964
CSC 1958[3]	–	x	s	x	x	x	x	x	1964
HSFC 1958[4]	x	x	x	x	x	–	–	x	1966
HSC 1958[5]	x	x	x	s	x	–	–	x	1962
SECTORIAL									
Whaling (IWC)[6]	–	x	x	x	x	x	x	x	1948
Load lines 1966[7]	x	x	x	x	x	x	x	x	1968
CLC 1969[8]	x	x	x	x	x	x	x	x	1975
Protocol 1976[9]	–	x	x	x	x	x	x	x	1981
Protocol 1984[10]	–	–	–	x	–	–	–	–	——
Intervention 1969[11]	x	s	x	x	x	x	x	x	1975
Protocol 1973[12]	x	x	–	–	x	x	x	x	1983
Fund 1971[13]	–	x	x	x	x	x	x	x	1978
Protocol 1976[14]	–	x	x	x	x	x	x	x	1981
Protocol 1984[15]	–	–	–	x	–	–	–	–	——
Ramsar 1971[16]	x	x	x	–	x	x	x	x	1975
Protocol 1982[17]	–	x	x	x	x	x	x	x	1986
LDC 1972[18]	x	x	x	x	x	x	x	x	1975
Incineration, Protocol 1978[19]	x	x	x	x	x	x	x	x	1979
COLREG 1972[20]	x	x	x	x	x	x	x	x	1977
CITES 1973[21]	x	x	x	x	x	x	x	x	1975
MARPOL 1973, 1978[22]	x	x	x	x	x	x	x	x	1983
annex I	x	x	x	x	x	x	x	x	1983
annex II	x	x	x	x	x	x	x	x	1987
annex III	–	x	x	x	x	x	x	x	1990
annex IV	–	x	x	x	–	–	x	–	——
annex V	–	x	x	x	x	x	x	x	1988
SOLAS 1974[23]	x	x	x	x	x	x	x	x	1980
Protocol 1978[24]	x	x	x	x	x	x	x	x	1981
STCW 1978[25]	x	x	x	x	x	x	x	x	1984
ILO 147[26]	x	x	x	x	x	x	x	x	1981
CMS (Bonn)[27]	–	x	x	s	x	x	x	x	1983
REGIONAL									
Berne 1979[28]	s	x	x	s	x	x	x	x	1982
Oslo Dumping 1972[29]	x	x	x	x	x	x	x	x	1974
Incineration Protocol 1983[30]	x	x	x	x	x	x	x	x	1989
Paris Land-based 1974[31]	x	x	x	x	x	x	x	x	1978
Protocol 1986[32]	x	–	x	x	x	x	x	x	——
Offshore liability 1977[33]	–	–	s	–	s	s	s	s	——
MOU 1982[34]	x	x	x	x	x	x	x	x	1982
Bonn 1983[35]	x	x	x	x	x	x	x	x	1989

s signatory
x ratified
– not ratified

Notes

[1] United Nations Convention on the Law of the Sea, Montego Bay, 10 December 1982 (not in force)
[2] Convention on the Territorial Sea and the Contiguous Zone, Geneva, 29 April 1958
[3] Convention on the Continental Shelf, Geneva, 29 April 1958
[4] Convention on Fishing and Conservation of the Living Resources of the High Seas, Geneva, 29 April 1958
[5] Convention on the High Seas, Geneva, 29 April 1958
[6] International Convention for the Regulations of Whaling, Washington, 2 December 1946
[7] International Convention on Load Lines (LL), London, 5 April 1966
[8] International Convention on Civil Liability for Oil Pollution Damage (CLC), Brussels, 29 November 1969
[9] Protocol to International Convention on Civil Liability for Oil Pollution Damage (CLC PROT), London, 19 November 1976
[10] Protocol to the International Convention on Civil Liability for Oil Pollution Damage (CLC PROT), London, 25 May 1984 (not in force)
[11] International Convention Relating to Intervention on the High Seas in Cases of Oil Pollution Casualties (INTERVENTION), Brussels, 29 November 1969
[12] Protocol Relating to Intervention on the High Seas in Cases of Marine Pollution by Substances Other than Oil (INTERVENTION PROT), London 2 November 1973
[13] International Convention on the Establishment of an International Fund for Compensation for Oil Pollution Damage (FUND), Brussels, 18 December 1971
[14] Protocol to the International Convention on the Establishment of an International Fund for Compensation for Oil Pollution Damage (FUND PROT 1976), London, 19 November 1976
[15] Protocol to the International Convention on the Establishment of an International Fund for Compensation for Oil Pollution Damage (FUND PROT 1984), London, 25 May 1984 (not in force)
[16] Convention on Wetlands of International Importance Especially as Waterfowl Habitat, Ramsar, 2 February 1971
[17] Protocol to Amend the Convention on Wetlands of International Importance Especially as Waterfowl Habitat, Paris, 3 December 1982
[18] Convention on the Prevention of Marine Pollution by Dumping of Wastes and Other Matter (LDC), London, 10 November 1972
[19] Amendments to Annexes to the Convention on the Prevention of Marine Pollution by Dumping of Wastes and other Matter, Concerning Incineration at Sea, London, 12 October 1978
[20] Convention on the International Regulations for Preventing Collisions as Sea (COLREG), London, 20 October 1972
[21] Convention on International Trade in Endangered Species of Wild Fauna and Flora (CITES), Washington, 3 March 1973
[22] International Convention for the Prevention of Pollution from Ships (MARPOL), London, 2 November 1973 (Annex V was amended in order to designate the North Sea as a special Area under that Annex; Annex III 1990 and IV are not in force); Protocol to the International Convention for the Prevention of Pollution from Ships, London, 16 February 1978
[23] International Convention for the Safety of Life at Sea (SOLAS), London, 1 November 1974
[24] Protocol Relating to the International Convention for the Safety of Life at Sea, London, 17 February 1978
[25] International Convention Concerning Standards, Training, Certification and Watchkeeping for Seafarers (STCW), London, 7 July 1978
[26] ILO Convention No. 147 Concerning Minimum Standards in Merchant Ships, 1976
[27] Convention on the Conservation of Migratory Species of Wild Animals, Bonn, 23 June 1979
[28] Convention on the Conservation of European Wildlife and Natural Habitats, Berne, 19 September 1979
[29] Convention for the Prevention of Marine Pollution By Dumping from Ships and Aircraft, Oslo, 15 February 1972
[30] Protocol to the Convention for the Prevention of Marine Pollution by Dumping from Ships and Aircraft, Oslo, 12 June 1981
[31] Convention for the Prevention of Marine Pollution From Land-Based Sources, Paris, 4 June 1974
[32] Protocol amending the Convention for the Prevention of Marine Pollution From Land-Based Sources, Paris, 26 March 1986

[33] Convention on Civil Liability for Oil Pollution Damage Resulting from Exploration for and Exploitation of Seabed Mineral Resources, London, 1 May 1977 (not in force)
[34] Memorandum of Understanding on Port State Control in Implementing Agreements on Maritime Safety and Protection of the Maritime Environment, Paris, 26 January 1982
[35] Agreement for Co-operation in Dealing with Pollution of the North Sea by Oil and Other Harmful Substances, Bonn, 13 September 1983

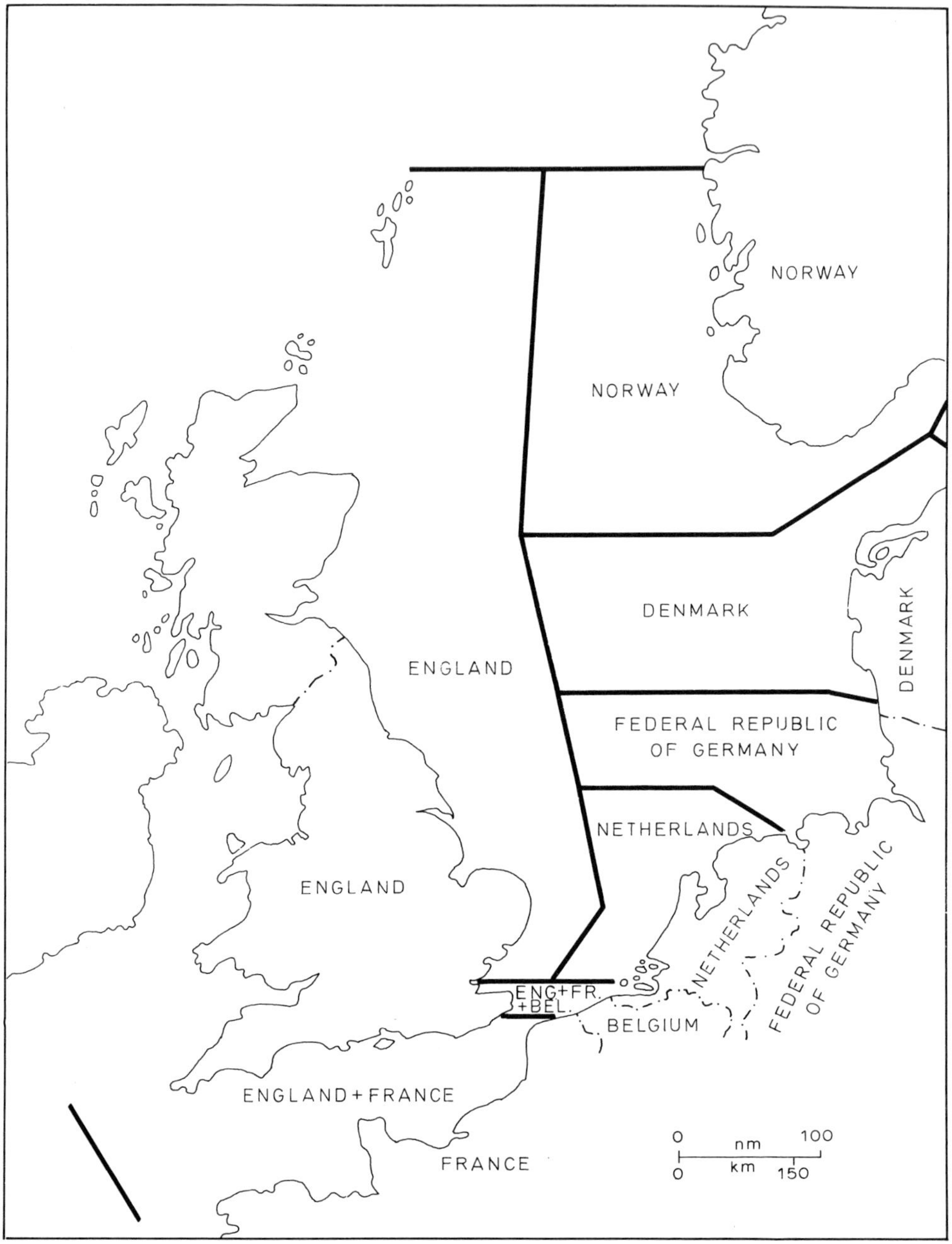

Figure A Pollution combating zones under the 1983 Bonn Agreement

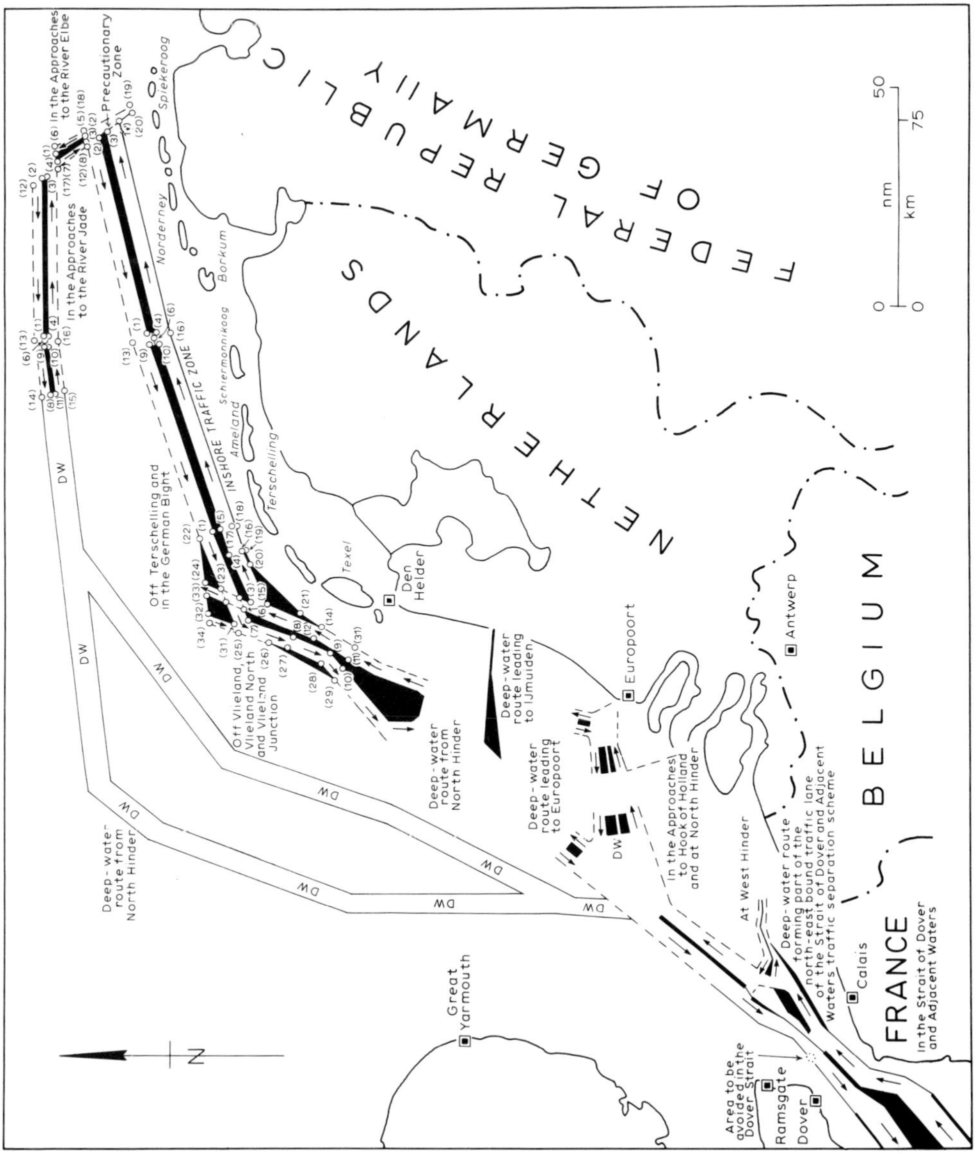

Figure B IMO traffic separation schemes in the North Sea

INDEX